Christianity:
Endangered or Extinct, Volume 2

A People's History of Christianity, The Consuming Force

THOMAS KESSLER

WIPF & STOCK · Eugene, Oregon

Wipf and Stock Publishers
199 W 8th Ave, Suite 3
Eugene, OR 97401

Christianity: Endangered or Extinct, Volume 2
A People's History of Christianity
(in the Mode of Howard Zinn's A People's History
of the United States), The Consuming Force
By Kessler, Thomas
Copyright©2015 by Kessler, Thomas
ISBN 13: 978-1-5326-7713-7
Publication date 12/7/2018
Previously published by Outskirts Press, 2015

Table of Contents

Preface to the 2019 Reprint Edition i
Preface iii
    Age of Power v

Chapter 1
The *Vaudois*, the Primitive Valley People of the Alps 1
    The Typography of the *Vaudois* Valley 1
    An Apostolic Community? 4
    Beliefs of the Vaudois 9
    Visiting the Former Residence of the Vaudois Valley 13
    Waldo, the Waldensians, and the Poor Men of Lyons 13
    The Waldensians and the Vaudois 15
    Persecutions of the Vaudois and the Waldensians 16
    The Albigensians and Other Missionary Endeavors 21
    Conclusion 24

Chapter 2
John Chrysostom (345-407), the Treasure from the East .. 26
    John's First Church, Antioch 30
    Family Background 33
    John the Ascetic 38
    Homilies and Sermons 40
        Husband and Wife 44
        The Arians and Manichaeans 45
        The Jews 46

    The Poor 49
    On Hatred and Violence 51
    John's Faults as a Preacher 51
    The Burdens John Felt as a Preacher 52
    John's Use of Rhetoric 53
  The Homilies on the Statues 54
  The Emperor Kidnaps John to be
  Constantinople's Patriarch 59
  John Chrysostom, Patriarch 60
  Olympias and Her Monastery of Nuns 63
  John's Other Activities 65
  The Affair of the Tall Brothers 65
  The Synod of the Oaks 67
  Conclusion 70

Chapter 3
Cyril and Nestorius 73
  Nestorius, Cyril, and the Council of Ephesus 74
  Nestorius 75
  Cyril 76
  Nestorius, Manipulated 77
  Politics Preceding the Council 78
  Nestorius, a Recluse in Constantinople 79
  The Impassibility of God 81
  The Theological Problem of the Council of Ephesus 83
  The Council of Ephesus (431) 86
  A Question or Two 90

Chapter 4
Leo the Great (390?-461) and the Dark Ages 93
  The Typography of Rome at Leo's Time 94
  Leo and Attila the Hun 95
  Leo and Papal Infallibility 97

Leo, His Tome, and the Council of Chalcedon 101
The 6th Century Onward 102
Theological Roots of The Dark Ages 106
The Primacy of the Number "3" 110
    The Warrior 113
    The Worker 114
    The Prayer 114
Slaves 116

Chapter 5
The Peace of God 118
Historical Setting 118
The Beginnings of the Stress on the Individual 120
The Peace of God Movement Stresses Individual Rights 123
Saint Martial 125
The Truce of God 127
Two Chroniclers of the Age 1000 128
Ademar of Chabannes 129
    The Debate 130
    How Do Good Historians Now Read Ademar? 132
    Ademar's Early Years 133
    Ademar and the Year 1000 134
Rodulfus, Apocalyptic Writer and the Peace of God 136
Conclusion 141

Chapter 6
The Albigensian Crusade (1209-1229) and Its Inquisition .. 143
Languedoc, the Center of the Fray 143
Internal Conflicts in Languedoc 147
The Beginnings of Conflict 150
Organization of the Crusade 151
The Good Men and Women, Victims of the Crusade 152
The Crusade Itself 153

- Massacre of Beziers 155
- Carcassone 157
- Other Tragedies 158
- Counter-Offensive of Raymond VI 159
- Continuance -- Louis VIII 162
- Conclusion of the Crusade 163
- Were They Really Cathars? 164
- The Reality of the Religion of Good Men and Women 167
- Beliefs of Good Men and Women 169
- The Good Men and Women: Victims of the Inquisition .. 170
- The Inept Albigensian Crusade 171
- The First Inquisitors 175
- Peace of God, Inquisition Style 176
- Effects of the Inquisition 177
- Conclusion 180

Chapter 7
The First Five Crusades, 1099-1221 183
- Lead-up to the Crusades 183
- The East and the West of the Middle Ages 185
- Fantasy Number 1: "Christian Violence" 185
- Fantasy Number 2: "Spirituality" of the Crusaders 187
- Fantasy Number 3: Matthew 16:17-19 and the Rise of Papal Power 190
- The Final Straw 194
- Clermont 197
- The Peasants' Crusade 201
- Anti-Jewish Sentiments 203
- The Peasant Crusade Reaches the East 204
- Nicaea and Antioch 205
- Byzantium's Political Acumen 207
- Europe's Complete Commitment 207

The Siege of Jerusalem 208
The Second Crusade, 1146-1148 209
Hildegard of Bingen 212
The Third Crusade 214
The Fourth Crusade 215
The Children's Crusade, 1212-1213 219
The Fifth Crusade 220
Passagium Particulare 222
Modern Crusades 223
Two Beautiful People in the Rubble 223
    Saladin's Death 224
    Francis of Assisi 224
Conclusion to the Crusades 227

Chapter 8
Religious Life: The Black Monks to Waldo 229
Religious Life in General in the Age 229
Religious Life of Old 230
Renewal of Hermit and Preacher Groups 235
The Lay Reform Movement 236
    The Humiliati 236
    Beguines and Beghards 238
    The Waldensians 239
Heresy in the Age 240

Chapter 9
Francis of Assisi 245
    Overview 245
    Early Years 248
    Conversion 254
    The Lepers and the Sultan 260
    Franciscan Growth 267

Chapter 10
Thomas Aquinas, The Angelic Doctor 270
   Basic Orientation 271
   Problem with the Thomists 273
   Life and Later Influences 274
   Quirks of Personality 277
   Continued Academic Work 278
   Dominican and Papal Acclamation 280
   Metaphysics 283
   Matter and Form and the 4 Causes 287
   Ethics 288
   Sacraments 291
   5 Natural Proofs for the Existence of God 294
   Immortality of the Soul 298
   The Literal Sense of the Bible 300
   Just War 303
   Political/Social Writings 305
   A Humane, Well-Ordered World 306
   Private Property 307
   Law 309
   Status, Wealth and Sainthood 310
   Summary and Analysis 311

Chapter 11
The Inquisitions in General 315
   Pre-Lateran IV Persecutions 317
   Lateran Council IV of 1215 321
   Innocent III 328
   Follow-up to Lateran Council IV 329
   Inquisitions and Jesus' Teachings 331
   The Popes and the Inquisitions 332

Inquisition, Politics, the Local Church and the Populace...333
Inquisition of the Theologians 336

Chapter 12
The Inquisition of the "Witches" 339
The Old Religion and Their Deeper Knowledge 339
The Neighborhood of the Impoverished Witches...........341
The Stereotypical Witch 344
The Fears Generated by the "Witches" 346
The Problem of the Intelligentsia and Witchcraft 347
The Stories of the Witches in Their Own Age................349
Who Were Called Witches? 351
The Church, Clergy, Torture and Execution of Witches..358
The Inquisition of the Witches – In Practice.................361
Conclusion 364

Chapter 13
The Spanish Inquisition..366
Lead Up to the Spanish Inquisition...............................369
Kingpins of the Early Inquisition in Spain 369
The Jews and the Inquisition in Spain 371
The Beginnings of the Inquisition in Spain...................373
The Marriage of Ferdinand and Isabella........................374
Plans for Inquisition and Elimination of
Muslims from Spain..375
Ferdinand and Isabella's Inquisition 377
The Inquisition of Torquemada 380
The Proceedings of the Inquisition 382
The Case of Elvira del Campo 385
The Inquisition and the Spanish People.......................393
Columbus and the Arawak Indians...............................394
Dostoyevsky, Jesus, and the Spanish Inquisition............395

Chapter 14
Dante, Florence and Boniface VIII 401
   Pope Boniface VIII 402
   Dante Alighieri 404
   The Guelphs and the Ghibellines of Florence 405
   Battle for Control of Florence 408
   Dante, the Exile 409
   The Comedy 412
      Inferno 413
      Purgatorio 414
      Paradiso 417
   The Essence of the Comedy 418
   The Demise of Boniface VIII 419

Epilogue: Synopsis of Events to Date 421
Bibliography 430

Preface to the 2019 Reprint Edition

Written by a respected religious scholar, this work continues the work of the groundbreaking book *Christianity: Endangered or Extinct—A People's History of Christianity, Volume 1*.

The first work dealt with Christianity up to c.300. This second volume continues to challenge long-held beliefs about Christianity from c.300 up to the twelfth century. It details a great divide between Jesus of Nazareth's teachings and Christianity as we know it even in our present day.

With comprehensive historical research over a twenty-year period, Thomas Kessler has analyzed the powerful, class struggle in the church. He shows in detail precisely how the church continued to choke the life out of the Christian community. Some of the churchmen of the period even committed genocide to attain their own personal ends. The reality is insidious.

It is clear that the church is not a perfect society. Knowing the facts about it grounds us in reality, the starting point of any solid Christian commitment.

This work will aid in perceiving Christianity in a brand-new light.

Thomas Kessler is a former Capuchin Franciscan friar and priest. He studied theology at St. Anthony Friary in Marathon, Wisconsin. He also conducted independent studies at the Graduate Theological Union in Berkeley, California, and in Assisi, Italy. His interests include Christian history, philosophy, theology, Greek, and Latin.

PREFACE

A young man or woman quits college or leaves children and spouse behind in order to enter the army to fight in Afghanistan. "My country needs me now," he or she says. "I must go and do my duty to my country." Where did he or she get such an idea? It is not only a recent concept arising among young people in the Empire of the United States. Although it might have been conceived even earlier in history, it certainly can be traced back as far as the Roman Empire.

In early Christianity, we know that events began to occur contrary to the early intent of the true Christian movement. A Roman general, Ambrose, became Bishop of Milan, and Augustine, a convinced Roman, became Bishop of Hippo in North Africa. Both were well trained in Greek/Roman literature; both were familiar with Virgil's writings.

Virgil, the ancient Roman classical writer created Aeneas to exemplify Roman *pietas*, the Latin word for the virtue of piety. For years to come, Virgil's Aeneas became the example of the true Roman citizen. *Pietas* meant three things to the Romans: primarily, it meant dedication to God or the gods; secondarily, it meant dedication to Rome, and thirdly, it meant dedication to one's family. A hierarchy exists here: first, God or the gods; second, Roman society, and then one's family. After the time of Virgil, this *pietas* was prized by Roman citizens.

Roman *pietas* explains not only the actions of the patriotic men and women in our own country, but those of Ambrose and Augustine as well. The difference between Ambrose and Augustine was that Ambrose had a family and Augustine's family had already died. If Virgil created Aeneas as the prime example of *pietas,* Ambrose and Augustine were *pietas* number two and *pietas* number three. Unfortunately, their piety was clearly not the piety of Jesus, who prized love of God and love of all neighbors, even one's enemies. (It must be noted here that a reading of volume 1, *Christianity, Endangered or Extinct: The Gathering Storm* is beneficial for an understanding of this present volume 2.)

In volume one we saw that Constantine's supposed vision at the Melbian bridge enabled him to bring Christendom to its knees as warriors before him. Ambrose, Augustine, Athanasius, and others then watered down Christianity until the thinking of the virtuous Roman became Christianity. Similar patriotism became Christianity not only for Romans, but for future generations to come: God, first; our country, second; family, third. This hierarchy of patriotism is one of the reasons so many young Americans are willing to go off to die in war, leaving their families behind.

Christianity agreed to other abominations to which Jesus would never have agreed: Christians permitted and even sanctified torture for the sake of the Kingdom of God; they agreed that obedience to their political leaders was Christianity; they agreed that Greek philosophy was the basis of Christianity; they agreed that obedience to masters and mistresses was Christianity; they agreed that slavery was acceptable in Christianity; they agreed that worshipping with certain specific rites and not others was an integral part of Christianity; they agreed that men, not women, should hold important offices in the Church, and that these men should be celibate. They agreed to a hierarchy of popes and bishops over everyone else in Christianity. All this is treated in much more detail in volume one.

I now approach the facts that necessitate a volume 2. Emperors began to dictate Christianity to the clergy. At the same time, the clergy put stress on the primacy of truth. Believing two dementional truths overshadowed acting in a just and loving way according to the words of Jesus. It was much easier for the politicians and clergy of the time to simply believe truths about Christianity without doing a thing. Then even truth lost its luster and became contaminated. Christianity had clearly lost much of its intrinsic meaning.

Something gradually died within Christianity, and what died was not peripheral, but basic and essential. Jesus and his message died. For years, Roman Catholics have said in the liturgy of the Eucharist: "Christ has died; Christ is risen; Christ will come again." Indeed, Christ has truly died.... But the rest is still a question. We have not yet allowed him to rise again in our midst.... Hopefully he will come again and be with us in ages to come. If he does, it will be because Christians, under the inspiration of the Holy Spirit, helped bring him back.

THE AGE OF POWER

In volume 2, I now continue to enter the age of power within the church. Howard Zinn in his *People's History of the United States* stood with the poor of the United States. He continues in volume 2 to be my mentor and guide in dealing with the ruse which the powerful have foisted upon the Christian world. As we recall from volume 1, Zinn admits that his history is "a history disrespectful of governments and respectful of people's movements of resistance." Both his and our books report that the dominant class in the church deceives and oppresses the poor. The elite in every age, including our own, have attempted to keep the common citizenry passive and powerless, dependent on some new savior, bishop, or pope to bring them justice (Zinn, 2003, 570; Zinn and Armove, 2004, 24).

In a taped lecture, Zinn spoke the following words:

> If you don't know history, it is like you were born yesterday. And if you were born yesterday, anyone up there can tell you anything, and you have no way of checking up on it. (Zinn, 1994)

You are as naive as a child, ready to accept anything "anyone up there" in the hierarchy tells you. You have no foundation in fact -- you are not grounded in reality.[1]

Zinn has more to say. Upon reception of the Eugene Debs Award for education, Zinn stated:

> When I started studying history in 1927 -- I was in graduate school -- I got my textbooks, so I started to page through them. I looked for the labor struggles in this country. They were not there. I looked for ... the Colorado Coal Strike of 1913-1914. It was not there. I looked for Mother Jones.... She was not there. I was in graduate school and my textbooks were the same as in grade school, except now they had footnotes. (Zinn, 1994)

Christianity also needs a counterforce in the face of mitered popes and bishops, scholarly theologians, and self-serving and self-righteous Christians. Zinn's words about United States history

---

[1] This and the following quote are taken from the movie about Howard Zinn *You Can't Be Neutral on a Moving Train.* Chicago Filmmakers, 1994.

are analogously true of the advanced theological history books in Roman Catholic schools in the 1960's and even later. Look through them and try to find the crusade and inquisition against the good people of Southern France. You will not find them. Look for the beautiful, apostolic community in the Alps founded by an apostle or disciple of Jesus. It is not there. Advanced students of theology have been spoon-fed by "anyone up there," and they have readily swallowed it all. Many things which the established church wished to be left out of the books were indeed left out, and other things of little consequence were included.

As Howard Zinn reported concerning the voices of the poor in secular history, Harvard theologian and biblical scholar Elisabeth Schüssler Fiorenza has reported on the state of women in the church. She has led us in attempting to establish women's voices lost within the graveyard of male-dominated church history. Schüssler-Fiorenza 1994, 1-2).

This, too, is our venture and our quest. In *Christianity: Endangered or Extinct? A People's History of Christianity*, volume 1 and 2, we bring out women's voices. The philosophers/theologians have already taken over, and they have cut male-domination in stone. This task becomes more and more difficult, but it is still possible.

The third influential voice is French psychologist, philosopher, and historian, Michel Foucault. We find that his approach is helpful in getting behind the language of the popes, the bishops, and other churchmen to see the oppression that exists in their wake. His "laboratory of power" puts some in high positions according to often-perverted value systems. Those who resist are often put down and destroyed.

Even though these three important guides are not often mentioned in this volume, they are always in the back of my mind. This work is going to continue to sort through the lives of the

Christians who lived before us. My goal has not changed in volume 2. I continue to try to ground myself, maintain a position in reality, enabling me to present as best as I can, with all my limitations, the life and words of Jesus. At the same time, I hope to restore justice to many Christians of merit who were denigrated and/or forced into oblivion, even burned at the stake, and establish that they indeed have been part of the Jesus movement.

Gone are the days when I say to myself: "Do not say this or that about the church, or you will give scandal." I believe that I can no longer worry about "scandal." Christianity must be saved. I feel that it is necessary to critically evaluate the spurious value systems that have become set in ecclesiastical stone and also the lives of some of the established "saints" who are not worth their salt. I also feel that I must continue to elevate others who have been sorely abused.

So my method has not changed in volume 2, only the material has changed. I am now dealing with the years 430 CE to the inquisitions, and the "missing persons" who have been obliterated by the established church hierarchies -- those who deserve recognition within Christianity and in the world. Even John Chrysostom, as he laid stress on a truly Jesus community, sometimes missed the "persons" in his own neighborhood, especially when he dealt with the Jewish people. Also, John's Greek brothers had trouble in the early Councils of the Church because the Greek language had no word for "person," a word that was forced upon them by the Romans. The Greek bishops had to dig deep into their language to find some semblance of understanding of the word.

Not that their Roman brother's understood the meaning of the word person and the dignity of the individual much better. They killed the valley people in the Alps; they ran rough-shod over their Eastern brothers in the Councils of Nicaea, Ephesus and Chalcedon; they misused their own poor people through slavery and warfare; they felt the need to have an infallible pope, who could tell every individual person what to believe; they condemned people with the "crime of heresy," even having them burned at the stake if they did not conform to the common group view; they annihilated most of the southern part of France, causing the persons there immense pain and suffering; they engaged in the crusades, viciously killing Muslims and Jews in order to save themselves from the perceived Muslim threat and perpetuate their rights of passage to the relics in the holy land.

I insist that I am not trying to demolish Christianity and the Catholic Church. I love both deeply. At the same time, I believe that it is necessary for Christians to ground themselves in the realities of history if Christianity and the Catholic Church are to survive into and even past the third millennium. Up to now, many in the church have tried to hide any history which places the church in a bad light. It has raised up some that have not deserved it; it has destroyed the bodies and writings of others who were worthy, even though they might have had different opinions on this point or that -- points which were seen as extremely important to the church of their own age. It is unfortunate, to say the least. Even today, who does not have different ideas of Christianity than the person next to him or her in the pews in the church in which he or she prays? The Church has never been monolithic.

I am not accusing anyone of bad intentions. Perhaps the church believes that, if it tells the truth, it will give scandal to some innocent Christians. Certainly many will be taken back a bit by the things that are written in this book, as they were in the first volume. But we have to be forthright if we are to find the way of Jesus.

It is time that knowledgeable churchmen, humbly and in the open, stand up and tell the whole story. When they do so, the church will be able to grow again from humbler roots. Until then, the church will not ground itself in the reality of history, and it will be sucked down into the quicksand of pride and unreality. Until the church does so, I feel that I am called to do so. We cannot build a Christian future on the foundation of a sanctimonious, liar filled past.

Much of the content of this book deals with atrocious and ugly material. The book is an easy read, but the content is not. So-called holy men, churchmen, are guilty of genocide, pride and extreme selfishness. It is history. It did happen.

Note that chronology is not easily followed in volume 2. While I try to follow a chronology, sometimes it has to be set aside in order to produce a clear picture of *The People's History*. Chapter 1 deals with the Vaudois, the valley people, whose origins go back to apostolic or near-apostolic times, and who were followers of Jesus in their mountain hovel in the Alps. Chapter 2 is concerned with John Chrysostom, who was a contemporary of Augustine, but generally took a more compassionate tack, except when he dealt with the Jews. Chapter 3 deals with Cyril, who mistreats a fellow patriarch, Nestorius. Chapter 4 considers the life of Leo the Great, who had great potential, but took up the quest for papal power and infallibility instead. Chapter 5 digs into the peace of God movement, which shows poor people rising up against oppression; chapter 6 delves into the great oppression of the Albigensian Crusade and the inquisition that followed, incidences which leave bitter tastes in the mouths of citizens in southern France even today. Chapter 7 explores the horror stories of the first five crusades against the Muslims, which also involved oppression and persecution of the Jews. Chapter 8 shows the development of religious life, the black monks up to the time of Waldo." Chapter 9 highlights Francis of Assisi, probably the greatest follower of Jesus in the whole Christian era. Chapter 10 explores the life and teachings of Thomas Aquinas who utilized Aristotle's teachings to set up a total Christian philosophical/theological system dealing with Christian issues in his age. Utilizing his great mind, Thomas tackled many issues successfully, and he limped on others, but his thinking has dominated the Roman Church up to our own age. Chapter 11 to 13 deals with the inquisitions, showing what a monster the search for truth can become in a church that originally was based on "love of enemies," but chose their own "truths" instead. Finally, Chapter 14 looks at Dante Alighieri, who suffered terribly from the church, but survived to give us one of the greatest works of literature ever written.

ACKNOWLEDGEMENTS

I wish to acknowledge Joyce, my wife and confidant, and my two daughters, Annette and Laura, and their children, Eddie, Miles, Ayla and Will. Of course, I want to mention Rodger Cragun, without whose aid volume 2 would never have been written. Rodger did invaluable research with and for me over the past 25 years, and I held invaluable and extensive discussions with him on the material. I also want to thank his wife, Penny, and all the Duluth, Minnesota community that rally around them. I want to mention James and his crew at the Amery, Wisconsin, public library, who found me many research books that I needed. I also wish to mention all those who work at living in the Spirit of Jesus, especially my Capuchin brothers, whom I still dearly love.

Chapter 1

THE *VAUDOIS*, THE PRIMITIVE VALLEY PEOPLE OF THE ALPS

THE TYPOGRAPHY OF THE *VAUDOIS* VALLEY

A great number of scholars, including the Roman Catholic hierarchy do not believe that the Alpine community ever existed before the Waldensians. For them *Vaudois* does not mean "Valley people," who lived in the Alpine Valley as far back as apostolic times, but Waldensian, who supposedly first entered the valley in the twelfth century, or some other group that happened to enter the valley a little earlier than Waldo and his group.

It takes much naivety to believe that such an intricate community as the *Vaudois* suddenly arose and ascended from the snows of the Alps around the twelfth century. The *Vaudois* were rather an established community that had its origins in apostolic or near apostolic times, and in the twelfth century, the Waldensians joined them. This chapter will show many proofs which indicate that the Valley People existed to apostolic times or near apostolic times. Perhaps it was one or two of the first apostles who started this exemplary community in the Alps. Maybe it was an apostle's disciple. We do not know for sure. But it is clear that the *Vaudois* go back that far in Christian history. Even though we and they were never sure which apostle or early disciple of Jesus brought the message of Jesus to them, undoubtedly it was some person or group who knew Jesus intimately. Whoever it was, they, he or she deeply influenced this band of people, who then raised their own and many generations of children to know Jesus. After intense preparation, they also followed Jesus' instructions to go two by two to other nations of Europe bearing Jesus' message of salvation.

The people who lived in the valley could not understand what the Roman Church was doing to them when they eventually raided their mountain homes. For in fact they did do so.

The Alpine hovels were excellent places to live and pray. The snow on the peaks was always white and beautiful. The sun was bright and warm as was the Christianity which they shared with one another. They studied. Though generally illiterate, some of them went so far as to memorize their bible. They cherished the stories of Jesus and made him present to one another by imitating his actions and teachings. Yet, eventually members of the Catholic Church entered their valley home, and with venom in their hearts, attacked them with every intention of destroying them.

R. M. Stephens tells us in *The Burning Bush:*"…If whilst in Rome we need to think imperially, in the Alpine Valleys we must think exceedingly locally. Few of the great figures of history have even cast a shadow across the Valleys. The stage is small, the people few…." (Stephens: 1963, 9). Their downfall as far as the Roman Church was concerned was that they were ignorant of the happenings in the Roman world. They were simple people, and they never knew about the great councils of the Church or the great Popes and scholars who influenced the Church. While barely knowing it, they were an intense threat, fair game for "heretic mongering" soldiers, bishops, popes, and secular authorities. Yet, in their own primitive way, they knew Jesus, his death, his rising, his beatitudes and all the essentials of Christianity. They lived a Christian life with all their hearts and souls. They were saints who rose above many of those who were recognized as such by the Catholic Church.

The hidden valley is in the Northwest corner of Italy, 35 miles from Turin. It is in the womb of the Alps, a guarded place approximately fifteen miles, north to south, and fifteen miles, east to west amidst the mountain peaks (Stephens:1963: 10).

Approaching on the level plain from the south, a visitor sees the Alps stretching its peaks into the skies along the horizon. About thirty miles from Turin in the Duchy of Savoy, a visitor sees a great mountain gate. According to James Aitken Wylie in his *History of Protestantism,* this is the entrance to the *Vaudois* valley (Wylie, 1878, I, 26). Here is a small hill. Near it, a great monolith, called the *Castelluzzo*, shoots into the clouds. Both stand in front of the opening to the valley. For centuries, both stood sentry for the protection of the people who lived within. Protector though it was intended to be, the *Castelluzzo* was not protector enough, as we shall see. It became the instrument of martyrdom for many of the fervent pastors and peasants, mothers and children, who lived their simple life and admired the beauty around them behind this beautiful shield.

At the time of the martyrdom, there were seven valley communities in the valley. The first three of the seven spanned out like spokes from a central axel. Beyond the first three communities were four more communities, forming the rim of a wheel. All of the valley people were enclosed tightly from the rest of the world by a line of lofty, craggy peaks.

Each single community within the group had a simple enclosure of its own with a gate for entering and exiting. Each was surrounded by caves and rocks and mighty chestnut trees which separated them not only from the outside world but even from the other communities in the valley. Each community lived their separate lives, but in communion with the other communities, as separate parishes are part of a diocese.

At the center-point of the communities, the axel, the valley people built a simple retreat center, college and meeting place, where all the pastors of the valley gathered together annually. Here they trained missionaries, who, in imitation of Jesus' message in the Gospels, were sent out two by two to all parts of the known world (Wylie, I, 27).

The whole valley was sealed from anyone else in the world. As added protection, the people within knew every crag and cave in the valley (Wylie, I, 26-27). If they should need protection for any reason, they knew where to go.

Few even knew that these Christian people were present in the Alps. Certainly, for many centuries, most of the official members of the Roman Catholic hierarchy were completely ignorant of the fact.

AN APOSTOLIC COMMUNITY?

For many years, the *Vaudois* lived a simple, crude, isolated Christian life. Alexis Muston states in *The Israel of the Alps: a History of the Waldenses* that these people lived such a quiet, independent, life, unattached from the community at large, that some historians write them off by saying that no documentation is available that would *absolutely prove* that they were present in the valley at all (Muston, 1875; 1978: I, 2).[2] Muston puts this line of thought in the best terms with a humorist's twist: "Numerous let it be granted that they were, although in strictness it might be disputed" (Muston, 1875; 1978: I: 2).

---

2   Muston here quotes a letter from M. Schmidt, author of the *History of the Cathari*, Strasburg, April 28, 1850, concerning the absence of absolute proof of the Vaudois' early existence. He tries to use some humor about the matter.

At the same time, the lack of "certain documentation" is not an unusual problem for historians. Historians, especially Roman Catholic historians, do not demand such excruciating and exacting "documentation" to prove historical existence in other cases, e. g., the existence of the first group of Popes immediately following Peter. Lining up a group of possible early Popes – Peter, Linus, Anacletus, Clement, Cornelius, etc.-- just to make the papacy historically righteous and integral is far more doubtful history than denying the presence of the Valley people in the Alpine valley in early times, even apostolic times. Of course, this is to some degree an argument *ad hominem,* and it does not prove that the valley people lived in the valley of the Alps. It merely throws a question mark in another area of history: whether Linus, Anacletus, and Clement were truly Popes. It also shows that such problems are not unusual.

Also, the valley people are not the only group in Europe whose roots are questioned in this era of history. Documentation is not a characteristic element of the age. Historians speak of other remote communities in Europe in the same era. The kings, we know; the popes we know; key individuals we know. Outside of that, the age between the death of Justinian I in 565 and the eleventh or twelfth century has little documented history. People lived, raised their children, and died. But who exactly they were is a mystery. We are certain about that. There is no problem with that. Questions about the ancient origins of the valley people arise as a problem because the Roman Church was and continues to be intensely eager that they did not exist as a community with anything near a direct line to the apostles.

In spite of some historians and the sparse historical data of the age, ample documentation can be made to prove the presence of the *Vaudois* in the valley at a very early age, even all the way back to the apostolic age. Tertullian knew that he was writing the obvious when he wrote about a certain community: " they are off-spring of the apostolic church born from the womb of the apostles."[3] *Allix*[4] *on the Churches of Piedmont* is quoted in Acland as taking Tertullian's words, and making a defining statement about the *Vaudois*:" ... it is sufficient to make them (the *Vaudois*) deserve the name of apostolic, that they received the doctrine of the apostles as a pledge from the hand of their disciples, which they have preserved so *very tenderly* throughout the following ages" (Acland, 1827, xxii).

In spite of himself, Pope Alexander III, gives one of the best proofs, even though he was not very complimentary about it. Presiding over a synod in Tours in 1167, he damned the heresy of the *Vaudois*, which, in his own words he had to admit, had endured for a long time (*quae iamdudum emersit*) (Acland, 1827, xxxvi).

In 1250, Reynerius the Jesuit, an inquisitor, was bent on destroying the *Vaudois*, and in 1517, Claude Seyssel of Turin committed himself to the same mission. The established Roman Church designated the *Vaudois* as "the most dangerous of all heretics, because they are the most ancient" (J. A. Wylie, *The History of Protestantism, vol. 1,* London, Cassell Petter & Galpin, 1878, 26).[5]

Claude Seyssel dates the origin of the *Vaudois* from Leo I, in the time of Constantine the Great (Acland: 1827, xxxviii). With all due respects to Seyssel, the origin of the group was much earlier.

---

3   Acland, 1827, xxii, quotes Tertullian: "*Nascentes ex matricibus apostolicis, deputantur ut suboles apostolicarum ecclesiarum.*"
4   Allix is a member of the Vaudois, the valley people.
5   Acland goes on to quote Reynerius in more detail: "While all other sects disgust the public by their blasphemies against God, this group, on the other hand, manifest great piety. For those who belong to it live justly among men; and they believe sound doctrine on all points concerning God, and they believe all the articles which are contained in the Apostle's Creed. They only persist in blaspheming the Roman church."

Also, in the 1500's, Cassini, a Franciscan, writing against the *Vaudois*, states: "The errors of the *Vaudois* consist in their denial that the Roman Church is the holy mother church, and in their refusal to obey her traditions. In other points they recognize the church of Christ; and, for my part, I cannot deny that they have always been members of his church" (Acland: 1827, *xxxviii)*. But looking at the matter from the other direction, from the point of view of the *Vaudois*, they did not deny the Roman Church: they did not even know that it existed.

Rorenco, Prior of St. Roch in Turin (1640) was commissioned to investigate the origin and antiquity of the *Vaudois*. He came to the conclusion that "they were not a new sect in the ninth and tenth centuries" (Wylie: 1878, p. 26; Acland: 1827, xxxix). Furthermore, those who consult the first two chapters of *Usher de Statu et Success. Eccles.*, Mosheim's ecclesiastical history of the first eight centuries, and the first nine chapters of *Allix on the Churches of Piedmont*, know that a visible, sound church existed in the north of Italy certainly by the end of the eighth century (Acland: 1827, xxiii). A minor synod at La Vaux during the same time period encouraged the Pope to exterminate the *Vaudois*, "an heretical pest of enormous growth and great antiquity, generated in olden times" (Acland: 1827, xxxvii).

The questioning of the *Vaudois'* existence is an exercise in historical futility. The *Vaudois* did exist in the bosom of the Alps for many years, going back to near apostolic times, perhaps even to apostolic times.

Stephens mentions that even though many of the mountaineers were unable to read, they did know how to memorize, so they started a college at the heart of the Alps which taught them the languages of all their neighbors. Also, by the 12th century, the New Testament was translated in their own tongue, and the bible, especially the New Testament, was well read and even memorized by the students, who came from all over Europe. All of this was done so that they could fulfill the mandate of Jesus that his disciples go out with the message "two by two." One of the questions asked of them in the Inquisition of 1260 was whether they knew the Bible by heart. An inquisitor remarked: "I have heard and seen a certain unlettered countryman who used to recite Job word for word, and many others who knew the whole New Testament perfectly. All men and women cease not to teach and learn night and day. To those who cannot learn they say, 'learn only one word a day and in a year's time you will learn more than 300 and thus you will grow proficient'" (Stephens, 1963, 11-12).

Historians are quite sure that the *Vaudois* prided themselves in their Christian heritage and in their knowledge of Jesus. A certain crude freshness, they believe, could be found among these Christians. They freely lived a life united in faith. It was not imposed on them by anyone (Muston: 1875; 1978, I, 4). The very typography of the Alpine valley gave the churches there a certain character: "Each of these churches thus had its independent organization, as each individual may have his particular constitution and mode of life, whilst the general characters of human life are common to all men" (Muston: 1875; 1978, I, 4).

Then we come to the era of the Waldensians who joined the *Vaudois*. Again, Waldo could not have initiated the *Vaudois* presence: "For can it be believed, that within forty years this excellent man of Lyons [Waldo], without any peculiar assistance, could have so extended his doctrine, that his disciples, according to their opponents, should abound all over France, and in Spain, Britain, Germany, Hungary, Bohemia, and, in fact, throughout Europe..." (Acland: 1827, xxxiv)?

Muston tells us that the edict of Otto IV in 1209, the first document we can rely on after this period, and other documents soon to come, ascribes to the *Vaudois* a notoriety and influence of long standing in the land: "Supposing that the disciples of Valdo had taken refuge in the Alps about the end of the 12th century, it would be very difficult to admit that they could have so filled both the *Vaudois* valleys of Dauphiny and those of Piedmont in less than one generation, as to have acquired that influence which is ascribed to them…" (Muston, 1875; 1978, I, 15).

In the beginning, Waldo started from a Catholic, conservative, base, and he was intent on remaining within the framework of the Catholic Church. The *Vaudois* were present to him as a second choice only after he perceived that Catholics were intransigent.

While Constantine was seeking the union of Christian churches by legislation of uniformity, thus ensuring his own position, and while the pope was storming up a Crusade in order to destroy the Muslims, the "Albigensians" and the "Cathars" of southern France, the valley people, the Piedmont people in the diocese of Milan, told one another the stories of Jesus and for a long period of time, enjoyed their own independence (Muston: 1875; 1978, I, 4-5).

BELIEFS OF THE VAUDOIS

Throughout Christian history, the Valley people followed the way of Jesus, their light. They did everything they could to imitate him in their valley homes. The independence granted them by the Alps allowed them to believe ideas that were at the same time simple and ancient without knowing that they were not in accord with the established Church. Only gradually did they realize the chasm which existed between them and the existing Catholic Church. They believed that they were completely and thoroughly Catholic. The Catholic Church changed, creating the chasm between the valley people and the Catholic Church, not the valley people.

Reynerius, a Jesuit inquisitor, bent on destroying the valley people, mentioned in his writings that he had to admit that they were unwearied students of scripture. Acland quotes De Thou, a candid historian, as saying:

> They keep the commandments, the rule of a pious and holy life. They expel from themselves and their assemblies all iniquity, unlawful oaths, perjury, curses, reproaches, strife, seditions, debauchery, drunkenness, fornication, divinations, sacrilege, witchcraft, theft, usury, deceit, and all such vices, which they flee and with their whole heart detest (Acland, 1827, lxxvi).

Acland speaks of simple rules that the *Vaudois* made for themselves, establishing the manner in which they would conduct themselves with strangers whom they met on the road or who might visit them in their homes:

- Do not love the world.
- Avoid bad company.
- If possible, live in peace with all men.
- Do not have recourse to the law of the land.
- Do not take revenge.
- Love your enemy.
- Suffer willingly all toils, calumny, threats, rejection of men, and all torments for truth's sake.
- Be patient.
- Do not make pacts with the unbeliever.
- Have no communication with evil or with anything that savors of idolatry or any semblance of suspicion (Ackland, 1827, lxxxv).

They wrote other simple rules for the faithful to teach them how they might imitate Jesus:

- Do not serve the mortal desires of the flesh.
- Watch over your members, lest they become members of iniquity.
- Keep control of your affections.
- Let your soul control your body.
- Mortify your members.
- Avoid idleness.
- Be sober and temperate in eating and drinking, in your words, and in the cares of this world.
- Do works of charity.
- Live a life of faith and morality.
- Control your desires.
- Mortify the works of the flesh.
- Regularly devote yourselves to your religious community.
- Confer with one another on what is the will of God.
- Examine your conscience diligently.
- Cleanse, amend, and pacify your minds.

The rules were simple and easily memorized. At the same time, their college taught them not only about Jesus and the Bible, but also the languages of many of the people whom they might visit in Europe as they moved about two by two (Acland: 1827, lxxxv-lxxvii).

These mountain people gradually came to realize other bits of information as they contacted Catholics along the way. For example, they became convinced that no man should pretend to call himself the successor of St. Peter unless he had the faith of St. Peter (Muston, I, 5-6). They also came to realize that the Archbishop of Milan was not more a believer in the presence of

Jesus in the Eucharist than their common farmer (Muston, 1875, I, 6). At the same time, they also believed from time immemorial that the presence of Jesus in the Eucharist was symbolic. In their minds, this took nothing away from the Eucharist, for in their teachings, a symbolic presence was a real presence. For them, the Eucharist was still the Lord's supper, and all participated in it with the reverence of any Roman Catholic (Muston, 1875, I: 9). They believed that God alone could pardon sins, and that any contrived expiation and satisfaction for sin was worthless (Muston, 1875, I: 6-7). They considered indulgences, images, holy water and litanies strange innovations to Jesus and his message. Jesus alone was Mediator between God and man (Muston, 1875, I: 7-8).

Furthermore, they believed that Jesus desired that they go two by two as missioners. They, men and women, flooded Europe with a solid message of Jesus' presence. They never disputed with the Roman Church over the number of the sacraments. They contented themselves with saying that Jesus instituted only two. But they insisted that the gospel did not indicate a number, nor did it even mention the word *sacrament* (Muston, 1875, I, 21).

Their pastors, called *barbas*, all had a trade to support themselves. They were expected to become missioners for a period in their lives. Most of the *barbas* were not married. They visited all their parishioners once a year. Each person in the valley went to what they called *confession*, which was private counseling for the betterment of the person's soul (Muston, 1875, I, 27).

The beliefs of the valley people were not rebellion on their part. They had no need to fight against anyone, let alone the Roman Church: they were content to live their pristine Gospel life in their own enclosed valley and on the missionary trail. Their belief system was formed around their simple faith in Jesus.

To their staunch Catholic neighbors, who got wind of their

teachings through their own missioners and merchants, the valley people became synonymous with *magicians* or *infidels*. These people from the valley spoke strange words to anyone who had inherited and walked the whole journey as Roman Catholics – people who believed every word that now came from the pope's mouth. Yet, the valley people of the Alps never felt that they were anything but Catholic through and through. They were simply sheltered from the happenings of the Church through the ages. If they learned about the happenings of the Church-at-large, they ignored them as simply inconsequential, irrelevant, or pitiful. From the beginning they were taught that Jesus was their guide. They relied on one another for both their physical and spiritual maintenance. They did not believe that they had ever left the Church of Jesus. If anything, they believed that the Roman Church had left them (Muston, 1875, I, 17).[6]

VISITING THE FORMER RESIDENCE OF THE VAUDOIS VALLEY

Today, people visiting the place where the *Valdese* (Italian), the *Vaudois* (French), or the valley people (English) lived, come for spiritual reasons. It is a place where years past a spiritual group of people lived, a people who followed the way of Jesus.

WALDO, THE WALDENSIANS, AND THE POOR MEN OF LYONS

The city of Lyons, a number of miles away, on the eastern edge of France, was much different than the valley people. Lyons held 10,000 to 15,000 people at the millennium. It was not a large city, but it buzzed with commerce and industry, based on cloth-making. The local archbishop controlled the city and the

---

[6] Muston quotes Mezeray and Michelet in saying that Joan of Arc was condemned as Vaudois.

surrounding area economically, politically, and ecclesiastically. He divvied out ecclesiastical and political authority with his cathedral chapter members. Thus, the chapter was an immensely wealthy organization, as was the archbishop and each single member of the group. Especially because these churchmen in 1170 owned the thriving cloth industry, their luxurious clothes and manner stood out among the populace. When a severe famine hit the city, these rich, clean, well fed, and immune clergymen stood out even more.

A rich man lived in Lyons named Waldo. Peter was his baptismal name. Waldo was not his family name either, for people in the age did not have second names as we know them. Later, Waldo was added as a reference to his relationship to the people in the valley.[7] Peter invested in, bought and sold cloth, and he lent out money at interest to the people in the area. He owned his house in the city, plus much beautiful land in the countryside. He was part of the establishment, part of the established wealthy organization of cloth makers and the Church.

At the time of the famine of 1170, he experienced a religious conversion. He read the verse from Matthew 19:21, "If you wish to go the whole way, sell everything, and give it to the poor." He surprised his friends by reimbursing money to several people whom he felt he had treated unjustly. He then provided for his daughters, and gave the rest of his fortune to the poor. He resolved to conform literally to Jesus' command. He began to preach the word as Jesus had told his disciples to do. Waldo believed that this Gospel message which had spelled life to him should become available to others.

He was surprised that the clergy of the day were affronted by his actions. When he preached, as Jesus had told his apostles and disciples to preach, he found a responsive audience. People from

---

7   Because history calls him Waldo, we will call him Waldo in this work.

all levels of society listened intently to his message. His preaching was strong, fresh and dynamic, a marked contrast to the messages of the existing clergy. A group gathered around him.

In 1179 he went to Rome, and the Pope embraced him and approved his life of poverty. The investigators in Rome were impressed that these people were following the example of Jesus and his apostles. Waldo and his followers had no permanent homes; they traveled two by two, barefoot, possessing nothing. They were nonviolent, and they followed the poor Christ.

In spite of the fact that Waldo was doing only what Jesus told his apostles to do, and in spite of the fact that he had obviously been given a gift to preach the word, the Pope insisted that he and his followers not preach. That job was for the clergy and the clergy alone.

In 1181 Peter faced a tribunal in Lyons. He was cleared of all doctrinal errors and he agreed with the profession of faith which was drawn up for the occasion by the tribunal. At that time, Peter readily agreed with the tribunal that not everyone had to follow his poverty to be saved. He received the approval of the tribunal.

THE WALDENSIANS AND THE VAUDOIS

What happened then is almost predictable, considering the missionary efforts of the *Vaudois* and the location of Lyons, so near to the valley of the Alps. The popes and bishops should have seen it coming. They also might have read their Gospels more carefully and been more tolerant of the preaching efforts of Waldo and his community. But they apparently were unable to be as tolerant as Jesus in letting his disciples go out and freely preach his message.

Waldo then became disenchanted with the established Church, and he and many of his group freely violated the agreement with the tribunal. Waldo began calling his followers the *Vaudois*; others called his group the Waldensians. A firm union was made between Waldo's group and the *Vaudois*. The rumors which surfaced concerning the *Vaudois* were now Waldo's own. In 1184 the Poor men of Lyons, Waldo's group, was condemned by Lucius III. They had become a threat to the Pope, the bishops and the clergy. The Pope noted what he called the group's defiance of church authority. Waldo and the Waldensians were disenchanted with the church, and they had already moved into or near the valley.

Some of Waldo's group stayed with the Roman Church. They changed their name, which had become a problem for them, and they became "Poor Catholics," a group of evangelical, "anti-heretical" preachers. This group was then approved by Innocent III (Little, 1978 p. 120-128).

PERSECUTIONS OF THE VAUDOIS AND THE WALDENSIANS

Neither the Waldensians who joined the valley people nor the valley people could remain forever without notice in a shrinking world. In the centuries following, they were persecuted by the Catholics who surrounded them, and none of the valley people, not their old people, women or their children were spared the tortures and burnings that became their lot (Muston, 1875, I, 31-71ff.). The *Vaudois*, the holy preachers of Jesus went out with their bibles, not written in ink on paper, but in their hearts and in their memories, spreading the Gospel message throughout much of Europe. (Stephens, 1963, 12). Many died at the hands of inquisitors and soldiers who descended upon these missioners as they roamed Europe. In 1142 the citizens of Oxford, England condemned and beat six *Vaudois*. The six were then thrown out of the city in midwinter to die in the cold. (Stephens, 1963, 12).

The inquisitors and their men even entered into the sacred valley itself (R.M. Stephens, *The Burning Bush*, 1963, pp. 18-21).

In 1235, in Avignon, an inquisition condemned the Waldensians, the *Vaudois*, and their "errors." Those condemned were a ridiculously extensive group: those who were Waldensians and *Vaudois*, those who believed their faith, those who supported them in the city of Arles, those who believed that they were good and holy men, those who confessed sins to them, those who ate bread and fish blessed by them, those who visited them often and heard them preach, those who gave them goods, and those who had even seen them without any intention of capturing them. That had to be just about everyone bar a handful of people out of touch with reality who could honestly say that none of the above was true as far as they were concerned.

The Avignon condemnation had the effect of strengthening the group. Many of the common people had their own inner perceptions of holiness, and they obviously did not agree with the condemnation. Furthermore, the Alps were still inaccessible to any undesirables who wished to enter it.

About 1308 inquisitors attempted to enter the valley, and the *Vaudois* defended themselves. The inquisitors left without consequence. (Muston, 1875, I, 30) The killings then began. In 1312 a Waldensian woman was burned at the stake at Pinerolo (Merlino:1980, 46). In 1332 Walter Lollard, a Waldensian, was burned at the stake at Cologne (Stephens, 1963, 12). In 1335 Pope Benedict XII issued an order and another group of indeterminate numbers were killed. In 1348 twelve *Vaudois* were tortured, taken to the Cathedral of Embrun and burned (Muston 1875, I, 39). The persecutions went on and on.

In 1393, an inquisitor named Borelli took armed troops into the valley. He summoned all the people of the valley to appear before him. None appeared. The inhabitants were then seized, some from the road, some from the field. Many were imprisoned; many were burned.

In 1485, Innocent VIII betrayed his own name.[8] He drew up a letter of extermination, calling on all temporal powers to arm and destroy the valley people. It was a letter legitimizing simple murder:

> ...absolving beforehand all who should take part in this crusade from all ecclesiastical penalties, general or special, setting them free from the obligation of vows which they might have made, legitimating their possession of goods which they might have wrongfully acquired, and concluding with a promise of the remission of all sins to everyone who should slay a heretic. Moreover, he annulled all contracts subscribed in favour of the *Vaudois*, commanded their domestics to abandon them, forbade any one to give them any assistance, and authorized all and sundry to seize upon their goods (Muston, 1875, I, 31).

The Papal Letter laid no crime at the door of the *Vaudois*. The Pope wrote that their principal seduction was their appearance of sanctity. As a consequence, in 1486, 18,000 regular troops of the king of France and the sovereign of Piedmont gathered forces with thousands of fanatics and adventurers from all parts of Italy, and they marched on the valley. While the approaching army spread itself over the whole plain, the valley people took to the most hidden parts of their own hiding places. For warmth and for camouflage, the *Vaudois* covered themselves with the armor of the thick hides of animals. The arrows of the approaching

---

[8] Innocent VIII fathered eight children. It was joked that "henceforth, deservedly, Rome was able to call him 'father.'"

army, shooting upward, did not penetrate them. Their own arrows drove the approaching army away (Muston, 1875, I, 33-35).

In June 1488, the *Vaudois* placed their women, children and old people in a secret cave, but the cave was not as safe as they thought. The commander of the imposing army, La Palud by name, found the cave, and he lit a great fire at the caves entrance. As the inhabitants of the cave came out they were killed, many thrown down the great cliff which had protected them for centuries. At least fifty little children died that night with their mothers beside them. At least 150 women and old people also perished (Stephens, 1963, 18; Muston, 1875, I, 43-44). In 1655, John Milton wrote the following sonnet to venerate the martyrs of that day and the slaughter of 1655:

> Avenge, O Lord, thy slaughter'd saints, whose bones
> Lie scattered on the Alpine mountains cold;
> E'en them who kept Thy truth so pure of old,
> When all our fathers worshipp'd stocks and stones,
>
> Forget not: in Thy book record their groans
> Who were Thy sheep, and in their ancient fold
> Slain by the bloody Piedmontese that roll'd
> Mother with infant down the rocks. Their moans
>
> The vales redoubled to the hills, and they
> To heaven. Their martyr'd blood and ashes sow
> O'er all the Italian fields, where still doth sway
> The triple tyrant; that from these may grow
> A hundred-fold, who having learn'd Thy way
> Early may fly the Babylonian woe.

The year 1655 commemorates much more than the year John

Milton wrote his poem. It was a year of infamy. On June 3rd, sad news came out of Piedmont that the Duke of Savoy decided that the people of the valley who followed the way of Jesus be converted by force to the Catholic religion. Blind John Milton wrote letters to all Protestant states asking them to intercede. Envoys were sent. All efforts were to no avail. Eventually, gradually, the valley was penetrated. In 1686 Louis XIV forced the Duke of Savoy to try to exterminate the valley people. All their churches were razed to the ground, all pastors were taken out of the valley, and all their children who endured the ordeal had to be raised as Roman Catholics. The *Vaudois* and the Waldensians were, for the time, conquered. In 1687, armies came and violently drove the valley people, those who faithfully walked the way of Jesus, out of their homes. On the road many were tortured and slaughtered (Stephens: 1963, 7).

After the massacre, according to Henri Arnaud in *The Glorious Recovery by the Vaudois of Their Valleys from the Original by Henri Arnaud, their Commander and Pastor,* 14,000 were thrown into prison under inhumane conditions. They endured many months of harassment, torture, burnings, imprisonment, and the galleys. Henri Arnaud tells the story from notes taken at the time (Arnaud: 1827, 3). The Duke did release the 3,000 remaining, but he did so in the dead of winter. He did not allow them to return to their mountain home, but he forced them to travel into the Alps. Some reached Geneva, where they were treated with compassion and care by the Genovese (Stephens, 1963, 20-21; Acland:1827, lx-lxvi; Arnaud:1827, 4).

Three years later, eight hundred of these refugees, led by Henri Arnaud, returned to their homeland. Only six hundred made it, and they did so only with much difficulty, opposition, and political maneuvering. The journey took ten days, but the *Vaudois* were again on native ground (Arnaud:1827, 27). The journey, its military strategies, its sorrows and its joys are told with great feeling by Arnaud.

The *Vaudois* again began their life and their missionary activities out of their valley home. But the Archbishop of Narbonne condemned them when they again became active in his diocese. King Alfonso II, King of Aragon, forbade them entrance into his territory. But Waldensian activity, headquartered in Milan, was noted in the Rhone Valley, north-east Spain, Lorraine, and Lombardy. Eventually some of their members even reached Germany. An edict of emancipation was given on February 17th, 1848. Today, 15,000 people, who follow the simple way of Jesus, continue to live in the valley.

In 1532, through all this turmoil, the Waldensian bible, the Olivetan Bible, became the first bible in the French language. It was such a good translation that it remained the standard French bible for three hundred years (Stephens, 1963, 12).

The *Vaudois* and the Waldensians never accepted the designation of heretic which was placed on them. In fact, they devoted much skill and energy opposing the Cathars, whom they and the hierarchy designated as heretics. Durand of Huesca wrote the earliest Waldensian writing against the Cathars, *The Book against Heresy (Liber Antiheresis)* in 1180 and discovered in 1946. But, the group had run headlong into the years of dogma, which had been Church-developed during the *Vaudois'* isolation in the valley of the Alps.

THE ALBIGENSIANS AND OTHER MISSIONARY ENDEAVORS

Earlier writers from the eighteenth and nineteenth century saw the *Vaudois* and the Waldensians as the parent tree of the Albigensians.[9] They state it as a clear historical fact that the faith

---

9   Usher agrees with the statement. He brings in historians of his time -- Popliniere, Pilichdorf, and De Thou to support his thesis.

of the people of Southern France owe their origin to the *Vaudois* and the Waldensians (Acland: 1827, xli-xlii). A third way exists which we would propose. Allix, who was a member of the *Vaudois*, stated that the *Vaudois* did not have to bring the faith to the people in southern France. When they arrived in southern France, they found it already established. Their missioners only needed to support what was already present, and the missioners joined themselves to what had already been established.

Later the Waldensians did naturally join in supporting the people of Southern France. They were neighbors to one another. Allix continues: "...those authors who have written with any degree of honesty, call the Albigenses by the name of Waldenses, because they hold the same faith and opinions." He quotes Ribera and Gretser, the Jesuits, with Cardinal Hosius and Andrew Farin, as acknowledging the Waldenses and Albigenses *to be the same, and differing only in their name* (Acland: 1827, xliii). If this is true, the Albigensians were not the heretics that they were made out to be.

Furthermore, *Vaudois* preachers in southern France are notable. Peter de Bruys and his brother Henri were celebrated preachers among the Albigenses, and their success was noted by St. Bernard. Arnaud and Esperon also preceded the famous preacher, Waldo in the area of southern France. All of these were pastors, or *barbes*, as was Bartholomew, who was *barbes* of Carcassone, who later went to Hungary, Dalmatia, and other countries in that area (Acland: 1825, xliv).

Granted, a few Cathars sojourned among the Albigensians and the *Vaudois*.[10] The fact that there was some intermingling

---

[10] Confusion reigns with the Cathars in Southern France. Even some so-called Cathars in Albigensian territories were not unChristian or unCatholic. They insisted that they were good men and good women with troubadour connections and graces. Certainly the so-called Cathars in Albigensian territory are not the Cathars of other parts of Europe. They were more or less Christians. Christians in Southern France were by and large upset with the Catholic Church's torturing and killing their good neighbors. Later, some of these Christians would not have anything to do with the Catholic Church.

of the groups in common projects can be ascribed to the fact that the so-called Cathars of the area were not truly Cathars, but they were, according to social custom, acting as though they were. Commingling with them did not dampen the apostolic spirit of the Christians of the area or the apostolic spirit of the *Vaudois*. They were doing only what Jesus would have done, showing kindness to their brothers in humanity, and joining with others in works of love.

The relationship between these groups and the interchange of pastors in certain situations is noticeable and remarkable. Certainly the people of Southern France and even some of the good men and women in this area of the world were Christian and even Catholic, even though they had the social graces of the troubadours and the Cathars.

The up-coming horrid persecution of the people of southern France shows unbelievable disregard for human life. Because of its ugliness and duration, it is treated separately as a chapter of its owns in this book. Suffice it to say here that the light of Jesus, carried by these men and women, was not extinguished. It re-lights in the next century in the persons of Wycliffe, Huss, and Jerome of Prague, to name but a few.

Acland refers to the writings of Reynerius, the inquisitor, who tells about the movement of the *Vaudois* to England: "Lollard ... having preached in Languedoc, Guienne, and Germany, etc., ended his doctrine to our country [England], to be preserved in it forever through Wycliffe and his followers...." The Valdensian origin of this reformer's doctrine is attested also by T. Walden,[11] Cardinal Bellarmine,[12] Alphonsus de Castro,[13] and Popeliniere"[14] (Acland: 1825, xliv-xlv). The message was transferred from hand

---

11 T. Wvi Tit. xii, c. 10. Perrin, book i. c. 8.
12 Bellarmine, ii, Book I, c. 26.
13 Castro, *Con. Heresias*, book vi., 99. Perrin.
14 Popeliniere, *Hist.*, book i

to hand until it reached Wycliffe. Wycliffe developed and propagated the message in England.

Commenius and Camerarius both ascribe the origin of the Bohemian church to the *Vaudois* in the valley of the Alps. Thus the Moravians claim pure apostolic descent (Acland:1827, xlvi-xlvii). A crusade was called by the Pope against the Bohemian branch of the *Vaudois* church. A large army was turned back by the Bohemians, then called Hussites (Acland: 1827, liii). Reynerius mentions that Bohemians and Germans habitually sent their clergy to be instructed by the *Vaudois*. They knew that the *Vaudois* preserved the apostolic standard and their missionary work was tireless. Not only Bohemia and Germany, but Dalmatia, Holland, and many other places also received the message from the Waldensians and the *Vaudois*.

CONCLUSION

The existence of the *Vaudois* at a very early age of Christianity is clear, except to those who refuse to see the facts. For many years, this group, living in the womb of the Alps, was oblivious to the Catholic Church synods, councils, bishops, popes, and emperors that constructed the Catholic Church as we know it. They lived the simple, sheltered life given to them by some apostle or disciple of Jesus, and they lived it in their sheltered Alpine conclave.

When they were ready, as the Gospel instructed them, they did go out two by two as Jesus instructed his apostles. They were often mistaken for heretics, and some of them were killed. Later, they probably supported the people of southern France and the Waldensians in their struggle with the popes and bishops. They were concerned about the intransigence of the Roman Church and the movement of the Catholic Church away from the values of Jesus.

Their condemnation and massacre by members of the Roman Church is difficult to understand or justify. Would that Rome would have befriended and learned from this simple Alpine group! If they would have offered them a friendly hand, the whole church would have benefitted. The Catholic Church would be better off today.

Chapter 2

JOHN CHRYSOSTOM (345-407), THE TREASURE FROM THE EAST

"There was at Antioch on the Orontes a certain presbyter named John, a man of noble birth and possessed of such wonderful powers of eloquence and persuasion that he was declared by the sophist Libanius to surpass all the orators of his age"(Sozomen, H.E. 8.2).

Chrysostom spoke:

"It is the rich men who encourage strife
and litigation, jealousy and murder,
and the general disorder that distracts us,
with their troops of slaves and swarms of parasites,
panting for more wealth and public importance,
building great houses, adding field to field....
They are the people who bring
down the anger of heaven on us...,
not the simple...wisdom-loving Christian who is content
with a modest house, poor clothes, and a small bit of land."
(See John Chrysostom, Homilies, 3, 6, 7, 50, 52, 53)

JOHN CHRYSOSTOM (345-407), THE TREASURE FROM THE EAST

It is not improper for us to continue our second volume by entering into the age of John Chrysostom, even though we are backtracking into the age of Ambrose and Augustine. We do so to show a contrast. Toward the end of our first book we showed how Ambrose and Augustine did violence to the message of Jesus. Now we will show how, in the same age, another person in the East tried to follow Jesus.

While Ambrose and Augustine sat in their glory in the Western Empire, John Chrysostom rose like a comet, a ball of fire, in the Eastern sky. He was different than Ambrose and Augustine who, knowingly or not, had attached themselves to the earth through their allegiance to the Roman Empire.

John walked the path of Jesus. He, like Jesus, spent time in the wilderness and came out a messenger for the poor and oppressed. He was a brilliant speaker confronting the established religious and political order of his time. Like Jesus, he was eventually accosted by his enemies and was walked to his death. In many ways, he reminds us today of Jesus.

His writings have come down to us well-preserved and uncontaminated. Wendy Mayer and Pauline Allen, in their book *John Chrysostom* state: In the case of John Chrysostom no single volume can do justice to a father of the church whose output was so prolific and is so well preserved" (Mayer/Allen 2000, vii). Donald Attwater goes even further in his commendations of John:

> It is difficult to realize that more than a millennium and a half has passed since the golden voice of Chrysostom was stilled and the heart of fire ceased to beat in the worn-out, wasted body. He is so close to us, so endeared in his affectionate letters, his deep human sympathies, his understanding of the heart of man, that he speaks to our age

in its own language, as he has spoken to every age preceding us (Attwater 1939, ix).

John Chrysostom (c354-407)[15] lived most of his life in the city of Antioch. He was born there, some thirty years after Constantine had accepted the Christian church as the state religion of Rome and a dozen years or so after the capital of the empire had been established at Byzantium, henceforth to be known as Constantinople, "the new Rome " (Attwater 1939, 1). Later, he became a presbyter in Antioch. Toward the end of his life he was whisked away from that place, and he was made the Patriarch of Constantinople, an upgrade which John did not expect but did not in any way refuse. He would now be able to do his reforming in the great city of Constantinople.

Aideen Hartney wrote that he was a complex man (Hartney, 2004, 1). People who know him do not find this difficult to understand. John was complex. At any moment after he became a presbyter, from Antioch to Constantinople, he was an ascetic, a private and prayerful man. At the same time, he had a sense of humor. He was an extemporaneous, persuasive, and exceptional preacher and church administrator who said and did exactly what he thought needed to be said and what he thought needed to be done to form his people into a Jesus community. For example, he spoke for the poor. He did not care who was incensed or took offense by what he said or did -- be that person an emperor, an emperor's wife, a political leader, another member of the Church hierarchy, an important person of another religious sect, or a member of his own congregation. But, as he attempted to form a Jesus community, he, in fact, did imprudently offend the emperor, the emperor's wife, and, it must be

---

15 Chrysostom Baur indicates that Palladius, an excellent source who lived in John's era concedes 354 is the earliest date for John's birth.

said, as John would later agree, most vehemently, imprudently and mistakenly, the Jews.

He was utterly "now" involved and Jesus directed, intent on forming a Jesus community, no matter the cost. He barged constantly forward while he continued his ascetical life, enclosed from his people.

He would not preach in the ambo in the sanctuary of his churches so he could be seen as one of his congregation, but he preached strong, sarcastic words at times which were difficult for his community to hear, let alone practice. His ascetical life made him distant from his people even though he paradoxically preached from a position in the church that was considered to be "among the people." John would have done a better job if he would have involved himself with his people after the manner of Jesus and Paolo Friere. Rather than utilizing the deacons and deaconesses, he could have regularly served his people, as he did, in fact, do at one horrible incident in Antioch. At the same time, John had a pleasant personality and he was compassionate.

Why did John not continue to maintain regular contact with his people after that incident in Antioch? We will never know the complete answer to that. Perhaps, simply, he felt that he was called to remain the ascetic from the caves, even though that asceticism overwhelmed and destroyed not only him but his best efforts as well. Granted, Jesus, too, at a period in his life, was an ascetic in the desert, but he knew when to stop and make people his top priority.

In his preaching, John used the Gospel and the words of scripture which supported that Gospel message. He knew all the words of Scripture because he memorized them during his stay as an ascetic in the desert.

He so excelled in preaching that after his death, he was known as "golden mouth." His message was as direct and pointed as Jesus' own words, getting him, as we will see, into as much trouble as Jesus. He gave all his energy to promote the Jesus movement as he perceived it from the cloistered walls which he built around himself. After he was murdered, and after all the jealousies and belligerences had settled, no one, not even the Jews, whom he maligned, doubted that John lived what he preached. John was clearly a complex man.

JOHN'S FIRST CHURCH, ANTIOCH

John was born, raised and began his ministry as presbyter in Antioch in the province of Syria (now Antakya, in southern Turkey.) For years Antioch had been known as one of the stars of the Roman Empire. It was approximately the same size as Constantinople and Alexandria, with a population of about 200,000. Its inhabitants included "a motley collection of native Syrians and Phoenicians, Greeks (who predominated), Romans, Jews and others. (Attwater 1939, 8)."

Antioch was positioned beautifully on the left bank of the Orontes River, which gently flowed past the city toward the sea twenty-five miles away. The Slopes of Mount Silpios (450 feet high) rose like an immense wall to the southeast of the city. Antioch had an abundance of water from the Daphne springs, only five miles from the city and positioned high enough that it flowed naturally downward in order to provide the city's needs (Harkin 1983, 1-2), support a public bath, supply the needs of the hypodrome, an arena specially made for horse racing, and a theatre. Its main street was laid with marble, and oil lamps were lit on it to brighten the night. The city took pride in its great temple to Apollo, which was famous for the oracles given there (Kelly 1995,1).

It was a city of commerce and agricultural products. It

possessed a mint and an arms factory. It housed the administrative staff for military operations of the empire in the east and it was an important military base for war operations in the war against the Persians -- soldiers flowed in and out of the city (Kelly 1995, 1-2). It was also one of the centers of intellectual and cultural life in the Empire (Kelly 1995, 1-2). While John Chrysostom admitted that approximately 90% of the population were people of means, he was quick to also say that 10% of the population was abjectly poor (*Homilies on Matthew*, 66.3: *PG* 58.630).

John Chrysostom lived in an unsettled society. Many people lived under conditions of grinding want and many in a state of formal slavery; rapacious fiscal systems were administered by corrupt officials. The governing class was selfish and predatory. Not only property, but life itself was insecure. On top of all this, barbarians constantly threatened the borders of the empire and even penetrated it, so that even those who lived in the middle of the empire could not feel secure from the weapons and whims of the barbarians' constant thrusts.

Furthermore, the citizens of Antioch, John Chrysostom's hometown and the city of his first ministry, had a vast reputation for pleasure-seeking. They loved the good life, and they lived it wholeheartedly. They were cynical and fickle to the point of being unreliable.

At the time, the populace celebrated pagan festivals with as much fervor as they did in pre-Christian days. If any calamity, big or small, should strike a family, the family members more than likely would seek out the aid of the pagan priests rather than the local presbyter. Nothing changed much in the daily life of the common citizenry even though Christianity, by all appearances, was superficially becoming more and more prominent.

Antioch was even more complex than John. Isabella Sandwell states: "...We know that many of the main temples in the city continued to stand for much of the period.... Similarly, many of the traditional pagan festivals appear to have survived in some form." (Sandwell 2007, 42) They celebrated New Year's, an early spring festival, a May festival, a wine festival, and the Olympic festival that was celebrated for forty-five days every four years. All of these were celebrated in honor of one pagan god or another. (Sandwell 2007, 42).

Even non-Christians came to hear John because he was such a good speaker. It was recreation for them. This upset John. At times, even the Christians were more fervently Christians than at other times. But the non-Christian milieu in and about their lives tended to intrude and smother the Christianity in them. They would listen to John, feel great in church, and then go home and live like the pagans that surrounded them. In his homilies, John raved on and on about that fact.

In Antioch, Christianity also had weakened its own self because it was not homogenous. Robert Wilkin in *John Chrysostom and the Jews in the Late Fourth Century* states: John himself grew up in a place in which three Christian bishops -- one year it was even four -- fought in a power struggle over one legitimate bishopric (Robert Wilken 1983, 10-16). They threw condemnations at one another convinced that the other groups were heretical. There were two Nicene groups, the Meletians, the group to which John belonged, the Eustathians, and the Arians (Sandwell 2007, 45).

Furthermore, the emperors from Constantine onward controlled the Church. The Church had little autonomy. Not even John Chrysostom with his "unmeasured freedom of speech," as Socrates called it (Socrates, *Hist. Eccl.* VI.3, *PG* 67.668), was unable to change that. Emperors had their hands on any significant move churchmen made. They decided when a council of the church was held and, according to their tastes, whether the

Nicenes or the Arians were in control or sent into exile. As John moved into the Church hierarchy, he was very aware of all these things. Nonetheless, he did not care about the sensitivities of emperors or anyone else. The Christian life of his people was his single occupation.

From Emperor Theodosius onwards the secular emperors became more or less permanently housed in Constantinople. Therefore, the Second Ecumenical Council of 381, as a political move, raised the status of the Church see of Constantinople. The Patriarch of Constantinople was then second in ranking hierarchically after the Pope in Rome. Bishops, monks, politicians and pagans, religiously-oriented or not, flooded into Constantinople in increasing numbers to reside there for lengthy periods in order to seek influence and favor.

Antioch, also, was an important city for the emperor. Sometimes it was the emperor's permanent residence. When it was not, it was the emperor's vacation home.

FAMILY BACKGROUND

For the most part, we get a glimpse of John's childhood from his own homilies and sermons. But other sources do exist. Socrates and Palladius, especially, give us insights into John's early days.

Socrates alone of John's contemporaries mentions that John's father's name was Secundus and his mother's name was Anthusa (Socrates, *HE* 6:3; Baur 1959, 1). In his own works, John never mentions his father by name. His mother was Christian and his father was apparently not so inclined. His father was a civil servant in the Bureau of the Commander of Military Operations. Palladius[16] indicates that John's father was military commander

---

16 Palladius is a good source. He was in close contact with John in Constantinople. He was ordained by John as a priest and probably as a bishop. He quotes John accurately. (Robert Meyer, tr. and ed., *Palladius: Dialogue on the Life of John Chrysostom,* Newman Press, 1985, 6.

of Syria but he was undoubtedly not that high in the hierarchy of the military to be the top commander. He died when John was an infant (Meyer *1985*, 1; *Dial* 5:34-35).

John had one sister, who died as a child. John hardly mentions her.

When his mother became a young widow, she decided not to remarry, a decision made by many Christian widows of independent means at that period of time in the Christian East. John's mother was not rich, but she had connections, and she had the intellectual ability to handle the money that was hers in order to comfortably raise John. She had to put relatives, tax-collectors, servants, and city officials in their place so that enough money would be available to give John the education he received. She supersedes Monica in the gallery of Christian wives and mothers. She, rather than Monica, is the one whom our own age and earlier ages have to thank for unselfishly raising an eminently Christian man (Baur 1959, 4).

John portrays Anthusa as rightfully complaining, as any mother in the same situation might, that while it was bad enough for her to be left with a baby daughter, it was infinitely worse to be left with a squirrelly infant son (Hartney 2004: 69). Anyone who has raised an intelligent boy with "ants in his pants" knows what Anthusa was talking about. At the same time, Chrysostom later wrote a memorial to his mother in his famous work "On the Priesthood." It is one of the most beautiful memorials of all Christian antiquity: full of gratitude, he emphasized in his mature age, that not a breath of discord had marred the beautiful tenderness of the relationship between his mother and him (Baur 1959, 4-5).

In one of his homilies, John recalls a life threatening incident from his childhood:

Long ago when he was a mere lad, he was walking with a friend through the gardens alongside the Orontes on his way to a martyr's shrine when his companion noticed a white object floating on the water. It looked like a piece of linen, but when they saw that it was in fact a book they vied with each other in sporting rivalry to fish it out. When they got hold of it and turned a page, they discovered to their horror that it was covered with magical formulae. Its terrified owner had tried to get rid of it, but they knew that even so he had been arrested and executed.... Anyone dabbling in sorcery or magic arts, or possessing books dealing with such ... subjects was liable to summary action. The city was everywhere patrolled by soldiers on the lookout, and as they handled the incriminating codex the young men saw one approaching. Rigid with fear, they managed to conceal it, and when he had passed on his way they flung it back into the river (found in Kelly, 1995, 25).

They had escaped certain death, John told the rapt audience that was listening to his homily.

John studied rhetoric under Libanius,[17] the professional orator. He studied philosophy under Andragathius, a man whom history otherwise does not recognize. It was then that he, unlike

---

17 Libanius was an excellent teacher who knew how to inspire youth. He was a genius at prose oratory, but he relied on others for his material. He looked after the welfare of his students in their needs. His students, in turn, were loyal to him. When Libanius was sick, they faithfully visited him and watched by his bed at night. He disliked Christianity, holding it responsible for the ills of the times, but he carefully distinguished between Christianity and Christians. He corresponded regularly with St. Basil, and he disapproved of persecutions of Christians. He taught many Christians, including Basil, Gregory Nazianzen and John Chrysostom (Baur, 1959, 18-21).

the other Church fathers in the West whom we have considered, became disenchanted with the philosophy of the time.

John knew no Latin, no Hebrew, nor any other language but Greek, yet he handled that Greek language with a dexterity and clarity rarely recognized. He was a master in the art of eloquence.

At some point c367, when he was approximately eighteen years old, John turned away from a secular, professional career. Palladius stated that "he revolted against the sophists of word-mongering" (Palladius *Dial* 5:35). He esteemed the philosophy of Jesus, Paul and the Apostles over the philosophy of Plato and Aristotle. For him, Jesus' words and deeds stood far above those of any other man (Attwater 1939 ,11).

It was not unusual in John's age for a person with John's talent and position in society to turn to the Church for a profession. It was an attractive move for a man in the middle class. His talents as a rhetorician could be amply used in his preaching and writing. Joining the clergy had its financial benefits as well. For example, in Carthage, a bishop received a salary five times that of a professor of rhetoric. John was not necessarily turning his back on either his social class or his education by becoming a cleric. In fact, the people John alluded to in his early writings were all from wealthy, reputable and powerful families (Harkin 1983, 6-7). Only gradually did John move toward a reclusive, prayerful form of life, away from affluent living (Harkin 1983, 7).

In 369, John was baptized by the bishop of Antioch, Meletius (360-381) (Palladius *Dial* 5: 35,). He spent the next three years as that bishop's aide (Palladius *Dial* 5:35). In actuality, Meletius was probably not a Nicene nor an Arian bishop. He professed that he just did not know.[18] In his wisdom, Meletius thought that not only was it impossible, but it was not important for us to know such intimate matters about God, such as, was the Son always

---

18   Such wisdom we have seen in few others since Athanasius and Arius began their feud

God, or was he created and then God poured himself totally into Him.[19] Some things were for God alone to know, not us mortals. Meletius had a gentle temperament which "promised a much desired peace for his subjects... who were weary of endless debate" (Harkins 1984, 20-21).

Valens (364-378) then became emperor of the east, and he favored the Arians. He expelled Meletius, the "fence-sitter," from the old Church and prohibited him from celebrating the liturgy within the city walls. Euzoius, an Arian, became bishop of the old church. Meletius's community was forced to assemble for worship outside the city walls, either on the mountain slopes or by the bank of the river (Sandwell 2007, 46). John was ordained a lector at this time (Palladius *Dial* 5:35).[20] A lector read the Old Testament passages and the Epistles during worship.

John then joined a theological school taught by Diodorus who eventually became Bishop of Tarsus. Diodorus had a profound influence on John. He laid emphasis on the literal and historical meaning of the texts of scripture rather than the allegorical and mystical interpretation taught by Origen, the Alexandrian and the Augustinian schools. John remained faithful to the literal interpretation taught by Diodorus throughout his life (Attwater 1939, 16). Diodorus's school was also connected to the church of Meletius, so it, too, met outside the city of Antioch. This group of theologians renounced marriage for themselves, adopted a distinctive dress, and gathered regularly for prayer (Sandwell 2007, 48). John lived at home during this period in his life.

It was not long before Bishop Meletius was sent into exile by the emperor. This was the fate of anyone who held beliefs not compatible with the beliefs of the emperor at the time.

---

[19] Another group, the Anomians, also entered the mix. They argued that God the Son was essentially different than God the Father. John often preached against them, considering them completely outside the walls of civilized debate.

[20] Lector is the ordination in the hierarchy which precedes sub-deacon.

JOHN THE ASCETIC

John eventually became unhappy with his life. Five or six years after his baptism, his mother died, leaving him more freedom. He decided to join a group of more rigorous ascetics who lived in the mountains around the city of Antioch (Attwater 1939, 19). The decision was not an easy one for John. He was afraid of leaving familiar comforts. He was a frail man. He was concerned that he would starve or be worked to death. So he did ask many pointed questions, but we do not know what answers he received to those questions. He asked, would he have the essentials of life? Would he have fresh bread? Would he have to use the same oil for his lamp as he used on his food? Would he have to eat ugly, tasteless vegetables every day? Would he be forced to do too much servile work, like digging holes in the ground and carrying heavy loads of water? In short, he asked all the questions about things which would drain his strength and leave him unable to pray. (See Harkin, 1983, 9)

It was apparent that John was accustomed to being a protected city boy. In spite of his fears, he was soon in the desert, vigorously living the life of an ascetic. He spent two years there tutored by an old Syrian ascetic. Attwater tells of the severe life of these people who lived in or near the mountains:

> These men, dressed in rough clothes, were up before sunrise to pray and praise together, and at dawn went to their work, which occupied them for most of the day – tilling the ground to raise their food, building dwellings for themselves, milling and baking, making mats and baskets, and so on. Five more times during the day there was an office of psalms and prayers, and there was but one full

meal, in the evening. Their food was bread and water, sometimes vegetables and oil, and it was eaten in their cells or sitting in the open air – there was no refectory, no cloister, even the nearest proper church might be some distance away (Attwater 1939, 20).

Though only a few of the monks attained to or even aimed at a religious life alone in a cave, a state called *megaloskhemos*, John lived for four years doing just that. It was then that he memorized the whole bible.

After these six years, John returned to Antioch. We can only guess why. Undoubtedly his health began to fail from his ascetical life and especially his years of rigorous cave living. John clearly overdid it. Upon returning, many thought that the desert had affected his personality. His enemies, even later in Constantinople, said that he was "hard, passionate, morose and arrogant" (Sozomen, *Hist. eccl.* 8.9; Harkin 1983, 9). Perhaps, rather, he had turned from the affluent to an ascetical life and was more rigorous with himself and others. He was unable to move away from the ascetical life. He ate alone from this time onward and he abstained from wine (Harkin 1983, 9).

Theodosius I (379-395), then, became emperor. In a decree of February 27th, 380, he made Nicene Christianity the religion of the empire. He expelled the Arians from the old church, recalled Meletius from exile, and set him up as bishop in the Great, or Golden Church (Sandwell 2007, 46). John must have been overjoyed that he could again join forces with his old friend in the cathedral church.

John was then ordained a deacon by Meletius (Palladius *Dial.*, 5: 35). It was one of the last acts of Meletius in Antioch. Meletius then went to the Second Ecumenical Council at Constantinople, which voted him "president" in the absence of legates from Rome. But Meletius was able to do little presiding. This wise man died at the Council. His wisdom and spirituality were recognized, and he later became a saint of the Church (Attwater 1939, 24-25).

In 386, the successor to Meletius, Flavian, ordained John a presbyter (Palladius *Dial* 5:36). John was approximately 42 years old at the time of his ordination (Attwater 1939, 25). He served an apprenticeship as a preacher in the Great Church and then he was given a congregation of his own in the Old Church (386-397) (Palladius *Dial* 5:36; Sandwell 2007, 54).

But the Arians did not go away. Later in 380 they began to have influence again in the city (Sandwell 2007, 46). Needless to say, much ambiguity and confusion reigned over the Nicaean doctrines. For many, the decrees of Nicaea introduced concepts which were not found in the bible and were therefore dangerous. They insisted that God the Father is one, the sole origin of everything that has been, is, and will be. The Council definitively stated that the Son is equal to the Father, thus compromising what they saw as basic Christian belief. (See Harkin, 1983, 11)

HOMILIES AND SERMONS

John's popularity as an orator of the Word of God soared, but he always tried to be a messenger of Jesus. Nine hundred of John's sermons and homilies survive to this day, most of them preached in Antioch. If there was a basic thrust of his sermons, it was that he showed compassion and empathy for the poor and the downtrodden.

John was not a handsome, vibrant preacher. His looks had nothing to do with his popularity. He likened himself to a spider in the pulpit. He was short and thin and he had a weak voice. His too large head was bald. He had bright deep-set eyes beneath a wrinkled forehead above hollow cheeks and he wore a straggly grey beard. His complexion was most often pale (Attwater 1939, 36).

In his preaching, he was especially critical of those who used intertextuality to the detriment of the true meaning of scripture. The text "should actually be proposed in its entirety, with nothing added. Many people, at any rate, [he never mentions Augustine and Ambrose by name] bandy about some other passages from the Scriptures as well, drawing out distorted interpretations" (Hill 2003, 10-11).

John loved to preach. It was as if he were created to do so. Wilken quotes John as saying: "Words rush from my mouth like a mighty torrent...." When he stepped before a congregation, he came alive. "As soon as I open my mouth, all weariness is gone; as soon as I begin to talk, all fatigue is over...." (Wilken 1983, 106).

John's homilies and sermons were usually given extemporaneously, without notes or with only a few notes scribbled on a piece of paper, a style which required intense preparation. George of Alexandria, a late biographer of John, said that people were amazed that he had no scrap of paper or text in his hand but held forth in an extemporaneous manner, something they had never seen before (Kelly 1995, 57-580). In many of his sermons he would run into a rut speaking this way. Two examples are the following. John spoke: "Yet, indeed, I do not know how I was led so far away from my topic in this sermon (Hartney 2004, 38)." He also said at another time: "But the chain is dragging me away still further from my subject, and pulling me back again, and I cannot bear to resist it, but am drawn along willingly..." (Hartney 2004, 201, footnote 16).

Some say that John entered such asides in a prepared text, either before giving it or after, when he was preparing it for publication. But this is not likely. As Hartney says:

> It would not always be practicable for a preacher to accurately predict audience reaction and respond to it in advance to the extent we see Chrysostom do. And if we consider the question of revisions for publication purposes another issue arises. I find it hard to accept that Chrysostom would have meticulously gone through his homilies to add in those little asides and pretended interactions with the audience, and yet leave untouched the many inconsistencies of argument, the contradictions, and the tangential ramblings that remain in the text. Such complex narratives point clearly to off-the-cuff speaking… (Hartney 2004, 39).

John did work on some of his homilies and sermons before publishing them. At the same time, many of his homilies were never touched again by him until they were included in the nine hundred works transmitted to history. Because of this fact, his works vary in quality. Indeed, we have every word he spoke. *Notarii* or scribes were present because people knew that he was a great preacher, and they wanted to preserve his words. The scribes sat in the back and recorded his messages in shorthand.

The general audience John addressed was, for the most part, not much different than the congregations in most of our city parishes today. His congregation was mainly the wealthy or at least the comfortable in society. He preached to artisans and business people. But there were also some noticeable differences between now and then. John preached to soldiers, ascetics, and church officials, especially in the later Constantinople church. He also preached to slaves who were forced to be present by their masters. It was a status thing – the wealthy in society wanted to parade the slaves they had because the more slaves you were able to buy the more important you were in society.

John Chrysostom did not believe, as did Augustine, that parts of the sermon on the Mount were meant only for monks. He said in his homilies:

> Speak not to me of mountain heights, of caves and gorges and inaccessible deserts; these alone are of no avail to soothe the unrest of the soul. Much more, to this end one needs... the love of Christ (*De Compunctiones*, 2,2 [47,413]; *De Sacerdotione*, 6,6-8 [48,682-5]; *De virginitate* 4 [48,536]; *Homily* 44,1; *Concerning Matthew's Gospel* N57, 463ff all found in Baur 1959, 111). All men are obliged to love; all are called to perfection; but not all are called to monastic life." Is it only monks who are obliged to please God? No! God wishes that all should become holy, and that none should neglect the practice of virtue."(*Homily* 21, 6 in *Gen*. [53,182-3]).

All things are the same for the monk and for the married person, except that the married person has a husband or wife and a family. The sermon on the Mount, in all its parts, refers to the married person as well as the monk. All are to "turn the other cheek"; all are to love their enemies. The difference between the two is environmental. The monk is free from the noise of the world, free from any clamor. Silence rules in his world, while the clamor of children and the desires of a wife or husband rules in the married person's life.

Husband and Wife

In his sermons and homilies, John stressed the equality of man and wife in sexual relations, insisting that neither deprive the other of intercourse without his or her consent, for "the love [*Eros*] of husband and wife is the force that welds society together" (*In Eph.*, 5:22-33 *Hom.* 20; In I Cor., 7 *Hom.* 19).

In *Homily XX, on the Ephesians*, John said that the love between a husband and wife quietly surpasses all other kinds of love. As they encourage one another to forge ties throughout the community, they ensure that the human race is not pulled asunder. The sound relationship between husband and wife enables sound relationships between parents and children, between other members of the household, between neighbors and between other members of the community. If husbands and wives do not enjoy a harmonious relationship, then chaos rules and the very structures of society come under threat.

John expressed the good marriage symbolically as a healthy body: the husband is the head and the wife is the body. Husbands are urged to love their wives, and wives their husbands, and they must be willing to undergo any kind of suffering for her or him. Their love for one another ensures their living together harmoniously. John at times stated, according to the common writings of the age, that the wife was inferior to the husband, and she must obey him. Nonetheless, if you read his messages in their entirety, it was clearly not the message he wished to convey. Such statements are some of the sorry effects of his contemporaneous style. It is clear that in practice he rose above such statements.[21]

---

21 John entrusted women with diplomatic and missionary roles, and Olympias was made head deacon in Constantinople. He was clearly willing to give women a co-worker's role. When, in his extemporaneous preaching, he fell into the fourth century rut of calling women weak and placing them in inferior roles, his congregation knew him too well to take these words seriously. His actions spoke louder than his words, and his demeanor in the pulpit when he made such slips showed his embarrassment..

He stated that even though a man might be able to rule over his servants through fear he should never treat his wife in such a way that she fears him. After all, she is his body. A good marriage owes nothing to the desires of the flesh, but is basically a union of the spirit and the soul. Respect is needed. If it is present, there will be no serious teasing or gossip. If it is present, a good wife will not be suspicious of her husband, and a good husband will not do anything to arouse suspicion. Furthermore, the wife will not nag.

He tells his married couples to look past external beauty to the beauty within (Hartney 2004, 59-65).

The Arians and Manichaeans

John was strongly Nicene. He was undoubtedly advised to be so by Flavian and even perhaps Meletius, who, as we have already said, thought that it was inappropriate, even impossible, for us to speculate on God's own domain, God's own inner life. But in his wisdom Meletius knew that a young presbyter must ride many rough waves without willingly steering himself into an avoidable storm. Clearly, Nicene was the only way for a presbyter or bishop to be if he was to have any influence within the Catholic Church.

In his homilies, John Chrysostom did feel the need for "intellectual correctness," and he did take off in a flurry whenever he noticed an error floating around his neighborhood. His first sermon against the Anomians is instructive in regard to John's feelings not only about the Anomians but the whole Nicaean debate. John makes this interesting statement: "... how meager and mediocre human knowledge is and what madness it is for men to pretend they possess the fullness of knowledge of God since God is incomprehensible to both men and angels (Cf. Harkins, FOTC 68.1.1 9 p. 1 and nn. 1 and 2; Harkins 1982, 24).

We cannot help but wonder if the great wisdom of John's

friend Meletius, the one who said "Who knows what happens in God?" was not shining forth here. Furthermore, we cannot help but believe that John Chrysostom, a wise man himself, did not see that his statement extended far beyond the Anomians, and was a criticism of Athanasius, Arius and the Council of Nicaea itself.

The Manichaeans were often targets. In one lengthy tirade he takes them to task for saying all wickedness came from some uncreated evil principle, wherein, in fact, it comes from our own perverse choices and negligences (Kelly 1995, 96).

The Jews

The Jews knew that John was a decent human being who deserved their respect. However, the feeling was not mutual. The pressures of trying to form a Christian community was the reason for the bad attitude John had for the Jews, but, morally speaking, a good goal does not justify the bad means used to attain it. Human beings, be they Gentiles, Jews or Muslims, deserve respect. John did not give that respect to his Jewish neighbors. From the perspective of a people's history, his attitude toward the Jews was one of the great mistakes in his life. It is easy to excuse John for having blind spots. But the Jews, who were his neighbors, had to suffer horribly from his attitude toward them.

He, therefore, spoke vehemently against his congregation going so far as to participate in Jewish life and celebrations (Wilken 1983, xvi-xvii, Lim 1995, 178). He saw this disintegration of his Christian community even in Antioch, where John spoke out most strongly against the Jews. It was in Antioch that he delivered his eight discourses *Adversus Iudaeos*, which are clearly polemic in nature."In them Chrysostom often spoke bitterly.... There is little of the gentle Christ weeping over Jerusalem" (Harkins, 1984, xxxi). "If you admire the Jewish way of life, what do you have in common with us?" he spoke. "If the Jewish rites are holy and venerable ... our way of life must be false." (*Adversus Iudaeos,* 1.6; 852; Wilken 1983, 68) Such statements, of course, were blatantly untrue. Certainly, if a person admired the Jewish way of life, he or she could still live an intense Christian life, and if a person held the Jewish rites as venerable, even supporting them by being with them as they celebrated, they did not have to believe that the Christian life was false.

John's rhetoric went on and on. And there was one painful difference between John's words and his predecessor preachers who spoke against Judaism: his predecessors spoke about Judaism in general while John spoke against a specific group of individuals in his own city. In a number of other places, he did, in the heat of his sermons, call the Jews "Christ-killers." In another place he elaborated on a broad theme: "Jeremiah said: 'Your house has become for me the den of a hyena.' He did not simply say 'Your house has become the den of a wild beasts, 'but the den of a filthy wild beast,' and again, he spoke: "I have abandoned my house, I have cast off my inheritance. But when God forsakes a people, what hope of salvation is left? When God forsakes a place, that place becomes the dwelling of demons." He then continues:

> But at any rate the Jews say that they, too, adore God. God forbid that I say that. No Jew adores God! Who says so? The Son of God says so. For he said: "If you were to know my Father, you would also know me. But you neither know me nor do you know my Father." Could I produce a witness more trustworthy than the Son of God?

> If, then, the Jews fail to know the Father, if they crucified the Son, if they thrust off the help of the Spirit, who should not make bold to declare plainly that the synagogue is a dwelling of demons? God is not worshipped there. Heaven forbid! From now on it remains a place of idolatry. But still some people pay it honor as a holy place (John Chrysostom, *Discourse*, 1).

Chrysostom's citation twists the facts. Jeremiah did not say: "Your house has become the den of a wild beast, the den of a hyena," but "Is not my inheritance to me a hyena's den?" (Jeremiah 12:7 LXX) Chrysostom also did not do justice to the quotation from John. Jesus said in John: "You know neither me nor my Father. If you knew me, you would also know my Father," (John 8:19 NAB) not "If you know my Father, you would know me." (Harkins 1984, 11) These are unfortunate statements. He also called the Jews "wretched" and used other rhetorical terms that he had no reason to use.

It is painful today for us to read such words in the writings of Chrysostom. After all, Jesus was a Jew, and Jesus participated in Jewish life and celebrations.

John went even further than verbally abusing the Jews. He said that those who persisted in celebrating Jewish festivals were to be refused communion. John's invectives against the Jews even caused violence against them. In Antioch in the closing years of the fourth century, a period of bloody collisions broke out between Christians and Jews. John's extemporaneous diatribes played a part in provoking them (Attwater 1939, 38).

Toward the end of his life, John tried to make amends. He stated that the Jews were the group most supportive of him in the difficult days preceding his exiles. If they were supportive of him at that time, they were kinder to him than he was to them. In this the Jews are to be admired. They are the ones who, in the words of Jesus, loved their enemy. John was not loving when it came to the Jews.

In regard to relations with the Jews, it was John Chrysostom's solid community members, who supported and respected Jewish life and rituals, not John Chrysostom, who were the true members of the people's history of the Church. When it came to the Jews, take John Chrysostom out of the picture and put his solid community members into *The Peoples' History*. Those solid members of his community who ignored John's diatribes and who supported and respected Jewish history were, in this regard, the giants of this part of history.

The Poor

But John again returns as a member of *The People's History* when he speaks of the poor. Nothing got John into more trouble politically than his love for the poor and his personal repulsion to affluence. John's graphic sermon on Psalm 48.8 tells the story:

> He pours contempt, for example on the luxurious mansions of the wealthy, with their lofty columns crowned with gold capitals, their marble-encrusted walls and their fountains of running water, their exotically carpeted floors... A man's true glory, does not consist in things like these, but in gentleness, humility, and unfeigned charity (See John Chrysostom, *Homilies*, 3, 6, 7, 50, 52, 53).

He is even more derisive of Christian women, even consecrated virgins, who attended church with elaborate, showy hair-styles, decked out in jewelry, gold, rubies and pearls, and dresses with long trains: "It is as if they were actresses, or even street walkers; they only succeed in making themselves laughing-stocks to pagans" (See John Chrysostom, *Homilies* 3, 6, 7, 50, 52, 53).

He is simply furious at the sumptuous banquets people put on "... at which the tables are laden with all kinds of luxurious meats, fowls, costly fish, pastries, and wine from Thasos, the guests reclining on ornate, softly draped couches while flute-players, dancers and buffoons are brought in to add to the fun."

These tirades are matched by other descriptions of a heart-rending nature:

> ...of impoverished outcasts stretched out all night, not on silver couches, but on dank straw in the colonnaded entrances to the public baths, frozen stiff with cold and racked with hunger; of the beggar who, while warmly clad citizens saunter home from the baths to well-prepared dinners... (See John Chrysostom, *Homilies* 3, 6, 7, 50, 52, 53).

Then he unites the above thoughts into one, and he speaks these condemning words from the pulpit:

> 'As for you, you would let your own children for your circus charioteers, you would throw away your very souls for your pantomime dancers, but to Christ when he is starving you would not hand over the smallest piece of money. ...But when we have to give an account of ourselves, when we hear Christ saying, 'You saw me hungry, and gave me nothing to eat, naked and you did not clothe me,"

what shall we say, and what shall we plead in our defense?' (See John Chrysostom *Homilies* 3, 6, 7, 50, 52, 53).

With such an agenda, is it any wonder that John was reamed out of Constantinople's elite society as Christ was reamed out of Jerusalem? Jesus, we know, spoke similar words. Those who lived in luxury, in the palaces, did not take kindly to John's words.

On Hatred and Violence

Even though he was a contemporary of Ambrose and Augustine in the West, John spoke a different word about hatred and violence. In his book *On Matthew*, he wrote: "It is certainly a finer and more wonderful thing to change the mind of enemies and bring them to another way of thinking than to kill them.... We ought to be ashamed of ourselves, we who act so differently, and rush like wolves upon our foes...." And further on he says: "If, led like sheep into the pasture, should we behave as though we were ravening lions? This mystery requires that we should be innocent, not only of violence, but of all enmity, however slight, for it is the mystery of peace." He then expressed concern that, when the celebrant prayed at the altar for true peace among people and nations, the people celebrating with him were inwardly calling down vengeance upon their enemies.

John's Faults as a Preacher

Besides his rhetoric against the Jews, John admitted other faults as a preacher. He admitted that his asceticism sometimes got in the way. He admitted toward the end of his life that he tended to be intolerant. He often spoke angrily, uncompromisingly, when he saw that his people did not match up immediately to Gospel norms. He admitted that he should have set up an agenda to bring his people along gradually and with a little more kindness. Although he certainly never knew the words to the twentieth century song by Arlo Guthrie, it was exactly what he thought he should have done: "Inch by inch, row by row, going to make this garden grow; going to mulch it deep and low, going to make it fertile ground." Furthermore, he could have gotten his fingers dirty by aiding in their projects.

Also he admitted that he often set himself up for problems with important people, problems he could have avoided if he would have been a bit more diplomatic and understanding. Yet he did have a great sense of humor which aided him to reach many. In a group of people who knew a certain proud teetotaler, he addressed the man as "my old soak." When he met the man who everyone in the group knew was trying to live in poverty, he said "look out for this guy, or he will steal your tunic when you are not looking." The man who was well known as a charitable man, he called "my old gangster" (Palladius 18, 128).

The Burdens John Felt as a Preacher

Preaching, especially extemporaneous preaching, was a burden for John Chrysostom, as well as a delight. The life of the serious, regular, extemporaneous Christian preacher was difficult. The total experience, even though it had its moments of joy for John, was, at times, a nailing to the cross. Preparation for a good, extemporaneous homily or sermon took John many hours of prayer and research. Sometime, to be true to Jesus, John had to treat some difficult issues. Other times what John thought was a delight struck painful chords in some listener or even in the whole congregation. Then John had to deal with the consequences. Sometimes the message was misunderstood or John said an unfortunate word or two which he later regretted. That set up the need for individual conversations, apologies, and regrouping afterwards. Then the next sermon or homily had to be readied.

John Chrysostom would have admitted that it was not an easy occupation. When he was in exile, he churned his words over and over in his mind wondering if he spoke the right word or if he should have used different words or phrases. Undoubtedly, John's "mission" against the Jews was foremost in his mind, as was his "mission" against the emperor and his court.

John's Use of Rhetoric

Of all the people who used rhetoric in the past, Tertullian, Justin Martyr, etc., no one used rhetoric more literally or effectively in his preaching than did John Chrysostom. But John was sincere from his head to his toes. He was generally not out to annihilate people with the tools he had been taught. He merely wanted to help his people to be better followers of Jesus.

Many attended his sermons and homilies "from the schools" simply to learn rhetoric from him. In fact, John was concerned that the rhetoric that he used became lessons which were analyzed and imbibed, and his message was completely missed by the scholars in his congregation. This, of course, was not his intent. Isabella Sandwell writes: "At various points in his sermons Chrysostom suggests that it was the rhetorical display, rather than the content of the sermon ... that his audience were interested in. His own audience also treated him like a sophist and acted "like spectators sitting in judgement [sic] on his speaking *(De Sac. 5.1 (SC 272.283);*Sandwell, 2007)."

THE HOMILIES ON THE STATUES

Twenty-two of the nine hundred homilies and sermons which were transmitted through history were preached from Lent to Easter during the persecution of Emperor Theodosius. Even though the incident was not history-making in comparison to other great events that influenced mankind, it was by no means a minor incident.

Emperor Theodosius I imposed a tax, the nature of which we do not know, but the people of Antioch felt that it was outrageous. John indicated that it was not only a poor person's problem (*Hom.* III:6). All felt that the tax was outrageous and most played some part in the uprising. Libanius stated that in all five of his orations on the riot, everyone first showed tears.

When supplication and tears did not work, some gave inflammatory speeches and then others became violent (van de Paverd 1991, 21). They threw stones at imperial portraits and tore down statues of Theodosius, Flacilla, his first wife who had died, Theodosius's father, and his sons Arcadias and Honorius (van de Paverd 1991,22). They then dragged the statues through the streets of the city, began to set fire to official places, and had designs on doing so to the palace of the emperor himself. The whole riot was over in three hours (Attwater, 1939).

John and Libanius both assert that even children were among those executed immediately after the riot. John states that with God it is sufficient to confess your sins to cancel the accusation, but the emperor is not so merciful. He continues:

> But with man it is altogether the reverse. When those who have sinned confess, then they are punished the more, which indeed has happened in the present instance. And some have perished by

the sword, some by the stake, some given to the beasts, and not men only, but children as well. And neither this immaturity of age, nor the tumult of the people..., nor poverty, nor having offended in company with all, nor promising that they would never hereafter dare to repeat such deeds, nor anything else, could at all rescue them. But they were led away to the *barathron*, without reprieve, armed soldiers conducting and guarding them on either side, lest anyone should carry off those condemned, whilst mothers also followed afar off, seeing their children beheaded, but not daring to bewail their calamity, for terror conquered grief and fear overcame nature (John Chrysostom, *Hom. III 6, 56, 32-48 as translated by van de Paverd, 1991, 37*).

He also stated that Celsus, the Consular, took pains to not pick innocent people off the streets, but only punish the guilty. But who knows that John was not using some type of conciliatory rhetoric here for the good of the rest of the city. John said that it was not necessary to leave the city unless persons were guilty (*Or. XIX and XXIII*). But he also said that Theodosius had no reason to punish anyone else. He had already inflicted punishment on those who did the rioting.

Poverty or youth was not accepted as an excuse for having participated in the riot. The riot was clearly much bigger than that, and Theodosius obviously felt threatened. Many from the city went to the church for asylum. The plan of Bishop Flavian and John was that the bishop would go to seek amnesty from the emperor, and John would keep peace among the people in the church.

In the meantime, Theodosius sent two judges, Caesarius and Hellebicus, to pass judgment on the rest of the people (Attwater

1939, 43). John states that Theodosius, utilizing his imperial absolutism, at one point, actually ordered the extermination of the whole city, with its men, children and buildings, reducing the city to a small village of women (See van de Paverd 1991,39). John certainly knew that the emperor could use his power to do anything he wished. The people knew it as well. That is why so many fled the city in small groups, going to the mountains or the desert, leaving the woes of the city to the few who remained. Those who left did so at the risk of their lives due to the oppressive environment that they were entering.

All knew that even if the whole city was not destroyed, other punishments could be expected, for the emperor had made it clear that he was not appeased. The city could be sacked, part of the population could be executed, especially the councilors of the city, property could be confiscated or, even more burdensome, fines and taxes could be imposed on the citizens.

Now that the people who remained in Antioch were in the church, they prayed and lived with John, who occasionally addressed them (van de Paverd 1991, 41). Some who never saw the inside of a church now spent their days, 24/7, within its walls (van de Paverd 1991,47). John's first homily opened with the following words: "What shall I say, or what shall I speak of? The present season is one for tears, and not for words; for lamentation, not for discourse; for prayer, not for preaching (*Hom. II:* 1, 33 as found in van de Paverd, 1991, 47)."

Many members of the city council and lawyers of the city were arrested. The judges conducted a court session which used torture of the *humiliores*, believe it or not, the little people who were witnesses, to obtain the convictions of the counselors and lawyers. John joined those who stood at the outer gates of the atrium. He testified as an eye-witness to what happened among the relatives of those tortured:

> A mother and a sister of a certain person, who was among those under trial within, sat at the very vestibule of the judges, rolling themselves on the pavement.... ...and hearing as they did the voice of the executioner, the stroke of the scourge, the wailing of those who were being scourged, the fearful threats of the judges, they themselves endured, at every scourging sharper pains than those who were beaten.
>
> For since in the confession of others there was a danger of accusations being proved, if they heard any one scourged, that he might mention those responsible, and uttering cries, they, looking up to heaven, besought God to give the sufferer some strength of endurance, lest the safety of their own relations should be betrayed by the weakness of others, while incapable of sustaining the sharp anguish of the strokes....
>
> There was lamentations within and without. Inside, on the part of those responsible; outside on the part of their relatives (John Chrysostom, *Hom.* XIII, 1, 137, 36-138, 16).

Towards evening the sentences were read. The orchestra, hippodrome, theatres and baths, the means of recreation in the city, were closed. Land was taken away from many, as well as metropolitan rank, and bread no longer could be distributed to the poor. (The poor? Why were the destitute innocents singled out?) The councilors were stripped of their authority, and that authority was given to Ellebichus, the military commander (van de Paverd 1991, 78-79).

Of those convicted, some were exiled; others were sentenced to be put to death. The carrying out of further capital punishments was suspended and left to Theodosius alone to decide. The property of those convicted was confiscated and their houses were sealed. The judges then took their rest (van de Paverd 1991, 78-79).

Were the councilors and lawyers guilty and deserving of the punishments they received? All agreed that not one of them participated in the acts of violence.

Before Easter, Theodosius acceded to the plea of Bishop Flavian and granted a full pardon. It would be an understatement to say that Theodosius overreacted, as he pulled men, women and children off the street and executed them. Theodosius, the one who introduced Christianity as the religion of the empire, and set himself up as a Christian leader, was a closet follower of the Divine Right of Kings, not Jesus. The whole event was not Christian. Jesus, who said "Blessed are the peacemakers; blessed are the meek" would never have held a city captive like Theodosius held Antioch. And why did he do so? Because they resisted a stiff tax and tore down statues of him and his family. Even if the tax was necessary, the proper response could have been compassion and understanding. No Christian leader would put its citizens and even children to death.

Because the baths, the theatre and the marketplace were closed, the Churches alone were filled to overflowing. It became the only recreation.

John had done the job of keeping the peace among the people while awaiting the bishop's return with a pardon. His prestige overflowed all the way to Constantinople. His sermons given at that time show that he was very much in touch with the fears of the people, and he was one with them in their situation. At the same time, he diplomatically maneuvered around the emperor and officialdom in doing the task at hand.

Unfortunately, this is probably one of the only times he was in contact, one-on-one, with the poor and the homeless in the streets. He undoubtedly got to know the poor personally and intimately. But characteristically, the bond would not last. Each had his own life style and would go back to it when the pardon was given. John was the establishment and the ascetic, even though he did not like to admit it; the poor had to scavenge for food.

But at that point, John gained the confidence he needed as an exceptional preacher, and from that time on he used his gift to its capacity, even if he, as did most preachers of his time, drifted out of touch with the real people whom he served.

THE EMPEROR KIDNAPS JOHN TO BE CONSTANTINOPLE'S PATRIARCH

Ten and a half years later, on September, 397, Nectarius, bishop and patriarch of Constantinople, died suddenly. Nectarius was known for his mediocrity, having done or said nothing worthy of note (Lim 1995, 171). Without John's knowledge, Eutropius, a high ranking imperial eunuch, nominated him to be the new Patriarch (Palladius *Dial* 5: 36). John was then elected by the synod of Bishops.

The powers that existed in Constantinople knew that the people of Antioch, and maybe even John Chrysostom, would resist this election, so one day in late October John received an urgent summons from Asterios, governor of Antioch. He was ordered to present himself immediately at the great martyr's shrine outside the gate. The shrine was by the road which led northward to Constantinople. John went as ordered. He was loaded in a carriage and was literally kidnapped. As the group road off with John in tow, they informed him that he was elected and appointed Bishop and Patriarch of Constantinople (Palladius *Dial* 5:36; Kelly 1995 104). The journey through Tarsus and then over the Tarsus range covered 736 miles.[22]

JOHN CHRYSOSTOM, PATRIARCH

Ironically, John was consecrated bishop by Theophilus, Patriarch of Alexandria, the person with whom John had problems the rest of his life (Palladius *Dial* 2: 17-18). Emperor Arcadias forced Theophilus to consecrate John on February 26, 398 ("Introduction," Palladius, *Dialogue on the Life of St. John Chrysostom*, p. 2).

John not only took the job, but he took up his official duties with vigor. As Aideen M. Hartney said: "Constantinople, as imperial capital of the eastern empire, provided a great challenge for Chrysostom's reforming instincts" (Hartney 2004, 20). He thought that he had much to do and he was not gentle in doing it. If he was Bishop of Constantinople some things had to change quickly.

John immediately stripped the patriarch's residence of all luxuries, an action which was not popular with the clergy and richer citizens of Constantinople. It and other events that followed corresponded to Jesus action of throwing over the tables of the money changers in the temple in Jerusalem. After stripping the bishop's residence, John dismissed recalcitrant clergy from their positions, and warned others to be more disciplined in their lifestyles. (Hartney 2004, 20) Then John scrutinized the finances. He cut back on all showiness in the churches, and he scaled back on the entertainment and hospitality functions, pocket money

---

[22] John was now known as probably the greatest preacher of his age.

which the Patriarchs previously held to accommodate dignitaries (Hartney 2004,20). This money was redistributed to care for the sick and the poor (Hartney 2004, 20).

His preaching did not change much. He encouraged the community to alter their life style to a more Christ-like mode. The great throne of the Patriarch of Constantinople, which was present in St. Sophia's Church, collected dust. John refused to use it because it was in the sanctuary, far from the people. Socrates tells us that John no longer stood, as he did in Antioch, but he sat in the deacon's station in the midst of the congregation (Mayer/Allen 2000, 26). He immediately attacked the greed and selfishness of the clergy and the richer element in society in his homilies.

In his homily "On Eutropius" John said before all the people assembled that even though the Imperial Court promoted him to his position, it did not necessarily mean that good relations would always exist between the emperor, the empress and himself. The emperor and empress apparently had not been warned of the internal workings of this man who they brought into Constantinople to be patriarch. John, in his turn, did not understand that a persuasive presbyter in Antioch could get away with saying things bluntly while the Patriarch of Constantinople might have to say basically the same things, but with a bit more tact. Or we can look at it from another angle: it was necessary that some bishop stand up and confront the established order no matter what the consequences might be for him personally. Enough toe kissing had taken place since Constantine. John and Jesus did just those confrontations for their respective ages.

Meanwhile, John straightened out ecclesiastical charities to preclude waste or misdirection of alms (Palladius, *Dial* 5: 39). He built hospitals, delegating two presbyters to administer them, and he hired cooks and other workers to look after them (Palladius, *Dial* 5: 39).

John's favor with the emperor, the empress, and many respected citizens of Constantinople constantly waned, and John in his zeal did not ease the situation. Eudoxia, the empress, was at the height of her influence, yet John admonished her for an act of injustice to a poor widow. He also gave a pointed sermon on the vain extravagance of women, and Eudoxia was told that he was pointing his finger at her personally (Palladius, *Dial.* 6:40). John never shook in his sandals before the power of the emperor or empress or anyone else. Rather, he complained:

> He [the bishop] is distracted on every side and is expected to do many things that are beyond his power. If he does not know how to speak effectively, there is much complaining; and if he can speak, then he is accused of being vainglorious. If he cannot raise the dead, he is worthless, they say: such a person is pious, but this man must not be. If he eats a moderate meal, he is accused on this account, and they say that he ought to be strangled. If he is seen at the bath, he is greatly criticized. In short, he should not even look at the sun (John Chrysostom, *Homily I on Titus*, NFPNF 13.523, PG 62.669).

John had to go back to Antioch to settle some matters that he had begun and never finished. After all, he had been kidnapped from the place, and he had left loose ends. Perhaps he chose a bad time to do so. He was gone for four months, and he missed the baptisms on Easter in Constantinople. He had to soothe those who were upset by his absence, and he probably was inserted on a number of "enemy" lists by doing so.

OLYMPIAS AND HER MONASTERY OF NUNS

According to the historian and bishop, Palladius, Bishop Nectarios, the previous bishop, had ordained a woman by the name of Olympias to the deaconate in the church. Olympias had her own monastery, but she spent much time serving the church of St. Sophia, the main church in Constantinople. She became the life-long friend of John. Palladius tells us about Olympias and John in interview fashion. In his interview, he does not recognize the fact that women, too, have knowledge and patient endurance:

> The Deacon speaks: Now, if it is not too much trouble, tell us about Olympias, if you have some knowledge of her.
>
> The Bishop: Which one. There are several.
>
> The Deacon: The deacon of Constantinople who was the bride of Nebridius, the former prefect.
>
> The Bishop: I know her well.
>
> The Deacon: What kind of women is she?
>
> The Bishop: Do not say "woman," but "manly" (*anthropos*) for she was a man (*aner*) despite her bodily appearance.
>
> The Deacon: How is that?
>
> The Bishop: By her life, her asceticism and knowledge, and her patient endurance in trials. (Palladius, *Dial* 16.179-190.)

Sozomen said much the same: "... Olympias the deacon

(*diakonos*) showed herself to have manly courage (*andreika*)" (Sozomen, *Ecclesiastical History 8:24*). John had a close relationship with the women in Olympias's monastery, and especially Olympias herself. As bishop and patriarch he was the only outsider, certainly the only man, permitted to enter the walls of its cloister. He did so to give instructions to the women.

According to Attwater, Olympias was about thirty-seven years of age in the year 400. She was indeed the widow of the prefect Nebridius. The emperor Theodosius had pressured her to marry a kinsman of his, but she rather devoted herself and her wealth to good works in Constantinople. Olympias had had many holy friends before John Chrysostom entered Constantinople: St. Gregory Nazianzen, St. Gregory of Nyssa, St. Amphilochius, and St. Epiphanius, but she was completely devoted to John's cause. She suffered much on John's behalf (Attwater 1939, 93).

Another woman friend of John's who suffered with him was Nicarete, who is mentioned in the Roman Martyrology on December 27. She was forced into exile from Constantinople because of her loyalty to John (Attwater 1939, 94).

John himself ordained other women deacons, Pentadia and Procla, from Olympias's monastery. All three, Olympias, Pentadia, and Procla, were well loved by John, and they insured the continuity of pastoral ministry within the greater community. Olympias also saw that John had food and provisions. The deaconesses were often at the Church of St. Sophia or working out of it. Palladius says of Olympias and by inference the other women deacons:

> These are those whom priests and levites passed by, and to the shame of men, a manly (*andreika*) woman took them in and to the shame of bishops, a female deacon (*diakonos*) gave them hospitality; she whose praise resounds in churches for many

other reasons, in imitation of the Samaritan, whoever he was. Going down from Jericho and finding a man beaten by thieves and half-dead, he put them on his own mount as far as the inn, mixing the oil of compassion with the wine that heals, and treated his wounds (Palladius, *Dial 17, 122-130).*

Their job at St. Sophia's Church was to assist in the baptism of women, to visit Christian women in their homes, to manage all the charitable work of the Church, and to tend to the pastoral and spiritual needs of the Church. Olympias was put in charge of all the deacons, men and women, at St. Sophia.

JOHN'S OTHER ACTIVITIES

In Constantinople, John was involved as peacemaker with the emperor and high ranking officials in time of dispute. In the year 400 he negotiated with the dissident Gothic general Gainas over hostages. He helped the once powerful eunuch, Eutropius, from the wrath of the military, turning antipathy into sympathy. He boldly reminded the emperor of his obligation to Nicene Christians. He convened synods and deposed bishops who were not doing their duties. He appointed replacement clergy when necessary.

He took special care in supporting a mission in Phoenicia, which he aided to help the orphans, widows and the poor there, sending sandals, clothing and food. He told the missioners working there that he would supply a constant line of support.

THE AFFAIR OF THE TALL BROTHERS

The Patriarch of Alexandria and the Patriarch of Antioch took careful notice of "how ridiculously" John was playing his cards.

By every standard of the world, they were correct. They were there to take advantage of John, to knock him down wherever they could for their own advantage. They were all patriarchs. Why should Constantinople stand above Alexandria and Antioch in church hierarchy? It was an on-going feud that the patriarch of Alexandria and Antioch carried on with the patriarch of Constantinople, but now it took an ugly turn.

Theophilus, the Patriarch of Alexandria, got his chance when John granted asylum to a group of Origenist monks who had fled from Theophilus's wrath. Origen died during the persecution of Emperor Decius from the effects of tortures endured for Christ. The erroneous teachings attributed to Origen were these: the divine persons are unequal; human souls existed before Adam; Christ's soul pre-existed; the human body, after the resurrection, will be non-material; no one will receive eternal punishment; all intelligences tend to reabsorb in the one Fount of Beauty; the allegorical sense of Scripture is the only sense that makes sense. Whether Origen actually taught these things was and still is a matter of dispute, but some of the statements attributed to him are intriguing. John, for one, while taking exception to this or that statement attributed to Origen, was a fervent admirer of the man (Attwater 1939, 106-107). And what was wrong with sincere theological debate?

Theophilus could have been tried for his misbehavior in pursuing these monks whom he had excommunicated, but he skillfully avoided that by taking the offensive (Hartney 2004, 20-21). Quoting the second canon of the First Council of Constantinople, held in 381, he said that John should be the one called to account: "The bishops are not to go beyond their dioceses to churches lying outside of their bounds, nor bring confusion on the churches; but let the Bishop of Alexandria, according to the canons, alone administer the affairs of Egypt; and let the bishops of the East manage the East alone...."

The whole matter would have been ludicrous if John had not amassed a great many enemies in Constantinople, including the Empress Eudoxia. The entire business with the empress extended over a two year period, during which John danced in and out of royal favor. But disfavor took over and deepened, and Eudoxia gradually agreed with Theophilus – John must go. The loss of imperial favor was the final straw and John was deposed and exiled in 403.

THE SYNOD OF THE OAKS

Then Theophilus held the Synod of Oaks, in which he accused John of other faults: he wrongfully dismissed a cleric; he ate alone; he diverted funds of the Church into his own coffers. Because of such matters, he declared John Chrysostom deposed.

The emperor and empress now turned on John. They exiled him under the Patriarch of Alexandria's recommendation (Palladius 1:19, 20). The extent of this first exile was merely one day, for the empress suffered a miscarriage and an earthquake hit the city on the same day. The empress was a superstitious person, and she felt that the wrath of God was falling on Constantinople. The emperor and empress also noted that many of the people of Constantinople objected strongly to the exile. So the emperor recalled John to Constantinople the very next day (Hartney 2004, 20-21; 72-73). John hesitated returning. He was not willing to be the ping-pong ball in an ecclesiastical/imperial ping-pong game played by this emperor, empress, and the Patriarch of Alexandria. But he did return, much to the joy of many of the people.

After his return from exile, the people insisted that he take the dust off the bishop's throne, give his usual benediction, and deliver a homily from that throne in order to show the people that he was resuming his patriarchal duties (Mayer/Allen 2000, 26).

Things proceeded calmly for a couple of months, until a silver statue of Eudoxia was dedicated amidst much celebration. The triumphant goings-on coincided with John's liturgy, and the singing and dancing drowned out John's preaching. John lashed out at this aberration, calling the event an insult to the Church. John further infuriated Eudoxia, this time comparing her to Herodias, who had John the Baptist beheaded (Hartney 2004, 21). Eudoxia was furious. New charges were brought against John, and John was exiled once more from Constantinople in June, 404 (Hartney 2004, 73). The emperor sent John to the farthest parts of Armenia (Palladius 1: 20-21; 10: 66, 69-70).

All the way down the halls of history we can hear Theophilus laughing at the incredible stupidity of John. But John was not sorry. When he had taken the job of patriarch, he vowed to throw caution to the wind. He was determined to sit there and say all that he had to say to form what he considered to be a Christian community after the person of Jesus. John did just that – even though they should murder him for doing it, as they murdered Jesus.

Then John kissed some of the bishops, who wept over his leaving (John's own grief prevented him from kissing them all). He then went into the baptistery and called on Olympias along with the deaconesses Pentadia and Procla, and Silvina, and he addressed them:

> Come here, my daughters, listen to me. I see that the things concerning me have an end. "I have finished my course" and perhaps "you shall see my face no more. This is what I ask of you. Let no one prevent you from the good will you have had towards the Church. And if anyone be brought forward for consecration as my successor, provided

he comes willingly and at the will of all, bow down to him as if it were to John (for the Church cannot exist without a bishop). And thus you will find mercy. Remember me in your prayers (Palladius *Dial* 10:66-67).

He was then removed by mule from Constantinople to his place of exile in the farthest part of Armenia. The Emperor Honorius of the West and Pope Innocent I attempted a new synod to stop the recall (Palladius *Dial* 1: 16; 3: 24-25; 3: 28-29), but Arcadias imprisoned the legates who brought news of the synod. (Palladius *Dial* 4: 29-31). The Pope then broke off all communion with the Patriarchs of Alexandria, Antioch, and the newly appointed Patriarch of Constantinople, the chief ecclesiastical connivers in this situation.

After John's exile Olympias was accused of setting fire to the Church of St. Sophia in protest. When brought before the prefect to answer the charges she replied, "My past life ought to avert all suspicion from me, for I have devoted my large property to the restoration of the temples of God."

As a testimony to her, John Chrysostom wrote to her:

> Now I am deeply joyful, not only because you have been delivered from sickness, but even more because you are bearing adversities with such fortitude, calling them trifles, a characteristic of a soul filled with power and abounding in the rich fruits of courage. You are not only enduring misfortune with fortitude, but are making light of it in a seemingly effortless way, rejoicing and triumphing over it. This is a proof of the greatest wisdom (John Chrysostom, *Letters 6).*

From 404-407, seventeen of his extant letters are addressed to her from his exile. His letters to her are passionate, intimate, pastoral and theologically profound. He called her "the reverend God-loved deacon, Olympias."

Because of his constant correspondence with the people of Constantinople, in 407 John Chrysostom was once more placed under heavy guard, and he was supposed to be transferred farther away to Pityus of the Caucasus, a journey of 400 miles. The guards were commissioned to move him as quickly as possible through difficult, often mountainous terrain (Palladius *Dial* 11: 72). No longer was John allowed to ride a mule or a litter. He was forced to walk as Jesus was forced to walk to the cross. The little party made forced marches of some 20 kilometers a day. On September 12 they reached Dazimon (today Tokat). John was utterly exhausted, feverish and burnt red by the sun, which alternated with the chilly, heavy fall rains. The guards pressed on. On September 14 John begged the soldiers to postpone departure until the fifth hour of the day to give him a chance to rest. But they refused his request. John walked on another four or five kilometers and collapsed. He died that night saying as he always did: "Glory be to God for everything." It was a death march all the way, and it was probably meant to be just that (Palladius *Dial* 11: 72-73). Thus the reign of John Chrysostom, Bishop and Patriarch of Constantinople, ended.

CONCLUSION

It would be unfortunate to close here without further comment on the complicated life of John Chrysostom, Patriarch of Constantinople. John Chrysostom certainly was an intense and knowledgeable lover of Jesus Christ and his message. For the most part, he was a compassionate lover of his fellow human beings. He was against intertextuality. And he definitely stood by the sermon on the mount as the 10 commandments for all Christians. This is what made the man the great saint which he certainly deserves to be.

To point out some of his flaws, we can use Levin in Leo Tolstoy's *Anna Karenina*. Levin was rejected in marriage by Kitty, whom he loved very much. He could have returned to his farm with a sour attitude and become a recluse, a hermit, forcing his peasant farmers to work his land, and make a living off of it. The peasants would have reluctantly worked for him because they had little choice in the matter. They would have done less than an adequate job because their heart would not have been in it. It was much like John Chrysostom's congregation. They listened to this Golden Mouth, were enthused by his words, then went home and lived their pagan life as they did before. Then, because he was so intent on forming a Christian community, John got frustrated with them and gave them "holy hell" next week when he again stood before them to preach.

Levin took a different tack. He started to go out with the peasants and helped them bring in the hay. He was the first one out there in the morning to help them plant the fields. He worked with them all day long, sweating with them. After long conversations with the peasants in the field, he found out their needs and desires. He decided to do profit sharing with them, and he found out that he got much more yield from his fields when the peasants were working for themselves.

Perhaps John could have learned from Levin. If John would have only learned to give up his hermit life, if he would have pitched in with his community in the work that had to be done for the community of Constantinople as he had to do during the riots in Antioch, he might have been more successful. If he had done so, he might have become a closer follower of Jesus Christ. He might have learned from his people, and he might have learned earlier that the Jewish people were truly fine human beings, deserving more of his respect. His congregation also might have learned from him how to follow Jesus more intensely. Furthermore, he would have lived a lot longer life than he did, learned even more, and done much more to develop a Christian community in his deeper respect for all individual persons.

Chapter 3

CYRIL AND NESTORIUS

The Roman Empire collapsed. With its collapse came also the complete collapse of Roman Catholicism in North Africa. The main reason that Catholicism collapsed so quickly in that region was the total disconnect between the people and the Roman Church. In The *Rise of Christianity,* W. H. C. Frend states: "Only when one reads that congregations had sometimes to be addressed through an interpreter does one realize the extent of the gap that divided the great majority of the clergy from part of their flock" (Frend 1985,700).

It was precisely the arrogance and self-righteousness of some of the believers in Roman Christianity which we have seen in Augustine and others that alienated the people of the entire region of North Africa. In North Africa, it is a myth maintained by the Christian faith that the believers of Islam contaminated Christianity in that area of the world and forced Christianity out. It was the Catholic faith itself that must be held responsible for the demise of any visible trace of the Jesus movement there. We only hope that someday, when North Africa becomes open to the rest of the world, Donatists may still be found in the hidden mountains of North Africa.

But North Africa was only symbolic of the total problem -- it was not the only problem that caused the church to flounder in the Empire. The problem was more wide-spread. Worse than losing North Africa to Christianity, many clergymen, including four in the same age of history -- Athanasius, Ambrose, Augustine, and Cyril of Alexandria -- reshaped the movement founded by Jesus of Nazareth so that it would be unrecognizable by him or his followers. Sadly, the Church canonized them saints, and even worse, proclaimed them doctors of the church (superb teachers of Christian belief). Ever since, the Church has gone steadily downhill, with only a few plateaus and small hills to hinder its freefall.

Falling off the cliff in freefall is also a good way to describe the church of Cyril (376-444) in Alexandria in the era immediately after the death of Augustine. Cyril, if we glance at him superficially, was a great theologian who led the Council of Ephesus to understand that Mary, Jesus' mother, was *theotokos* (the God-bearer).

In reality, Cyril was a self-centered, manipulative Patriarch of Alexandria, who was interested in defending only himself and perhaps the patriarchate which he owned in Alexandria. He manipulated events and destroyed anyone who got in his way as he stomped over the terrain of the church to obtain his own glory. He was in actuality no great doctor of the church. He was no doctor of the church at all.

NESTORIUS, CYRIL, AND THE COUNCIL OF EPHESUS

The Council of Ephesus was held in 431. One of the main purposes of the Council was to declare Mary, mother of Jesus, *theotokos* (the God-bearer). It also declared that Nestorius, the young Patriarch of Constantinople (428-431) was a heretic. Cyril of Alexandria orchestrated the whole procedings. This book has already leveled some strong statements against Cyril, an established doctor of the church. It is time to explain the what's and the why's of the matter.

NESTORIUS

Nestorius was born in the late fourth century in Syria. He became a monk and studied under Theodore of Mopsuestia. He was a great preacher and likewise a great fighter against heretics. The Emperor Theodosius II appointed him Patriarch of Constantinople in 428, approximately 20 years after John Chrysostom died. He remained Patriarch of Constantinople until 431, and he died about 451.

Nestorius strove to be an immovable force against heresy when he became Patriarch of Constantinople. The young Patriarch thought it was his mission to be a strong voice in the Church of his times. But he ran headlong into an immovable object, Cyril, the Patriarch of Alexandria.

Until recently, scholarship shredded Nestorius. The following statement of Niceta of Rimesiana is typical of writings about him in our church history books throughout the ages of church history. It, and other writings about him down to recent ages, could have come from the pen of Cyril of Alexandria himself:

> Nestorius ... suddenly introduces two persons while pretending to distinguish two substances in Christ. In his unheard-of wickedness he assumes that there are two sons of God, two Christ's -- the one God, the other man; one, begotten of the Father, the other, of the mother. Thus he asserts that Holy Mary is not to be called *theotòkos* [Mother of God], but *christotòkos* [Mother of Christ], since she gave birth not to Christ-God, but Christ-man. But, if one believes that he speaks in his writings of one Christ and that he teaches one Person of Christ, let him be careful not to give

too easy credence to such an interpretation (Niceta of Rimesiana, Chapter 12).

Such statements do not do justice to Nestorius's beliefs.

CYRIL

Cyril succeeded his uncle, Theophilus, as Patriarch of Alexandria, following a bloody, disputed election (Von Dehsen 1999, 46). Cyril's activity as patriarch led to riots started by his cohorts, which culminated in the torture and murder of the distinguished female scientist and philosopher, Hypatia (Russell 2000, i; Von Dehsen 1999, 46). As we will see, he also destroyed the naïve Patriarch of Constantinople, Nestorius, as well. Self serving, he found that he could borrow the common Christology of his age, disguise himself as the mind behind that Christology, and use it as a tool to help him rise out of the difficult position in which he found himself within the Church. He later purported to generously give that Christology as a gift to the Church (Fairbairn 2003, 6). This ruse was so well executed that he fooled everyone and became a saint and doctor of the Church.

The events are a bit difficult to follow. A group of Egyptian monks who fled from Alexandria brought charges to the imperial court in Constantinople against Cyril. Emperor Theodosius asked Nestorius to look into the matter. Nestorius took his time in investigating the matter. He realized that charges against another patriarch were serious matters and would have serious consequences. The monks told Nestorius that Cyril was responsible for expelling serious minded Christians from the church; he expelled numerous members of the Jewish community from Alexandria; he was responsible for torturing and killing the woman, Hypatia. Rather than defending himself before Theodosius or Nestorius,

Cyril slyly took a diversionary tack and went on the offensive against his judge, Nestorius. That offensive attack was an insidious one, an only apparently theological one.

Suddenly, Cyril immersed himself in Christological doctrine, something that was not characteristic of him. John J. O'Keefe states: "From the time of his ordination to the episcopacy in 412 until the eruption of the conflict with Nestorius in 428, Cyril's works reveal no sense of Christological crisis (O'Keefe 1997)." It was out of fear for his own well-being that he dug up a theology of Christ in order to take the offensive against Nestorius. Bishop Theodoret of Cyrrhus, a contemporary of Cyril and Nestorius wrote that he was convinced that Cyril's attacks on Nestorius were driven by non-theological motives (ACO I i/7, 141 as found in Chadwick 2001,538). This is not to say that Cyril, previously, never wrote commentaries on biblical theology. He did. However, most of these are insignificant. They have never been translated or studied (O'Keefe,1997).

The simple monk, Patriarch Nestorius, was the pawn, the object of Cyril's manipulation of reality. Cyril was out to destroy the person who was supposed to investigate him. Nestorius was naïve: he was mystified and baffled by Cyril's actions.

NESTORIUS, MANIPULATED

Nestorius, fresh from a monastery just outside of Antioch in Syria, was well-trained in theology by Theodore of Mopsuestia (Chadwick 2001, 527). His theology was not heretical. But it was in the Greek mode, and it was a slightly different slant on the theology of the times.

Cyril rightfully feared Nestorius, the Patriarch of Constantinople, whose views inevitably commanded a wide audience. Cyril knew that he had to call on all the resources that he could muster, including spending time learning Christology (Russell 2000, 31). Cyril also knew that Nestorius could destroy him for his behavior in Alexandria. He attacked the Christology of Nestorius to create a stir throughout the Christian world. Cyril was not a man who would easily be destroyed by an up-start (Fairbairn 2003, 5).

POLITICS PRECEDING THE COUNCIL

Nestorius was eloquent. His first sermon on the day of his inauguration was a diatribe against all heretics. He was intent on worming all of them out of their holes, wherever they might be. No heretic was exempt, not even a saintly Bishop Paul, who was well-known and respected by the aristocrats among the populace of Constantinople. Nestorius's zealous frontal attacks caused Nestorius's, not Bishop Paul's popularity to wane. Cyril noted all of this.

Furthermore, Nestorius soon found out that the Church of Constantinople which he inherited was, for him, a strange place. He was not used to urban monasteries with monks in the city exercising a ministry among the people. One of those revered by the citizenry was the archimandrite, Dalmatius, who had been offered the Patriarchate of Constantinople before the See was given to Nestorius. But Dalmatius claimed himself a recluse, and he refused the patriarchate, because, as he said, he wished to continue to live an enclosed life, separated from society (Russell: 32). In the summer of 431, he clearly broke from his recluse life, and with great ranting and raving, demanded that Nestorius's views be rejected, and Cyril's claims be accepted by all (Russell 2000, 32).

Another monk, Hypatius, archimandrite of a monastery in Chalcedon, wandered hither and thither about the city of Constantinople as Pulcheria's spiritual director. Pulcheria was the sister of the Emperor Theodosius, and a psychological case in her own right.

Nestorius gave an order that all monks busy themselves with the sacred rites in their own monasteries and not concern themselves with the spiritual life of the lay people in the city. This, of course, made Nestorius' popularity fall further, crashing thunderously like lightning from the sky.

Then Nestorius made an enemy of Pulcheria herself. Pulcheria was not a nun, but even though she was sister of the emperor, she lived a life of a consecrated virgin in the palace of the emperor. She had brought up her brother after the early death of their parents, and she held a heavy influence over him and the decisions he made by him as emperor. When Nestorius took over his church in Constantinople, Pulcheria's picture was hanging over the main altar. Nestorius immediately had the picture removed. He also said that the robe which she donated as an altar cloth should be removed and never be used again (Russell 2000, 32; Limberis, 58). Pulcheria was also used to receiving communion in the sanctuary with the clergy. At Easter, she tried to enter the sanctuary and Nestorius closed the sanctuary doors to her, saying that no woman ever should enter therein. "Why?" she said. "Have I not given birth to God?" She was obviously convinced that, as a consecrated virgin, she was equivalent to Mary herself. Nestorius threw up his hands at the statement. All he could think to say to her was the unfortunate statement: "You have given birth to Satan (Russell, 32; Limberis 1994, 54-55)!"

NESTORIUS, A RECLUSE IN CONSTANTINOPLE

At that point, Nestorius, not Dalmatius, became the recluse in his own home. His popularity with the general Christian populace was meager, and his popularity with his own Christian people of Constantinople was not much better. Chadwick tells us politely that Nestorius was "cordially hated at the imperial court" (Chadwick 2001, 542). He was easy prey to Cyril who sought to destroy him.

Then Nestorius began to preach sermons which apparently made certain distinctions to *theotokos*, literally "The bearer of God," or as we would say "the mother of God." At that point, some were incensed. They went to Nestorius with a question: "Was it proper to say Mary was *theotokos* (mother of God) or *anthropotokos* (Mother of the man, Jesus)?" Clearly they were trying to trip Nestorius with his own words. At the same time, they asked Nestorius a legitimate question.

Nestorius answer was wise and also legitimate. He said that both were correct, but, he admitted, the New Testament text appears to accentuate *theotokos* more than *anthropotokos* (Russell 2000, 33). His own preference, of course was that *theotokos*, although correct, not be used. He found it an ambiguous word, open to aberrations of all kinds in an age that was paying more and more undue honor to Mary's virginity (Fisher 1896, 152-153). Pulcheria's statement above is an excellent example of such aberrations. Also, for many, veneration of Mary was becoming adoration -- she was becoming a goddess for them, an Athena, Christianized.

Cyril caught word of all of Nestorius' difficulties as quickly as his messengers could make it to Alexandria. He was delighted at the supposed "mistakes" of this young Patriarch of Constantinople. He would use them to escape the wrath of the emperor. Cyril rebuked Nestorius publicly.

Nestorius, not Cyril, went on the defensive. He wrote to Cyril that he was confused by Cyril's activities. If Cyril had a problem with any of Nestorius's words, he, as a fellow patriarch, should have approached him privately and discussed the matter with him in a spirit of brotherly love. He did countercharge that Cyril was expressing bountifully his own personal piety, while his love for his own brother was clearly sparse. Nestorius ended by writing that he was ready to die for the faith of Christ (Russell 2000,35-36).

Cyril then knew that Nestorius was vulnerable, and he began an all out attack on him. The hornet's nest which Cyril aroused eventually enveloped the Church in the whole Mediterranean region (Baum and Winkler 2003, 23). It was like the present day weapons of mass destruction in Iraq insofar as there was no substance to any of it.

Cyril contacted the Emperor Theodosius and Pulcheria. He also contacted significant clergy. For Nestorius's part, he gave a sermon on December 6, 430, in which he complained about the "golden arrows" of Cyril, bribes given by him to officers of state to keep his diversion afloat (ACO I, v. 43.17, as found in Chadwick 2001, 531). Bishop Theodoret of Cyrrhus also said that he was outraged by the hard evidence of bribery (ACO I, iv. 85 as found in Chadwick 2001, 538).

But Cyril gained the ear of Celestine, the Pope and Bishop of Rome. Celestine gathered his Italian bishops together and condemned Nestorius. The Bishop of Rome first wrote Cyril to tell him of his decision and then he wrote to Nestorius complaining of the "poison" that came from his lips. (Baum and Winkler: 24) After hearing from the Bishop of Rome, Cyril tried to get Nestorius to recant or resign.

THE IMPASSIBILITY OF GOD

As the Council of Ephesus approached, the perennial problem arose, the same problem faced at the Council of Nicaea. Nestorius's problem cannot be understood unless Eastern mentality and language is understood. Christians who spoke only Greek or used the Greek language in their theology had no word for "person." While the Westerners were thinking of one person, the Son of God, with two natures, one human and one divine, Nestorius was thinking: what does "person" mean, and how can God suffer? It is impossible. Paul Gavrilyuk enters Nestorius mind when he writes:

> Nestorius of Constantinople (d. c.451), following his teacher Theodore of Mopsuestia (c.350-428), claimed that since God is impassible, the divine subject cannot be involved in the suffering of Christ. According to Nestorius, it is possible to distinguish two subjects in Christ, one human and one divine; the human experiences of Christ are to be ascribed to the former and not to the latter. For Nestorius, the divine impassibility entailed that under no circumstances could God be the subject of birth, suffering, and death on the cross (Gavrilyuk 2004, 18-19).

At the same time, Nestorius struggled with the very word "person." He could not find adequate words in the Greek language to give him the same meaning. Yet he felt he had to find them.

An ecumenical council of the Church was called. It was to be held at Ephesus on June 7, 431. Ephesus was a Metropolitan See known for its devotion to the Virgin and for its hostility to Nestorius (Russell 2000, 38).

Nestorius was not against a general council, but he would have preferred that it be held in more friendly surroundings. Out of touch as he was concerning his diminishing popularity, he was shocked that the emperor agreed to hold it in Ephesus rather than

Constantinople. Furthermore, in his naivety, he thought that if theological experts would be present to listen carefully to the subtleties of his arguments, he need not worry. Young Nestorius did not see the political web that Cyril had slowly weaved around him.

THE THEOLOGICAL PROBLEM OF THE COUNCIL OF EPHESUS

Cyril and Nestorius both believed in the Council of Nicaea. Both believed that Jesus was both truly God and truly man. Both denied the caricatures of the other's arguments. Nestorius denied that he believed that Jesus contained, in his makeup, two sons – one human and one divine. Cyril, in his turn denied that he did not believe that Jesus was really human. (Russell 2000, 39-40) But each continued to charge the other with defending the Christological error which the other pinned on him (Herzog 1908, 562).

The differences between the two clearly arose from the theological language of the age in the Greek world. It is clear that the Greeks would have a problem when the only words that they had available to them were the following: *ousia* (Heidegger says that it has been mistakenly translated "substance," but it really means "being"), *physis* (nature), *hypostasis* (essence, e.g., the essential nature of Christ, divine and human) and *prosopon* (which means "face" or "mask"). Actually, these words also meant different things depending on who was using them in Greek, and even though the Christian Greek theologians tried to use one or the other for "person," none of them quite worked. It shows the intense difficulty the Greeks were having in sorting out exactly what *persona* meant in a world that had no word for *persona*.

So Nestorius, a student of Theodore of Mopsuestia, seriously struggled. To tell the truth, "person" is a difficult word for modern philosophers and theologians in the West to understand. But the theologians from the West at Nicaea and Ephesus thought that they understood the word perfectly. It would have been best if the councils had taken into consideration the different cultures of the world when making their decrees. In this case they were laying a heavy burden on the Greek culture to use their own language to try to understand the meaning of the councils.

Theodore and Nestorius wished to understand the Council correctly and struggled to do so. Frederick G. McLeod in *Theodore of Mopsuestia Revisited* describes the intense struggle the Greeks had with the word "person." He writes that Nestorius, at first, described "person" in a way that is at best confusing. But it is the struggle of an intelligent man to find an answer to a nearly impossible dilemma. Nestorius said: a king dresses in the clothes of an ordinary soldier. The human nature of the king, which he shares with all other human beings is called *ousia* in Greek; his human nature as a king is called *physis;* all the characteristics of this particular king is called *hypostasis;* all the characteristics as seen by others is called *prosopon;* the characteristics of the king which change with time are called *schema*. (McLeod, *Theological Studies*, vol. 61) Cyril insisted that *hypostasis* is the "person" of Nicaea. This was the tangle that arose among sincere Greek theologians, including Nestorius, at the Council of Nicaea. It arose again at Ephesus.

More modern writings have recognized Nestorius' struggles. They have placed him in better perspective, while recognizing that Cyril, his life-long adversary, had his own agenda which did not necessarily conform to "correct theology." Cyril was deliberately self-righteous, most visibly the most manipulative ecclesiastical man of his age, maybe of any age, in Christianity.

Nestorius ended up with a simpler solution to try to conform to Cyril and Roman thought, but it involved much theological and philosophical gymnastics on his part: when he spoke of *prosopon*, Nestorius meant not two persons, but two different roles played by the one person Jesus. When Cyril brought charges against Nestorius regarding his use of the word *prosopon*, he said that Nestorius meant two persons. But that is not what he meant, and Cyril probably knew it. When he spoke of *physis* or *hypostasis*, Nestorius distinguished between the human and the divine in Jesus.

If the theologians around Cyril and Nestorius would have come to Ephesus to listen rather than to argue, they could have come to an understanding (Fairbairn 2003, 7). After all the sweat and worry about the matter, the two sides had come close to an understanding (Russell, 2000, 39-46). If Cyril and John of Antioch could later come to an understanding in the time it takes to blink an eye, so could have Cyril and Nestorius – if Cyril sincerely sought an understanding.

The bottom line is that Nestorius did not support the doctrine of two sons, two persons in Christ, two subjects, as Cyril said he did. For Nestorius, Christ was fully God and fully man. Nestorius, then, was clearly not the heretic Cyril made him out to be (Baum and Winkler: 4).

"Yet Nestorius was never able to resolve the relationship of the two natures in Christ in a way that would guarantee the unity of Christ" (Benko 2004, 255). But it was merely a language problem for him, not a theological one. In other words, he had difficulty finding the right words to describe the two natures to the satisfaction of Cyril, the Romans, and even himself. This was the perennial problem which the Greek Church had with the Romans. And this made Nestorius vulnerable to anyone like Cyril of Alexandria who wished to take advantage of him.

THE COUNCIL OF EPHESUS (431)

Nestorius and sixteen of his bishops were the first to arrive at Ephesus. Nestorius was wise enough to come with armed guard. He was not received well in the city. He was received more like a defendant in a trial (Russell 2000, 46). Others followed, including the bishops from Rome. The bishops coming overland from the East were late. The Council began on June 22, 431 without the Pope's proxy and without the absent Eastern bishops. All of them had difficulty getting to Ephesus (Russell, 2000, 47). Realizing that their absence might be beneficial to his cause, Cyril wished to move in haste in order to achieve his intended results. Later, sixty-eight bishops signed a letter urging Cyril to wait for the Easterners. But, as we will see, the bishops at the council were weak, naïve, and easily swayed.

Cyril, in spite of everything, proceeded at all times according to the letter of the ecclesiastical canons and imperial regulations that governed councils. His right to preside was undisputed. Cyril was the most senior hierarch present and therefore, until the arrival of the papal legates, he was Celestine's proxy. Even if the Easterners had been there he would have been the natural president. Nestorius was under canonical censure from Rome. He complained that Cyril took over the council and dominated it completely. Cyril certainly did, but it was his right to do so. Cyril actually did not intervene very much in the proceedings. Nor did he force the bishops to keep to his agenda. The business side was handled by a certain Peter, the chief notary, but Cyril did prepare the agenda with Peter and supplied him with the dossier of documents and the books which he would later lay before the fathers.

All depended on the mood of the assembly…. But a result could only be attained if there was unanimity. Those who were sincere, but naïve among the bishops did not come to the council

CYRIL AND NESTORIUS

to negotiate a compromise. They came to recognize the moving of the Holy Spirit, and under the Holy Spirit to affirm the true faith. Unanimity was the guarantee that the Holy Spirit was speaking. Without it a council would fail.

But, Cyril was clearly not sincere, and he was intensely manipulative. He judged that conditions were favorable for the positive result of his quest, and they were unlikely to occur again, so he moved quickly. The present bishops were easy prey to Cyril's manipulations (Russell, 2000, 48). The present Eastern bishops insisted three times that Nestorius be invited to attend the council proceedings. They did not feel right about his absence. But Nestorius was frankly afraid to attend. His house in Ephesus was surrounded by unfriendly soldiers. He did indicate to the Council that he would come when all the bishops had arrived (Chadwick 2001, 533). Security and Cyril's stacked deck kept Nestorius in his place of residence.

The Council then proceeded unabated without him. Some of the bishops, no doubt spurred on by Cyril and his cohorts, showed how weak and easily influenced they were. At one point they cried out: "If anyone does not anathematize Nestorius, let him be anathema" (Russell, 2000, 49)!

But after that explosion of sentiments by some, noticeable unease settled upon some of the bishops. They were uncomfortable with the proceedings and its internal movements. Cyril noticed that the group was turning against not Nestorius, but Cyril himself. At the same time, some of the bishops from the East who supported Nestorius, began to arrive. As far as Cyril was concerned, the goal of the Council was beginning to fall apart in his own hands.

Cyril, seeking unanimity, quickly softened some of the decrees. In desperation, he then had carefully pre-selected writings of the fathers of the Church read to the assembled bishops. The bishops listened carefully to these readings, and they were actually, but naively, deeply moved by them. After Cyril's select readings from the fathers, he stood before the bishops to make his do-or-die pitch. It was now or never, and he knew it. Other bishops with other views would soon arrive and he would have increasing difficulty getting agreement, let alone unanimity. He spoke: "Is it your wish to affirm the primitive doctrines of the faith and depose the innovator? He had judged the moment well. The decision was unanimous" (Russell 2000, 50). All 197 bishops at the first session, easily swayed as they were by the emotion of the moment, filed up to the altar and put their signatures to the deed of deposition" (Russell 2000, 50).

Cyril quickly sent his messengers to Constantinople to arouse public opinion. Public opinion more than anything would sway the emperor. Nothing, of course, was law in the empire under Theodosius until Theodosius ratified it (Russell 2000, 50).

John of Antioch and his party of 46 bishops from the East arrived on June 26. They were furious with Cyril for, in effect, holding his own Council without their input. After reading the proceedings of the Council, they found errors therein which touched on heresy. They immediately sent their own messengers to the emperor, and they had Cyril deposed. The Church of Ephesus, which was in accord with the proceedings of Cyril's Council, closed its doors to John and the 46 bishops (Russell 2000, 50).

Upon receiving many conflicting reports, Theodosius annulled all the proceedings of the gatherings of Cyril. He told the bishops to stop the petty nonsense and to reassemble in order to affirm the true faith. After all this bickering, the Council proceedings were debated on September 11 in the presence of the emperor. One result of the proceedings was that all did accept the formulation of Mary as *theotokos* (the God-bearer; the Mother of God) (Russell 2000, 51).

Nestorius, who had been imprisoned in the disgraceful happenings at Ephesus, no longer had any stomach for such Church politics, and returned to his monastery, near Antioch. He was replaced by Maximian, who was well-liked by all. Cyril returned to Alexandria, where he was greeted by parades as a hero (Russell 2000, 51).

The fact of the matter was, however, that the council had failed. Cyril's gamble in presenting John of Antioch with a *fait accompli* on his arrival at Ephesus had not paid off. Instead of accepting the majority decision, the Easterners repudiated what was done on June 22nd, thereby denying the council the unanimity that would have brought peace to the Church (Russell 2000, 53).

While everything fell apart around him, Cyril fell into deep depression. Peace began to grow out of chaos when Paul of Emesa, the representative of John of Antioch came to Alexandria, Cyril's own church, and preached a sermon. He started by calling Mary the *theotokos*, and the whole congregation broke into applause. He continued:

> Mary the *Theotokos* therefore gave birth to *Emmanuel*, and *Emmanuel* is God incarnate. For God the Word who before the ages was ineffably and inexpressibly begotten of the Father in the last days was born of a woman. Having assumed our nature perfectly, and having taken humanity to himself from the first moment of conception, and having made our body a temple for himself, he came forth from the *Theotokos*, the same perfect God and perfect man. By a union (*syndromē*) of the two perfect natures, I mean the Godhead and the manhood; he became for us one Son, one

Christ, one Lord.(Paul of Emesa, ACO I, 1, 4, p. 10. 15-22, translated by Russell, 2000, 54-55).

This was a paraphrase of the words that Cyril had sent to John of Antioch, and it was the expression of the Alexandrian Church. If Paul of Emesa, John of Antioch's representative, spoke these words in the basilica in Alexandria, then peace again, for the time, returned to the Church (Russell 2000, 55). Peace was John and Paul's intent.

But John of Antioch, weak-kneed, was then dragged into signing a condemnation of Nestorius. His true feelings were that Nestorius was orthodox, even if, at times, imprudent (Chadwick 2001, 542). At the same time, John did accept the transition from Nestorius to Maximian as Patriarch of Constantinople, creating unity in the church. Theodoret insisted on a distinction: he condemned Nestorianism, that there were two persons in Jesus, but he refused to condemn Nestorius, who insisted, with the other bishops, with Paul of Emesa and John of Antioch and the Council, that there was only one person in Jesus, and He was God incarnate (Rainy 1902, 400).

A QUESTION OR TWO

What was the problem the Greeks had with the word "person? Obviously, confusion reigned. The Greeks were not quite sure what "person" meant in regard to fellow human beings. Being solidly community-minded, they still had no word for "person." They had to dig into their philosophy and do some deep thinking to come up with some approximate understanding of the word. To call a human being a person separated from close community ties was difficult for them. The Romans did not realize the trauma they caused the Greeks when they started to throw the word around. It was merely a linguistic/cultural problem.

Cyril and the Romans were quite sure of the meaning of the word. If they truly did understand it, all humankind would have benefitted from their deep knowledge. We wish that they would have explained it more fully so the Western world and generations following them could also understand it. But it is doubtful that they had such deep knowledge of the words meaning.

Then these same Romans started using the word "person" to describe the inner life of God. Philosophers in the West even today are not sure of the full ramifications of the word "person" when used to identify separate human beings, let alone "person" in relation to God the Father and the Son, and Jesus in relationship to the Father in the Godhead. What are the extended ramifications of the word in relationship to God? We are not denying what the council enacted, but was the council not trying to describe what goes on in the intimate realms of the life of God. We do know from revelation that Jesus called God, "Father." We also know from revelation that Jesus spoke of being united with his Father. But that is just scratching the surface of the relationship. Are we talking about what the Roman churchmen called "person" here, or are we talking about something which far exceeds what the Roman churchmen called "person"?

And what does it mean that this person, *Emmanuel,* became man? After all, we also know that he suffered in life, and he suffered and died on the cross. What are the full ramifications of Jesus suffering and dying? Again, we are not denying any statement of the council. Yet there is deep mystery about all this that transcends our, and even Cyril's or the council's, ability to understand.

And, could we not leave some privacy in the intimate life of the God-head -- leave something of the deity for which we can stand in awe? Do we have to go barging in even here with our meager concepts?

Finally, what was Cyril trying to accomplish? He was obviously trying to protect himself and promote his own image, which had nothing to do with the Jesus movement. The amazing thing is that, as far as the church is concerned, he got away with it. If Cyril was a great teacher in the church, it is no wonder that the church continued its freefall into the abyss. He joins Athanasius, Ambrose, and Augustine in carrying the church further and further from Jesus, its true light. Cyril spent his whole life manipulating and lying to gain his own advantage. If Cyril is a great saint of the church, none of the rest of us need worry a bit. He is a sign for us of the universality of salvation. All of the rest of us sinners are going to make it.

Cyril died in June, 444. Nestorius continued to write. He was eventually banished from his monastery, and he died in some unknown place around 450. Much disaster washed onto the human shores in the wake of Cyril. To this day, Nestorius is honored in the East as a great teacher and a saint.

Chapter 4

LEO THE GREAT (390?-461) AND THE DARK AGES

In many ways, empires stand eyeball to eyeball with one another as they share their likenesses. The fall of the Roman Empire unfolded much like other empires in history. Politicians were self-serving, ruthless, or weak-kneed. Religious leaders enjoyed the good life, licked their own wisdom and liked it. The rich took every means their conniving minds could entertain to protect and increase their wealth. The poor became unbelievably poor. Only when they had suffered much more than anyone should even think about suffering did they begin to rise and organize.

In other ways, the Roman Empire was even more extreme than other empires. Literacy dropped in the decadence of the Roman Empire until it reached the extremes of illiteracy. The elite who should have been literate were barely functionally so. The rulers and the rich faked it, while they relied on the monks in the monastery to do their reading and writing for them. General knowledge degenerated accordingly.

At the same time, the immigrants, the so-called barbarians, banged on the door of the Empire, demanding entrance until no emperor, prefect, or soldier could keep them out. The fortifications of the Empire began to disintegrate.

The plague then ravished the citizens, rich and poor, killing a great number of the people. Disease became rampant.

Eventually, the empire fell into pieces under the tensions within and the pressures without. It is chilling to note that from the 5th to the 11th century someone took Julius Caesar's and Constantine's empire, the cultured society of the Roman Empire, and shot it with some infernal bow back into the backwaters of pre-history.

THE TYPOGRAPHY OF ROME AT LEO'S TIME

It is difficult to describe accurately the typography of Rome in the fifth century. One description is given in "a regionary survey attributed to Constantine I, preserved in a slightly modified form in order to fit the fifth century in a *notitia* appended to the *Philocalian Kalendar A.D. 336-354* and in the *Curiosum*" (Jalland 1941, 22). A summary of the source paints an interesting picture. In the fifth century the population of Rome was one to two million. Its walls were 11 ¾ miles long. It had 15 gates and 9 bridges spanned the Tiber, 11 forums dotted the city, as well as 10 basilicas, 28 public libraries, 290 public warehouses, 46,102 tenement houses (*insulae*) which were nothing but blocks of flats let out to poor people, and 1,790 mansions (*domus*), homes of the rich. For the most part, this was the scene that Leo the Great saw as he looked out the windows of his own home in Rome (Jalland 1941, 22).

Unlike John Chrysostom, we know nothing about Leo before he became an ecclesiastical figure (Gore 1887, 5-7). He rises, like Melchizedech, from nowhere. If we cannot say for sure that he was Roman by birth, he was certainly aristocratic Roman by sentiment and Catholic by religion.

If he ever secretly frolicked as a teenager with his peers, we will never know about it. In fact, not only his youth, but nothing that we know about Leo was private. He is presented as living wholly for the Church. Everything about the man was stern and, as far as we can tell, without feeling. Yet, he is eminently the ecclesiastical figure of the age (Gore 1887, 6). In fact, he is not only the most important figure of the fifth century, but he stands mightily above anyone else (Gore 1887, 17-24).

Some peripherals in Leo's world we do know. When Leo became pope, Jerome was already dead for 20 years and Augustine was dead for 10. Spain and all of Africa was lost to the Empire and Africa was lost to the Church; Sicily was devastated; Rome had already been plundered. Attila, as well, was standing at the gates of Rome, ready to conquer it.

When Pope Sixtus III died in 440, the Church considered no other candidate to fill the position of pope but Leo. Leo became pope on September 29, 440, and he held center stage in the totality of Europe for his entire reign (Jalland 1941, 38). He received respect far and above that which any human being should ever receive. While he was undoubtedly among the greatest diplomats the world has seen, at times Leo's own sense of importance overtook his better judgment. He began to see himself as others perceived him – as something special. If there was any defect in Leo's personality, this was it.

LEO AND ATTILA THE HUN

Leo did actually meet with Attila the Hun, but the symbolism that grew up and surrounded the meeting in Catholic circles overwhelms the reality. Let us look at the meeting as it is portrayed in Catholic circles even today. The exaggerated myth that was generated and continues to exist in popular church history books was instigated or supported by a painting transmitted to us by the artist, Raphael (1483-1520), a millennium later, showing us Leo overawing and disciplining the barbarians. This myth goes as follows:

> The Huns, with their hideous features and grotesque appearance, the very emblems of uncivilized force, headed by their powerful and fierce monarch, Attila, are threatening Italy and Rome. The empire is paralyzed with fear; it turns to the Church. Leo, the representative of religion, in his sacerdotal robes meets the wild conqueror before his own camp, and he whom arms could not stay trembles and bows before the peaceful priest (Gore 1887, 26).

If you believe this, you are as naïve as the history books that promote the idea. This representation is certainly not true to historical fact. While the representation painted by Raphael and its interpretation described by Gore, was not true to history. Today's serious historian can only project what happened in that diplomatic meeting. Undoubtedly, Leo did not wear his sacerdotal robes, with stole and chasuble, but he met Attila in more simple garments. The meeting demanded that he not enflame the ire of Attila. We can only project the words that were spoken between Attila and the diplomatic group, not only Leo, who went to speak with him. The group included Leo, Leo's Consular Avienus, and the Prefect of the city of Rome, Trigetius (Gore 1887, 28).

We know that Attila had a terrible presence about him. He was proud in his gait, powerful at council, and a lover of war. But we also know that he was capable of controlling his warrior side, and he was obviously ready to welcome and spare a suppliant who came humbly to him (Gore 1887, 27).

The diplomatic group had some things which they could lay on the table next to the good Italian food, which Attila undoubtedly shared with them on the shores of Lake Benacus. After all, as is true of any immigrant, it was the good life that Attila had come to Italy to enjoy, not the woes that could entangle an invader. Certainly the group of diplomats undoubtedly carefully and gently pointed out such entangling snares to him. Alaric, for example, had not done well for himself by conquering the huge city of Rome. He had more problems than he could reasonably endure. Did Attila need all these troubles? Many of his warriors would die. Did he need that (Gore, 1887, 27-28)?

At the same time, Attila received messages from the east that his own land was in danger of invasion. He was a great warrior, but he was also intelligent enough to know when to stop. Attila left, but as he did so, he raised his fist threateningly at Italy (Gore 1887, 28). The diplomatic mission, then, was successful. Leo, Avienus and Trigetius must all go down in history as brave and skilled diplomats.

LEO AND PAPAL INFALLIBILITY

Leo, whose popularity, as we can imagine, increased overwhelmingly after Attila left, soon began to show another side of his respected self. In a conflict with Hilary of Arles, he stated that the secular powers should back the pope's spiritual authority, and that all bishops should do the same: "the peace of the Church will not be secured," he proclaimed, "till, with one consent, it recognize its ruler" (Gore 1887, 32). But then he went further than voicing his own opinion and made an injunction which he thought should last in perpetuity: "this is our perpetual injunction, that the bishops, neither of Gaul, nor any other province, be allowed ... to attempt anything without the authority of the pope of the Eternal City; but that for them, and for all, the law shall be whatever the authority of the Apostolic See has or shall have ordained" (Gore 1887, 32-33).

Pope Leo the Great had gone further than expressing a need of the time. He was claiming a very special role for the papacy. He was stating something much more than "Bishops, in this particular period of time, I do not trust you. Please run everything you do past me so that you do not mess up the whole Church." He was saying that inherently the Pope had special powers, beyond which no pope had ever insisted upon before him.

Leo gradually solidified his own thought on the matter in *Ep.* 14, II. He proclaimed three points:

> 1. Whatever Peter was to the apostles, the pope is to the bishops.
>
> 2. Peter was not merely "first among equals" or "superior among inferiors." Peter was mediator between Christ and the other apostles. What the other apostles received from Jesus, they received from Peter.
>
> 3. The pope has immediate authority over the whole Church, East and West. He is the immediate recipient of sacerdotal grace, and what others receive is received from him (Gore 1887, 92-93).

The first thought which comes to mind is the obvious one: in light of the Gospels, how could Leo come to such conclusions? Jesus only spoke three statements in Peter's favor, but they were ambiguous statements. Furthermore, these could have easily been spoken to bolster Peter's sagging spirits: "Peter ... you are rock..." (Matt. 16:1 NAB). "...Strengthen your brothers" (Luke 22:32 NAB). "Feed my sheep" (John 21: 17 NAB). He also spoke other scorching statements to Peter: "Get out of my sight, you Satan" (Matt. 16: 23 NAB)! "I tell you, Peter, the cock will not crow today until you have three times denied that you know me" (Luke 22:34 NAB). "Asleep, Simon? You could not stay awake for even an hour" (Mark 14: 37 NAB)? "Put your sword back in its sheath" (John 18:11 NAB). Furthermore, the other apostles never appeared to accept Peter as a person superior to themselves, but always as an equal. (*Acts*, 10)

I wonder what would have happened if Leo would have married. He was not in fact married. I am merely saying "what if..." Of course, I am now writing as a married man. I am not here speaking about having a concubine -- concubines, we can expect, would flatter the Pope, as apparently did his advisors -- but truly married for life to one woman whom he loved and cherished. Would things have looked different in Leo's eyes? Envision the scene:

> His wife enters into the pope's den, perhaps with a pot of tea, and she asks him: "What are you working on, Lee?
>
> He says to her: "Oh, I am just putting the final touches on this decree that I am going to send out tomorrow to all the churches that reads that I am infallible."
>
> There is a long pause. "Infallible, you say? What do you mean?"

"Well, Peter was the superior apostle, and the rest of the apostles and the other Christians received everything from him? Well, I am now Peter for the Church."

She begins to fidget a bit, and she then says, "Lee, Peter denied Jesus three times, and Christ told him, 'Get behind me, you Satan! You think like men think, not God.' Do you really think Peter had such an exalted position? Certainly he ended up a saint, but the other apostles also contributed and became saints. Maybe if your message had a meek and humble attitude about it, it would be a better example. Maybe you should think this out again. You have done some great work, Lee, and you have even persuaded Attila to leave Italy. But 'infallible' is going a bit far for any human being."

Pope Leo says, "I will. I will think it over."

A very different decree, I would think, one that took into consideration human realities and human weakness, would have come out from Pope Leo.

If Leo had faced more of the humiliations of life, if he had faced the wall of human reality: poverty, ignorance, helplessness, and marriage, like Peter, he might never have come to his three conclusions. A good historian today cannot help but think that if Leo the Great had a different *modus vivendi*, he would have been a better Bishop of Rome, and albeit, follower of Peter. Clerics, in imitation of Peter, might have even walked humbly through the world in sandals.

Leo prided himself in speaking *ex sede Petri* (*from the throne of Peter*). He never did seem to realize that the only chair Peter is famous for sitting upon was the chair of the cross. Leo was the first Pope to think that other Catholics should look to him as the last word in everything. Regarding "the infallibility of the pope," Charles Gore stated:

> Theory of Papacy is more the result of conscious effort than the papacy itself. When the power and influence of the popes was continually growing, they and their supporters began to look about for arguments to justify their position, but the position itself was in very large measure the product of circumstances. No doubt there was much of personal ambition that went to build up the fabric, no doubt much unscrupulousness may be laid to the charge of popes and those who worked for them, in the way of misquotation and falsification of documents… (Gore 1887, 94).

LEO, HIS TOME, AND THE COUNCIL OF CHALCEDON

In the Council of Chalcedon, in the year 451, the Church fathers again gathered to determine the doctrine regarding the Person of Jesus Christ. To review a bit, Nestorius, newly consecrated bishop of Constantinople, had delivered a Christmas homily in 428 on the correctness of calling the Virgin Mary, "Mother of God." In doing so, he laid stress on the differences between the Godhead and the manhood of Jesus Christ. Cyril, the bishop of Alexandria, pounced on the words of Nestorius, calling him a heretic. Cyril was interested in making the Patriarch of Alexandria higher in status than that of Constantinople. Here was his chance (Sellers 1953, xi). The dispute created by Cyril eventually gave rise to the Council of Chalcedon and the Tome of Leo which influenced the proceedings. The conclusion of the Council was that Jesus Christ was declared to be one person, who was the Son of God, and that one person had a human and a Godly nature (Seller 1953, 211).

This, of course, again threw the whole Church of the East into consternation. Some of their great bishops were excommunicated over the matter. The problem they had was again a cultural and language problem. "Person" was important to the Romans, not the Greeks. As Sellers stated: "…Leo… was handicapped through not being able to appreciate that when the Greeks used the word *natura* they meant the same thing that he did when he used the word *persona*…" (Sellers 1953, 233). It was again these cultural, language differences, coupled with political problems between the East and the West, which made the Council of Chalcedon, as well as the Council of Nicaea and Ephesus, a failure (Seller 1953, 254).

THE 6TH CENTURY ONWARD

In the first sentence of his book, Georges Duby states: "At the end of the sixth century Europe was a profoundly uncivilized place" (Duby 1973: 3). Marc Bloch, the traditional historian of feudalism, admits the limitations which the lack of civilization during this point in history has meant for scholars: "Of the past he [the historian] knows only so much as the past is willing to yield to him" (Bloch 1961, xxi). The feudal ages, Bloch admits, is stingy in the information it is able to yield.

What we do know is that between the sixth and seventh

century the economic situation in the Roman Empire grew progressively worse. The clever and the lucky among the citizens thrived at the expense of the others, but the numbers of the clever and the lucky was growing fewer in number. The few rich, as they have in every age, firmly believed that their riches either came from God or fate or from their own hard work. Most of them believed that they would violate their heritage and that of their sons and daughters if they shared their wealth. The rest of the citizens continued their slide into poverty, dependency and helplessness. Eventually, the situation got so dire that the poor gave themselves to the rich as slaves or as free peasants in order to feed themselves and their families. Thus, the dark ages clouded the skies of the Empire.

Furthermore, inheriting its position given to it by Constantine, the medieval Church played a key role not only in the spiritual realm, but in the economic realm of Europe. Robert D. Tollison and his group of fellow scholars states: "Before the year A. D. 900, the Church directly owned approximately one-third of all cultivated land in western Europe, including 31 percent of such land in Italy, 35 per-cent in Germany, and 44 percent in northern France… (Tollison 1996, 8)." It is unclear how much uncultivated land was owned by the Church, but the proportion was likely considerable.

We sit with the books of Georges Duby and Marc Bloch and others, researchers of the dark ages, in our hands. They record the devastation of most of the people who lived in Europe at that time. In the work *The Three Orders: Feudal Society Imagined* Duby presents the picture. He states that the dark ages owes its origins to the greed of the wealthy nobles, including the churchmen, who survived with wealth, but also maintained control of a bleeding society (Duby 1980, 35, 68). In the same book he also writes of certain fathers of the Church whose ignorance or lack of backbone led them to compromise the teachings of Jesus and justify the grossness of that society. Duby's conception of the dark ages leaves us breathless when we consider its consequences for poor people, who searched and scratched day by day to survive.

As luck would have it, the migrants, who wanted a piece of the "good life," continued to further complicate the issue. No matter what the Romans did, they could not keep people out of the Roman Empire. They could not build a wall big enough. They could and they did make laws, but they could not find anyone who could effectively enforce them.

Then the bubonic plague demolished the people as well. No one could heal the people who became infected by it. The Roman Empire, which seemed so immortal for so many years, whose emperors were considered gods, could not deal with such a disease. Rome was as mortal as the rest of the world. The empire was not able to deal with suffering, death, and its own weakness. As a consequence, it fell into a pre-historic state.

Early medieval history has baffled historians. It is not part of the gradual development of humanity. Few written documents exist because writing went out of style. Historians have in hand mainly archaeological documents. It is very similar to the period characterized by ancients painting buffalos and mammoths on caves. (Duby 1973: 3).

So Duby admits that we do know a few things, but not many, regarding the decadence of Roman society after Constantine. One fact we do know was the rampant, growing illiteracy. Bloch goes into detail in describing it:

> The relatively brilliant culture of a few great royal or noble families should not deceive us; nor should the exceptional fidelity of the knightly classes of Italy and Spain held to pedagogical traditions,

somewhat rudimentary though these were: the Cid and Ximenes, if their knowledge perhaps did not extend much farther, at least they knew how to sign their names... (Bloch 1961, 80).

Both Duby and Bloch plunge headlong into the culturally vacated dark ages knowing that there is not much other data to examine. It is impossible to underestimate the technical problems which these historians faced (Duby 1973:12).

As far as we can know, the population of Europe decreased in number from the second century onward, a decrease which was aided by the aforementioned bubonic plague in the sixth century, which killed hundreds of thousands of people (Duby 1973,12-13).

Our period of concern includes but also precedes the period of Duby's and Bloch's concerns. Their concerns are respectively the years 1000 to 1250 C. E and 900 to 1300 C. E.. but to discover the underpinnings of the later periods, both deal with the socio-politico-economic situation which endured from the years 500 C. E. to 1000 C. E., the years of the demise of the Roman Empire.

Bloch states: "the princes were obliged to rely on the clerical element ...for services that the rest of their entourage would have been incapable of rendering" (Bloch 1961, 80). By "clerical element" Bloch, for the most part, means the scholars from the monastery, who were the persons from the age who took time to learn. Furthermore, an essential part of the knowledge of these monks came from Christian scholars from the Church's past. Now we face head-on, not only the degeneration of the Roman Empire, but the degeneration of Christianity which took place in an earlier period, and influenced the later period as well. For Augustine, Gregory the Great, Jerome, Dionysius the Areopagite, and others arise from the dead as major influences. They were the ones who either formed the dark ages from their own theological roots or influenced it in principle during a broad period from Constantine to 1000 C. E.

THEOLOGICAL ROOTS OF THE DARK AGES

Culture and literature during the early dark ages, as Duby stated, was a barren waste. The ones who were educated in the age, as we have in general mentioned were certain clergymen. Unfortunately, significant churchmen of the time did not have the backbone or the deep knowledge that was necessary to resurrect society. They catered to the reigning thoughts of the rich and supported the dominant environment and superstitions. Tollison and his fellow scholars, who were interested merely in the economic factors of the Church in the era, states:

> The primary service supplied by the medieval Church to its customers was information about and guidance toward the attainment of eternal salvation. At issue here is not the veracity of the Church's theological claims, nor its ability to guarantee the end-product, but rather the fact that whatever knowledge consumers possessed in this regard was provided entirely and exclusively by the Church. An important aspect of this service concerned the afterlife: the idea that the soul continues to exist for all eternity after the death of the body. To a medieval Christian, one's existence on earth was a tiny part of 'life' -- while the average person might live a mere forty or fifty years in the earthly realm, the soul's existence in heaven or hell would be forever (Tollison, 1996, 25).

Tollison's statement concerning eternal life certainly might be true, but it was used by the medieval church to capture the minds and hearts of the people. Individual rich persons, in order to ensure their "salvation," bequeathed their riches to the Church upon their death. Wealthy heretics were dispossessed of their riches, and those fortunes were given to the Church. Clergy were also given "stipends" for their services. The Church was indeed becoming big business. The clergymen of Jesus continued to look less and less like their founder.

Duby continues, using as sources the *Gesta Episcoporum Cameracensium* of Gerard of Cambrai, written in 1024 C. E., and the *Charmes* of Adalbero of Laon, a brilliant satire written at the end of the first millennium. Both sources say the same thing: "three's" became a sacred number: "Here below, 'some pray, others fight, still others work ...'; 'men of prayer, farmers, and men of war.'" Three types of action: *orare, pugnare, agricolari-laborare*. Two speakers (Duby, 1980, 13).

These two bishops shout at us from the swamps of oblivion, a fete so rare in the age, we best heed them some interest. They are two of the few voices from that era that we will ever hear.

Adalbero is the elder of the two and the most known, for he was a traitor, carrying the crown of the French king from one opposing dynasty to another, from the Carolingian dynasty to the Capetian dynasty. Adalbero was a nobleman from head to toe, a descendant of Charlemagne. Educated at Rheims, he became the Bishop of Laon. In 977 he was entrusted with the job of chancellor to Lothar, the Carolingian king of Western France.

Gerard was of the same family. By marriage, he was a relative of Adalbero. He journeyed East to become one of the churchmen serving the emperor Henry II, a Capetian King. In 1012, in a political, ecclesiastical squabble with the Count of Flanders,

Henry II made him Bishop of Cambrai. He was a young Bishop, but at least a trustworthy one.

These two bishops shout the song of "social trifunctionality" -- men who went to war, men who prayed, and men who worked -- which smothered individuality, the value of the person, in the dark feudal ages. Their words spoke of a carefully knit ordering of society. Each person in that society knew the place that God wanted for him or her. It was, they were told, the creator's destiny from the beginning.

Paul, misquoted though he was, started building the foundations of feudalism by bringing up the concept of "order," a characteristic essential to feudalism. From the grave, certainly, he must have wished that he had never said it, never brought it up. Paul wrote: Just as in Adam all die, so in Christ all will come to life again, but each one in proper order: Christ, the first fruits and then, at his coming, all those who belong to him" (I Corinthians 15: 22-23 NAB). Like a balloon, certain rulers, clerics, monks, and fathers of the Church put helium into Paul's "order," and used it to fly into the sky to their own never-never land.

Augustine of Hippo (354-430) took Paul's words and wrote about authority and the moral necessity to submit to it in his *Enarratio in Psalmis*, 39, c. 6 (PL 36: 436): "For in the Church this *ordo* is established: some precede, others follow.... And those who follow imitate the leaders. But those who set the example for those who follow, do they not follow anyone? If they do not, they will go astray. Hence, they, too, follow someone, Christ himself" (*Enarratio in Psalmis*, 39, c. 6 [PL 36: 436]).

The Catholic Encyclopedia states that Pope Gregory the Great (540?-604), was the father of the medieval papacy. Gregory was no theologian or philosopher, but his influence in the church was indeed huge, even up to our present day. Gregory states: "Although all men are born equal by nature, sin subordinates some to others in accordance with the variable order [*ordo*] of merits; this diversity arising from vice is established by divine judgment. Thus, man, who is not intended to live in equality, can be ruled by another (*Regula Pastoralis*, Gregory the Great)." In a *Letter* to a bishop, he wrote: "Almighty God places good men in authority that He may impart through them the gifts of his mercy to their subjects...that through the blessings bestowed on you the blessings of heaven might be bestowed on your people also (*Letter*, Gregory the Great).

Where "sin" and "vice" fit into Gregory's script is problematic. Gregory himself does not indicate where they fit. He is more interested in cracking out principles for the divine right of kings, which, of course, included in the same nutshell the divine right of popes and bishops. For, in the feudal system, kings, popes and bishops were the leaders of those who pray, war, farm and labor. To summarize his thought, Gregory is insistent on one point in particular: "Everybody, know your place and stay there." This, of course, was easy for him to say. He was on top.

It was not until the reign of Charlemagne (742-814), who became St. Charlemagne until he was later demoted to Blessed Charlemagne, that the feudal system was cemented into law. Charlemagne stated simply: "Harmoniously every man shall keep to his own life's purpose and to his own profession." "Harmoniously" needs explanation, lest it muddies the waters. Today it is too easy to say, "That is peace-loving of him. Charlemagne seeks harmony in the world." Charlemagne did not only seek harmony, he needed it and demanded it, as did every other emperor and king. He was thinking not of the well-being of his people when he spoke the words, but the well-being of himself, the emperor. Harmony gave the emperor security. Charlemagne was, first of all, insisting that everyone should stay in the social position in which he was born, thus mandating the dark ages, pure and simple. "Harmoniously" was added to add years to Charlemagne's life.

The image we thus uncover is one based on the major teachings upon which Latin Christendom has never ceased to meditate, the writings of Ambrose, Augustine, Gregory and all the others who promoted the hierarchy which we have inherited from history. It is the concept of a pyramid of obedience, a phalanx subjecting the subordinate to the discipline of superiors, the idea of the necessity of closed ranks, of punishment for failure to execute orders. All of this Christendom took for its own.

THE PRIMACY OF THE NUMBER "3"

Then the theologians of the lords of the age took up the number "3" and soared with it to the heavenly gates. It became a sacred number, a proper number, a number that had an essence of its own. We have already mentioned that there were three groups, three orders in the feudal social order: those who pray, those who fight, and those who work. The theologians mused that this order was appropriate because it reflected the very image of God: there were also three persons in God. Society, then, made of prayers, warriors and workers, imaged God. It would have been good if they had stopped there. Even this is difficult to swallow. But they continued to cook up other "3's" for us.

Gregory the Great and Augustine of Hippo are now joined by Jerome (340?-420) and Dionysius the Areopagite (6th Century?) who also bring the other half of the human race, women, into the scene, a group whom Augustine and Gregory did not often address. Women now were also included in the theological trinities. Inclusion is often a good thing, but I am sure women are not pleased with the context.

Jerome in *Adversus Jovinianum* said it simply: there are three degrees of sexual purity: that of virgins, that of the continent, and that of the married couple (PL 23:225; cf. 213-216). Augustine also categorized the Christian community in three groups: the leaders – noted for their purity --, the continent; and couples joined in matrimony (PL 76:976-77). Gregory the Great followed Augustine's lead, but gives pointed detail to his classifications: The leaders were now the bishops; the continents were the monks; the last group were the "good" married couples (*Moralia*, I: 14).

Two question are in order here? 1) If the group included the "good" married couples, who were the "bad" married couples? 2) Why were married couples singled out as "good" or "bad," and the monks and bishops were not?

Dionysius the Areopagite in *Ecclesiastical Hierarchy*, takes the supremacy of the "3's" to its ridiculous heights:

> The division of every hierarchy is ternary [in three's]....The word of God attributes nine revelatory names to the angels according to their hierarchy.... In immediate contact with God were the Seraphim, the Cherubim, and the Thrones, "constituting a single hierarchical triad and truly the highest...; to enable lesser natures to rival themselves, they raise them up imitating the supreme goodness, and communicating to them thereby the splendor visited upon themselves. In turn, these natures of secondary rank [another triad: the Dominations, the Virtues, the Powers] transmit to the next lesser grade this splendor, and at each degree the superior distributes to the lesser a portion of the gift of divine light." Through this third

angelic triad (comprising Principates, Archangels, and Angels), illumination "revelatory for human hierarchies," finally came to cover the earth. In the lowest rank of the "celestial hierarchies" stood the angels; in the highest rank of the "ecclesiastical hierarchies," the bishops: from the former to the latter the message was transmitted (Dionysius, *Ecclesiastical Hierarchy*, c. 1).

No wonder Jesus has been having such a difficult time getting his message across! I speak satirically, of course. According to Dionysius, he must communicate some of his brilliance through nine different sets of angels (three groups of three's) before he gets to the bishops, who then must share some of his episcopal brilliance with the people -- with those who pray, with those who war, and with those who work. Jesus would have to work through a rat-maze of heavenly and hierarchical red tape before people could even begin to hear his message.

Augustine, Gregory and Dionysius the Areopagite and even Jerome were utilizing theology not to promote the words of Jesus, but to protect an accepted socio-political system, and to promote harmony within that system. No matter what else can be said about the social theology of the "3's" and the theological imagery of Dionysius, very little of Jesus ever did trickle down to the lords, the warriors, the prayers, the workers -- or the bishops, for that matter.

Duby also informs us that in 747 Pope Zachary gave an address which supported the "theology of the "3's":

> ... to the princes, to the men of the world, and to the warriors [bellatores] fall the task of guarding against the enemy's cunning and of defending

the country; to bishops, priests, and servants of God, it is given to act by offering salutary counsel and prayer – so that thanks to God, with our praying [*orantibus*] and their fighting (*ballantibus*), the country may remain safe (Pope Zachary, *Dissertation*).

Although the role of the worker is not explicitly mentioned by Pope Zachary, it is implied. They are part of the community that must remain safe.

The Warrior

Duby goes on to show the primacy of the warrior, the protector of society, in the post-Constantine period of the sixth, seventh and eighth centuries of the Christian era: "The culture... was a culture of war and aggression; the status of freedom was first of all defined as fitness to participate in military expeditions, and the principal earthly mission of kingship was to lead the army, in other words, the whole folk massed together for the attack (Duby 1973, 48).

He continues by giving us an example, a rare peek into the turmoil and moral destitution in the era:

> Grierson has drawn attention to stipulations in the laws of Ine, king of Wessex, which call for the following distinctions to be made between aggressors: if there are less than seven, they are simply thieves; if they are more numerous, they constitute a band of brigands; but if there are over thirty-five, they may fairly be taken for an army.... Beyond the natural frontiers marked out by marshland, forest

and wilderness, any territory they occupied was regarded as a hunting preserve. Every year, the young men would set out in a body to roam round it, with their chieftains as guides. They would try to despoil the enemy, to lay their hands on everything they could carry off from his lands: ornaments, weapons, cattle and if possible men, women and children (Duby 1973, 49).

The Worker

The king also had his workers, who, for the most part, did not go to war. First mentioned are the goldsmiths, like St. Eligius who served King Dagobert I. The goldsmith's job was to take all the king's gold and gems, bought, borrowed or stolen, and make them into a collection that could be managed and displayed.

The farmer (agricola) too, was an indispensable member of society. The farmer brought in the bread-stuffs, wine, beans, peas, herbs, roots and olive oil, which were part of the diet of the populace, foremost the king, his court, and then the rest of the people. Meat was also part of the diet, so farmers herded and tended the animals. Tool makers were also in great demand to make the instruments of war and farm.

The Prayer

The people and the king provided the monastery with its own store of food and gems. The monks in the monastery received the first fruits, every tenth cutting of wheat and produce, one tenth of the raids made by the warriors, and a portion of the riches of the dead. Sacrifice of this type was considered the surest way to acquire divine favor. Taboos protected the monastery from pillage, elsewise they were easy prey, like cutting warm butter. In return, the monks were to pray and offer sacred rites for the community and its people.

Bishops and members of the aristocracy managed to live contrasting lives from the multitude. They decked their dainty dinner dishes with delicious food and filled their lives to the brim with sumptuous luxuries. In 585, Fortunatus describes the residence of Bishop Nicetius of Trier:

> ...an enclosure flanked by thirty towers encircles the mountain; a building rises up on a spot covered until recently with forest; the wall spreads its wings and drops down to the valley floor.... Its walls encompass an immense area and the house alone constitutes a veritable fortress. Marble columns hold up the imposing structure....The tower commanding the sloping approachway contains a chapel dedicated to the saints, as well as weapons for the warriors' use. There an engine of war still stands.... Water is channeled off along ducts following the contours of the mountain; the mill which it turns grinds corn.... (Duby 1973, 58).

As Duby mentions, we must make allowances for rhetorical grandiloquence in this description. It does show a striking picture for the age, and it does show how entrenched was the identities of the religious, military and the farmer in society, and how oppressed was the multitude.

SLAVES

Slavery was nothing new in the Roman Empire. But it increased during the decline of the Empire. During this time, the Church hierarchy was in its ascendancy. Society was made up of another triad: the noblemen, including the bishops, a somewhat free peasantry, and slaves.

In the seventh and eighth century Europe was made up of a large number of *servi* and *ancillae*, who were often called by the neuter name *mancipia* (sellable goods) indicating their status as things rather than persons (Duby,1973, 32). They had nothing they could call their own, and they were totally at the mercy of their masters. Their master could do with them as he pleased. Sons and daughters of slaves also became slaves of the same lord, and they, too, suffered the same fate as their mothers and fathers.

Slaves of the lords were, then, replenished by the reproduction of the present slave stock. It was also replenished by raids on neighbors, by warfare, and by trade. Slavery was a fundamental structure of the economy of Europe.

The free peasant is probably a misnomer, because he or she, too, was a slave, totally dependent on a lord or bishop. Duby indicates a formulary, an oath, which Merovingian lords forced their free peasants to say when poverty forced them to enter their custody: "As it is well known to all that I have not the means to feed and clothe myself, I have begged your pity, and your will has granted it to me, to allow me to be delivered into and consigned to your protection...."(Duby 1973,45).

At the will of his lord, the free peasant was forced to bear arms, to follow his Lord in order to foster justice and the law, or to become a monk and serve God in a monastery. Women and girls were also on call to serve the lord in whatever tasks the lord should give her. Apparently free, they were totally burdened by the services which the lord or the bishop forced them to render.

The lords and bishops, then, dwelt at the center of a large household called the palace. Large groups of various kinds of people hummed around them, serving them. The lords and bishops were the privileged ones who owned the land, dealt with the slaves, directed the free peasants, and went to war.

We return to the theology of the "3's, the very image of the Trinity, God himself. "The feudal system consisted of those who prayed, those who warred, and those who worked. God was a Trinity. On the theology of the "3's" the literate theologians of the age hung their feudal theologies.

Chapter 5

THE PEACE OF GOD

HISTORICAL SETTING

Approaching the millennium, a growing middle class arose. Individual farmers, artisans, merchants and common laborers had struggled and establish themselves in a new growing economy. When Hugh Capet took the throne of France in 987, his weaknesses as king generated a whole new ruling dynamic, not only in France, but in other places in Europe. Hugh was unable to exert authority over lesser lords. Castles and their rich owners, the castellans, rose everywhere. The castellans began to take over and flex their muscles.

According to Colin Morris, because of their new position of power, the castellans bowed ever so nicely to the king, and then with their *milites* or *cabalarius* (Morris 1972, 41) began to exert more and more control over the lands around them. The *cabalarius* of the age were not soldiers. They were free and generally unattached men of modest wealth. While not rich, they had enough resources to at least own a war horse and the equipment to go with it (Bonnassie 1991, 208). They were the type of person who would be a villain, or, at rare times, the hero in *The Three Musketeer* literature and movies of recent times. Generally, they were men who were capable and willing to bleed the unarmed people until they were pale and anemic (Duby 1980, 135). Together with the owners of the castles, these men became the newest dominators of the population and the Church. While Castellan control had a certain flair, it lacked justice and disturbed the peace. "Whoever held the castle enjoyed military control of the region. Meanwhile, the general breakdown of royal authority which had taken place in France in the tenth century had left local lords free to develop their own pattern of exploitation (Morris 1972, 40-41).

The head of the castle and his men peered down on the citizenry. They knew everything that was happening beneath them, and they controlled the populace. Such sudden power in the hands of the castellans brought the whole ascending, working middle class to its knees. Once again, these middle classes were once more not only poor, but slaves on the land. The free laborer was forced to join with the slave in an unhappy union, and they became one, inert, passive group unable to do anything for their own benefit. They were a group simply used by others. The local lord and his *cabalarius (soldiers)* demanded labor, taxes, and the use of the women of all who lived beneath the castle walls. In return, the poor received a certain "protection" from outlaws and prowlers from other castles. When abused or raped, they only had the small consolation that a local soldier or castellan was the culprit, not a foreigner. They "had to take whatever was dealt them" without recourse to the king and his men.

At the same time, inheritance patterns changed. The castle demanded constant, one man control. Land that had been shared by inheritance among the members of the castle family, now went to one person, the eldest son. The feuds and instability which this caused among the castellan families lasted for centuries (Landes 1, pp. 26-27).

The hierarchy also suffered the loss of much land to the castellan and the *cabalarius,* who floated here and there doing anything they wished, taking away the possessions of even the church by extortion, by force, and by claim of the right of accession. They now exerted the right to place ministers and bishops of their own choice in local dioceses (Landes 1995, 27-28).

The word spread among the owners of castles that it was possible for them to exert all this control. Castellans cropped up in England, Germany, and the rest of Europe. Castellans everywhere in Europe exerted the same power. They saw it as too good to be true, but it was indeed true. All of them began to pay the required due homage to their kings, only to turn their backs and sap the king's royal powers by taking control over their areas. They leeched onto their subjects, enslaving them all.

The former doctrine of the "3's," the trinity of God's community on earth -- the harmony among those who prayed, those who went to war, and those who worked -- was in jeopardy. Ironically, it was being replaced by a new doctrine of the "3's," the castellan, including most bishops and some clergy who somehow, by inheritance, hook or crook, managed to slither to the top of the pack, the cabalarius and the oppressed, which included another inferior group of "3's," the monks, the inferior clergy, and the free peasants and slaves.

THE BEGINNINGS OF THE STRESS ON THE INDIVIDUAL

Such a situation could not last. The person had tasted freedom, and it now considered itself as human as the castellan and the cabalarius. A protest movement arose. The populace united with the monks and some clergymen to demand the rights inherent in every human being. The poet W. H. Auden gives us one of the best descriptions of the feelings of the individual in the age:

> Some thirty inches from my nose
> The frontier of my Person goes;
> And all the untilled air between
> Is private pagus or demesne.
> Stranger, unless with bedroom eyes
> I beckon you to fraternize,
> Beware of rudely crossing it;
> I have no gun, but I can spit. (p. 14)

Such feelings concerning personal rights were innovations to the poor person who lived before the beginning of the second millenium. They had to battle through the theology of the "3's" to arrive at such feelings of freedom. They had no tradition of individualism to fall back on. Colin Morris tells us that the learned fathers of the Church, who were steeped in Greek philosophy had words to express "community of being," but they never came up with a word which could adequately translate the word "person"-- the clear distinction between one human being and another" (Morris 1972, 2-3). This was a problem that had to be worked through.

Not that the value of individualism was foreign to our Christian tradition for those who relished it. Before the age of the fathers of the Church, the value of the individual was found in the Old Testament, and was enhanced by the true Christian community as they worked at living according to the words and deeds of Jesus. However, because the Church quickly became inundated by Greek philosophic thought, Christians have suffered to this day from a lack of appreciation of the individual person.

In the Old Testament, God called all humans by name. People were important because of their position in the community of God's people, but they were also important as individuals: Adam, Noah, Abraham, Isaac, Jacob, Joseph, Moses, Miriam, Aaron,

Gideon, Deborah, Judith, David, Amos, Isaiah, Jeremiah and all the rest were individuals in their own right before they were positioned as special community members.

The Psalms also stress the value of individuals. In spite of the works of liturgists, ancient and recent, who rightfully stress that the bulk of the psalms are liturgical, community prayer, many of the psalms still stand out clearly as prayers of individuals to their God: "O Lord, how many are my adversaries…" (Psalm 3 NAB); "God, reprove me not in your anger" (Psalm 6 NAB). We could go on and on.

Jesus, while not de-emphasizing the importance of community, stressed the importance of the individual. He, of course, followed the example of the Old Testament by placing a premium on individual names. But he went much further than that. The Sermon on the Mount teaches us that everyone is so important that he or she deserves to be treated well by others, even if they be an enemy. Jesus was tender with the sick, with the lame, with the dying; he relished the company of Mary, Martha, and Lazarus, and he was generous with the thief next to him on the cross. Some of his parables also stress the importance of the individual: the parable of the lost sheep (Luke 15:1-7 NAB); the prodigal son (Luke 15: 11-32 NAB). The value of individual human life owes a great deal to the Old Testament and to Jesus.

Paul was one of the first Christian writers to place a heavy emphasis on community. He saw the need to weld his communities into a united force. Amongst other statements he wrote: "There does not exist among you Jew nor Greek, slave or freeman, male or female. All are one in Christ Jesus" (Galatians 3:28 NAB) The statement is clear. Nothing is important for us except our membership in the Body of Christ, the Church. Duby, when he deals with the slavery that lingered on and on throughout human history, condemns Paul for placing such a stress on the Church community and emphasizing slavery. He states "Christianity did not condemn slavery; it dealt it barely a glancing blow" (Duby 1980, 138). Paul's letter to Philemon regarding slavery is a stark example of Duby's contention.

Then, after the age of the fathers of the Church who were trained by Greek philosophers, the value of individuality was, for the most part, lost for another time and place.

THE PEACE OF GOD MOVEMENT STRESSES INDIVIDUAL RIGHTS

The citizenry responded to the disorders and general violence caused by the castellans and their henchmen by peace demonstrations, huge gatherings assembled in open fields to denounce injustices. If the king, the counts and the dukes could not be relied on, the people could and they did call on the church and the monks to help them to do so. Modern peace movements carry banners with clever sayings. The citizenry and the monks of the middle ages hauled out the bodies of local saints which the people marched behind, protesting the injustices being inflicted on them and the church. People assembled from all ranks of society to the fields where the peace of God councils were held, and castellan and *cabalarius* were forced to swear in the presence of the relics and the people that the oppression would cease.

Peace assemblies started in the latter part of the 980's. They became popular, and they spread across Europe. The first was held in central Aquitane, at Charroux in 989. Daniel F. Callahan tells us that at Aquitane at this very time the last of the three strophes of the *Agnus Dei* in the liturgy of the Eucharist was changed from *miserere nobis* [have mercy on us] to *dona nobis pacem* [grant us peace]. The change can be linked to the peace of God movement there (Callahan 1992, 7, 173).

Nothing shows the intensity of popular enthusiasm for peace than the first peace council of Limoges. The cult of Saint Martial, the first missionary of Limoges, was on the increase. Charles the Bald gave Saint Martial a new life by wrongly associating him with Saint Peter. In November, 994, according to Ademar, a plague of "holy fire," broke out in Limoges, creating panic and widespread fatality. What the plague was, we are not completely sure, but Ademar's description would point to an outbreak of ergotism. The Bishop and abbot called a three day fast. Then the body of Saint Martial was taken to a hill outside the city. There, before a great crowd, the plague was lifted, the people were seized with joy, and the duke and his men repented and signed a pact of peace and justice. This was the most famous of the "sanctified" peace councils, one with, not only large crowds of all classes of people, but also miracles and spiritual experiences (Head and Landes 1992, 1-3).

Later in this chapter, many of Ademar's works come under grave suspicion, but his writings on these local events, by and large, are safe and are quoted and supported by an unusual amount of other independent writers from the age. At this point, we have no reason to dispute the authenticity of the events. Their spiritual impact and the number of people present were impressive (Head and Landes1992, 8, 186).

But sadly the impact of the first peace movements had little apparent effect. The castellans and *cabalarius* went back to their oppressive ways, and the poor went back to serving them -- now with less power than they had before (Landes 1995, 32).

The poor could only recall the memory of their bishops, stark naked, beating their breasts, wailing against the misdeeds of the counts and their horsemen. They remembered the bishops walking along side them behind the bodies of local saints, and they knew it was a charade of mammoth proportions staged to gain their favor. So the poor returned to serving the castellans – much too little was done to relieve their plight. If there was a change, it happened only in the minds, resentments, and secret efforts of the citizenry and the monks. The chronicles of the monastery of Saint Martial, for example, inscribed a damning curse aimed at peace breakers which had to rattle the consciences of castellans and cabalarius alike.

SAINT MARTIAL

In Limoges, Saint Martial was growing in stature in the minds of some who spoke of the saint as Saint Peter's younger cousin and an apostle of Jesus. Stories abounded among the poor that Saint Martial converted tens of thousands at one time and resurrected more people from the dead than Jesus (Landes 1992, 191). Such spiritual yarns are understandable – they rise and they fall according to times and cold seasons among the hopeful poor and oppressed. However the monks of Saint Martial also took the new myths and ran with them. Saint Martial was their new hero.

Between 1020 and 1030, approximately 20 peace councils were held in Europe (Head and Landes 1992, 6). One of these took place in Limoges in 1031 with Saint Martial in the lead. The Peace of God movement, with the relics of various saints leading the way, continued into most of the eleventh century (Head and Landes 1992, 9).

Richard Landes continues in his article "While God Tarried: Disappointed Millennialism and the Making of the Modern West":

> The year 1000 thus came without the world-ending Terrors and went without the long hoped

for Millenium. It did, however, galvanize a generation that viewed its passage as the dawn of a new stage in the redemptive process in history.... 'It was,' wrote one spokesman for Cluny '... as if the whole world were shaking itself free, shrugging off its old age, and covering itself everywhere in a white mantle of churches (Landes 1997, 22-27).'

But then, in the course of time, the year 1033, the commonly believed millennial year of the death of Jesus, arrived. It had become the new date for the end of the world, especially after a European-wide savage famine, eclipses, a new star in the heavens (a nova spotted around 1006) and the destruction of the holy sepulcher in Jerusalem. Attempts by some to convert the Jews *en masse* resulted in pogroms in Europe. An increased number of Peace of God councils flooded Europe in anticipation of expected events (Landes 1997, 22-27). But gradually, after nothing of consequence happened, some of the common people came to the realization that if anything was to happen, they would have to do it. Landes continues:

> Among the responses ... was the emergence of groups of people – commoners, clerics, aristocrats, both sexes – who formed apostolic communities, pursuing a life of manual labor and common property, refusing to enter churches, rejecting idols (crucifixes) and sacraments (mass, baptism).... (Landes, 1997, 22-27).

THE TRUCE OF GOD

In the 1040's and 1050's, the Truce of God joined the Peace of God movement. The Truce of God councils were attended, not by lay people, but by bishops and clergy to deal with matters of injustice and oppression. They generally found their expression in new church laws.

The Council of Elne was one of the first. This was followed by the Synod of Arles in 1041, which put in place a law which is humorous to 21st century ears, but it was progress. It prohibited fighting from Thursday to Monday morning (in commemoration of Christ's passion), on important feast days of the Church, and during Advent and Lent (Head and Landes,1992, 7).

Frederick S. Paxton stated in his brilliant analysis of the evolution of historical studies on the Peace of God, "History, Historians and the Peace of God: "Medieval Europeans did not draw lines between the sacred and the secular in the way we do" ((Head and Landes,1992, 32-33). While the Peace of God insisted upon the needs of the helpless, the poor and the unarmed, the Truce of God followed in its path, stating that the very shedding of blood was sinful. The Canon of Narbonne (1054) stated the following words: "No Christian should kill another Christian since whoever kills a Christian doubtless sheds the blood of Christ" (Head and Landes,1992, 8; Bloch 1961, 413).

Furthermore, Paxton's analysis of the data indicates that the clergy were often as afraid of the Truce of God movement as was the soldiers, but they felt that they had to do something to appease the people, who were growing angry in their oppression.

The people were angry about the selling of indulgences and other religious graces by the clergy. They were also concerned about the hidden wives of the priests. But they were most concerned about the destructiveness of the *castellans* and their *milites*, simply because they infringed on their own lives. The common masses were fed up with their religion as well as the oppression they faced day by day. They desired respect for their individual lives and a common religious life in which all could join together in social and symbolic unity (Paxton 1992, 36-37).

Gradually the laws established by the peace of God movement were established by the truce of God and became part of the established order regarding peacekeeping. By the mid-twelfth century, the king took on the peace of God as his own peace (Head and Landes 1992, 8).

TWO CHRONICLERS OF THE AGE 1000

One of the problems historians have with documenting anything in the age 1000 is a significant one. Only a few minor chroniclers existed who wrote extensively about the events of the age. We know of only two who wrote considerable works during this transition period, Ademar of Chabannes and Rodulfus Graber. Both told us about the peace of God, and because the peace of God did not play into their pathologies and are documented from other minor sources, their words are credible. But both ended up causing their own oppression of the people by raising fears and false hopes among them, and both, at times, purposely lied to history on other matters.

If these chroniclers would have committed honest mistakes, we could, as we write *The People's History*, bypass them. But here were two chroniclers: one was a pathological liar and the other was a belligerent person whom no one could endure. Nonetheless, they were able to manipulate many historians with their lies and exaggerations. We must handle them and their data with discernment.

ADEMAR OF CHABANNES

On August 3, 1029 Ademar of Chabannes jumped out of his bed into his sandals. He threw on his habit, and with great piety, walked solemnly to the cathedral of Limoges through the crowds assembled for a great celebration. The people watched him as he knelt in prayer in the cathedral at the place where the body of Saint Martial lay.

Behind the prayerful Ademar, kneeling there, were his aging, but proud parents who had made the grueling journey of one hundred kilometers to be present at the celebration.

Ademar was once a monk of Saint-Cybard of Angouleme, France. He had recently transferred to the monastery of St. Martial in Limoges, also in France, to prepare the great celebration of this day. The great gathering of the peace of God members in Limoges in 994 had propelled St. Martial as an apostle of Jesus, the mediator between heaven and earth. Ademar, an archivist and chronicler, tried to further the case of St. Martial, the patron saint and the first bishop of Limoges by insisting that he had the documentation that would prove that St. Martial was not merely a saintly confessor, but also an apostle of Jesus. After making the promise to the people, he took the matter to his back room (Landes 1995, 286-287).

Bishop Jordan trusted Ademar, his chronicler, and he had decreed the apostolicity of St. Martial, threatening with excommunication anyone who contradicted it (Landes 1995, 226). On August 2, the monks transferred the body of St. Martial in procession to the cathedral. All was prepared. Not only St. Martial, but Ademar was star of this show. He had filed the papal and council documents. He felt that he had handled the manuscripts and made the necessary adjustments in order to make them say that St. Martial was an apostle of Jesus Christ.

After considerable work, the documents now carefully stated not only that St. Martial was not only an apostle, but St. Peter's own nephew. Ademar also prepared a new liturgy for the celebration. He had convinced Bishop Jordan that this was an ancient liturgy used by St. Martial, lost by negligence ages past (Landes 1995, 210).

With all the care he had taken, Ademar made two crucial mistakes. While he did change all mention of *confessor* to *apostolus*, he was not able to forge two large initials onto the manuscript — initials which would have verified ancient authenticity. Also the manuscripts copied were not taken directly from "original" folios (Landes 1995, 216). A forger can only go so far.

The Debate

As Ademar knelt in prayer before his beloved saint, he was interrupted by a loud disturbance in the cathedral square. A renegade assistant of Ademar, Benedict of Chiusa, stood outside, boisterously denouncing as a monstrous fraud the nonsense about "Saint Martial, the apostle." Ademar ran out of the cathedral to silence Benedict. If he did not stop him, the carefully scripted project would crumble in front of the bishop and in front of the eyes of the whole assembly. He would certainly then be exposed as a forger. Ademar confronted Benedict, but Benedict had the evidence and carefully proved the fraud to all. As R. I. Moore states in a postscript: "Popular endorsement of Benedict's claim that the apostolicity of Saint Martial, the cause of which Ademar had dedicated his work and passion, was no more than a fraudulent attempt to raise money and power on false pretenses...." (Head and Landes 1992, 323)

To their credit, people listened to the arguments, agreed that the reason for a holiday was a fraud, shook off the holiday from work, and walked home murmuring, knowing that they had plowing or something else to do. Ademar stood in shame. There would be no celebration on that day.

Anyone who thinks that the people of the middle ages were dolts have to stand in amazement at these people. They processed all the information on the spot, realized that Ademar was a forger, turned on their heels, and went back home to their family duties. After all, they were present for a big celebration, and every one of them were primed to celebrate. That day, every single one of them proved to be staunch members of *The Peoples' History of Christianity* by refusing to do so.

After all, their discernment was subtle. Certainly, all of the spiritual writers of the age, with their apocalyptic bent, were expected to write in superlatives, and everyone in the age would have understood simple exaggerations. But Ademar had crossed a fine line. He had gone too far, further than the ancient manuscripts indicated. And the people recognized it and walked away. The ordinary people had to make a quick decision on that morning. They decided rightly, and in the process, took away from themselves a day without work, a day of celebration.

The confrontation between Benedict of Chiusa and Ademar and the response of the people are surprises to anyone who thinks of the year 1000 as an age of spurious relics, superstitions, witches, goblins, quests, and general unrealities. Ademar's claims of apostleship for St. Martial were not grease for the wheels of the cart which the people of the age were riding. The people of the age were clearly intelligent and discerning. Landes is correct when he states:

> Both he and we tend to assume (not without reason) that, with very few exceptions, early eleventh-century people had not the critical faculties by

which to tame their devotional fervor.... And yet it turned out...that there were men of sharp and skeptical intellect like Benedict to question and mock these fabrications and, still more unexpectedly, crowds who would listen to them (Landes, 1995, 15).

The very next day, drenched in shame, Ademar, now an unwanted commodity at St. Martial, returned to his first monastery, Saint Cybard in Angouleme, where he went into seclusion. He was unwanted there as well, and he received little solace from his now hostile brother monks on his return.

How Do Good Historians Now Read Ademar?

How do we find true history in the writings of Ademar, who has a wealth of information about an age which yields very little knowledge, but who suffers from a psychotic disorganization which makes him prone to lie? Of course, the answer is: the historian handles him very carefully and as intelligently as possible. At the same time, Landes relies on R. G. Collingwood who insists that the historian is forced, because of the lack of information in the age, to use his a priori imaginations. Landes goes on: "By this he meant our ability to think about what we know existed but for which we have no direct data; just as we know there is a far side of the moon without (normally) [until recently] being able to see it... [T]he historian's a priori imagination must not only be possible, it must conform with the available evidence (Landes, 1995, 19-20)."

Most historians do this whether they intend to do so or not, whether they admit it or not. Evidence gives them the dots, and they must put in the lines between the dots (Landes, 1995, 20).

As demented a person as Ademar was, he was close to the history of his times. If the historian who knows him well works carefully with his writings, Ademar can tell them something about his times (Landes, 1995, 21). "This approach amounts to a juggling act between the ever-changing world of Ademar's texts, contexts, and personal dispositions" (Landes 1995, 22).

So we believe Ademar concerning the "peace of God" events, but we do not believe him when he writes about Saint Martial, apostle of Jesus Christ. Others were eye-witnesses to the "peace of God" events, and they verify Ademar's reporting of those event. At the same time, Ademar tells us much more than the others about the peace of God events. Historians tend to believe him regarding this matter.

Ademar's Early Years

Ademar of Chabannes was born into a minor aristocratic family in 989, the year of the first peace council. The credentials of his ancestors were formidable. In the family line was Turio (897-944), a bishop of Limoges, Aimo (897-944), an abbot of Saint-Martial. His uncles, Adalbert and Roger, became respectively deacon and cantor of Saint-Martial. His mother's father was Ainard, one of the most powerful castellans of the region north of Limoges.

Ainard ably supported his cousins, the counts of the Marche, in their fight against the Duke of Aquitaine and the King of France (Landes, 1995, 78). "Ademar makes no mention of his family's participation in the numerous castellan wars he describes, and outside of Ademar himself, no trace of his own family appears in the documents" (Landes, 1995, 79).

Ademar entered the monastery of Saint-Cybard. He was trained as a scribe. He worked on the *Lives of the Fathers* (fols.

43-50). Not long thereafter, he went to study at Saint-Martial of Limoges. Here he became a much more accomplished scribe (Landes, 1995, 88-101). He certainly expected an exulted position in the monastery hierarchy when he returned to Saint-Cybard (Landes, 1995, 109).

Ademar, then, over a four year period, wrote three different recensions of his *Historia*. Each took on different tones, depending on the changes of his own political aims, the likes and dislikes of his audience, and its reception by the general populace (Landes, 1995, 129).

Ademar and the Year 1000

Marjorie Reeves from St. Anne's College, Oxford, writes about millennialism:

> The history of Christian apocalyptic reveals one thing very clearly: the desire of the human soul to find a significant place for itself in the time process..., and belief in the soul's immortality is intimately linked with the place of the human personality in an ongoing historical process which has two terminals – an individual one in death and a universal one in the end of the world. This sense of "place" and of "end" is one of the chief roots of morality...(Reeves, preface, 1979 xiii).

But the millennium did not mean much to Ademar. He was not emotionally involved in it and he was only historically involved in the peace of God movement. In fact, he at times resisted the millennium. He was detached from it, endured it passively (Landes, 1, 1995, 287).

He was ten years old in the year 1000, a year which did not mean much to him, but the year 1010 was the first documentable time when Ademar's apocalyptic fears coincided with that of the ordinary populace. At that time, he was twenty years old, and many believed that this same year, 1010, was the year that the Anti-Christ would appear on earth. Ademar claims that he walked into the open and saw a terrifying vision of Christ nailed to a celestial cross, weeping over the city. But he kept his thoughts inside himself. In fact, later, he manipulated this date, as well as many others, changing it to 1009 in order to play down its apocalyptic references (Landes, 1, 1995, 300). Otherwise, he had no interest in millennial implications.

In relationship to previous and following centuries, Bernard McGinn, professor of historical theology and history of Christianity at the Divinity School of the University of Chicago tells us that the year 1000 did not produce much out of the ordinary in the area of apocalypticism (McGinn 1979, 88). Certainly, in some quarters, millennial scares existed. But historians can exaggerate them. Even then, some with an apocalyptic nature were able to see through the panic, transcend it, and see a vision of the glory which was to come. What we find in the year 1000 is a continuity of the millennial expressions which were common throughout the ages of Christianity (McGinn, 1979, 88). Abbo of Fleury gives an intimate statement of the apocalyptic stress, or lack of it in the age. Here is another example of the discernment of some of the people in the age:

> When I was a young man I heard a sermon about the End of the world preached before the people in the cathedral of Paris. According to this, as soon as the number of a thousand years was completed, the Antichrist would come and the Last Judgment

would follow in a brief time. I opposed this sermon with what force I could from passages in the Gospels, Revelation, and the Book of Daniel. (Translated from *PL* 139, cc. 471-72 by McGinn, 1979, 89-90).

Ademar, also, was not often expressive about the millennium. The millennium does not seem to play into his psychosis. He mentions neither the year 1000, 1003, the supposed date of Christ's birth, nor 1033, the supposed date of Jesus' death on the cross. He does mention a vision of Christ in 1010 which he dated as 1009 to avoid millennial interpretations. Outside of that, only in his unedited final scribblings do we find apocalyptic, but indifferent and detached ravings.

RODULFUS, APOCALYPTIC WRITER AND THE PEACE OF GOD

Rodulfus Glaber (c980-c1046), on the other hand, an unbalanced, cranky eccentric, and gossip-mongering extrovert, presented apocalyptic writings with vitality. He was tormented by the millennium:

> When some of the more truthful of that time were asked by many what might be the meaning of such a great flocking together of people to Jerusalem, unheard of in previous centuries, they cautiously responded that it presaged nothing else but the coming of the Lost One, the Antichrist, who according to divine authority stands ready to come at the End of the age. (Translated from *PL* 142, cc, 681D-682A by McGinn, p. 90).

At about the same time that Ademar was struggling at Saint-Martial and Saint Cybard, Rodulfus Glaber, a self proclaimed, self-willed, and self-indulgent child was placed by his uncle in some monastery in France. He behaved so badly there that he was booted out of the place (Glaber 1989, xxv). In fact, he spent most of his life moving from one monastery to the next. We get the impression that the constant movements were not merely because of Rodulfus' need to do research. Other monks found him neither a gentle nor generous companion.

But Rodulfus Glaber did write *The Five Books of the Histories* and a minor work called the *Life of St. William*. In contrast to Ademar, he was obviously convinced of A. D. dating and the importance of the millennium after the birth and death of Jesus:

> ...furthermore, in the space of nearly two hundred years, no one, except Bede in England and Paul in Italy...who wrote only about their own people and nations -- has come along a person who was anxious to transmit the deeds of the past for posterity. It is clear that across the sea and in the barbarian provinces of the Roman world many events have taken place which would have been a powerful and profitable lesson for men – if they had only been written down. This is especially true of the many events which took place around the millennium of the Incarnation of Christ, the Savior (Glaber, *Histories,* I, 1).

The millennium certainly did inspire and influence Glaber's writing of *The Five Books of the Histories*. Rodulfus noticed that at the millennium, in the whole world, but especially in Italy and France, men began to rebuild churches. It was as though "the whole world were shaking itself free, casting off the past, and dressing itself in a white mantel of churches. But in this new white shining landscape, according to Rodulfus, hiding behind the white columns, darker, more sinister, images appeared – nasty, demonic heretics. "All of this bore out the prophecy of John, who said that the devil would be freed after a thousand years." Rodulfus saw evil lurking in everything that happened, the good, bad, or indifferent (Pegg 2008, 8). He was convinced that the Church could only be purified through famine, war, destruction, and an abundance of heretics. Again, at the millennium, Christian writers began to worry about heresy and other grave evils that could happen to humanity. Glaber was influential in deceiving ages to come that "heretics" of every age can be gathered together in one big pile.

It is questionable whether such concern was necessary beyond the written manuscripts of this man. Rodulfus then set out on an ambitious task which he nor anyone else was ever able to accomplish: "Furthermore, since we are going to relate the events which happened on all of the four corners of the earth, it is only right that we give a dissertation on the divine power of the Lord who made this earth (*quaternitatis*)." (Glaber, *Histories,* I, 1; Pegg 2008, 8).

Rodulfus had difficulty being anything but a busybody and a gossip. He provided, as Bulst indicates, "a keyhole view of the great" of his age (Glaber 1989 xx). Of his work historians agree: it is without plan or organization; it is badly written; it is gossipy and full of hear-say. Its value is that it is one view of the times, written by a contemporary.

Rodulfus had connections. He enjoyed a special relationship with St. William, "who under the influence of the monastery of Cluny came to be one of the leading monastic reformers of the early eleventh century, and [Rodulfus] accompanied him

[William] on a visit to Italy." (Graber 1989, lxx) It is clear that William sought out monks who he thought had special talent and encouraged them to develop those talents. He encouraged Rodulfus to write the *Histories.* "However the relationship between Rodulfus and William did not last long. Neithard tells us that he later quarreled with his patron and left him for another monastery not under his jurisdiction.... (Glaber 1989, lxxi).

It is not surprising that Rodulfus eventually quarreled with William on some unknown issue. Rodulphus continued to be a quarrelsome, bombastic, and generally speaking, a mettlesome monk. Nonetheless, Rodulfus waxed eloquent and true when he wrote of the Peace of God counsels which happened before his eyes:

> In the millennial year of the passion of the Lord after the disaster of years of want, thanks to the divine goodness and mercy, the violent rains ceased. The gloomy face of the heavens cleared, and gentle breezes began to blow. Amiably, the Creator made the surface of the earth verdant, giving us abundant fruits to expel our needs. Then the bishops, the abbots and other holy and devote religious people in the whole surrounding area of Aquitaine gathered their people together in councils. Many bodies of the saints and other relics were brought there in procession. The movement then spread to Arles and Lyons, then to Burgundy and to the furthest parts of France. Throughout all the dioceses it was decreed that in a certain place the bishops and rulers would gather their people to re-establish peace and the institutions of the holy faith. When they heard this, the nobles, the middle class and

the poor came rejoicing to obey the commands of the pastors of the church, as though these words were spoken from heaven to earth. For all were still terrified by the death and horror of recent times, and they feared that the instability might stand in the way of any good times enduring into the future. The peace councils in the fields of France did their work: The scribes drew up a description of the decrees which were explained until they were understood by all. They contained a list of things which were prohibited. The most important of these was to the keeping of the peace, so that everyone, whether lay or religious, could go about his business unarmed and without fear. The scribes at the councils recorded the names of those who swore to God to keep those decrees. Robbers and those who violated the rights of others in any way would suffer the full rigors of the law, either by heavy fines or by corporal punishment. Unless a person violated the peace oath, even if he committed some crime, he could still seek refuge in a church, because it is a place of reverence. But if he violated the peace oath, he would be seized even at the altar and made to suffer the established penalty. Everyone agreed to show reverence to clerics, monks, nuns, and anyone traveling with them. They were not to be harmed by anyone. Many decisions were made at these councils which we wish to relate at length (Rodulphus Glaber, IV, 14-16).

Glaber then left the essence of the peace movement behind and went into detail on issues of little consequence which must have been decided at one or the other peace of God councils which he attended regarding abstaining from wine on the sixth day of the week and from sex on the seventh day of the week. Those who violated these laws had to give assistance or money to three poor people. He then goes into a long dissertation on the multiple healings and miracles which took place which, he said, gave credence to the events and made all cry to God with extended hands. He adds that in that year the harvest of corn and wine was so abundant that it equaled that of the next five years. He then comes back down to earth and adds notes of reality. He states that "all food was inexpensive that year except for meat and rare spices" (Glaber,1989, 16). He then adds that it did not take long for everyone to return to former evil ways (Glaber, 1089, 17).

CONCLUSION

We have completed our trek through the peace of God movements which happened around the end of the first millennium of Christianity. In doing so, we have waded through the pathologies of two men, Adamar of Chabannes and Rodulfus Glaber, who have given us the greatest insight into those movements. Their accounts ring true in spite of their psychological problems: they are both capable writers; their expositions are detailed; their commentaries do not play into their pathologies; some minor sources support their expositions of the events.

The peace of God movements fit into the scheme of history. They were long over-due. Common Christians finally had had enough. They rose up and objected to their oppressions.

Their actions gave them only temporary relief, but they did lead to the truce of God of the bishops and the eventual support of kings. *The People's History of Christianity* recognizes the value of these first peace of God marches, and the courage of those who organized them.

Furthermore, it was only a beginning. Other protest marches of the populace have taken place throughout history. Some of these marches were more successful than others. Yet all of them were last ditch efforts by common people to lift ridiculous, oppressive systems.

Chapter 6

THE ALBIGENSIAN CRUSADE (1209-1229) AND ITS INQUISITION

LANGUEDOC, THE CENTER OF THE FRAY

The Albigensian Crusade is certainly one of the most infamous moments in the history of Christianity. Today, many Christians never heard of the catastrophe. Others who did hear of it say the Albigenses deserved it.[23] Most others who are knowledgeable of

---

[23] Such appears to be the view of Andre Vauchez, *Francis of Assisi: the Life and Afterlife of a Medieval Saint*, tr. by Michael Cusato. Yale University Press, 2012, 51. Vauchez is professor emeritus at the University of Paris X, and an expert on religious movements, saints, and the dynamics of the Middle Ages. He writes: "The Roman Pontiff [Innocent III], at the head of this battle, endeavored to distinguish those currents which were clearly heretical, like Albigensianism (against which he launched a crusade in 1209), from those whose doctrine seemed essentially in conformity with the beliefs of the Church...." Perhaps he is writing what he believes was Innocent III's mindset, not necessarily his own beliefs. It is difficult to believe that Vauchez, from a prestigious university in France, could make such a statement. First, if any of the so-called Albigensians firmly believed in Catharism, they were not heretics: they were in no way Catholic or even Christian at all. *Consolamentum* was not Christian baptism; and the *perfecti* and their other beliefs and religious rites were in no way Christian. They certainly were religious, but their unique religion was outside the realm of the Christian or Catholic religion and therefore outside the jurisdiction of the Pope. Second, a few Catholics formed some customs akin to Catharism and the troubadours in Southern France. These people were more or less Catholic, depending on the individual. But they were peace-loving, community-involved and careful not to criticize the Roman Church. They were simply not a threat to the church. Certainly, the pope did not need to canonize them as saints, but burning them at the stake and destroying the group, as well as thousands of Catholics in the process, was uncalled for and clear genocide. Third, the pope killed 10,000 at Beziers alone (it may have been more), and only 222 were good men and good women. No more than 2% took on themselves the "Catharism" or "semi-Catharism." This is a minute number of the population, and the community-at-large certainly could and did absorb them with no harm done to Christianity. Fourth, the people of Beziers were willing to die rather than give these 222 over to the crusaders. Does this not say something? 10,000 Catholics gave

the event, including some living in the Languedoc area today, consider it one of the greatest injustices of history, second only to the holocaust in Germany in the 1940's.

While Francis of Assisi, with love and devotion, was enflaming the hearts of followers of Jesus in central Italy, crusaders were burning the towns in southern France. While Francis was mapping out the way of Jesus, the Albigensian Crusade was carefully and logically ushering genocide into the whole Western world under the guise of Christianity.

Some people were trying to form a distinct Christian culture in the rich fertile lands of Toulouse and its neighborhood, utilizing some of the social characteristics of the troubadours and the Cathars. A person might rightfully call it a fad of the age. Mark Gregory Pegg emphatically states in his work *A Most Holy War: the Albigensian Crusade and the Battle for Christendom:* "The Albigensian Crusade is one of the great pivotal moments in world history.... The crusade ushered genocide into the West, changing forever what it meant to be Christian, what it meant to be like Christ.... What it meant to be a Christian...would never be the same again (Pegg 2008, xiv, 5)." In short, what Augustine perverted when he permitted just war, the Albigensian Crusade took to its ultimate limits.

Around 1900, historical scholars mistakenly supported a fiction that equated *Albigensian* and *Cathar,* a mistake which has been perpetuated in many circles and in dictionaries today. In all truth, the Albigenses or Albigensians were people, most of them Roman Catholics, who lived in the city of Albi.[24] The Cathar,

---

their lives to save 222 good citizens, their neighbors, who had new and different customs. The 10,000 Catholics might be considered for canonization as martyrs, if we think about it. Five, Innocent III and Gregory IX should have been held accountable for their genocides.

24 Albi is a city 85 kilometers northeast of Toulouse on the river Tarn. It is the seat of the Archbishop of Albi, and its inhabitants are called Albigensians. There might have been some good men and good women in Albi. But to link Albigensianism with Catharism is a grave misnomer of early 20th century historians.

on the other hand, was a designation for individuals in Europe who held to certain teachings which were foreign to Roman Catholicism, foreign to even Christian beliefs. Their beliefs were various and disparate according to individuals and cultures . Now a small group with some so-called Cathar and troubadour customs, who preferred to be called good men and good women, did live in southern France. They did not hold to the beliefs of the Cathars in Europe, but they did think it stylish to imitate some of their customs. Their beliefs and customs, too, were disparate depending on the individual, but they were not those of Catharism. Mark Gregory Pegg goes so far as to state: everything about these good men and good women, so-called Cathars and their supposed secret "Albigensian" knowledge "...is utter fantasy, even down to their name [Cathar or Albigensian]. In fact...more than a century of scholarship on both the Albigensian Crusade and heresy hasn't been vaguely mistaken, or somewhat misguided, it has been breathtakingly wrong (Pegg 2008, x).

Some other historians have told other fairy-tales and myths about Languedoc, the southern part of France. Once upon a time, they have told us, in a land called Languedoc, lived a count who loved his people. He lived in a great castle in Toulouse, which, to his delight, was a center of love and romance. Arts and sciences flourished in Languedoc. The count brought in troubadours to play there. Farmers brought their harvest to sell there. Merchants from all over the Mediterranean brought their fine cloth and rugs to its market. The Count took pride in his castle, in his community, in the merchants and troubadours he was able to attract -- for it was a center of peace and prosperity. Then evil counts and knights came from the north to destroy the good life that was thriving there.

It sounds like *The Lord of the Rings, Game of Thrones,* or some other similar work of fiction. It is the fairy-tale many nineteenth to twentieth century historians want us to believe. Actually, much of the story is true, but not the part that tells us that Toulouse was filled with "peace and prosperity." If we take "peace and prosperity" out of the story, the beautiful fairy tale falls apart in our hands. It is diluted to the point of being meaningless. Life was not glamorous in Languedoc. Troubadours sang there, but their songs were a diversion from an otherwise tedious, even horrible life.

Elaine Graham-Leigh in her book *The Southern French Nobility and the Albigensian Crusade* (Graham-Leigh, 2005) drove the spike in the heart of this fairy tale. She states: "Beginning in the 1870's ... a view of the crusade was developed in which the pre-crusade Languedoc was cast as a lost idyll of tolerance and civilization. This remains one of its most influential guises" (Graham-Leigh 1995, 3).

Graham-Leigh points out that the Albigensian Crusade was, first, internal conflicts over land among the Counts of Languedoc. The common people, indeed everyone, suffered mightily under the burden of such conflicts. Those with Cathar customs were not on center stage then. Later, the horror story grew in intensity as the Counts and knights of Europe entered the fray, and finally, even later, the King of France decided to enter the conflict— all primarily because of land rights and material greed. The revenge concerning those who were developing customs akin to Catharism was an afterthought of two popes, Innocent III and Gregory IX.

Geoffroi de Breuil first extended "heresy" to all the Albigenses. Many historians, even to this day, follow his lead. The Popes at the time also fell into the trap. It is untrue to say that more than a few people in Albi, indeed in Languedoc, were true Cathars. Most were trying to find more meaning in an otherwise brutal world around them. As Pegg states: "Regrettably, the name [Cathar] is used with such an appalling lack of discrimination by modern scholars – it gets thrown around like so much Cathar-confetti, lazily adorning almost all heretics before the fourteenth century – that it is an epithet of confusion rather than clarity (Pegg 2008, 23)."

In summary on this point, it has become clearer and clearer that there existed in Languedoc no Cathar Church. "Good men" and "good women" made individual or small group decisions to do what they did, and their customs varied from village to village. They, in fact, never called themselves Cathars. Only Roman Catholics and historians down the ages designated them as such. Furthermore, their customs were almost exclusively cultural, not religious, beliefs. Certainly, the lack of knowledge of religion and scripture in some of the good men and women was the fruit of a degenerate clergy and a failing Christendom (Pegg 2008, 25-26).

Mixed with the cultural reform of the good men and the good women was a love of the culture of the troubadours, song writers who had a certain flair about them and sang of courtly love, respect for women, and the dignity of the person. They went from city to city, singing as they went.[25]

INTERNAL CONFLICTS IN LANGUEDOC

The language spoken in Southern France, also called Languedoc, was a refined language. It was a development of the ancient Latin, easily translated into poetry and song. That is why the troubadours loved it. Dante was enamored by the language.

---

[25] Colin Moore in *Discovery of the Individual* wrote about the troubadours who played for the count of Toulouse. The Count paid these songster well for their songs. The central theme of their love poetry was called *fin'amors* or *verai'amors*. Translate these words as "true love" if you like, or "courtly love." But the troubadours would have frowned on such a translation.. They were songwriters. The words that they used were words of songs. They were interested in music and they played with the complex and rich rhymes that could be achieved in the local language. Thus the works of the troubadours are untranslatable unless a person knows the full culture of the time and area.

At one point, he considered writing his *Divine Comedy* in the Languedoc language (Oldenbourg 2001, 26). Some elements of the language influenced Dante's work.

On the other hand, the bishops of Maguelonne in Languedoc, who were considered Counts in their own right, made the silver coinage, the *sols,* which were used for most of the monetary transactions in the area. The local bishops had become affluent and decadent. They were often more interested in money than anything else. Where were they when their people needed them? They are noted for their silence throughout the conflict between the Counts, the whole up-coming crusade and the inquisition that followed.

The good men and women found respectable places within the local societies. At the same time, they lived among people who were clearly suffering because of the constant internal wars caused by the constant bickering of their counts and minions over land rights, which continued on and on through the whole of the 11th into the 12th and even into the beginning of the 13th century.[26] The people turned to whomever would give them spiritual solace, and that was often the good men and women.

Also, the *Vaudois*, who entered the area, were able to distinguish local customs from hardcore religious beliefs. The Popes had trouble doing so. The *Vaudois* also gave much support to the people of the area.

All the castles of Languedoc, including that of Toulouse, lay at the foothills of the Pyrenees Mountains. The counts controlled not only their own lands, but the roads and the trade routes to the Mediterranean Sea (Graham-Leigh 1995, 52). Tolls paid at every intersection kept these counts wealthy. In the twelfth and thirteenth century, the counts of Languedoc were by far the most prosperous royalty of all of Europe (Sumption

---

[26] See Jean Dunbabin's fine work, *France in the Making, 843-1180,* Oxford, 1985, 300-301.

1978, 40; Hamilton 1979, VIII, 10). Huge individual fortresses dotted the landscape of Languedoc. Some were family castles. Some were walled villages of about 250-500 people. A few of them were larger cities. Local lords together with their councils controlled the politics. Foreigners and even various religious sects were not only tolerated, they were welcomed by the counts in order to contribute to the social environment (Sumption 1978, 22; Strayer 1972, 8).

The count who was most successful in the fray was the politically wise Raymond VI whose castle was in Toulouse in southern France in the year 1209. Although he took his lumps, the castle walls of Toulouse, manned as they were by knights with military expertise, protected well the people who lived there. Other castles in Languedoc were not so lucky. Others became the sites of horror stories – horror stories as real as the knights who attacked and defended them, the weapons they wielded, and the warm-bodies of those who once lived there and were soon scattered cold on the ground. Some of these victims were children; some were young maidens; some were very old.

A small population of good men and good women involved themselves in the community-- some of them even became members of the ruling councils of their cities. Their widows took in the orphan children who needed homes. It was clear that the counts and the ordinary Catholic population respected their faith and sincerity. While they developed a somewhat different social atmosphere than the Christian majority, their customs and activities developed within the respected society.

However, ostensibly their presence and their beliefs were a threat and a painful thorn in the sensitive foot of Church authorities. The good men and women became scapegoats of an ugly war to come – a war in which the Pope was a central figure.

THE BEGINNINGS OF CONFLICT

Innocent III took the position of sitting on the chair of Peter as the vicar of Christ between God and all of mankind. No Pope before him, not even Leo the Great, saw himself in such an exulted position. Religiously and politically, he thought that he had his ear to God for what he considered the benefit and, as he determined it, the necessary destruction of some of mankind. He was right and everyone on earth either agreed with him or was wrong. He was the supreme judge of God on earth, judging all, but he was judged by no man.

On March 10, 1208, Pope Innocent III (1198-1216), called the Albigensian Crusade, not in response to some "Cathar" threat, but in response to the murder of the papal legate Pierre de Castelnau, (Graham-Leigh1995, 2). The wily Innocent III would soon make what he perceived as the "Cathar" threat as a secondary purpose.

Pierre de Castelnau had been sent to Raymond VI to discuss some matter of concern to the Pope. The papal legate was murdered, some say by Raymond VI, Count of Toulouse (1194-1222). Before sunrise on Monday, the 14th of January, 1208, Pierre, the Cistercian monk, was about to cross the Rhone River near Toulouse when a squire trotted up behind him, took a lance and pushed it into his spine. As the sun was rising, the legate forgave his murderer, received the Eucharist, and died. Raymond VI probably did not have the legate killed, but his squire thought that he was doing him a favor by doing so. Innocent III would have done well if he had imitated Pierre de Castelnau in forgiving his enemies.

The Pope was often an angry man, and he was also worldly-wise and shrewd. When told of the murder, Innocent III did not forgive his enemy. He screamed to the heavens that the murderer should be cast into hell. As Pegg says, quoting the troubadour Guilhem de Tudela, he "chose a course of action that would leave many brave men dead, 'their entrails pouring out,' and many young girls stripped raw, 'with neither covering nor robe'" (Pegg 2008, 5). He did so simply because he was convinced that Raymond VI was the murderer.

He called on the knights of the rest of Europe "to be signed with the cross, that all their sins would be taken away if they went on a crusade against Languedoc." But he knew that forgiveness of sins was not incentive enough to pry enough knights out of their castles to do the job there. At the same time, he knew that all the knights of Europe were aware of the rich land that existed in Languedoc. The pope made the material wealth of the area fair game to any crusader. In so doing, he knew that he could attract the knights he needed. Knights flocked into the area to get whatever booty they could. Certainly, as it turned out, the Pope offered the knights more than he ever delivered (Sumption 1978, 73; Strayer, 1972, 53).

The great question which thunders down the ages is this: if Pope Innocent III called this Crusade because he considered himself to be the successor of St. Peter, was he denying Jesus (John 18:15-27) or loving him (John 21:15-17) when he condemned his enemies and killed thousands of citizens of Languedoc...?

ORGANIZATION OF THE CRUSADE

The Pope excommunicated Raymond VI in May, 1207 (Sumption 1978, 40: Hamilton 1979, VIII, 10). Thereafter, Raymond VI noticeably co-existed with both the good men and women as well as the Catholics who were true to the pope. Most likely the excommunication freed him to serve the welfare of all the people who relied on him for safety. Perhaps he was not sure himself whether the Pope or the good men and women were correct. He probably saw virtue in the good men and women, which he had to balance against the angry vindictiveness of the Pope. He even aided one of his four wives to enter the convent of the strict good women, and she became one of the leaders of the group. At the same time he treated the Catholic clergy with respect, promoted monasteries, and made donations to religious institutions.

But Pope Innocent III followed through -- using the incident of the assassination to justify a Crusade not only against Raymond VI, but against "the sinister race of Languedoc." All of Languedoc was sentenced for distruction. In the letter of proclamation of the Albigensian Crusade the Pope offered indulgences "equal to those fighting in the Holy Land" for any knight who joined in the effort for at least 40 days (Sumption 1978, 73; Strayer, 1972, 53). But who or why the pope wanted them to fight was not at all clear.

THE GOOD MEN AND WOMEN, VICTIMS OF THE CRUSADE

Sumption says that already in 1179 the Third Lateran Council had placed the label "heretic" on the good men and women. Heresy had become a fetish of churchmen. The Council had invited all the faithful to take up arms against them. It even went so far as to say that anyone who killed one of the group would receive an indulgence of two years (Weis 2001, xxiii). This effectively put not only "the faithful," but also the good men and women in the mix of the conflict between the aristocrats from Europe and Languedoc.

Early in his pontificate, Innocent III issued a decree *Vergentis* to the people of Viterbo. In it he equated heresy with the Roman crime of treason against the emperor. In July 1200 he extended the decree to Languedoc (Barber 120).

But it must be remembered that the citizens of Languedoc, even the good men and women were not the primary reason for the Albigensian conflict, but an afterthought. Primarily, Innocent III was after Raymond VI. Innocent III's anger skewered his logic. All the people of Languedoc, and especially the good men and good women were an added dimension. Innocent III and the invading armies which he was responsible for sending decided that the war was also a prime opportunity to rid Languedoc of the "threat" of the good men and women.

THE CRUSADE ITSELF

The crusade ravaged the whole territory, destroyed crops, razed towns, and indiscriminately annihilated whole populations of people. It had elements of a genocide, a mass persecution, and an invasion. But its most noted element, as it developed, was the gradual degeneration of humanity in the conflict between Crusaders and defenders. The highly civilized community of Languedoc was completely dehumanized.

Because many knights found the offer of booty in rich Languedoc an attractive incentive, an army of 10,000 - 20,000 knights gathered in Lyon to begin the march southward. One of those knights was Simon IV de Montfort l'Aumary (1165-1218) who was disinherited from the land of his uncle's estate in Leicester, England. Montfort was appointed the military leader of the Crusade. As recompense for his efforts, he was offered any land he could conquer (Sumption 1978, 86). The leaders of the knights met with Arnauld Amaury, the newly appointed Papal legate and the "spiritual advisor" of the Crusaders.

Meanwhile, Raymond VI of Toulouse got word of the

powerful approaching army. Realizing his own risk and the risk to his people, he had a sudden but prudent conversion. To get in good graces with the Crusade and the Pope, Raymond VI handed over seven strongholds to the crusaders and pledged to expel the good men and women from Toulouse, a pledge he never kept. He was looking out for his own interests and his own responsibilities, the interests of the people of Toulouse. According to Peter of Vaux-de-Cernay, as told in Sumption, he also had to submit to an embarrassing punishment:

> The count was required to appear naked before the cathedral and an assembly of twenty-two bishops to swear an oath of obedience. The papal legate thereupon absolved him, placed a stole around his neck, and, while beating him, dragged him into the church. To the populace this was high drama, but to the knightly class it was nearly an execution (Sumption 1978, 86).

The Pope then did an unbelievable thing: he lifted the excommunication, and Raymond VI joined the group of Crusaders. Was not Raymond VI the expressed reason the pope gave for sending the troops? Now, in the strange world of papal alliances, Raymond VI became one of the attacking force. Were the people of Languedoc or were the good men and good women now the papal reason for the attack? For the insurgent knights, it was simply the fertile land of southern France, the most fertile land in all of Europe, which the knights wished to own.

For his part, Raymond VI was boldly playing every angle. He hoped for personal gain, as did every other knight who came to the crusade. Secondarily, he desperately sought to ensure the well-being of his people.

Another Raymond, Raymond-Roger III de Trencavel (1194-1209), Count of the City of Beziers, also heard about the vast army coming. Raymond-Roger was actually an enemy of Raymond VI. The two, and their families before them, had an internal war. Raymond VI believed that Raymond-Roger lacked courage and had no political sense. Raymond-Roger, too, tried to join the knightly effort, but he was rejected.

The crusaders set their first sites on the city of Beziers. Raymond-Roger III de Trencavel was in charge of that city. He did not know what to do. His political acumen was clearly meager. Strayer says he gave the city of Beziers general instructions and then said he would go quickly to round up more defenders (Sumption 1978, 89-94; Strayer 1972, 61). He reneged on sending the defenders.

Massacre of Beziers

On July 21, 1209 the crusaders captured the village of Servian, to the north of Beziers. They then turned immediately on Beziers, demanding that the city hand over its 222 good men and women. The Catholics in the city supported these 222 virtuous people, and the city refused to hand them over (Wakefield 1974, 102). What happened then was the greatest massacre of Christians by Christians in history.

Raymond-Rogers was gone, and no one with any military ability came to the fore in Beziers. The Crusaders were able to enter the city because of a blunder on the part of a small group of unorganized defenders of the city. On July 22nd, this small group of light armored defenders made the huge mistake of opening a gate in order to make a small attack on the huge army now starting to encamp outside its walls. Some of the crusaders noticed that a gate was open. They stormed it before it could be closed and held it open for the whole invading army.

The crusaders took the city before they were even able to plan its attack. It was simple access, much like walking into your own home after a day of hunting. Surprised by the easy access, the knights asked Arnauld Amaury, their "spiritual leader": "Whom should we kill?" He, too, was undoubtedly surprised by the sudden turn of events, and in his enthusiasm he responded, "Kill them all. God will know his own." It is a strange statement from a man who promoted himself to be a follower of Jesus, but it is certainly the statement of one who had completely and enthusiastically supported the pope and the war effort.

At any rate, it is clear that Arnauld Amaury was in charge, and he was guilty of giving the order. It was also clear that the Crusaders massacred the populace. Peter of Les Veux-de-Cernay, an eye-witness who was always prejudiced in favor of the Church position very generously estimated the number of good men and women in the Beziers area to be 700 out of a population of 8,000 to 9,000 (Barber, 121). The Bishop of Beziers said that he knew every good man and woman in the city. Other sources say 10,000 to 20,000 Beziers residents and visitors (for people came into the city of Beziers from outlying areas because of the military threat) were murdered by the Crusading army, and only 222 of them were good men and women. The command to "kill them all," was obeyed by the attacking soldiers. The slaughter ended only when heat from the burning city drove the Crusaders out. The city of Beziers was filled with burning corpses, and most of them were Catholics without any particular good men and good women connections (Wakefield 1974, 94; Baigent 1983, 49).

Afterward, Arnauld Amaury wrote to Innocent III boasting that "neither age, nor sex, nor status was spared" (Oldenbourg, 2001, 116). Here was a "shock and awe" invasion which any human being should have difficulty understanding, and it was all done in the name of Jesus. It was a genocide by any human standards.

Carcassone

The crusaders had to remain in the Beziers area for three days, recapturing frightened horses, getting ash off their tents, and doctoring their own singed lungs. 40 days was approaching when most of the knights would have served their term of service and would go home. Simon knew that no time could be lost -- the Crusade must quickly continue in earnest.

Terror then seized all of Languedoc. Many towns quickly took stock of their resources to wage war against the crusading army. Narbonne was on the main road from Beziers to Carcassone, and it submitted before the invaders arrived. The army passed through a series of other empty towns (Wakefield 1974, 103-106), empty because people fled from their homes.

The Crusaders immediately set their sights on Carcassone, fifty miles away. Raymond-Rogers was in charge of Carcassone's defense as he was in charge of defending Beziers. The population of this fortification had swelled to thirty or forty thousand because of those who had fled other areas to seek refuge there. The castle with its 30 towers, had strong walls and was militarily defendable, but it had one weakness --it relied on the nearby Aude River for water.

The weather was hot. The sun wilted the people therein. The crusaders cut off the water supply, and within two weeks, thirst, disease, and black flies forced the city to submit. Simon IV de Montfort l'Aumary, the military leader of the invaders did not massacre the people. Rather, he forced every man, woman and child to leave the city with only the one shirt and breeches on his or her body -- and nothing else. The citizens left the city without water, but with their diseases. The black flies continued to bite them as they went. Some went to Spain, others to Toulouse. Carcassonne was desolate and stinking.

Raymond-Rogers, who poorly defended Carcassone and Beziers was taken prisoner and died soon after in a dark, cold prison. Raymond-Rogers, the Viscount of Carcassone, Beziers, Albi and Razes (1194-1209) was "the first member of the higher nobility of Languedoc to fall victim to the Albigensian crusade" (Graham-Leigh 1995, 1- 2; Strayer, 1972, 70; Oldenbourg, 2001, 122-125).

Armand Amaury inventoried the riches of the city. It must have been considerable, but no one today knows what the final figures were. We do know that no knight received any of it. According to Oldenburg, Armand Amaury declared: "We shall hand over these goods to some rich baron, who will maintain the land in a way pleasing to God."

At the same time, Amaury was getting nervous. He wrote a letter to the Pope saying that he expected more than moral support from him. Raymond VI was one of the knights preparing to leave the force – Raymond VI had seen and heard enough evil done to the people in his neighborhood. Indeed, by September, 1209, Amaury had only twenty six knights supporting his effort. Each knight had a few hundred soldiers around him (Sumption 1978, 178-182; 191-198).

Other Tragedies

In November of 1209, the Crusaders attacked the City of Puisserguier. The defenders of Puisserguier blinded and mutilated two of Simon de Montfort l'Aumary's men. The tortured men were then thrown into the moat and garbage was thrown on top of them. They were sent naked into a very cold night. One died of exposure and the other barely survived.

From March to July, 1210, Simon de Montfort l'Aumary captured Bram and then Minerva. He mutilated over 100 members of the castle garrison, blinding them, cutting off their noses and upper lips-- leaving only one of them with one eye so he could lead the others to the next town. This, of course, was in retaliation for the mutilations at Puisserguier. According to Weis, he burned 140 good men and women at the stake in Minerva (Oldenbourg, 2001, 136; Weis 2001, xxiii). Oldenbourg says it best:

> Throughout the war, one of the cruelest known from the Middle Ages, both sides had instances of knights being flayed alive, chopped into pieces, or otherwise mutilated: faith, patriotism and vengeance between them legitimized every kind of savagery. From the sack of Beziers onwards, it looks as though both sides developed a total contempt for their opponents as human beings (Oldenbourg 2001,150).

Counter-Offensive of Raymond VI

Meanwhile, Raymond VI continued to dance in and out of the church, apparently doing whatever was necessary to save his people. Arnauld-Amaury accused several prominent citizens of Toulouse of being heretics, and he wanted Raymond VI to punish them accordingly, but again Raymond VI stood with his citizens. He was again excommunicated. Raymond plainly had taken enough from Amaury and the Church -- he began to organize a coalition of neighboring lords and knights to fight against the invading force.

Between July and December, Amaury besieged Termes, which

was north of Carcassone. Some of his soldiers were caught by the defenders. They were either killed or they faced a worse fate -- their eyes were put out, their noses cut off along with other members of their body, and they were sent back to the Crusade.

From this time onward, Simon de Montfort l'Aumary had his eyes on the stronghold of Toulouse. The castle and its inhabitants bent to the point of breaking, but never did completely break.

In May, 1211, while Raymond VI and his neighbors were busy organizing a defense, Simon de Montfort l'Aumary took Lavaur in a two month period and then Casses. In the process he gathered and burned 350 to 450 good men and women from the towns. He handed the sister of the defender of Lavaur over to his soldiers. He told them to abuse her in any way they pleased, then throw her into a well and stone her to death (Sumption 1978, 178-182; 191-198).

In 1212, some Crusaders were caught near Narbonne. They were subjected to whatever tortures their torturers could think of. They were found suspended by their genitals.

The Crusaders seized San Marcel on May of 1212. Twenty eight citizens were killed. Others fled to the Church seeking refuge. No refuge was allowed. Everyone, including women and children, were stripped naked and robbed of all their goods. The terror went on and on. Each day the indignations and tortures inflicted grew in number and in intensity.

Approximately six hundred were burnt alive in Minerva, Lavaur, and Casses. They were leaders of the good men and women, but none of them were the main leaders. The good men and women were coming together and doing what was necessary to protect themselves from the onslaught. Undoubtedly the leaders prudently looked elsewhere than castles to hide. They felt that such fortresses were unsafe, especially after the massacre of Beziers (Oldenbourg 2001, 150).

While it is clear that the good men and women tried their best to hide themselves, no evidence exists that, when captured, any put up a fight against his or her attackers. Their passive resistance was certainly not weakness.

A number of Church people put themselves forward as spiritual men in this era, but few were actually examples of virtue. Unbelievably, Arnauld-Amaury believed himself to be holy. Innocent III thought himself to be a man of God, but he showed few signs of sanctity. Dominic actually became St. Dominic, but he often distributed more blows than blessings. Francis of Assisi did not propose to be, but he was certainly a spiritual man. However, he lived in Italy, a land near Languedoc but with the great Alps in between, and he professed complete obedience to the Pope. Every indication leads us to believe that he would have opposed the war, but as far as we know, he did not know about it.

The common citizen hated the knights who continued their incessant fighting for the riches of southern France. It is no wonder that the good men and women could count on the support of the common people in Languedoc. Instinctively Christian people knew the words of Jesus, "by their fruits you shall know them...." Certainly, the good men and women had some different customs. While the leaders of the people, ecclesiastical and secular, fought their wars and sought their own gains, the good men and women and the common people of Languedoc were peacemakers who were dying in their midst.

In September, 1215 Raymond VI and Raymond VII, his son, began a counter-offensive. Castelnaudary fell. Then sixty other fortresses and towns also fell. The good men and women returned from hiding, and after six years of war and murder, everything quickly returned to 1209 status (Weis 2001, 382).

Simon de Montfort l'Aumary, while carrying out yet another

of his attacks on Toulouse finally met his match. On June 25, 1218, Oldenbourg says that he was killed with a stone gun fired by women and young girls (Oldenbourg 2001, 198).

The Fourth Lateran Council in 1215 protected the rights of Raymond VI's son, Raymond VII, reserving for him the Provencal lands of the house of Toulouse. The knights of Europe came to fight for nothing. They were completely hoodwinked by the pope.

Continuance -- Louis VIII

Oldenburg wrote that Prince Louis VIII of France took Simon IV de Montfort l'Aumary place as the leader of the Crusade. He attacked Marmande and massacred 5,000 people in a merciless and meaningless attack:

> Men and women, barons, ladies, babes in arms, were all stripped and despoiled and put to the sword. The ground was littered with blood, brains, fragments of flesh, limbless trunks, hacked-off arms and legs, bodies ripped up ..., livers and hearts that had been chopped to pieces or ground into mash. It was as though they had rained down from the sky. The whole place ran with blood -- streets, fields, river-bank. Neither man nor woman, young or old, survived: not a single person escaped unless they remained in hiding. The town was destroyed also; fire consumed it (Oldenbourg 2001, 202).

Raymond VII gradually recaptured Marmande. In 1221 the beliefs of the good men and women resurfaced one more time, and many Catholic bishops fled. One more time, nothing basically had changed except the memory of war, destruction, mayhem and death --and the absence of a number of Catholic bishops who had fled the terror and bloodshed.

Arnold states that the Peace of Paris in 1229 allowed Raymond VII to keep his lands until his death unless his daughter married a Capetian. But Raymond did not give up without fighting the inevitable. It was not until 1249 that Alphonse of Poitiers, brother of King and Saint Louis IX took control of Languedoc (Oldenbourg 2001:32; Barber, 4).

In 1233 a new Pope, Gregory IX, had the insidious sensibility to begin applying brakes on the reckless Albigensian Crusade. European knights had murdered one another. The war upon the good men and women was always the hidden main reason. More Catholics were killed than good men and good women.

The beginning of the end of the war came with the fall of the fortresses of Montsegur in 1244. 200 good men and women were burned at the stake on the day it was taken. Queribus was taken much later, in 1255.

Conclusion of the Crusade

So the fighting ceased when Innocent III died. But the persecution of the Cathars would now take center stage and continue under another form – that of an inquisition. The new aggressors would be the inquisitors, not the knights (Weis 2001, 379). The church still felt threatened by the group.

In summary, the tenor of the Albigensian Crusade was one of revenge and dehumanization. The Pope was after revenge; the crusading counts and knights were after land and riches; the defenders were after more land. Everyone ended the crusade in a revenge mode, inflicting inhumanity upon one another. The supposed "enemy" of the Church, the Cathars, the side issue in the conflict, either stood bravely and humanly in the flames, or walked away from the fray and hid. Jesus was crucified anew, and his message had no influence at all on any of the inquisitors.

The Albigensian Crusade ushered genocide into Western civilization. Henceforth, whether we are talking about the future inquisition, purging the heretics, the Crusades decimating the Muslims and the Jews, we are talking about genocide. Other genocides, too numerous to mention, have taken place in the name of Jesus. As Mark Gregory Pegg states: we are talking about an essentially different type of killing than before the 13th century. From the Albigensian Crusade onward mass murders took on a new dimension. Pegg categorizes genocide in the following manner: "First and foremost, it is an irrevocable moral obligation to eliminate specific people from the world who, if not wiped out rather sooner than later, will poison and destroy all human existence." (Pegg 2008, 188-189) These evil people who are killed existed many years on earth, but now they are threatening the pure. They look much like the rest of us, but their similarity to the rest of us only makes them difficult to sort out. Those guilty of genocide feel joy that the relationship between heaven and earth are preserved by the extermination of these men, women, and children. God smiles on us for doing these killings. This is an extended definition of genocide, this is a definition of the Albigensian Crusade.

Were They Really Cathars?

Barber's implication that Catharism spread far and wide in France is incorrect. He quotes Chanson (volume 1, laisse 2, pages 8-11, translated by Shirley, pages 11-12) who refers to a poem written by William of Tudela, a clerk in holy orders. The poem expresses the fears the good men and women instilled in the Roman Catholic clergy of the age.

> Of course you all know how this heresy
> --God sent his curse on it!--
> Became so strong that it gained control of the whole of the
> Albigeois, of the Carcasses' and most of the Lauragais.
> All the way from Beziers to Bordeaux many,
> or indeed, most people believed in or supported it.
> When the Lord Pope and the other clergy saw this lunacy
> spreading so much faster than before and tightening its grip every day, each of them in his own jurisdiction sent out preachers.
> The Cistercian order led the campaign and time and again it
> sent out its own men.
> Next the Bishop of Osma arranged a meeting between himself
> and other legates with these Bulgars at Carcassonne.
> This was very well attended, and the king of Aragon and his
> nobles.
> Once the king had heard the speakers and discovered how heretical they were, he withdrew, and sent a letter about this to Rome
> in Lombardy.
> God grant me his blessing, what shall I say?
> They think more of a rotten apple than of sermons, and went
> on just the same for about five years. These lost fools refused to
> repent, so that many were killed, many people perished, and still
> more will die before the fighting ends.
> It cannot be otherwise.

According to Lester K. Little, the medieval historian, the "Cathars" who were so oppressed in southern France, "constituted a loose amalgamation of sects, established in various parts of Europe in the twelfth and thirteenth centuries, with the heaviest concentrations in southern France, the Low Countries, the Rhine valley, and northern Italy" (Little 1978, 134). We would question Little's statement that their heaviest concentration was in southern France. Furthermore, were they really Cathars? If you would have asked them they would have said, "No! We are good men and women. We take in orphans and do good to as many people as we can." They probably were not true Cathars, but they had developed many Cathar customs. In looking at what they suffered, we can add, if they were, so what? Are we unable to live with others who are different? Do we not believe that the tolerance of Jesus is a virtue? Remember how he treated the Samaritan woman and the thief on the cross. No Christian should treat anyone as the people of southern France were treated.

According to Walter L. Wakefield, the population of these people grew in small numbers in the Languedoc area from approximately 1150 through the thirteenth century (Wakefield 1974, 30).

Jean Duvernoy, a historian and a statistician quoted by Wakefield, states that historians actually know the names of 1,015 members of the sect who lived in Languedoc in the period between 1100 and 1245. The total number ever to live in Languedoc can only be estimated, but it would not be more than 2,000 to 3,000, perhaps 2% or 3% of the total population. From 1200-1209, approximately 1,000 to 1,500 lived there. These numbers are important. They show that contrary to the fears of the pope and church authorities, the good men and good women did not have the people power to "flood" Languedoc with heresy.

Both Wakefield and Strayer say that the "Albigensian Crusade" slaughtered 25,000 to 35,000 men, women, and children. Of course, the good men and women could only be a small part of the casualties. The suffering of the whole population in the community is beyond human comprehension. As the Crusade developed, the good men and good women and the total community of Languedoc protected themselves as best they could against the army of invading knights.

But Christian authorities and Christian knights in Languedoc, both crusaders and defenders, felt that they had the right to dehumanize all opponents. They were merciless in their quest, and, to achieve their temporal goals, they murdered, tortured, and forced any degradation on others that their imaginations could dream up.

The Reality of the Religion of Good Men and Women

Unfortunately, as was the custom with the Church in dealing with its opponents, the writings of the group were destroyed. Their own writings might have given us a much better impression of their lives and beliefs. What we know of them comes mainly from the official transcripts of the Albigensian Inquisition. Portraying them from such a source, of course, is like portraying the German underground from the records of the Gestapo, or like portraying the Iraqi underground from the transcripts of Abu-Graibe. Even then, we do know from these prejudiced official transcripts of the inquisition which followed the war that the "Cathars" called themselves "good men" and "good women," not Cathars.

The good men and good women insisted that the group was Christian. They claimed that Jesus was their model and John's Gospel and the Acts were their spiritual books. They were not an organized group. Their relationship to one another and their belief systems were loose. They gathered together more as the persecution evolved. But those who chose to join the group did so intentionally and with an internal enthusiasm. They were staunch in their beliefs and they were not influenced by the Church leaders or any other force. They were ready to die for the beliefs they held.

The good men and women desired an uncluttered Christian

life in a simple Church dedicated to Christ and his message. This desire stood in sharp contrast to the extravagance of some of the clergy and the elaborate Church symbols that surrounded them. Because of the vacuum created within the Church by members of the clergy and because of sheer frustration, sincere good men and good women with meager ecclesiastical-theological background actively gathered and formed their own theologies and spiritual lives. They had their own characteristics, but they were not part of the reform movement called the Cathars. The good men and women were more similar to the Vaudois, the Bogomils, the Humiliati, the Waldensians, the beghards and the beguines, and the Franciscans in their love of simplicity and poverty. Many of them were educated and made their own living.

The movement differed in many ways from their Franciscan brothers and sisters of their age. One of the main differences was that the Franciscans took the practical, prudent step, if we are speaking of survival, to always carefully remain within the Church. As Francis said in his rule of 1221, "All the friars are bound to be Catholics..." (See *Rule of St. Francis*, 1209, 1221, 1223).

Some of the good men and women ran into difficulty with the Church when they explained the existence of evil in the world -- an enigma which, down the ages, has challenged the greatest theologians. The great minds of the established Church became comfortable with an ethical dualism -- good and evil are both present in the world, but they exist here only through the actions of human beings. Some did believe that both good and evil existed equally as separate gods in creation (Little 1978, 134; Barber, 2).

Some did not believe that Christ actually became man in the same way Christians do. He only took on the form of a human. These, of course, would no longer be Christian as we know it. Nonetheless, they were crude, but sincere attempts by untrained "theologians" of the age, who were demonstrably abandoned by any knowledgeable theologians, attempting to understand Jesus Christ and his message.

Some, we would suspect, held more to the Catholic faith, but thought that many of the customs of the good men and good women were "chic" or "neat." These people would have remained within the Christian belief system.

As they formed their beliefs, some of them in opposition to the firmly established, Catholic Church, this otherwise mild-mannered group developed another problem in unison with other Christian Churches, firmly established or not. They chose pet passages in revelation, de-emphasizing other passages of significance.

Many of the good men and women were not strictly heretics. Some existed within the Catholic belief system. Others appear to be complete outsiders and might be called infidels or apostates, but not heretics (See Little1978, 135). They considered themselves Christians. They quoted scripture, and used some of the same myths as did the Catholic Church. They were not theologians, but they were obviously sincere people. However, according to the Church, they were misguided and wrong. Their knowledge of the Gospel and Jesus were truly meager, and this was the fault of the clergy of the time.

Beliefs of Good Men and Women

Good men and women were generally a sincere, humble, and intelligent group of people. They did not think themselves superior to others. They were peacemakers, and worked with their hands at their trades. They took in orphans and did good deeds in the community.

Some few did reject some of the essentials and some of the trappings of the Church. They refused to take oaths; they rejected the priesthood and baptism as the Church knew it; they rejected the cross as a symbol, individual confession, religious ornamentation. They were careful not to openly oppose the Church, but they did not believe all of its teachings. Their church services were deliberately simple: a Gospel reading, a short sermon, a benediction, and the Lord's Prayer. The dove was an important symbol for them -- it represented peace and the state of existing in God's love. A flying dove represented the flight and the freedom of the soul (Strayer 1972, 31).

Some of the faithful accused the good men and women of fornication and many other sins. The words of Albert the Great were ascribed to them by the ignorant. Albert was quoted as saying, "Whatever is done by the good 'under the belt' is not sinful." We need not present a great amount of evidence to prove that the good men and women did not believe the words of Albert the Great. But fables grew among groups of Christians who did not know the group (Weis 2001, xxiii; Sumption 1978, 53).

The good men and women never slept naked. They refused to kill other human beings. They forgave those who persecuted them. In fact, they were moral and spiritual models seen but rarely in Christianity. They impressed even St. Bernard of Clairvaux. As Christian knights were preparing to war against one another, he admitted, "No sermons are more Christian than theirs [the good men and women], and their morals are pure" (Lerner 1972, 20; Weis 2001, xxiii). St. Bernard also said sympathetically and wisely, "Errors are refuted by argument, not by force."

The Good Men and Women: Victims of the Inquisition

The Albigensian Crusade had ended – but the attacks on the so-called Cathars and the people of Languedoc did not. The endurance of the people of Languedoc could not sustain what happened next. The people of Languedoc were like the injured rabbit that was played with by the lion, or the mouse being tortured by a cat.

Pope Gregory IX was painfully aware that, as he saw it, "Cathars" still moved across the land of Languedoc. It was a fetish for him. It was his intent to force an inquisition on that war-torn land. Even though Gregory IX initiated the inquisition there between the years 1231 and 1233, he was not the only one to blame for the inquisition which followed. The reality was much more complex. The great pile of legislation and activity before and during the Albigensian Crusade produced the groundwork for that inquisition. Bishops, priests, friars, kings, noblemen, knights, and soldiers all added their part to further torment the people of Languedoc after the bitter Crusade had crushed them. The nerves of the common people of Languedoc was worn to shreds.

Some Catholics held firm. They certainly were saints of the ordeal. But some of the ordinary Catholic people also caved into the pressures. Some, under pressures of interrogation, accused their neighbors of heresy in order to get inquisitors off their backs. In a way, we cannot lay blame at their doorsteps -- not everyone is heroic. The war and the inquisition were long, hard struggles for them. Many of their close relatives and friends had suffered and died in the ordeals. The pressures on them were intense. Their beautiful land, once the most prosperous of Europe had become a wasteland, and their joyful city squares had become silent and deadly quiet. The people were left to deal, not only with the waste which surrounded them, but now with an intense inquisition as well.

The Inept Albigensian Crusade

The Albigensian Crusade had lingered on and on for years, and it was clearly inept and devastating. The pope saw it one way, and the people of Southern France saw it another way.

The pope did not believe that the Albigensian Crusade against the Cathars dealt with the evils in Languedoc. Indeed, the Crusade had so many purposes and involved so many intrigues, it could not possibly have accomplished anything. Few good men and women who were not Catholics converted, and many of them went underground, often hidden by their neighbors. Certainly, after the evils of the crusade, none of them were inclined to "convert."

Basically, invading foreign knights had fought with local knights, and each side did horrible things to one another and to the local people. Many more Catholics suffered and died than good men and women, who were smart enough to find havens in which to hide, probably mainly in homes of Catholics. The ordinary citizen saw all this.

Both the people and the pope knew that the Albigensian Crusade was a disaster. But the disaster had different faces for each. For the people of Languedoc, the disaster was the devastation of their homeland, their relatives, friends and neighbors. For Pope Gregory IX the disaster was the continued existence of the "Cathars" in Languedoc.

The Pope was now intent on wiping out the "Cathars" and correcting the errors of the people in the area, no matter the cost (Arnold, 2001, p. 35). He sent investigators to Languedoc. One more time, the whole population of Languedoc, both Catholic and good men and women, suffered intolerable oppression.

Pope Gregory IX first wrote a letter to the bishops of southern France. In his plans for inquisition, he was intent now on by-passing the bishops, and giving the job of rooting out the "Cathars" to special inquisitors, whom he believed would do a much better job. He wrote to the bishops of France:

> Seeing you wrapped in the whirlwind of cares, and scarce able to breathe under the pressure of

overwhelming anxieties, we think it well to divide your burdens, that they may be more easily borne. We have therefore determined to send preaching friars against the heretics of France and the adjoining provinces; and we beg, warn and exhort you ... to receive them kindly, and to treat them well, giving them ... favor, counsel and aid, that they may fulfill their office (Gregory IX, *Letters*).

In 1233 the Pope appointed Peter Seila, one of St. Dominic's first companions, and William Arnauld, both Dominicans from Toulouse, as the first inquisitors for Languedoc. The Dominican Order was formed to promote "truth," so it is not surprising that the Pope turned to two Dominican friars to carry out his inquisition. The Pope gave them specific instructions, creating a new dynamics for dealing with heretics.

Walsh states:

> Into a town, reported to be infected with heresy, the friars were to go and publicly proclaim that all guilty of offenses against the Faith must appear and abjure their errors. Those who did so were to be forgiven. To detect those who did not, the friars were to set in motion an *Inquiry*; and if two witnesses testified that such and such a man was a heretic, they must place him on trial, acting at all times, of course, in cooperation with, and only with the consent of, the Bishop. There was no provision for torture. It was the job of the state to decide whether or not to inflict civil penalties (Walsh 1940, 45).

The task of the inquisitor was clear. By whatever means was available to them they were to decide whether persons were heretics or not, and if they were heretics, whether they were repentant or not. If the persons were heretics, it was the job of the bishop or pope to decide whether to reconcile or excommunicate him or her. It was then the job of the state to inflict civil penalties, which could include imprisonment for life in very dank prisons or burning at the stake.

The inquisitors were to choose a suitable central place which would allow them to deal with a number of localities in the area at the same time. "The inquisitors called all the people together and one of them preached a sermon in which he first cited their own authority in the matter. The preacher then went on to urge the people to identify heretics or those which they suspected to be heretics. He then announced a period of grace in which voluntary confessions to the inquisition would be accepted without consequences -- if the person repented. Within the same sermon, the preacher indicated that, for the most part, they would work in compliance with 'established legal procedure,' except for one, which the inquisitor made clear to the people: 'we do not make public the names of witnesses...' (Peters 1988, 58)."

Not making public names of witnesses was a huge difference from past proceedings, and it had great consequences. The person on trial could not face his or her accusers. Witnesses could come forward without retaliation. It also gave the inquisition secrecy and a fear factor that facilitated the proceedings and helped to bring the inquisition to a quick end. More insidiously, it encouraged hear-say evidence, evidence motivated by revenge, and completely bogus evidence given by those who had had enough, and were willing to cave in to whatever the inquisitors wanted them to say (See Cohn, p. 24). The inquisitor ended up as the sole judge of guilt or innocence.

After the sermon, during the period of grace, the inquisitors went to work. They drew up a list of suspects to be interrogated and they interviewed the witnesses. After the grace period, they promptly arrested those whom they concluded were guilty. On the decision of the inquisitors, the person arrested was presumed guilty from the start.

At that point, the accused needed to plead guilty to the specific crime which existed in the minds of the inquisitors. If the accusation was untrue and the accused did not know the specific accusation, the accused could only stand mute before the court, and he or she would be considered obstinate. An innocent victim could be tortured for days while trying his best to discern the crime.

Those who pleaded guilty, and were willing to return to the Church, renounced their heresy and accepted a penance. Those accused, convicted, or considered obstinate were excommunicated. Their sentences were read aloud in a public liturgical ceremony, and they were then handed over to the civil authority for punishment (Peters, 1988, p. 59-60).

The First Inquisitors

The two new inquisitors took their new job seriously, but they were too involved in the squabbles which arose from the heat of the Albigensian Crusade to do a creditable job (Oldenbourg, Pantheon, p. 286). It was not until 1240 that the inquisition had evolved into the working machine it was intended to be.

Arnold states: "Between 1245 and 1249 just two of the several inquisitors – Bernard of Caux and Jean de St. Pierre – interrogated over six thousand individuals....They created an inquisition manual which was called the *Ordo processus Narbonensis*" (2001;48). The manual emphasized the need for the people "to come 'spontaneously and penitently' to tell 'the pure and full truth on themselves and others.'" These inquisitors had developed "a mechanism for interrogating the whole flock" (Arnold, 2001: 51).

The inquisition was growing in intensity in its efforts to give power and authority back to the clergy. Arnold tells us that "... the inquisitorial task was ... becoming increasingly professionalized ... in the abstraction and systemization of procedures and principles..." (Arnold, 2001: 50).

Peace of God, Inquisition Style

Languedoc had its own version of "the Peace of God," an organized peace movement. It was a twisted perversion of any peace movement the world has ever seen.

The people of Languedoc did not organize to demand peace from structures that oppressed them. Rather the structures of the inquisition formed an organization to demand certain things from the people if the people wanted to live in peace.

Four canons of the Council of Toulouse in 1229 and the Statutes of Raymond VII in the same year demand repeatedly "the conservation of the peace" from the people. The statutes of Raymond VII set out the program in more detail. In order to preserve the peace, parish priests and laymen were to seek out those who broke it, namely, "heretics, those who believed what the heretics taught, those who received heretics into their homes or defended them, and those who showed heretics any kindness at all. In order to know the peace of God, they were especially to seek out the offenders in every house and in all secret places." (Arnold, 2001: 35-36) The search for heretics and heretic sympathizers were to take place in "the cellars, houses, and the woods" of all of Languedoc (Arnold, 2001: 37).

The Council of Toulouse also demanded that every man over the age of fourteen and every woman over the age of twelve swear an oath to reject heretics and heresy, to serve the Catholic Church, to persecute heretics and "manifest the good faith." The oath was to be renewed every other year, and the names of those who took the oath were to be recorded (Arnold, 2001: 37).

Between 1245 and 1249, two inquisitors in the region between Toulouse and Carcassonne forced whole villages and parishes to come to Toulouse for questioning. "...the inquisitors aimed to examine every single male over the age of fourteen, and every female over twelve" (Arnold, 2001: 48).

Effects of the Inquisition

The first action of the Inquisitors of Toulouse was the capture, trial, condemnation and execution of Vigoros de Baconia, one of the most dynamic leaders of the good men and women. The inquisitors efficiently performed this task in a matter of days. Vigoros de Baconia was burned at the stake.

Immediately upon hearing of the inquisition, the other good men and women went underground and fear continued to fill the hearts of the total population of Languedoc. *Montaillou,* a book on the transcripts of the inquisition in Languedoc by Emmanuel Le Roy Ladurie, tells us how the once free society had been transformed:

> ...for anyone who did not keep absolutely to the straight and narrow path it was a Kafka-esque world of spies and betrayals. Even up in the mountains, the last refuge of freedom of expression, one might be trapped at any moment because of a careless word -- trapped by the priest, by the *bayle,* by the *vicaire,* or by a neighbor. One piece of tittle-tattle

might mean prison, or having to wear stitched to one's clothes the yellow cross, symbol of ignominy imposed by the Inquisition on heretics (Ladurie 1975, p. 14).

Eventually, gradually, the inquisitors got the information they sought.

Raymond VII complained to the Pope about the extreme zeal of the two Dominicans: "They lay aside proper procedures, denied individuals the aid of lawyers, and generally provoked acute terror. ...they are causing great disturbance in the country, and by their excesses are stirring up the people against clergy and monastics alike" (Oldenbourg, p. 287).

In 1306, Bernard Gui, another Dominican, was appointed Inquisitor at Toulouse. For seventeen years, until 1323, Bernard directed the rooting out, the reconciliation or punishment of heretics. He presided over only 18 general sessions during that period during which time he tried 930 cases. He preferred to deal with his cases in groups. He wrote the lengthy manual *Practica Inquisitionis* which brought the 'professionalization' of the inquisition to maturity (Arnold, 2001: 53). Gui pointed out various elements of the demeanor of the guilty. He also blatantly stated that the inquisitor ought to feign that he knows certain things in order to entice the guilty person and help him label the person as guilty (Arnold, 2001: 56).

In 1310, we know that Gui discovered other "Cathar" stalwarts -- Pierre Authie, Arnaud Marty, Prudes Tavernier, Philippe d'Aylanae, Amiel de Perle, Sybille Baille, Pons Sicre and others. They and ten others perished in the flames of the Inquisition at the hands of this brilliant inquisitor.

In the official papers of Toulouse, historians found the record of the sentences of Bernard Gui:

132 -- released

9 --sentenced to make pilgrimages

143 -- sentenced to wear a cross for the rest of their lives (meaning they were considered "heretics") and they had to undergo regular humiliations and beatings

307 imprisoned in the dank, cold prisons at the time

42 burned at the stake

17 dead persons sentenced "in absentia" to imprisonment

3 dead persons burned at the stake "in absentia"

69 dead persons had their bones exhumed and burned "in absentia"

40 excommunicated from the Church

2 sentenced to be exposed in the town square in the pillory (an apparatus with holes where the head, arms and legs could be locked, and a person could be placed for a time to be ridiculed and abused)

2 priests degraded

1 priest sent into exile

22 had their houses burned

2 cartloads of the Talmud were condemned & burned

139 released from prison

1 interdict by which the sacraments and Christian burial were denied was lifted

Total, 930 (Peters, 1988, p. 151).

Virtually, the good men and women were finished. The group never had many members. It certainly had few reserves. As the Inquisition whisked away the last of its more charismatic members, little was left.

The number of those burned at the stake need not be exaggerated -- one group of numbers says only 8.5% of those accused met capital punishment. But many of the others were imprisoned. Imprisonment in the cold and damp prisons of the age was at least as brutal as burning at the stake.[27]

A decade later the Bishop of Pauriers, Jacques Pournier, prided himself in bringing two more solid members of the Cathar group to the flames. Guillaume Belibasta (Ewen 1929,13). was burned at the stake on August 2, 1321 and Bernard Clergne was convicted and burned in 1324 (Ewen 1929,14).

CONCLUSION

Inquisitions, as we have said elsewhere in this book, were usually not the same in all locations. They were different in procedure and content in the various places where inquisitors of various authenticities prowled and roamed. But certainly in Languedoc, it was a monster which moved toward two goals – the elimination of the so-called "Cathars" and the correction of the Catholic people. No person of consequence was concerned about the continued pain this inquisition caused the people (Arnold, 2001: 33).

The inquisitors firmly believed that heretics were one group among the dark forces aligned against the power of the Church and the authority of its clergy. Jews, Muslims, beguines, magicians and sorcerers were also included among the forces of evil, and

---

[27] I had the opportunity to visit some of the prisons in the medieval castles. Even though I was dressed warmly, I was chilled to the bone in half an hour. C. L'Estrange Ewen writes about the jails at the time: "This punishment sometimes meant death in a more lingering form.... Occasionally considerable numbers died during their term of incarceration." (Ewen 1920, 7)

they, also, suffered from the inquisition in Languedoc (Arnold, 2001: 56). The inquisitors presumed to have an authority to know which bordered on God's own authority, and it extended to all aspects of society -- not only to heretics, but to all hidden relationships. In true Augustinian fashion, the inquisitors were not squeamish about spreading guilt around the land. They were intent on cleaning up all of society, making the guilty stand out, and even making the innocent experience the consequences of the guilty (Arnold, 2001: 55). Languedoc was held in an era of intense fear. No one knew when some neighbor, priest, or passing teenager should whisper an intimidating word to the inquisitor.

The desire to know and the presumption of the authority to know everything was insidious. Thus, the age of the Albigensians ended. The people of the time looked on in wonderment, as do we. Here were good neighbors, who had lived their lives loveably, calmly, and peacefully, now had been taken out and burned at the stake. Later, their bones, if any were left, were dumped on a cart and thrown into a common grave. All this was done in the name of the Spirit of God, in the name of Jesus. Why?

By the end of the crusade, the inquisition had plunged Languedoc into inhumanity. The human life of the area wilted for isolation and lack of trust. No room was there anymore for any semblance of a good life -- for the arts and sciences, for a good laugh in the city square. No room was there for the troubadours who sang songs of love. Humanity was destroyed by Jesus' own followers.

The clergy, who had preached love at the Sunday liturgy, killed their fellow human beings after the service. Belief in their own right to power had blinded them to all else.

The Albigensian Crusade and the inquisition which followed were specifically directed at the heresy of Albigensians, (a misnomer, if there ever was one), the good men and women, who were few in number. More faithful Roman Catholics than good men and women suffered and died. The war and inquisition, once unleashed, like many wars to follow, did not know any bounds, any borders. The truth they proposed to hold so dearly had lost all intelligence.

The residue of these killings, with its bitterness, continued through history even into the modern era. Today many peasants in the area of southern France once known as Languedoc openly proclaim anti-Catholic sympathies. Generations after, the effects of violence does not die easily in their hearts (Moore 1975, p. 1).

Chapter 7

THE FIRST FIVE CRUSADES, 1099-1221

LEAD-UP TO THE CRUSADES

From the end of the fifth century to the eleventh century, cultural and commercial exchanges between Muslims and Christians East and West grew to be common and ordinary. The people who engaged in these exchanges were hospitable, cultured, talented and tolerant. Art, food, and products of all sorts were exchanged across the Mediterranean Sea.

Aziz S. Atiya, the prominent historian and linguist, who wrote invaluable works on the crusades, writes the following: "...the birth of the economic revolution of the Middle Ages took place, not in the static agrarian feudal society of Western Europe, but rather in the dynamism of trade and industry inherent in most of the countries of the Eastern Mediterranean (Atiya 1962, 19-38).

The fortunes of the trade and industry of the Mediterranean world were, then, shared fortunes. They happened in a shared environment of good will. Much credit must be given to the Muslims for this. As Thomas Asbridge states: "...if anything, Islam had proved over the preceding centuries to be more tolerant of other religions than Catholic Christendom." (Asbridge

2004, 3). Asbridge elaborates: " Muslim power held fast for generations, allowing culture, learning and trade to flourish, and Islamic Iberia blossomed into one of the greatest centres of civilization in the known world (Asbridge 2004, 17).

All told, Asbridge concludes that life under Muslim rule was not a bad life for Christians. Christians were not only allowed freedom of religion, but they were given respect. They not only survived: they thrived: "...indigenous Christians actually living under Islamic law, be it in Iberia or the Holy Land, were generally treated with remarkable clemency....Christian subjects may not have been able to share power with their Muslim masters, but they were given freedom to worship (Asbridge 2004, 19)."

Western Christians, Jews and Muslims in large numbers also maintained contact with one another in the East through their pilgrimages to their holy places in Syria, Palestine and Egypt. Christians of Central Europe regularly came on pilgrimage to the East. They revered relics in medieval times, and they considered the Holy Sepulcher, the site of Jesus' execution, and the other sites where Jesus lived and died as the holiest relics of all. The historian of the Crusades, Sylvia Schein, says that the attraction of these sites "was too powerful to be suppressed by learned exegesis" (Schein 2005, 5). They journeyed to these shrines with great reverence, thinking that journeying to the earthly Jerusalem would get rid of their sins and attain for them the heavenly Jerusalem (Schein, 2005, 5). Although they tended to stay with other Christians on these journeys, they also communicated with and bought from Muslim merchants on the way, and they were generally treated fairly and with respect by them.

THE EAST AND THE WEST OF THE MIDDLE AGES

On the other hand, the Muslim world had made great in-roads into Europe. Thomas Madden, states that "fully two-thirds of the old Christian world had been conquered by Muslim armies. Aside from the Holy Land, Muslims had conquered all of Syria, Egypt, North Africa and Spain. In addition, Asia Minor (modern Turkey) had only recently been conquered by the Seljuk Turks" (Madden 2006, 42, 13-17). Increased conquests of the Muslims caused fear in the pope, in the rulers in Byzantium, and in the rulers of Western Europe.

Furthermore, differences and fears continued to grow among pilgrims until contact between the groups became brash and bristly. Especially after the first millennium, Christians West, Christians East, Muslims and Jews at times looked down on one another. Some of the pilgrims, in fact, crossed the lines of religious fervor, and became increasingly fanatical.

Then certain Muslim nomadic tribes began to harass Christian, Muslim and Jews. Groups like the Seljuk Turks prowled about, making life intolerable for everyone in the area. Christian pilgrims brought the news back to Europe and the European Christian elite became incensed. With wisdom learned from the ages, Will Durant states that Christians and Muslims were doomed to soon meet at the supreme court of arbitration -- war (Durant 1950, 585).

In order to "go crusading," a Christian had to first of all, twist and contort the teachings of Jesus. In the process, he had to believe in at least one of a number of fantasies.

FANTASY NUMBER 1: "CHRISTIAN VIOLENCE"

Christianity in the post-Constantine and post Augustinian era took on an increasingly belligerent tone. By the time of Urban

II, Clermont, and the first Crusade, not only were the crusading "followers of Jesus" allowed to war against and kill the Muslims, but most Christians believed that they would be serving Christ by doing so. As incredible as it might seem, with apparent integrity, saints of the Church considered it a sacred act to say their prayers the night before and then, the next day, take to the road on their way to the Crusade. One of these crusaders, Louis IX, was canonized a saint by the Christian church by doing just that. The Gospel of Jesus Christ was about to be trampled on by marching soldiers with crosses on their armor.

In time, the Christian religious motivations for these approaching Crusades would have to lay open before the eyes of future Church historians and theologians. In view of the teachings of Jesus of Nazareth, it is difficult to understand how they would be able to stand such openness. The Crusades needed the added dress of gallant armor, fancy swords, and noble crosses on breastplates to put on any semblance of virtue. Otherwise, the contradictions would be too obvious, too difficult to lace together with the Jesus movement.

Nonetheless, the Crusades, with all their fervor, have continued to this very day. Even today, in Crusades which defy numbering, Christians, clothed in helmet and protective breast plates, and utilizing brilliant shock and awe displays, continue to kill Muslim men and women, children and elderly. Only the purported reasons have changed: then it was, "we must free Jerusalem and the holy relics of the city from the infidel. Today, "we must save our own country from invasion by the infidels." In both scenarios the one constant is "they are infidels," even though they are in truth a Godly people. Though the ugly "Christian" Crusade has truly never ended to this very day, it can never stand with integrity in the presence of the life and the teaching of Jesus of Nazareth.

Jonathan Riley-Smith in an insightful work states that in

the Middle Ages the Christian theory of positive violence had already gained respectability. This Christian theory maintained that, in spite of all that Jesus believed and said, popes, bishops and Christian lay people convinced one another that reasons existed for Christian nations to commit acts of violence. Such violence, they believed, was lofty, noble, right, and just. The Church thereby gave birth to generations of violent Christian "heroes"(Riley-Smith 1995, 6-7). The Knights Templar are a good example. They were a religious order of soldiers intent on fighting the Muslims and protecting those on pilgrimage. In this respect, the Church became more the followers of Augustine, Constantine and the later Roman Emperors than the followers of Jesus.

FANTASY NUMBER 2: "SPIRITUALITY" OF THE CRUSADERS

The medieval Christian held a spirituality which had elements of fantasy about it. The mission that the Crusaders set upon was unattainable and unrealistic, a venture into fantasyland. The long respected Edwin Pears describes "the noble and lofty" ideal which the early Crusaders had tried to realize:

> The Crusader affixed the cross to his shoulder in order that he might offer to God cross for cross, passion for passion, and that by mortifying his desires and making himself like unto Christ he might share with him in the resurrection (*Lect. Long. Exuv. Sac.*, ii, 11). ...To the Christian of the twelfth century [Jerusalem] was very far distant, the marvel of the earth, and so filled with relics and other memorials of the Divine Life, that it was readily

confounded with the heavenly Jerusalem (Pears 1886, p. 119).

The Muslims were clearly the menace standing in the way of reaching that heavenly city. They became the adversaries, the demons, if you will, hindering those who bore the cross. Unrealistic popes and "holy men" demonized the Muslims so that the Crusaders thought it virtuous to trample upon their land and kill them.

St Bernard of Clairvaux, the prime promoter of the Second Crusade and the author of the rule for the Knights Templar, expressed the fantasy well in his "Hortative Sermon to the Knights Templar": "...this is a new sort of chivalry, unknown through the centuries, because it tirelessly wages an equal and double war, both against flesh and blood and against the spiritual forces of evil in the other world" (Speed 1997, 194). He went on to state: "They fear not at all the sin of killing an enemy or the peril of their own death, inasmuch as death either inflicted or borne for Christ has no taint of crime and rather merits the greater glory. The one clearly serves Christ; the other brings union with Him" (Speed, p. 194). Andre Vauchez, professor at the University of Paris and expert on the Middle ages and religious movements, says it well: "With the Crusades, new avenues were opened to Christian warriors. Assured of their salvation, they placed their weapons at the service of God and the Church in the Holy Land. (Vauchez, 2012, 28)."

Of course, not all of the crusaders who would journey as conquerors to the East were on the spiritual venture spoken of by St. Bernard of Clairvaux. Crusaders approached the walls of Jerusalem and Constantinople with many various religious, political, social, economic and personal agendas. They came from all over Europe -- some with the highest, most spiritual, but diluted motivations; others with practical political reasons, and still others with the most primitive reasons imaginable. Peare said that they ranged "from the peaks of moral righteousness to the troughs of anti-Semitic prejudice" (Peare 1886, 119).

Some even used the Crusades as a good excuse for escaping sin while hoarding whatever they might steal. They felt that personally they had the better of both worlds -- they could kill and steal while bearing in hand the papal indulgence necessary to skateboard into heaven.

It is still fair to say that, to some degree, a common belief united all of them -- they all firmly believed in the legitimacy, even the virtues of the Christian violence they were perpetrating.

The spirit of the crusade did not wane. Quite frankly, up to our day it has not yet ended – Muslims continue to be the target of our sophisticated weaponry. This is almost beyond belief. Every one of the Crusades up to our present day has been burdensome, dangerous, frightening and expensive. The crusaders ventured into arid foreign lands with the hot armor of the north on their bodies. They ventured blindly into never-never land. Yet one army after another was sucked into the quest. At times, kings, counts, and barons have led their own soldiers into battle. Frederick Barbarossa and Louis IX, for example, accompanied their knights and soldiers, and they suffered with them in the struggle. Others like George W. Bush and Barack Obama preferred to let the soldiers do the fighting in nonsensical conflicts on the other side of the world.

The Muslims were not the only victims of "Christian positive violence." Jews, pagans, and even other Christians felt the wrath of the Christian who stood before them with the Bible in one hand and the sword in the other.

Christians somehow sincerely believed that they were supporting Jesus and his Father by wielding their swords and catapults, then guns, and eventually, high powered weaponry down through history at the people of the East. At every turn, the Christian West firmly believed that they were striking out as a moral imperative, or as a quest for Christianity, or even as an act of charity. They all thought they were self-righteously doing it in accord with the intentions of Jesus.

FANTASY NUMBER 3: MATTHEW 16:17-19 AND THE RISE OF PAPAL POWER

Between the eleventh and the late twelfth century, political power of the Popes grew within the confines of Europe. In that era the Popes attempted to balance religious as well as secular leadership. In the First Crusade especially, the Pope's plea received almost unanimous and immediate response from Europe.

But, except for the First Crusade, papal power was certainly not accepted without question by everyone in Europe. Many nations and individuals often maintained a greater or lesser amount of autonomy. To the extent that an area of Europe had weak secular governments and the populace had strong Catholic religious convictions, ambitious and politically powerful popes were ready and willing to fill the void and spread papal influence to spread violence across the earth.

In the minds of some popes and those who stood behind their thrones, in the eleventh through the fifteenth century, papal dominion reached much further than even the confines of Europe. The Catholic Encyclopedia says succinctly: "The idea of the crusades corresponds to a political conception which was realized in Christendom only from the eleventh to the fifteenth century; this supposes a union of all peoples and sovereigns under the direction of the Popes" (Brehier, Louis, "The Crusades").

Brehier, of course, is not correct if he believes that such a union was anything but a concept held by a few from the eleventh to the fifteenth century. Not everyone even in Europe bought into such a ruse – except at a few designated points in time during that long period of history.

The origin of such papal power comes from the stretching and extending of a passage of the Gospel of Matthew, 16:17-19. In that passage of scripture, Jesus gave Simon Peter the power of the keys. Matthew's Gospel reads as follows:

> When Jesus came to the neighborhood of Caesarea Philippi, he asked His disciples this question: "Who do people say that the Son of Man is? They replied, "Some say John the Baptizer, others Elijah, still others Jeremiah or one of the prophets." "And you," he said to them, "who do you say that I am?" "You are the Messiah," Simon Peter answered, "the Son of the living God!" Jesus replied: "Happy are you, Simon, son of Jonah! No mere man has revealed this to you, but my heavenly Father. So I now say to you: You are Peter [rock] and on this rock I will build my Church. And the jaws of death will never prevail against it. I will give you the keys of the kingdom of heaven: whatever you bind on earth shall be considered bound in heaven; whatever you loose on earth shall be considered loosed in heaven (Matthew 16:17-19).

In this passage, *kepa* (*petra* or rock) is possibly a reference to Isaiah 28:16, where the rock is Mount Zion on which the temple was built (See Isaiah 28:16). In this context, Jesus would mean that he was forming his church around Peter and the new group of apostles. Of course, Jesus would have expected this "Church of

Jesus" to live according to his word and example. The "keys" could be a reference to Isaiah 22:22, where Eliakim is given "the key of the house of David ... when he opens, no one shall shut, when he shuts no one shall open." Jesus referred to the new "house of David," his Church, formed on the apostles. Binding and loosing are Jewish legal terms referring to powers of interpreting the law. The apostles were to interpret the new law of Jesus correctly.

In any case, Jesus was speaking here about his new apostolic community. If he was speaking of successors of Peter, those who followed him would have the responsibility to interpret correctly the message of Jesus.[28]

Jesus was not endorsing carte blanche anything that would contradict his own words and deeds. This is proven in the very next section of Matthew's Gospel. After Jesus said that he would go to Jerusalem to suffer and die: "At this, Peter took him [Jesus] aside and began to remonstrate with him. May you be spared, Master! God forbid that any such thing ever happen to you!" Jesus turned on Peter and said, "Get out of my sight, you Satan! You are trying to make me trip and fall. You are not judging by God's standards, but by man's" (Matthew 16: 21-23). This passage

---

28 See Donald Senior's *Invitation to Matthew: a Commentary on the Gospel of Matthew with Complete Text from the Jerusalem Bible*, Garden City, New York, 1966, 160-161. In the explanation of the text, Senior says: "The material Matthew incorporates here may actually be playing on the identity of the Aramaic words for rock *(kepa)* and *Peter (kepa)*. But behind the wordplay an intriguing symbol is at work. Jewish reflection on the origin of the world had led to the belief that the foundation of the entire universe had been laid at Mount Zion, upon which stood the Temple., Peter is given "the keys to the kingdom," a reference to Isaiah 22:22, where Eliakim is given "the keys to the house of David...; should he open, no one shall close; should he close, no one shall open." Then, Peter, too, shall have such powers. He can bind and loose. In Jewish legal terminology, this meant the power to interpret the obligations of the law or to excommunicate from the synagogue. It is not clear which of these was given Peter--or was it both? Similar powers are given to the community in 18:18 (160-161). Senior goes on to explain that there is lack of clarity in this text. It is ambiguous. "Certainly there is nothing here to convince us that Popes down the ages have the same powers given to Peter, whatever that power was." In our volumes we have constantly come across popes who have insisted on their power of infallibility, both in the religious and political realm. The Roman Catholic Church, in its tradition, defined dogmatically in Vatican Council I that the pope has special powers of infallibility when defining matters of faith and morals.

seriously deflates any imperial "executive power" which not even Peter, let alone his successors, might have thought they had. The total Gospel passage, then, must be taken in context, and it is, at best, ambiguous, with many threads of possible meanings.

One thing, and only one thing is clear from the scripture passage -- neither Peter nor any pope ever had or ever will have the right to contradict the basic teaching of Jesus. Since the year 200, some members of the Church in the Christian West have paid much respect to the Pope as the successor of Peter. In fact, Popes, in grand fashion, took to themselves this "power of the keys." They believed that they had an imperial right to decree whatever they believed to be right, politically or personally expedient, and they firmly believed that all of Christendom had the responsibility to follow their decrees as they enacted them.

Pope Gregory VII boldly generalized this belief into "a call to Empire" in his "The Dictate of the Pope" written in 1075. The following is a summary of some of the "dictates":

1. The Roman Church was founded by God.

9. Only the pope's feet may be kissed by princes.

12. The pope may depose emperors.

18. No one may revoke the pope's sentences.

19. No one may judge a pope.

22. The Roman Church has never erred, and, according to the Scriptures, never will err.

23. The Pope is sanctified, because of the merits of the blessed Peter (Speed 1997, 252).

These writings of Gregory VII show the mind of Urban II when he called the First Crusade. He was in charge. He had been given the power from Jesus, the power of the keys, to make his decree, and all Christendom had the responsibility to follow.

In like manner, Louis Brehier in *The Catholic Encyclopedia* also tries to defend the Pope and the spiritualizing of the crusades. He defends both Pope and Crusader by saying: "The Crusades were expeditions undertaken in fulfillment of a solemn vow to deliver the Holy Places from Mohammedan tyranny." The Encyclopedia, then, sees the crusades only from the viewpoint of the pope and the "virtuous," if diluted, Christian crusader. He does not see it from the perspective of the Muslim victims, Jesus and his Sermon on the Mount.

THE FINAL STRAW

The politically astute leaders of Christian Europe, especially Pope Urban II and his immediate successors, took the lead in spiritualizing the Crusade for their citizen warriors. But they had some help from the Muslims.

The final straw came in 1009. Hakim, the Fatimid's Caliph of Egypt, started to harass Christian pilgrims. Why did they do so? Perhaps Christians forgot their manners and called him "uncivilized" and "infidel" one too many times. Perhaps, as *The Catholic Encyclopedia* says, Hakim was unreasonable and did it "in a fit of madness." At any rate, from that time onward, the Christian quarter in Jerusalem had to be surrounded by a wall and Christians had to protect themselves (Brehier). The Knights Templar, a monastic order of knights, disciplined and highly trained, were instrumental in doing so.

In the fervent mix of religions in the area around Jerusalem, many on both sides began to call the other "infidel." Eventual clashes were inevitable. Both sides were convinced that they were defending their own turf, their own land, and their own spiritual heritage. Christians, for example, who felt that the Holy Land was their heritage, constantly plodded across the land which Muslims and Jews considered their own. All sides began to figuratively stack sticks of dynamite near the bon-fire, and, whether they knew it or not, the dynamite would soon explode into all out war.

Yet in the face of harassment, the number of Christian pilgrims increased. For example, in 1065, 12,000 Germans came to the Holy Land in pilgrimage. They must have appeared to the resident population to be an invading army. At one point the *Catholic Encyclopedia* admits that the group was forced to seek shelter in a ruined fortress in order to defend themselves from a troop of Bedouins. Knights Templar were undoubtedly involved in their defense.

Then, another group of nomadic Muslims, the ascending Seljuk Turks further compromised the safety of the pilgrims and soon closed Jerusalem completely to Christians. Pears tells the story of Seljuk, the founder of the tribe bearing his name. He was banished from Turkistan by his father and fled to the northern territories in order to organize a group of soldiers. The group was accustomed to the cold climate and the hard times of their ancestors. They were nomads who had no towns or fortifications. They pitched their tents wherever they found themselves, and for their survival they preyed on those they contacted on the way (Pears 1886, 16).

In 1070 the Seljuk Turks took Jerusalem from the Fatimid's, closing it completely to pilgrims. In 1071 they nearly annihilated the Byzantine army at Manzikert. In 1085, they captured Edessa in Antioch, Tarsus and then Nicaea. In 1091 they defeated Diogenes the Greek emperor. Then they began to harass Syria. By

1092 every big city in the area was under their control. The emperor of Constantinople sent delegates to Urban II urging Europe to help him drive them back lest all of Europe fall. But Urban II had already begun making plans for the Crusade (Durant 1950, 586).

Urban II had many reasons for initiating the Crusades. He too feared an invasion by them. He also feared the restlessness of the Muslims, the perils to the Holy Sepulcher, the problems of Christians in Byzantium, and dangers to the pilgrims.

Over and above all this, the Pope was concerned that internal violence among the local counts, knights and lords back home was destroying Europe, and needed a common outside enemy to distract them from their petty squabbles. The great historian, Dana Munro states that for ages in Europe, brothers bitterly fought against brothers over small parcels of inherited land. As families grew in size down the generations, the large open land which great grandfather used to own became a pittance of land filtered down to many great grandchildren. Family strife increased on a daily basis (Munro 1895, 586). The Pope knew a crafty little secret about internal violence known to wise leaders of nations throughout history -- "If you have too much violence and upheaval in your homeland, get rid of it by exporting it."

From the viewpoint of Urban II, all of these problems together made the Crusades a political if not a religious necessity. Nonetheless, the Pope had to do almost the impossible – turn Christianity, which was originally a pacifist religion into a religion which not only allowed, but actually condoned not only violence, but all out war. He had the previous help of such politicians as Constantine, the war in southern France, and such theologians as Ambrose and Augustine in making his decision.

CLERMONT

In fact, the final decision to call the first Crusade came from Pope Urban II. According to Durant, from March to October of 1095 he toured northern Italy and southern France, sounding out leaders and drumming up support.

Then on a cold November day, writes Bongars in *Gesta Dei per Francos*, after much public relations, people gathered in an outdoor assembly, because the Pope anticipated that no building in the area was large enough to accommodate all of them. He expected a large crowd, but in reality only approximately 300 to 400 people braved the cold damp air (Asbridge 2004, 32). They cheered and pulsed with emotion as men raised the pope on a platform in their midst. It was theatre -- a daring one given the risk involved in an out-door event in the beginning of winter. But the risk was calculated because the actions of the leading actors were carefully scripted in advance.

We will never know exactly what Urban II said that day. But we can come close. We have the eyewitness reports of three people who were there, and wrote about it many years later. We also have Urban II's letters at the time which we can co-relate with the eyewitness reports.

As far as we can determine, his speech stood closely behind St. Augustine's conditions for a just war (Asbridge 2004, 33). In Augustine's and Urban II's mind, a just war needed to be proclaimed by a legitimate authority (and the Pope clearly felt that he met the requirements of a legitimate authority); it had to be for a just cause; and it had to be fought with a right intention, and out of love -- without cruelty or excessive bloodshed. The Pope took one more step toward making the Church the Augustinian Church, rather than the Church of Jesus Christ.

Augustine never did explain how a war can be waged out of

love and "without cruelty," nor did he explain how much bloodshed was excessive. What was Augustine thinking when he spoke these words to the scribes who followed him? In spite of the fact that Christian nations have relied on his "just war theory" and have used it time and time again in Christian history, it makes little Christian sense. The Christian cannot clear cut the forests of the world for ecology's sake. He cannot drink all night for sobriety. He cannot fornicate for virginity. And he cannot go to war out of love. Jesus was the one who said, "Put your sword into its scabbard"; "turn the other cheek"; "blessed are the peacemakers."

It is a mistake to state that the crusade was called to convert the Muslims. Urban II was knowledgeable enough to know that such a plan would be impossible. Urban II, rather, portrayed the Muslims as clear outsiders and brutal oppressors. Asbridge says these words were pure propaganda (Asbridge 2004, 3).

Rather, the Crusade was called to re-conquer land taken by certain tribes of Muslims. It was also called to conquer the Holy Land, especially the city of Jerusalem. A side issue was that the Pope wanted to support the Christian East, but this was a weak issue in his mind. In deed and in fact, the Christian East preferred to handle its own affairs with the Muslims.

Asbridge states a central element of Urban's speech which unfortunately goes along with Urban II's desire to re-conquer lands conquered by the Muslims, and his desire to conquer the Holy Land, especially Jerusalem: "A central feature of Urban's doctrine was the denigration and dehumanization of Islam. He set out from the start to launch a holy war against what he called 'the savagery of the Saracens', a 'barbarian' people capable of incomprehensible levels of cruelty and brutality" (Asbridge 2004, 33).

The pope quoted Jesus frequently: "He that does not take his cross and follow me, is not worthy of me," he said. The people shouted "God wills it," and the Crusade began. As Dana Munro, states: many orations have been delivered with as much eloquence and in as fiery words as the Pope used, but no other oration has been able to boast of such results (Munro 1895, 586).

The knights of Europe immediately embraced the scripture passage quoted from the Gospels, and made it a proverb -- "To take the cross" became another way of saying "to go on the crusade." Asbridge states that "Urban was activating one of the most potent impulses in human society: the definition of the 'other' as evil. Across countless generations of human history, tribes, cities, nations and peoples have sought to delineate their own identities through comparison to their neighbours or enemies" (Asbridge 2004, 34-35).

On-lookers had to wait in the cold until the end of the speech, for the pontiff to reveal internal strife in Europe as the other reason for the Crusades. The pope stated:

> For this land which you now inhabit, shut in on all sides by the sea and by the mountain peaks, is too narrow for your large population; it scarcely furnishes food enough for the cultivators. Hence it is that you murder and devour one another, that you wage wars, and that many among you perish in civil strife. Let hatred, therefore, depart from among you; let your quarrels end. Enter upon the road to the Holy Sepulcher, wrest that land from a wicked race, and subject it to yourselves.... (Urban II, *Letters*).

After that unfortunate statement, the pope's very last words were the most unfortunate of all: "Undertake this journey eagerly for the remission of your sins, and be assured of the reward of imperishable glory in the Kingdom of Heaven" (Munro 1895,

588). All who died in battle against the pagans, he said, would have immediate remission of all their sins -- just the words needed to spur the knights in the Middle Ages, an age which propagated guilt. He had no authority to give such an assurance.

The Crusades were thus announced by "Christian preaching." Each crusader was given a cross from the pope, and each was considered "a soldier of the Church." If the knight died in battle he was assured of eternal life in the form of an indulgence. Also any knight who took the Cross earned the remission of all his temporal debts, and he received other temporal privileges as well.

Durant says that Urban II traveled throughout Europe for the next nine months preaching the Crusade to the nobility. The bishops who returned from Clermont also did their part in promoting it. All Christendom moved as one as it prepared for war -- more united than it had been for centuries.

The war propaganda was filled with lies and half truths. The people were told about atrocities of the Muslims and infirmities of the Christians in Palestine. Muslims, they were told, worshipped a statue of Mohammed, a prophet who had been eaten by hogs. They were told that the Orient was extremely wealthy, and that dark beauties there waited to be liberated by brave men (Munro 1895, 588).

The Pope intended his message mainly for the knights of Europe. He wanted and needed trained knights who knew the nature, ways, and means of war. The rulers of Europe, and even Urban II, were amazed at the quick and uncontrollable response the Pope received from the totality of Christendom. Robert Chazan states: "The great rulers of western Christendom -- the emperor and monarchs -- were utterly unprepared for the explosive aggressions unleashed by the papal initiative....the minor barons and the lower classes enthusiastically took the cross (Chazan 1996, 3).

THE PEASANTS' CRUSADE

The propaganda and the preached word about the Crusade ran out of control. Zealous prophets reached the ears of poor people who were ready to go to the "heavenly" Jerusalem. The most celebrated of those preachers was Peter the Hermit. Munro states that a local abbot described Peter in the following manner:

> 'He was from the city of Amiens, if I am not mistaken, and we learned that he had lived as a hermit in the garb of a monk somewhere in northern Gaul, I know not where. We beheld him leaving there, with what intent I do not know, and going about through cities and towns under the pretext of preaching. He was surrounded by such throngs, received such enormous gifts, and was lauded with such fame for holiness that I do not remember anyone to have been held in like honor. He was very generous to the poor from the wealth that had been given him. He reclaimed prostitutes and provided them with husbands, not without dowry from him; and everywhere, with an amazing authority, he restored peace and concord in place of strife. Whatever he did or said was regarded as little short of divine, to such an extent that hairs were snatched from his mule as relics (Munro, 1895, p. 34).

In Peter's zeal he called the poor to take the mission of the Crusade into their own hands. If they were the poor of Christ, and they certainly were, he told them that then they were the true Crusaders. This was something Urban II did not intend.

Certainly, Urban II wanted knights trained in war and its strategies, not the poor of the land, to plan and be in charge of the crusade.

Due to Peter and others, Munro continues, an army of vagrant Crusaders left their homelands. Sinful and pious men, adulterers, murderers, thieves, perjurers, robbers, and women sold what they had, bought simple traveling kits and whatever weapons they could afford, and stomped down the road (Asbridge 2004, 82). These throngs had no means to sustain themselves. 12,000 left France to follow Peter. 5,000 followed a priest named Gottschalk from Germany. A third group followed Count Emichio of Leiningen (Munro 1895, 588).

Four months before the official crusade of knights was ready -- as the knights were strategizing in their castles -- the hordes were already on their way down the Rhine toward the Holy Land. What they lacked in strategy and wealth, they possessed in sheer, primitive enthusiasm. But they had little to eat, so they were not anxious to sit around talking to one another about the venture.

These poor people were escaping from lands where life had been intolerable. An almost unbroken series of floods, droughts, famines and plagues devastated their homelands. A Holy War was just what they needed -- with all the indulgences and civil benefits that went along with it.

The capture of Jerusalem was not the immediate objective of the knights in their castles, who were carefully planning an official series of attacks, but it was the only goal of the poor who followed their prophets. These poor had oversimplified the crusade. In their minds, the full burden of the crusade rested on their shoulders. Jerusalem became not only their only destination, but also the symbol of their hope. The earthly Jerusalem was their heavenly Jerusalem, and nothing was going to stand in the way of them receiving the heavenly reward which it offered them. They were gung-ho for the holy city.

If the poor considered themselves to be the only true crusaders, they became disillusioned when their meager resources ran out and they began to starve. Those who were able to continue onward had to pillage the fields and homes, the cities and towns, of the people they came upon on the way. Others died in the inevitable armed clashes, not yet with the Muslims, but with the local citizens of Europe.

ANTI-JEWISH SENTIMENTS

As they journeyed on, the crusading poor stirred up gross anti-Jewish sentiments among themselves. The Jews were the reason for all their ills: they were the people who killed Jesus, and they were the people who ruined the economy of Europe. They would not be poor if it was not for the Jews. If they were to enter into the glories of Jerusalem, it was appropriate that the Jews should be eliminated. The poor crusaders were of one mind and one heart regarding this point.

In May, 1096, the horde of poor warriors moved quickly down the Rhine River to the city of Mainz. The municipal authorities and the archbishop were well informed about the group, and they did everything they could to keep them out of the city. Wanting to protect their Jewish citizens, the city fathers closed the gates to them. This, of course did not sit well with the approaching warriors, who needed not only food and drink, but Jewish lives as well. The anti-Jewish, poor army would not be put off. Foreseeing this, Robert Chazan tells us, the Jewish citizens did not trust the walls of the city, but sought safety behind yet a second barrier, the fortified walls of the archbishop's palace.

Chazan continues to tell the story. The hordes had no need to break down the walls of the city. On the 25th of May, sympathetic burghers, the businessmen of the city, opened them from within. Some of these burghers were financially in debt to their Jewish neighbors. Some were in open competition with them for daily buying and selling. Their feelings also had turned to hatred for the Jews, and they were convinced that their survival involved the death of their Jewish competition. Without effort, the hordes secretly entered the city.

The soldiers defending the archbishop's palace fled in fear, effectively turning the Jews over to the invaders. The hordes gave the Jews an ugly alternative -- conversion to Christianity or death. Many took the opportunity to commit suicide or mercifully kill one another. Others submitted passively to a brutal death at the hands of the ugly invaders.

More than a thousand Jews died that day. The Jews in the city of Worms met the same fate days earlier, and those in the city of Cologne a few weeks later. The attackers were brutal, and the moral strength of most of the Jewish resisters never wavered. Even though the First Crusade was intended to be a war against the Muslims, the Jewish people were its first victims (Chazan, 1996, xii-xiii).

THE PEASANT CRUSADE REACHES THE EAST

Those from the hordes who did eventually make it through Europe to Constantinople were no boon to any society. Lloyd Simon tells us that they were hurriedly shipped across the

Bosporus[29] in August 1096.[30] They then broke into two groups. One group were killed by disciplined Muslim warriors as they attempted to take Nicaea. The other group was surrounded and massacred near Civetot two months later. Only a small group of the hardiest and the luckiest were able to retreat to Constantinople to join the knights and the second wave of Crusaders (Simon 1995, 34).

Durant says that these survivors became a fighting corps called the *tafurs,* the ugliest, filthiest, and most ferocious fighters of the crusade. The Muslims were terrified of them, and called them "living devils." The *tafurs* were an embarrassment to the knights of the crusade and even to Peter the Hermit. Peter lost control of his group, left them, and lived safely in Constantinople until 1115 (Durant 1950, 590ff).

The *tafurs* pressed onward with misdirected spiritual fervor. Completely out of control, they ended up assisting the conquest of Jerusalem. They brutally slaughtered Jews and Muslims alike as they entered the city.

NICAEA AND ANTIOCH

Durant continues to tell the story: early in 1097 four regular armies of knights numbering at least 100,000 followed the old pilgrim routes to Constantinople (Durant 1950, 590ff). Emperor Alexios I and his advisers were wary that the group

---

[29] Robert Chazan (1996, vii) states that usual sources for the crusades are useless when dealing with the hordes that made up the poor Crusades. Little is written about the assaults of these hordes on the cities of Worms, Mainz and Cologne. Jewish material does survive, including lists of victims, and poetic dirges in memory of the Jewish martyrs. The hordes supported one another in a great hatred for the Jews, and they killed many Jews as they approached and entered these cities. All is recorded in three Hebrew narratives. Especially one of these, *The Mainz Anonymous* is as trustworthy as all the Christian sources which scholars of the Crusades have sifted through for centuries. Another is a work attributed to Solomon bar Simson. It, too, is reliable, if not as tightly organized as *Mainz Anonymous.* Other works also exist which tell us of the Jewish haters who trudged down the Rhine to Jerusalem. (Chazan (1996, xii-xiii)

[30] The Bosporus is a strait between Turkey in Asia and Turkey Europe. It is about 20 miles long., connecting the Marmara Sea with the Black Sea.

might become a threat to Constantinople itself. Oaths were forced on the crusaders, and gifts of money were given them to try to keep them in line (Harris 1993, 54). Almost immediately, Byzantine soldiers began to follow the Crusaders wherever they went (Harris 2003, 60). Jonathan Riley-Smith states that plundering by the crusaders was not reserved to the poor crusader, but to the knightly crusaders as well: "... one cannot disregard the fact that, because the armies of the First Crusade had no proper system of provisioning, plundering was essential for their survival, particularly when they were far from supply points.... (Riley-Smith 1995, 246)."

This plundering must have been a traumatic experience for those who had their possessions and gardens ripped away from them by armies of soldiers with crosses on their armor, and it is no wonder that Byzantine soldiers kept an eye on them.

The campaign was strategically started with the capture of Nicaea. After resting a week, the crusaders moved through Syria toward Antioch. Antioch was the place where followers of Jesus were called Christians for the first time -- it was a special place for the crusaders. On the march the only enemy that opposed them was the heat and the short supply of water and food. Many died on the 500 mile trek.

For eight months, Antioch resisted their siege. Then in May word came to the crusaders' camp that a huge Muslim army was approaching, and many crusaders fled. The crusaders that remained were inspired by a priest by the name of Peter Bartholomew, who pretended that he found the spear that pierced Jesus' side. Inspired by Peter's words, the crusaders defeated the mighty Muslim army and took the city. The leaders of the army divided the conquered lands among themselves, creating Latin satellites in those eastern lands.

BYZANTIUM'S POLITICAL ACUMEN

Alexios I, from Byzantium, was invited to ride at the head of the Crusaders on their march to Jerusalem. He successfully side-stepped the whole issue. He told the crusader, Raymond of Toulouse, that "he was worried that his empire would be invaded by foreign enemies if he left the capital" (Harris 2003, 65).

The Byzantine Empire was reluctant at every turn to aggravate the Muslims, and consequently, they gave the crusaders very little aid throughout the battles of the crusades. It was not Byzantine policy to affront and aggravate the Muslims in such a way. As Harris states so well: "In the case of the Arabs, the Byzantines were dealing with a power that was stronger than their own empire and which had a religion and ideology every bit as compelling as their own.... They...established a *modus vivendi* with their powerful neighbours (Harris 2003, 29).

The "art of politics" used by the Byzantine rulers was not weakness. It was the wisdom learned from the ages on how best to protect their own communities. Wise though it might have been, animosity grew among the crusaders as they realized that the Byzantine Empire was reluctant to play a part. That animosity undoubtedly was one of the main reasons for the invasion of Constantinople in the Fourth Crusade. (See Harris, *Byzantium and the Crusades*)

EUROPE'S COMPLETE COMMITMENT

While the Byzantine Empire wavered in its commitment because of political prudence, Europe bulled ahead with complete commitment to save Jerusalem and the Holy Sepulcher. The victims were the Muslims and the Jews. Its all-out efforts are manifest between 1099-1187 in everything from military movement, international relations, and art. (Schein 2005, 7).

THE SIEGE OF JERUSALEM

After spending six months refreshing themselves and reorganizing, the Crusaders marched toward Jerusalem. On June 7, 1099, the Crusaders stood before its walls with their battering rams, ladders, catapults, wheels, and all the other medieval instruments of war. The Muslims, in their turn, attempted to use diplomacy. They proposed a peace plan guaranteeing the safety of pilgrims and worshipers to Jerusalem. The Crusaders would have none of it, but demanded unconditional surrender.

The garrison of the Muslims resisted for forty days, then gave in. The Crusaders were ecstatic. They had accomplished their high purpose. Raymond of Agiles, an eye witness reports what happened next: "Numbers of the Saracens were beheaded...others were shot with arrows, or forced to jump from the towers, others were tortured for several days and then burned in flames. In the streets were seen piles of heads and hands and feet (Durant 1950, 590ff)." Other eye-witnesses give more detail. Babies were snatched from their mothers and thrown over the walls of the city. Then their mothers were stabbed to death. 70,000 Muslims were slaughtered in Jerusalem. The Jews were herded into a synagogue and burned alive.

Atiya quotes Archbishop William of Tyre who placed the whole scene in perspective. He said that the worst part of the invasion of Jerusalem was not the mutilated, dead corpses on the ground, but the greedy eyes of the crusading invaders who were dripping with blood from head to toe. In the midst of the blood all that was left was the possession of the homes of those who once lived in them and now were dead. Ataya continues:

> The pilgrims had agreed that, after it had been taken by force, whatever each man might win for

himself should be his forever by right of possession, without molestation. Consequently the pilgrims reached the city most carefully and boldly killed the citizens. They penetrated into the most retired and out-of-the-way places and broke open the most private apartments of the foe. At each, the marauder claimed as his own in perpetuity the particular houses which he had entered, together with all it contained (Ataya 1962, p. 62).

Durant says that the Crusaders then flocked to the Church of the Holy Sepulcher, whose grotto, they believed, had once held the crucified Jesus. "There, embracing one another, they wept with joy and release, and thanked the God of Mercies for their victory" (Durant 1950, 592).

Godfrey of Bouillon was chosen to rule Jerusalem under the title of Defender of the Holy Sepulcher. Jerusalem was now a Latin kingdom. Godfrey's first duty was to insure the safety of the conquest. This he did the very next month at Escalon. He defeated the first Egyptian army arriving from Cairo intent on retaking the city. Thus, the first Crusade ended. The local *emirs* sent Godfrey gifts of gold and horses loaded with provisions and fruits, but the taste in their mouths had to be sour because of the conduct of the Christian soldiers from the north.

THE SECOND CRUSADE, 1146-1148

In a papal decree named *Quantum praedecessores* written in 1145, Pope Eugenius III called the second Crusade. This Crusade received strong support from the great spiritual leader, St. Bernard of Clairvaux, a French saint highly venerated in the Europe of his day.

The Muslims had successfully fought and took al-Ruah and Edessa in 1144. Eugenius III and Bernard were upset by the Muslim advances and convinced Louis VII of France and Emperor Conrad III of Germany to attack the well trained, well disciplined Muslim army. Clumsily, the two leaders from Europe moved their armies of about 140,000 recruits, their women, and their entourage from their homes to confront the Muslim forces.

As they traveled, Pears cites the developing problems between the Crusaders, the Eastern emperor, Manuel, and the Christian people of the East. Manuel was intent on protecting his empire and extracting whatever advantage he could from the crusade. The crusaders had other ideas: "[The crusaders] were ready to plunder the inhabitants of the districts through which they passed [the region of the Eastern Christian Church....] As great numbers of them were without money, plunder was indeed necessary if they were to live (Pears 1886, 134)."

Also, Harris indicates that Manuel "had an army on hand to shadow the crusaders and intervene if necessary" (Harris 2003, 95).

Through the gossip line, every misfortune the crusaders experienced was blamed on the "intrigues" and "hostilities" of the emperor of Constantinople. This disposition developed early among the crusaders and made them willing to punish the Christian people of the East when they were unable to conquer the Muslims. Common gossip circulating among the crusaders concluded that the Christians from Constantinople had betrayed Christ. They had assisted the enemy in order to defeat the cause of the cross.

Crusaders' battles with the Muslims were no contest, according to Durant. The crusaders' military ability was simply pathetic, almost non-existent, in the face of the well managed Muslim forces, led by Saladin. The Muslims crippled the crusaders by destroying the crops along the way and by poisoning the water springs as the crusaders approached. In the time and place of their choosing, they simply massacred the European armies (Durant 1950, 121 & 123).

Saladin was a great Mohammedan diplomat and military strategist. Munro says he belonged to the tribe of the Kurds. He was born in 1137 or 1138 in Tikrit, a fortress on the River Tigris. In time, he became ruler of both Egypt and Syria. He is the one who demolished not only the second crusade, but Christian rule within the Holy Land (Munro 1895, 148).

Saladin was a religious man. Even though he was accomplished at the art of war, he did not take war lightly. Twice, in 1180 and 1185, he concluded and maintained his part in treaties which he made with the Christians. But he could be driven too far.

A Christian by the name of Reginald of Monreale continually molested Egyptian traders and pilgrims from his own little desert haven. Reginald constructed a fleet of five ships and set out to destroy the holy cities of the Muslims, Mecca and Medina. It was a mad and futile project – one example of the insanity which the spirit of the Crusades drew out of people with personality problems.

In 1187 Reginald made the sad mistake of seizing the sultan's sister who was in one of the caravans which passed his desert hovel. Saladin lost all patience with the man. He made a vow to separate Reginald's head from his body with his own scimitar.

On May 1, 1187, Saladin engaged the Christians at Nazareth. The Christians suffered heavy losses. He then moved toward Tiberias. The Christian force numbered 10,000 knights and 18,000 foot soldiers, but, as we have already implied, they had poor leadership. Saladin enticed them into the waterless desert just before Tiberias.[31]

---

31 Speed mentions that the soldiers of Saladin mastered the art of shooting arrows while riding. (Speed, 1997, 190)

The battle began on July 4, 1187. The sun beat down on the Christian army, and Saladin surrounded them and harassed them with archers from their horses. The dismounted iron-clad crusaders were weighed down by armor in a waterless inferno. They eventually threw off their armor and surrendered, begging for water. The noblemen among the crusaders were treated royally by Saladin. They were given cool water to drink and were allowed to return after paying a ransom. Saladin himself then killed Reginald with his own scimitar, as he had promised. The rest of the crusaders were killed or sold in the slave markets. Because of the great number of new slaves, the slave markets became oversaturated and slave prices reached a new low.

Atiya goes on to say that the way to Jerusalem was now open to Saladin. Tiberias fell the next day. Acre fell on July 9. Tripoli then fell and Antioch fell as well. Jerusalem fell on October 2nd. The seizure of Christian Jerusalem by Saladin stood in sharp contrast to the taking of the city by the Christians in the First Crusade. Saladin checked the fury of his men and forbade any abuse. He gave the rich Christians forty days to pay a ransom and leave the city. He accepted small sums for the ransom of groups of poor Christians in the city. He delivered another 1,000 poor Christians who had no ransom. Finally he released 15,000 elderly crusaders, a charitable gesture, he said, which he did "for the solace of his own soul." He protected the Holy Sepulcher and allowed unarmed Christians to visit it. In short, he gave the Christians an example of the humane way to take a city, the proper way, as he saw it, to wage war -- if warfare ever there should be (Ataya 1962, 72).

HILDEGARD OF BINGEN

Miriam Rita Tessera (2002, 77-93) found a revealing letter of Hildegard of Bingen (b1098 CE), a prophetess, whose visions

Pope Eugenius III approved at the synod of Trier in 1147-1148 CE., during her own life-time. Hildegard was an abbess who, Tessera states, claimed to be "a weak woman sent by God to confound the powerful, including the clergy" (Tessera 2002, 77). Tessera continues that this holy prophetess was "able to expound causes and consequences of present events through the Spirit's shining shadow" (Tessera 2002, 78).

Philip of Flanders wrote to Hildegard in 1177 CE on the eve of his departure to the Holy Land. Philip hoped that he could soothe his own troubled soul as well as further his own floundering prestige by leaving his own land and going to the Holy Land to fight the Crusade. After all, had he not "taken the cross" in 1175? Furthermore, he considered himself a pious man. Yet he was anchored in Flanders due to many administrative odds and ends.

He asked Hildegard, the handmaid of Christ (*ancilla Christi*) to mediate between the divine will and him, an unworthy sinner (*peccator et indignus*). And unworthy sinner Philip apparently was. He committed atrocities in the war with England, and he had the knight, Walter of Fontaines beaten to death because he was thought to be Philip's wife's, Countess Isabel's, lover (Tessera 2002, 80).

Hildegard responded, centering almost exclusively on the need for Philip to purge his own heart from his sins. She gave Philip only one sentence regarding the Crusade: "And if the time shall have come that the infidels are working to destroy the font of faith, resist them as much as by the help of grace you are able to resist them." (Tessera 2002, 86) *Et si tempus advenerit quod infideles fontem fidei destruere laborant, tunc eis, quantum per adjutorium gratiae Dei potueris, eis resiste*" (Letter of Hildegard of Bingen to Philip, Count of Flanders).

The "if clause" in the text is significant. Hildegard meant to turn the mind of Philip from the Crusade in Jerusalem to a more spiritual vision. She was, in effect, saying: "But, by the way, what in reality have the Muslims done to destroy the Christian font of faith? Philip, take another look."

THE THIRD CRUSADE

Peters tells the story of the beginning of the Third Crusade. Word of the tragedy of the capture of Jerusalem reached Europe. The three great kings of Europe, then, immediately "took the cross." The third Crusade against Saladin took place from 1189-1192, and it was pathetically catastrophic (Peters 1971, x).

Emperor Frederick Barbarossa, sixty-seven years old, set out with his army. All Christendom applauded him as the new Moses. But Turkish bands harassed him as he marched, cutting off his supplies. Hundreds starved to death and Frederick drowned in a river in Cilicia before reaching the Holy Land.

Richard the Lion Hearted and Philip Augustus then tried their hand at crusading by attacking Acre and conquering it. The two did not get along before they came on the Crusade. Inevitably, they had another dispute and Philip went home.

According to Durant, Richard, now alone, met his match in a war of give and take with Saladin, the Muslim. Saladin clearly won the war on every level (Durant 1950, 598-612). On his way home, Richard was captured by the Duke of Austria in complete violation of the privileges given him as a Crusader. He was held for a huge ransom.

Pears states that this failure further increased the animosity of the Crusaders from the West towards Constantinople. The very passivity of Constantinople was now held against them. One chronicler wrote that the thought in the mind of the Crusaders was "Those who are not with us, are against us" (Pears 1886, 134).

Thus, the third Crusade ended in bickering and complete failure. But this did not dampen the crusading spirit of Christendom. The Crusades would go on.

Peters says it well: "Visionaries, lawyers, calculating and idealistic rulers, and calculating and idealistic popes expressed again and again the view that only by regaining the 'Vision of Peace' -- the allegorical meaning of Jerusalem -- could Christian society be certain of divine favor" (Peters 1971, x). The Crusade had become a Christian institution.

THE FOURTH CRUSADE

Pope Innocent III called the fourth crusade. He was intent on recapturing Jerusalem. This, of course, was nothing new. Every Pope since 1198 was intent on the "liberation" of the Holy Lands. But now the enthusiasm was gone. Some elements which spirited the first, the second and even to some extent the third crusade were lacking, and other more sinister elements were added.

The Crusaders originally planned to conquer first Egypt and then Jerusalem, but instead of fighting the infidel, they turned toward Christian Constantinople. They not only attacked and captured Constantinople, the capital of the Christian Byzantine empire, they systematically looted its palaces and churches, expelled its rulers and crowned Baldwin as the new emperor of the city.

The Christian world is full of surprises. We would expect that Innocent III would be horrified by the actions of his crusaders. Harris gives us the essence of Innocent's letter to the Crusaders after the incident. The letter is a dilemma to anyone trying to establish a consistent Catholic war morality: "When Innocent replied in November 1204, he ... placed the new emperor, his lands and his people under his protection, and commanded that the crusading army, rather than going on to Egypt, should stay to protect Constantinople from any attempt by the Byzantines to retake the city (Harris 2003, xiii)."

Certainly something was amiss. Something had happened to change the minds of key people in the Christian West, including the Pope, about Byzantium. The Crusading army, instead of retaking Jerusalem, turned and brutally sacked the greatest city of the whole Christian world, Constantinople.

Innocent III clearly agreed and applauded the sacking of Constantinople. In effect, he told the Crusaders, "Forget about Nicaea and Jerusalem. Stay in Constantinople and maintain the city against counterattacks from the Christians in the East." One of the reasons for the First Crusade, launched in 1095 by Urban II, was to aid Constantinople against the Muslims who were knocking at their door. Now, Innocent III and the soldiers of the Fourth Crusade somehow felt themselves completely justified in attacking and slaughtering the good people of Constantinople and taking control of that great center of Eastern culture. The whole event is not only problematic, but undoubtedly unjustified -- even if we use Augustine's just war theory, which is also problematic.

Historians have puzzled over the reasons for this turn-around in mid-stream, but nothing seems to justify such an action. Some events can explain it, but only to some degree.

Some have blamed the doge (the head magistrate of Venice), Enrico Dandolo and the merchants of Venice, who did not wish an attack on Egypt, because Venice had supposedly concluded a commercial treaty with Egypt in 1202. Constantinople was a better target, as far as the merchants were concerned because the Emperor of Byzantium was obstructing Venice's trade activities. In the process of granting the Crusaders transportation, the merchants goaded them on to run up an enormous debt (Pears

1886,120). The problem with this theory is that the treaty between Venice and Egypt is now known to have taken place in 1208 or 1212, long after the Crusaders took Constantinople. The doge of Venice was not the main reason for the war with Constantinople.

We also know that industrial Byzantium did become rich by charging a custom duty of 10%, the *kommerkion,* on all imports and exports. We know that the custom duty of 10% was considered exorbitant by traders, and did not make the establishment of Byzantium many friends.

Other theories have fallen apart in the context of history. No apparent escalating estrangement existed between the two societies in the twelfth century. East and West were closely intertwined. Intermarriages regularly took place, and Western Christians made up the best part of the Byzantine army. Because historians struggle to find a causal link between east-west relations to warrant the open attack and sacking of Constantinople, we have to conclude that it was not a planned aggression. The idea arose when a Byzantine prince of the politically involved Angelos family mentioned it to the Crusaders as an option in order to restore his father to the throne. It was a diversion, an after-thought. Also, the customs of 10% did not help, nor did the fact that Byzantine politicians thought it prudent to dance around the crusaders, but not give them much help, less they antagonize the Muslims.

Even so, many knights left the group in disgust when they heard that Constantinople was their destination, and many others who stayed had serious doubts about its legitimacy. Finally, later, few were willing to help Baldwin of Flanders and his successors defend the city. Constantinople remained a Latin city for only fifty-seven years (Harris 2003, xvi).

While Harris is correct in stating that clash of civilizations is too dramatic and too simple a reason for the fall of Constantinople, certainly misunderstandings of the *modus operandi,* concerning how problems were solved between Christian nations East and West, was a major problem, leading to the fall of Constantinople. In the West, the offended were more inclined to put on their armor, grab their swords, jump on their horses, and ride off to war. Negotiations, then, were easy and one-sided, because they took place after the offenders, their wives, and their children were not only vanquished, but oftentimes dead. (Harris 2003, 16).

So the Crusaders decided out of frustration and on a whim to conquer, not Jerusalem, but Constantinople, the most civilized city in Christendom. From 1202-1204 the Crusaders were intent on capturing not Jerusalem, but Constantinople (Durant 1950, 598-602).

The misunderstanding of politics and the petty feuds which had broken out since the first Crusade between the Christian East and Crusaders West finally reaped its harvest. It ended in a greed-fest. Even Pears, who is constantly sympathetic to the Western Crusaders, admits that the soldiers of the West were "comparatively a horde of barbarians," upon entering the great city of Constantinople. (Pears 1886, 120) Pears wastes no words: "They were rough, drunken and licentious, and at times false and cruel. ...the Byzantines wrote and spoke of them as barbarians, recognized their superiority in strength and energy, but thought of them in return as ignorant men and as fanatics" (Pears 1886, 120).

The contemporary French eyewitness and chronicler of the event, Villehardouin, who was sympathetic, even prejudiced, when writing of the French Crusaders can be trusted when he speaks of the three day sack of the city: "Since the world was created, never has so much booty been won in any city!" Robbers and even Christian ecclesiastics in holy orders shared equally in taking what they could carry. Works of art and precious manuscripts were plundered or destroyed. Rare scrolls of Aristotle or Demosthenes were sold for next to nothing. Palaces were plundered. Churches were looted. The four bronze horses over the portals of San Marco's basilica were snatched. The altar of St. Sophia was swept away (Atiya, p. 84). The warriors of the cross then committed open rape -- even the women religious were not spared (Atiya 1962, 84).

In this way the Byzantine Empire was replaced by the Latin Empire of Constantinople. The Christian Crusaders had learned nothing from the example of the Mohammedan Prince Saladin.

Durant tells us that by 1207 the Western soldiers who parceled out and shared the conquered city of Constantinople were afterwards ashamed to call themselves Crusaders (Durant1950, xv). This conquest and looting had the side effect of weakening the great city making it vulnerable to its eventual capture by the Muslims (Durant1950, xv).

THE CHILDREN'S CRUSADE, 1212-1213

The complete collapse of the Fourth Crusade was the greatest disappointment of Innocent III's pontificate. But the Pope was undaunted. He planned yet another Crusade (Powell 1986, 6).

Not only the Pope, but others found the spirit as well. James Powell in *Anatomy of a Crusade* tells about the Children's Crusade which showed "the depth of popular frustration over the failure of the highest leaders of medieval society to liberate the Holy Places from the hands of the Muslims" (Powell 1986, 6). Powell and other recent authors think that the *pueri* who went on the crusade were in fact not children. *Pueri* has related meanings beside "children." "Dependents" is one of those meanings. They believe that the Children's Crusade was made up of "dependents," that is, those who subscribed to the religious poverty movement of the time and were dependent on others for their up-keep. These poor people saw themselves as the elect of God, the imitators of Jesus, who would take the Holy Land when military strategists, the rich and the powerful failed (Powell 1986, 6).

One of these, named Nicholas, appeared at the court of Philip Augustus with an alleged letter from Jesus to the king urging a holy war under the leadership of the poor. So in 1212 and 1213, some 30,000 from France and Germany joined the new crusade following Nicholas down the road toward the Mediterranean Sea. Crowds greeted them with enthusiasm. Some of these Crusaders said they would walk across the sea to get to Jerusalem. Others were certain that the sea would open miraculously in front of them.

But most of these poor zealots never got out of Europe. They either died of starvation or turned back. Those who did make it through Europe, Atiya says, were given free transport to slave markets in North Africa or Egypt (Atiya, p. 85-86).

THE FIFTH CRUSADE

The Fifth Crusade (1217-29), like the Fourth, was called by Pope Innocent III. He called the Crusade at the close of the Fourth Lateran Council in 1215. This Crusade was well planned. The armies took a different route than crusaders previously took, going through Damietta, Egypt. When the Crusaders took Damietta, they were elated.

Francis of Assisi visited the crusader's camp in Damietta. Powell says he did so not on a whim. Certainly he was not interested in cheering on the Crusade. He had prayed long and hard about the relationship between Christians and Muslims, and he came on a mission of peace. He told the Crusaders that they would be defeated if they continued their venture (Powell

1986, 158). He told them that Jesus desired that they change their hearts, not their military strategies. Jesus could do without military strategy, but he did desire that they change their hearts.

Francis also visited the Sultan's camp. We know that in both the Christian and Muslim camps Francis taught "a change of heart" as the way to stop this constant fighting. Some later biographers of Francis say that Francis tried to convert the sultan to Christianity, but this is undoubtedly mere legend. Francis was a wiser man than to expect that.

The Muslim holy people wanted Francis killed, but the Sultan would not touch this holy man from the West. The Sultan tried to give Francis gifts, but he ended up giving him only one, a ram horn to call people to prayer. Then the Sultan respectfully let Francis go on his way.

Francis was correct. Atiya tells us that the crusaders were attacked and were defeated as they advanced down the road along the Nile between Damietta and al-Mansurah (Atiya 1962, 72). Powell says that the failure of the Fifth Crusade marked the last time a medieval Pope succeeded in mounting a major Crusade (Powell 1986, 1).

Frederick II, who was at the time excommunicated, arrived late for the fray because of urgent matters at home. He was blamed by the Christians at home for the Crusade's collapse. However, by diplomacy this excommunicated monarch managed to arrange bloodlessly what all the other Crusaders could not do.

Admittedly, Frederick II was lucky enough to reach the East at a bad time politically for the Sultan, and the Sultan, who never really wanted war did not want to go to war again. Peters tells us that Frederick II wrote this letter to Henry III of England in 1229, entitled "The Imperial Achievement":

...be it known to you that not only is the body of the aforesaid city [Jerusalem] restored to us, but also the whole of the country extending from thence to the sea-coast near the castle of Joppa, so that for the future pilgrims will have free passage and a safe return to and from the sepulcher; provided, however, that the Saracens of that part of the country, since they hold the temple in great veneration, may come there as often as they choose in the character of pilgrims, to worship according to their custom....Moreover the city of Bethlehem is restored to us, and all the country between Jerusalem and that city; as also the city of Nazareth, and all the country between Acre and that city....(*Letters of Frederick II;* Peters 1971,162-165).

In later years, in a minor effort, the First Crusade of King Louis IX of France (1248-54) also failed. Saint Louis IX actually died at Tunis in 1270 on his Second Crusade. This, according to Lloyd, was the last of the international crusades before 1300 (Simon Lloyd, 1995, p. 39).

PASSAGIUM PARTICULARE

Slightly before the death of King Louis IX, in the 1260's, a strategy called *passagium particulare* gained more and more acceptance in the crusades. This strategy did not rely upon large invasions, demanding large movements of troops across Europe. Rather, it took a more stable tack. Rather, it established permanent satellites in the Holy Land with troops manning the satellites. Small expeditions moved from Europe to support the efforts of these satellites (Sylvia Schein, 1991, pp. 20-21).

Schein quotes Humbert of the Romans ('Opus tripartitum', pp. 191-198) to summarize the guiding thought in Europe at the time: "... the Saracens, if left in peace, would already have overwhelmed the whole of Christendom" (Schein, 1991, p. 30). At this point it is clearly the theory of pre-emptive war, which has come down to us, was used in dealing with the Muslim states — do it to them before they have a chance to do it to us.

MODERN CRUSADES

But more "Crusades" would come. A case could be made that they never stopped -- that they continue until this very day with the war in Iraq. Today as in days of yore spiritual Christians continue to fight wars with the Muslims. Jerusalem, of course, is not as attractive to Christians of our day. But Christians continue to speak of "Muslim" and "terrorist" as though they are wedded to each other. Al-Qaida, they believe, is at least as evil as the Seljuk Turks. They together with Muslims in general are demonized in order that Christians might legitimately kill them by shock and awe tactics. Words and actions of modern politicians mimic the speeches given by Pope Urban II and Pope Innocent III many years ago. These speeches express *the Christian theory of positive violence.*

TWO BEAUTIFUL PEOPLE IN THE RUBBLE

Two beautiful people arise from otherwise disastrous crusades, one from the Muslim side, and the other from the Christian side. The first is Saladin, and the second is Francis of Assisi. Certainly more choice people could be mentioned here, like Hildegard of Bingen. Paul Sabatier mentions in his book *Life of Saint Francis of Assisi* (1919): in order to save Sodom, God sent Lot to find five good men in that city. Lot could not find them. If, on the other hand, the Almighty Himself would have done the search, He certainly would have found many more than five good men in that great city. (p. 30) God could record thousands of people of merit during this period in history. We only mention two.

Saladin's Death

Many examples are recorded of Saladin's compassion for those in tribulation, especially for the Christian elderly, women, and children. He was a gallant man, so generous with everyone that his servants had to scrounge lest he leave himself without necessary provisions. Munro says that when he died, the man was almost penniless. Durant says that shortly before his death at fifty-five years of age, he had nothing he could call his own. Without anything to his name, he said these words to his son:

> My son, I commend thee to the most high God.... Do His will, for [in] that way lies peace. Abstain from shedding blood...for blood that is spilt never sleeps. Seek to win the hearts of thy people, and watch over their prosperity; for it is to secure their happiness that thou art appointed by God and me. Try to gain the hearts of thy ministers, nobles, and emirs. If I have become great it is because I have won men's hearts by kindness and gentleness (Durant 1950, 598-602).

Francis of Assisi

Francis of Assisi was the son of a rich cloth merchant. He was intelligent and well liked. Early in his life, he led his friends through the streets of Assisi and enjoyed the good life.

When the time came, he tried to make himself a knight-in-armor, but he was not very successful at it. On November, 1202, he fought for Assisi in an ill-conceived war against the much larger city of Perugia and was taken prisoner. He lay in a cold, damp prison for approximately one year.

In 1204, he armed himself as a crusader and road triumphantly with other knights from the area. But on the way Francis came to know in his heart that something was radically wrong. He turned around and went back to Assisi.

The troubadour and knight from Assisi then became ill and spent more and more time by himself. His friends asked him why he no longer kept them company. "Are you planning on getting married? And has your sweetheart turned your head" (I Celano, 7)? Then Francis spoke with bravado as was his way with his friends: "You're right! I am thinking of marrying! And the girl to whom I intend to marry is so noble, so rich, and so good, that none of you ever saw anything like her" (I Celano, 7)! Paul Sabatier said: His friends understood nothing of what he was speaking, "[Francis] had become aware of the abyss that was opening between them and him." (*Life of St. Francis of Assisi*, p. 25). The *Sacrum Commercium*, a religious allegory, written about 1227, one year after Francis's death, tells of Francis's search for his "bride":

> Francis began to go about in the streets and crossings of the city ... diligently seeking whom his heart loved. He inquired of those standing about, he questioned those who came near to him, saying: "Have you seen her whom my heart loves?" But this saying was hidden from them, as though it were in a foreign language. Not understanding him, they said to him: "Sir, we do not know what you are asking. Speak to us in our own language and we

will give you an answer" (*Sacrum Commercium*, Section 5).

At the time his statement was simply bravado. But he continued to read the Gospels and pray until the message for his life became clear. It was Lady Poverty whom he sought. He would marry Poverty whom he found in Jesus and the Gospels. This baffled everyone: his friends, his family, the clergy, and even the bishop of Assisi. No one understood how he could seek, of all things, poverty. He was certainly insane?

> For there was no voice nor sense among the sons of Adam in that day that they might want to confer together or speak about poverty. They hated poverty bitterly then, as they do today, nor could they speak peaceably about it to any one asking about it. Therefore, they answered him as they would an unknown person and they said they knew nothing about what he was seeking (*Sacrum Commercium*, Section 5).

As the Church was jousting for wealth and power, Francis sought, eventually found, and never wavered in following the poverty of Jesus and his teachings, especially his teachings on the beatitudes. Jesus, he came to realize, turned the value system of the world upside down. His secret insight into the Beatitudes of Jesus was: in order to live the Beatitudes, a person must change value systems; a person cannot seek above all else, the riches, power and prestige of this world. Francis forced the rich, crusading Church -- Pope Innocent III, the bishops, its Crusaders, and all its conniving theologians and clergy – all who believed that power, prestige and money were its legacy -- to face his life and that of his beautiful bride, Lady Poverty. So did he force the Sultan and the Muslim world to face her. In return, Francis received from the Sultan and the Muslim world, the gift of hospitality to even one's enemy, daily prayer and dedication to God.

CONCLUSION TO THE CRUSADES

Back in the first century Ignatius of Antioch in his *Letter to the Ephesians* told us how Christians were to behave in the world. His words stand in sharp contrast to the "crusading spirit:"

> And so do not cease to pray for all other men, for there is hope of their conversion and of their finding God. Give them the chance to be instructed, at least by the way you behave. When they are angry with you, be meek; answer their words of pride by your humility, their blasphemies by your prayers, their error by your steadfastness in faith, their bullying by your gentleness. Let us not be in a hurry to give them tit for tat but, by our sweet reasonableness, show that we are their brothers (Ignatius of Antioch, *Letter to the Ephesians*).

Cases can always be made for wars. At any point in time, they continue by some to be considered right and just. The distance and perspective of history tells us how embarrassing wars truly were and continue to be. Christians everywhere live with the horrible reality the Crusades lay before them.

At the end of his *History of the Crusades,* S. Runciman lays the historian inside him aside as he editorializes:

> The triumphs of the Crusade were the triumphs of faith. But faith without wisdom is a dangerous thing.... The Crusades were a tragic and destructive episode.... There was so much courage and so little honour, so much devotion and so little understanding. High ideals were besmirched by cruelty and greed, enterprise and endurance by a blind and narrow self-righteousness and the Holy War itself was nothing more than a long act of intolerance in the name of God, which is a sin against the Holy Ghost (Simon, p. 6).

True Christians have to be appalled by the nature and the intent of the Crusades. How they can be justified by any legitimate view of Jesus' teachings is problematic. At best, they were an attempt to protect pilgrims who wished to go to Jerusalem. At worst, they were the activities of marauding Crusaders, who wished to kill and gain new property for themselves in Jerusalem and Constantinople. They were assured by unbelievably dense or evil popes that they would go to heaven for their efforts.

Christians have considered that they have been right throughout history. They have contorted history to justify any action. They have blocked out, watered down, or merely justified anything that would be considered questionable or evil in their actions. Saying and believing that "we are extremely right, and you are extremely wrong" has been and continues to be one of the gravest sins of the Christian fellowships.

Chapter 8

Religious Life: The Black Monks to Waldo

RELIGIOUS LIFE IN GENERAL IN THE AGE

Religious life of various forms was a dazzling element of the Church in the West. Like the fine work of Michelangelo or Leonardo Da Vinci, inventiveness and creativity were the dominant themes. The creator of the Mona Lisa and the Pieta had extreme difficulty doing creative work. Supreme dedication was necessary. Such dedication was also needed by the founders of various forms of religious life and their close followers, anyone who attempted to form a Christian life in accord with their own convictions and charisma. Inventiveness and creativity were used to survive, thrive, and occasionally even thrive well, without suspicion, socially and ecclesiastically. In these matters, the great artists of the time and the founders of religious life could have sat together, shared brews from the keg or glasses of wine, and discussed many interesting stories concerning not so much their dealings with the common folk, but mainly their dealings with the kings, popes, prelates, and clergy of the time.

Granted, sometimes the formulated religious lives that evolved were ill-founded and, justifiably, were looked upon with bewilderment, but not with awe, by the general population of Christians.

Certain individuals lived out their fantasies, their neuroses and even their psychoses in the bedazzled public domain.

But for the most part, if the founder found a following, the general population was indulgent and accepting of those who desired to live a spiritual life in their midst. The major problem arose from the jittery, established hierarchy, who felt threatened by ideas which might infringe on their domain and threaten their authority. They watched carefully for anyone who might, intentionally or unintentionally, steal the power of the coveted gold-threaded stoles they wore, or who might throw a little dirt on their beautiful robes.

At times, as well, the religious lives formulated were brilliant at their inception, but eventually got entangled and went astray because of wayward second or third generation leaders, who lost their first fervor. At other times they became entangled and choked by the various practicalities of survival, and were not able to free themselves from "the realities of life."

RELIGIOUS LIFE OF OLD

Earliest of all were the Augustinians who we have mentioned in previous chapters, and the Benedictines, both formed by the founders whose communities bore their names. These groups came upon rough times and disintegrated. They did not survive their own internal disputes, difficulties with civil and ecclesiastical authorities, and the disruptions caused by the migrants, the so-called hordes, that descended upon Europe.

As a consequence, Lester K. Little writes: "The tenth century fostered one form alone of the religious life, that of the monastic community" (Little, 1978: p. 61). They were called "black monks" because of the woolen habit, dyed black, which they wore. These monks lived, for the most part, in monasteries near cities and towns, and they maintained the spirituality, learning and culture which were able to exist in these times. Some of these monasteries flourished and became rich from the gifts of beautiful land and good food given them from generous endowments, wills, and from the land given to them from heretics through the justice system of the day.

Each monastery was an independent corporation. Today, we do not even know how many there were. Certainly, the monasteries of Cluny, Saint Martial, Fleury, and Solignac existed and stood out among the rest. But thousands of others also existed on the countryside. Affiliations existed between monasteries, especially between those that branched from one another. Such affiliations varied from mere vague past remembrances to strong institutional bonds (Little: 1978, 62).

In exchange for the generous endowments of kings, counts and dukes, the monasteries gave these rich, noble people divine protection, fishing rights, manual labor and the fruits of their labors, such as wine and other produce. Many of the monasteries had monks who were moneywise, and some of those became rich moneylenders. The following story told by Little probably is an exaggeration, as most stories are, but it probably has some truth in it: "…at Saint Paul's-Outside-the-Walls, during the first proclaimed holy year (decreed by Boniface VIII in 1300): two clerics stood day and night by the altar holding rakes in their hands, raking in 'infinite amounts of money' (*die acnocte clerici stabant ad altare Sancti Pauli tenentes in eorum minibus rastellos rastellantes pecuniam infinitam*) (Little: 1978, p. 65)."

The abbeys of Saint Philibert, Cluny and other monasteries gained complete control of the economies of the villages around them. Cluny, in fact, constructed a new Church which was the largest building in Europe until St. Peter's Basilica was constructed in Rome.

These monasteries held on by their fingernails to the power and prestige which they had inherited from the Roman Empire. Without the Empire, these monasteries would never have existed. Monks were recruited from the ruling and the warrior class. Successful abbots became, of necessity, administrators of money rather than holy men. These monks "...made themselves voluntarily weak – or 'poor'...[but] felt no disturbing contradiction between 'wealth' and 'poverty' while living by a rule in the setting of a materially comfortable, in some cases, even magnificent and luxurious, monastery (Little: 1978, p. 68)."

As seen in *Canterbury Tales* and other writings of the time, the "holy monk" often became a cartoon of his own self. For example, in "The General Prologue" to his *Canterbury Tales,* Chaucer (c1343-1400) wrote:

> There was a monk, a nonpareil was he,
> Who rode, as steward of his monastery,
> The country round; a lover of good sport,
> A manly man, and fit to be an abbot.
> He'd plenty of good horses in his stable,
> And when he went out riding, you could hear
> His bridle jingle in the wind, as clear
> And loud as the monastery chapel-bell.
> Inasmuch as he was keeper of the cell,
> The rule of St. Maurus or St. Benedict
> Being out of date, and also somewhat strict,
> This monk I speak of let old precepts slide
> And took the modern practice as his guide....
> In other words, a monk out of his cloister.
> But that's a text he thought not worth an oyster;
> And I remarked his opinion was sound.
> What use to study, why go round the bend

> With poring over some book in a cloister,
> Or drudging with his hands, to toil and labour
> As Augustine bids? How shall the world go on?
> You can keep your labour, Augustine!
> So he rode hard -- no questions about that --
> Kept greyhounds swifter than a bird in flight.
> Hard riding, and the hunting of the hare,
> Were what he loved, and opened his purse for.
> I noticed that his sleeves were edged and trimmed
> With squirrel fur, the finest in the land.
> For fastening his hood beneath his chin,
> He wore an elaborate golden pin,
> Twined with a love-knot at the larger end.
> His head was bald and glistened like glass
> As if anointed, and likewise his face.
> A fine patrician, in prime condition,
> His bright and restless eyes danced in his head,
> And sparkled like the fire beneath a pot;
> Boots of soft leather, horse in perfect trim:
> No question but he was a fine prelate!
> Not pale and wan like some tormented spirit.
> A fat roast swan was what he loved the best.
> (Chaucer, *Canterbury Tales*, "The General Prologue")

This "holy monk" was obsessed by the hundreds in his monastery who were once rich and then came upon hard times, so they entered the monastery. Certainly "bad times" is not a good reason to enter religious life, and if it was considered a good reason at the time, the monastery must have been a sour place to live. No wonder this monk took himself away from that rancid life and lived the high life of a hunter and keeper of horses and dogs. At any rate, the monk preached about his obsession. His tale was an *Apologia pro Vita Sua,* the reason he left his horrid monks behind, as well as an extended sermon characteristic of the sermons given by the monks of the time. The monk was preachy in spite of his wild life. In any public forum it was undoubtedly the way of the black monks. He started with Lucifer and then gave seventeen detailed examples of great men and women (and one angel) who were at the top of their game and then fell into the worst of times. His discourse caused this response from the knight:

> Mr. Monk, no more of this, the Lord bless you!
> Your tales are boring us to death,
> And all of this kind of talk is waste of breath,
> No fun in it, it doesn't entertain....
> I'd have dropped off to sleep long before this,
> And fallen in the mud, deep as it is,
> And then your tale would have been told in vain.
> You know, the scholars have an axiom:
> If a man's got no audience -- why then.
> It's no use to go on lecturing.
> (*Canterbury Tales,* "Prologue to the Nun's Priest's Tale")

Chaucer was making a clear point here. He was showing how the monks of his day, in spite of themselves, showed exaggerated piety before the people -- to the point of making themselves repulsively preachy, whether their lives were truly pious or not.

Even though he called this monk "nonpareil," and he certainly dressed him quaintly and gave him individuality, it is appropriate to draw some conclusions here. Chaucer intended to generalize on the monks manner of discourse. He purposely never gave the monk a name. He has the knight say: "But on my honour, I don't know your name,/ Whether to call you milord Brother

John,/ Or Brother Thomas, or else Brother Alban?/ Which monastery's yours, in heaven's name." (*Canterbury Tales*, "Prologue to the Nun's Priest's Tale") After the great sermon, the knight said: "So, Brother Peter --if that's your right name -- I beg you on my knees, tell something else...."

Chaucer implied here that it was the way of monks, even those who were nonpariel, to sermonize in a fire and brimstone manner. He purposely refused to give the monk a name in order to make him a caricature of monks of his age. So the quaint monk's tales are, characteristically, monks of his age's "hell and damnation" stories. He meant to say that other monk preachers were as quaint and told similar sermons. Chaucer had hit a universal chord here. Which Christian person since then has not experienced the same frustration at one time or another while listening to churchmen sermonize on and on with multiple religious clichés? Chaucer spoke a message for all ages of Christianity.

RENEWAL OF HERMIT AND PREACHER GROUPS

Peter Damian (1007-1072) was distinguished for starting a reform movement. Peter was a hermit. He taught in various abbeys in his vicinity, but when he did so, he was careful not to receive any pay for his knowledge. He also wrote letters to Pope Stephen IX about the need for reform in the monasteries in light of the poor Jesus. The Pope was so intrigued with this poor hermit that he made him a Cardinal of the Church, a position which took him away from his hermitage more than Peter would have liked. In essence, Peter's message was: "the task of clerical reform meant depriving clerics of comfortable incomes and getting them to live from the labour of their own hands" (Little: 1978, p. 73). Peter told the Pope many horror stories concerning the goings-on, some of them sexual, in the monasteries. Morally sensitive, He was a true light of his age.

Robert of Molesme (c1027-1110) started the Cistercian Order, re-introducing the Rule of St. Benedict. The Cistercians strove for intense poverty. If benefactors gave them too many goods, they moved to another area for the sake of Gospel austerity.

Bruno of Colgne (1030-1101) started the Carthusian Order, which united the hermit life with poverty. The Carthusians had a monastic rule appropriate for a hermit.

Norbert of Xanten (1080-1134) started an Order of Preachers called the Praemonstratensians. They sought to interpret the Gospels for the political life which buzzed awry around them.

All of these men, following Peter, saw a need for change in monastic life. Their religious communities sought a new authenticity in that life, striving in various ways, according to each one's charism to follow the Jesus they knew in their own hearts. They were all valiant and authentic Christians in their age, saints who must be commended for their efforts.

THE LAY REFORM MOVEMENT

Due to the fact that many of the clergy tended to be a lecherous and greedy group, lay people began to leave the clutches of their clergy for more sincere Christian grounds. These lay people were confident that they could find their own way, and Christ would be their light.

The Humiliati

Somewhere between 1170 and 1220, lay people began to meet informally in one another's houses. They discussed the poverty of Jesus, his life, his death and resurrection. There was nothing inherently secret about their meetings, but only a few of the more upright clergy were welcomed at their discussions. The apparent secrecy of the meetings made the established hierarchy nervous. Lack of knowledge of their people meant lack of control.

Eventually, the gathering groups called themselves the Humiliati. They formed a community life together. The married members continued to live at home, but some of the single members decided to live together in one place, sharing a common life in an urban environment as they associated work with prayer. They were obliged to distribute to the poor all goods that exceeded their means. Some of these groups lived in various cities of Lombardy and at the Casa di Brera near Milan (Little: 1978, p. 113-114). Vauchez tells us:

> They did not flout orthodoxy, but other aspects of their life appeared shocking to churchmen, especially the mixed genders of their communities, where men and women coexisted on the level of strict equality, and their refusal to swear oaths before the courts, based on the words of Christ: "Let your 'yes' mean 'yes' and your 'no' mean 'no'" (Vauchez, 2112, 41).

They wore garments of un-dyed, virgin wool, and some of them began to reach out to the community around them by preaching to them, an activity which Pope Alexander III (1159-81) tried to stop. He also forbade the Humiliati from holding "secret" meetings. But "secret" was not the Humiliati's intent. They just did not want any clergyman present who would disrupt their gatherings by preaching at them.

Pope Lucius III (1181-5), Alexander's successor, called the Humiliati schismatic, and he placed an anathema on all of them. In spite of this serious action of the Pope, the Humiliati continued to grow. People saw through the clutches of a power hungry clergy.

Pope Innocent III (1198-1216) brought together a group of clergy to study the group, and he decided that by no means should all of them be excommunicated. He made them into an official religious community in the Church. The community consisted of a 1st order of priests, a 2nd order which was monastic (made up of separate male and female communities), and a 3rd order made up of lay people who continued to live secular, familial lives. He decreed that the Humiliati could preach by example. He did not allow them to preach doctrine. The Humiliati grew quickly in number. In 1216 there were 150 convents or congregations near Milan alone (Little: 1978, pp. 114-120).

The Humiliati are best known in the economic field for their woolen cloth. The trademark which was placed on every woolen piece which they produced was the lamb. In the course of the thirteenth century, they became entrepreneurs and some of them grew rich (Little: 1978, 119). They gradually phased themselves out of existence by their growing affluence.

Beguines and Beghards

Around the turn of the 13th century, men known as *beghards* and women known as *beguines* popped up in Europe. They were lay people who sought to live the "apostolic life," a life committed to poverty, begging, and preaching (Lerner, 1972, pp. 35-60). The *beguines*, the women, committed themselves to chastity and community in *beguinages*. The *beghards* were often free-spirited beggars, religious troubadours. They were the religious "hippies" of their age. They were less formal about their religion than other religious in their time, and they often aroused the hostility and suspicions of religious, clergy, and even lay people.

The Franciscans in Italy might have been considered members of this wayward movement, but the Franciscans had the friendship and guidance of Cardinal John of St. Paul, and after him, Cardinal Hugolino, the future Pope Gregory IX. With help from them -- which made Rome less nervous -- and with the guidance of Francis of Assisi, a man who had within himself the rare combination of genius and mystic, they came through the era surprisingly well, and were quickly considered a religious order within the Church.

The Waldensians

In the face of a deteriorated Church, the Waldensians, with sincerity in their hearts, sought a reform of the Church. Peter Waldo, in his early days, was very much like Francis of Assisi. He heard the beatitudes and took to heart the fact that the poor were exalted. So he started to preach the Gospel. He was soon joined by many other men and women. He gave his money away after taking care of his daughters, and paid off people whom he thought he might have defrauded. Peter Waldo and his group, the Waldensians, preached Gospel poverty and reform. He also preached equality among men and women. Women in his group were just as likely to preach the word as men. If the Waldensians would have been more successful with their endeavors within the Church, perhaps Francis would have joined them rather than starting his own movement.

Before going to the valley people, Peter, accompanied by a few followers, did go to Rome in 1179 to gain the acceptance of the Pope for his translation of Scriptures, and also to gain his permission to preach. Permission was granted for his translation of Scriptures. The Pope also granted Peter permission to preach, but only if he could gain the approval of the local clergy. But, the local clergy thought that the Waldensians lacked the necessary knowledge to preach, and an even greater reason was that they were afraid that the group would take over their own pulpits. Peter later joined the Vaudois, the valley people, out of desperation with the church, saying "It is better to obey God than men." He believed that he was only doing what Jesus told him to do.

Two or three years later, in 1184, the group was condemned by Rome at the Council of Verona. Peter and his group had had enough of Rome. They joined the Vaudois and their group then expanded rapidly. Pope Innocent III was able to eventually keep some of the group in the Church. With the advent of Francis of Assisi, many of the Waldensians became part and parcel of the Vaudois. Those looking to live a poor, Christ-like life within the church joined the Franciscans.

HERESY IN THE AGE

The so called heretic was much closer to the saint than most people realize. Both the heretic and the Church-proclaimed "saint" were, for the most part, good men and women. Both were Church people. Some were more educated in theology, it is true, but most tended to spend much time developing spiritual and theological concepts, and most of them developed a deep spiritual life. They were passionate about their religious beliefs. All of them agreed with one another on most of Jesus' teachings and the theological concepts of Christianity, and they lived it to the best of their ability. When they differed with one another or the main stream of Christianity, they differed on only one or two issues – differences which both the church and the projected heretic obviously felt were very important; differences which some of them argued about amongst themselves or with church authorities as though their life and the life of God depended on them.

When they were in conflict with the Church, their greatest problem was this: even though their differences revolved around one or two or, at most, a narrow circle of dogmas and ideas, they tended to be passionately intolerant of others who held other ideas. They stressed the differences they had rather than the whole rest of the body of Christian doctrine upon which they agreed. Those who won the battles of words and pleased the ruling church authorities became the Church's proclaimed saints. Those who lost became the heretics. Francis of Assisi's genius was that he decided never to get caught in such a rat maze of argumentation, which lowered a person's energy level and rendered a person unable to carry out effectively the mission given him or her by Jesus.

Most of those who at one time or another were called heretics (Marcion, the Montanists, the Donatists, Arius, Priscillian, etc.) came from different schools than the in-group of the established Church. Some might have even taken the time to teach themselves. They learned certain different theological concepts and frameworks than did the saints. Marcion, the Montanists, Arius, and Priscillian, to name only a few, were treated unjustly: though they were sincere in their beliefs, they had their names degraded and their works burned. Priscillian paid the ultimate price. He was burned at the stake. Today, we struggle to learn any little tidbit of information we can gain about the writings of these "heretics," while the works of Justin Martyr and Augustine thrive and have influence to this very day. For the ecclesiastical, hierarchical Church was, for whatever reason, convinced of the correctness of its own theologies, and they had the power to back them.

In the thirteenth century, the heretic was a different type of person than the heretics of earlier history. The Waldensian and the Humiliati began as spiritually starved, but sincere persons. The jealousies and the riches of the clergy of the day were a problem for them. The Popes or authorities who were "in charge" had difficulty with their message, sometimes for selfish or political reasons -- not reasons inherent in Jesus own teachings. Innocent III commanded emperors and kings, as well as bishops, priests and lay folk. He sat with great dignity on his throne in Rome. In doing so he showed little similarity to Peter, whose only throne was the cross on which he was crucified, or to the rest of the apostles, who never even thought about sitting on a throne, or to Jesus, the poor man from Nazareth, who was too busy disseminating his message and, in his temptation in the desert, spurned thrones.

The clergy sold spiritual favors and blessings. Priests and bishops who did not sell them were looked down on as either naïve or as neophytes by the rest of the clergy. Paul Sabatier gives a pointed description of the Roman *curia* in the thirteenth century: "They are stones for understanding ... wood for justice, fire for wrath, iron for forgiveness, deceitful as foxes, proud as bulls, greedy and insatiate as the minotaur" (Sabatier, 1894:28). Then Sabatier speaks of the bishops and priests: "The bishops, on their part, found a thousand methods ... for extorting money from the simple priest. Violent, contentious, they were held up to ridicule in popular ballads from one end of Europe to the other. As to the priests, they bent all their powers to accumulate benefices, and secure inheritances from the dying, stooping to the most despicable measures for providing for their bastards." (Sabatier, 1894:29) Now Sabatier is not above exaggerating, but his general message is clear and true.

Certainly not all bishops and priests were so inclined. But the situation was bad enough and extensive enough that certain conscientious lay-people rose to the occasion to deal with the situation. Sometimes we judge them today as being wrong, sometimes we consider them "right on." Among them were the Humiliati and the Waldensians. Being accused of heresy or schism did not mean that they were not following in the footsteps of Jesus. Being pegged a heretic had nothing to do with sanctity or a virtuous life. It only meant that a person was not keeping his or her theological concepts in a row as far as the Pope and the bishops were concerned.

This leads us to question the theology behind the whole concept of the importance and value of heresy for Christians. Churches have divided too many times. Too much hate has been thrown around over minute intellectual differences. Too many local churches hate one another. This is clearly not the intention of Jesus who wished us to be one.

If a person disagrees with the established Church on a matter of intellectual concern, is that not human? The Pope, bishop, or church authority might wish to discuss the matter with the person. He might send others to the person to discuss the matter further. If the person were approached humbly and sincerely, certainly these religious, spiritual people would in turn listen respectfully, consider the matter carefully, and then voice his or her own concerns in return. But if the person sincerely considered the Pope's, the bishop's, or church authority's ideas, and yet, with all personal integrity, continued to believe as before, the heavens and the earth did not therefore fall apart at the seams for them or for the Church.[32] They could still love one another as brothers and sisters. Were such minute intellectual differences of opinion on matters of faith of grave concern to anyone on a broad scale? Were they reason to deny communion to the person on the following day? Were they reason to burn the person's books or burn the person's body in the public square? Is it not time to seriously think about such matters?

---

32 The case of Galileo is a case in point. The Pope, not Galileo, was clearly wrong in his insistence that the sun moves in orbit around the earth. Why could the pope not have said: "You do not believe as I do, but let us respect one another's beliefs, and live at peace with one another?

Furthermore, were such intellectual differences of opinion really that important to Jesus? If there was a heresy in the church, perhaps it laid in the insistence on Aristotle/Thomas Aquinas/Justin Martyr's intellectualism. It seems to me that the Sermon on the Mount is tremendously more important. The Sermon is action based, not intellectually based: be poor, be meek, hunger and thirst for holiness, be single-hearted, be peacemakers, be willing to suffer persecution for Jesus' sake, be salt of the earth, be deeper than those who insist on the letter of the law, do not sit in the anger you have for another, do not sit in the lust you have for another, do not easily divorce your wife or husband, let your "yes" mean "yes" and your "no" mean "no," turn the other cheek when struck by another, and love even your enemies. (Matthew 5 NAB) And his deepest prayer was, "…that all may be one as you, Father, are in me, and I in you, I pray that they may be [one] in us…." (John 17: 21 NAB)

I do not read: "Make sure that your concepts coincide with those of your bishop or Pope." Or "All of you must celebrate Eucharist with the same words -- those dictated by your Bishops." The greatest heresies among Christians in years past and today is the insistence on intellectual trivialities.

Chapter 9

FRANCIS OF ASSISI

OVERVIEW

Francis of Assisi (1181-1226) not only knew the catastrophic state of the Church, but he developed the insight, the spirituality, and the practical good sense to move the poverty movements of the day to complete acceptability. He became respected by practically everyone of all nuances of belief. He is arguably the closest follower of Jesus in all of history, challenging the Church to become what Jesus intended it to be, a poor, peaceful servant of humankind.[33] The *People's History of the Church* needs to give him

---

[33] The early sources for the life of Francis of Assisi are his own writings, mainly dictations, given, for the most part, to Brother Leo. They also include mainly the two *Lives of Francis* written by Brother Thomas of Celano, which contain precious material that was gathered soon after Francis's death and the *Life of Francis* written by St. Bonaventure. All of these sources were able to be verified by friars who were contemporaries of Francis. For the most part, we can be confident of their authenticity.

These early sources need some explanation. Francis died in 1226. Pope Gregory IX, who was Cardinal Hugolino, Francis's mentor, immediately made arrangements for Francis's canonization as a saint. Francis was made a saint just two years after his death. The pope asked Brother Thomas of Celano, a Franciscan friar, to write the life of Francis to help celebrate the event. Quickly, Thomas used his own knowledge and experiences, the knowledge of Francis's close companions, Leo, Rufino, Angelo, Elias, Clare, Gregory IX, and others whom we do not know. The life that he wrote, known as *I Celano* is probably the best of all the lives written. Celano knew that it would be scrutinized by all who knew Francis well. As we might expect, it is a bit sketchy because Thomas had so little time to write it. Also, because the biography was written for the celebration of Francis as a saint, it has a flair about it which boosts Francis above the human realm into that of the saintly. Francis would have agreed with much of the work, but he would have probably laughed at the elevations above the human. Nonetheless, it was typical of the lives of the saints at the time. In our work, we call this *I Celano*.

In 1244, Crescentius of Iesi, head of the Franciscans at the time, asked the friars to send him

intense reflection.

The early sources for Francis of Assisi's life insist that after his conversion Francis sought to imbibe the life and teachings of the poor, peaceful servant, Jesus. Centered on this, he immediately eliminated some of the common religious practices at the time. For example, he resisted the compulsion of the age to parade the relics of saints around cities and fields or to build huge cathedrals to honor a fantasized, majestic king, Jesus. Furthermore, simply because Jesus considered them unimportant and detrimental, he was not interested in money, earthly power and esteem. Rather, he insisted on remaining centered and focused, convinced that Jesus, whom he knew not only from the Gospels, but also from remarkably accurate private inspiration, was the example for his age and ours. The compassion of that Jesus and Jesus' intentional shunning of earthly riches and glory became paramount goals in his life. He walked the world in sandals and a peasant's robe,

---

all they knew of Francis. The response was generous. Especially Leo, Rufino and Angelo, the closest companions of Francis, gathered what they knew. The three, interestingly enough, were not excited about writing a new biography of Francis, a fact that further supports the authenticity of *I Celano*. They wrote at the end of their letter introducing their new information: "These few things which we have written you can insert in the legends already mentioned, if your discretion sees fit to do so.... We believe that if these things had been known to the venerable men who wrote the legends mentioned before, they would certainly not have passed them by, but would have embellished them with their own style and handed them down for a remembrance to those who would come after them" (*Legend of the Three Companions*, Letter) So Crescentius gave all the data to Thomas of Celano, and Thomas was commissioned to write *II Celano*, which contains information he missed when he so quickly wrote *I Celano*.

Unfortunately, the life of Francis that bears the name *The Legend of the Three Companions* is not, for the most part, the writings of Leo, Rufino, and Angelo which was sent to Crescentius of Iesi, but a later life of Francis. Only the "introduction" is authentic. The present so-called *Legend of the Three Companions* was written in the years 1244-1246...to correct certain details about the life led by the saint...in terms too general and moralistic" (Vauchez, 2012, 7). It does read much like the other best sources, with a few more realistic exceptions. In spite of its spurious name, this work follows all others in calling it *The Legend of the Three Companions*.

The assembly of the friars in 1260 asked the head of the Franciscans at the time, St. Bonaventure, an excellent writer, to write what they called "the official" life of St. Francis. He completed it in 1262 or 1263. The next assembly received it with enthusiasm. We call this biography *Bonaventure*.

The works of Thomas of Celano had a rocky start. At one time after Bonaventure's "official" biography was approved in 1263, Celano's works were burned by the friars. Copies of the work were saved only because they were found in the library of a Benedictine monastery. Ironically, good Franciscan history was maintained thanks to the Benedictines.

greeting everyone with the message which Jesus inspired him to say, "The Lord give you His peace" (*Testament of Francis*)! As Andre Vauchez writes: "For the Poor Man of Assisi, it [peace] was an essential aspect of the Gospel message" (Vauchez, 2112, 67). The friars, and especially Francis, became peacemakers.

He intervened to put an end to factions in the city of Arezzo in Tuscany (Vauchez, 2112, 69). He pulled no punches when he addressed the people of Perugia for plundering and killing their neighbors, promising that the Lord would not let such injustices go unpunished. He said that the punishment would come in the form of an absence of peace within the realm of the city itself, and it happened as he predicted (Vauchez, 2012, 69-70). In Parma, a war-like town, as was many towns in Italy, his words brought peace: weapons were put aside, and a time of happiness prevailed (Vauchez, 70-71). This he did in other cities of Italy, as well.

He proposed a new affluence -- his riches were his deep, intimate relationship with Jesus and his positive regard for everyone, no matter their class or their social and economic background. Pope, cardinal, king, nobleman, crusader, Muslim, leper, and the poor were all the same to him. He treated them all with the greatest dignity. They were all one in Christ. Highlights of his social life are certainly his humanity and his sincere compassion. He became a popular spiritual man of his age, attracting a community of thousands of Franciscan brothers within the decade between 1209 and 1219. In the process, when the rest of Christianity was marching to the tune of the Crusades, he was able to bring Jesus' peace to the sultan, and reciprocally receive the sultan's peace and that of the Muslim community. In fact, he learned much more from the Muslim community than his own community and the Catholic Church ever recognized.

Economically, he was a poor man, and he desired that his brothers be poor men as well. For example, at the gathering of the brothers at the Chapter(s) of Mats at Pentecost in 1221 or 1222 and perhaps also in the Chapters of 1217, 1219, 1223 and 1224[34] the friars slept on straw mats out in the open as a sign of the poverty which they vowed. Francis was upset when the people of Assisi built a building for the friars for their meetings at the Portiuncula, the place where the Chapter(s) were held (II Celano, XXVII, 57; Legend of the Three Companions, IV: 11; Legend of Perugia,[35] 114; Bonaventure VII: 2).

EARLY YEARS

Francis was born in 1182. We are told that Pica, his mother, baptized him with the name "John" (II Celano, I, 3; Bonaventure I, 6; 3 Companions I, 2). The "John" anecdote is questionable. It bears nuances of biographers' attempting to make Francis the precursor of the coming of Christ. Hagiographers at the time did such intricate swan dives into fantasy in order to enhance their saints.

In order to complete the fantasy, one of the biographers wrote that Francis's father, Peter Bernardone, was off on a business trip to France when Francis was born. The trip went well, so he renamed his new-born son "Francis" after he returned (3 Companions, I, 2). This was probably also not true to fact. Francis was baptized with the name Francesco di Bernardone. Granted, Francesco was an odd name in Italy at the time, but it was true that his father was in love with France, where he bought many beautiful cloths to sell (Vauchez, 2112, 8). But Francis's father was probably not in France at the birthing. The birthing was too important an

---

[34] Some say only one assembly of the brothers was called "The Chapter of Mats". Others say it was a number of assemblies.

[35] Some say this is the work of Brother Leo. It does come from the 1300's. It was mutilated, and it bears indications of a copyist. Notebooks XI, XII, and XIII lack a beginning and a conclusion, X lacks a conclusion, LVIII is truncated, and notebook XV is completely missing. Also, there is clear indication that some of the original text is missing at the beginning, before notebook I. It might be better to call it the "Compilation of Perugia."

event for the Bernardone family for him to be gallivanting around Europe.

His father was a good man in spite of the biographers' attempts to make him an ogre. He merely took responsibility for raising his family and, in this case, his rebellious son, Francis. Francis, indeed, was a bundle to handle when he was a young man. Peter Bernardone should not be blamed for his actions. He was trying to do the best he could for the welfare of his son and the respect of the Bernardone family. Francis lived dangerously by doing many of the things that he did. He was not a normal young man of his age, as we will see. In fact, his actions were similar to a modern day son who runs off to join a cult. It is time to take Peter Bernardone out of the trash can in which the biographers placed him.

Francis probably received his early formal education, meager though it might have been, at the church school at San Giorgio in Assisi. How long he spent there is questionable. Questionable also is the education and abilities of his teachers. However, Francis was clearly an intelligent young man. While he might not have been a master of the Latin language, he was clearly knowledgeable in it. Furthermore, he showed great interest in the songs of the troubadours from southern France. He thus had to know the troubadour's Provencal tongue. These bards moved through Assisi singing their songs of the Holy Grail. In Francis's youth, Arthur, Queen Guinevere, and Merlin, the magician, were Hollywood for him. In addition, he was trained by his father, Peter Bernardone, on the ins and outs of running a business. In other words, Francis was undoubtedly more educated than the average young man of his age. He was clearly not an ignorant person. His writing ability was limited, but, even in his last days on earth, he showed that he could take a piece of paper and pen in hand and write a message.

Francis always was a courteous and refined young man (II

Celano I, 4; 3 Companions I.2; Bonaventure I, 1). At the same time, he was the gang leader of the youth of Assisi. He fit well into the local milieu as the young light and the "king of youth" in Assisi. He did, however, have a problem with his father, for he abundantly spent his father's money on the good things of the world (I Celano, I, 1-2; 3 Companions I, 3; Bonaventure I, 1).

But all was not rosy in Assisi, even though Francis would have liked it to be. The merchants and shopkeepers desired to form a commune type government under their own control. At the same time, the emperor, Henry VI, desired to take control of Assisi. Francis's father and the other shopkeepers resisted Henry VI's desires. Suddenly Henry VI died, just as he was ready to establish his authority there. The people of Assisi then stormed the citadel of the noblemen and drove them out. Many of these noblemen, about 20 families, went to the nearby city of Perugia to live. Among them, interestingly enough, was Clare's family. Clare was a close friend of Francis. She started the Poor Clare's, a woman's group of cloistered nuns (Vauchez, 2112, 11-12). Clare would eventually become St. Clare. But in Perugia, these Assisi noblemen stirred up the people of Perugia, who needed little persuasion to move against the uppity people of Assisi.

Pope Innocent III, then, thought that he could step in and, with the power of the papacy, fill the vacuum of leadership which he perceived in Assisi. He tried to take control of the town. When the town resisted even him, Pope Innocent III excommunicated the whole town.[36] Francis as a young man, suffered the wrath of the pope. He was excommunicated with the rest of the town, and he probably learned a life-long lesson about dealing with popes, especially Pope Innocent III.

Assisi was sitting in the middle of Italy, vulnerable on two

---

36 This shows how easily excommunications were distributed during the era of Innocent III. Certainly, this one was purely political.

fronts. The townspeople quickly built a wall around the town to protect themselves. Francis, who was 20 years old at the time, and his companions laid down their songs and partying and picked up weapons to fight a bloody war against the Perugians (II Celano, I, 4), and then, they thought, against anyone Pope Innocent III could recruit to move against them.

It was 1202. The world was smaller in those days. Soldiers did not go halfway around the world to fight a war. They only needed to go to San Giovanni bridge, just outside of town, down the road a ways. There the army of Perugia eagerly awaited them. Some of the Assisi youth were on horseback, with full armor and weapons in hand, as were some of the Perugians. Francis of Assisi was one of these armored warriors on horseback. His father was a wealthy merchant who could afford a horse and the equipment for war. Other young men, both citizens of Assisi and Perugia -- those who could not afford such luxuries -- walked to the battlefield, unarmored, wielding whatever weapons they could find. These foot soldiers from both cities, of course, were more vulnerable in the battle than those armored and on horseback. At any rate, the odds were against Assisi. Perugia was a much larger city.

Their citizens fought fierce wars against their neighboring cities and towns. The victors burned, plundered, and captured their foes. People thought it necessary. It was easy to see, was it not? Every city of Italy was a separate nation. Either their city or town destroyed the enemy or the enemy destroyed them (Englebert, 1965, 43-44) Not much has changed from then until today, except then it was city nation marching against neighboring city nations. Now it is one larger nation of the world marching against another larger nation.

Francis, we are told by the sources, fought bravely in the skirmish at San Giovanni bridge in November 1202, but the Assisi forces were grossly outnumbered by the larger city of Perugia.

Because he was on horseback, he undoubtedly killed some of the young foot soldiers of Perugia, the poorer soldiers from that city. This would have been a heavy load to carry for the rest of his life. Was this part of what he meant in his *Testament*[37] at the end of his life and in other places when he wrote, "The Lord led me to a life of penance. So I went to befriend the lepers"? Otherwise, what did the words "doing penance" -- words which he was constantly mentioning-- mean in the context of his life? It could have meant merely that Francis was doing penance for the free living that he did with his gang from Assisi. But we will never be sure, because the sources, and not even Francis's words tell us the particulars. One thing is sure. He fought bravely in the war, and it is difficult to understand how a person could not kill someone when he was fighting bravely, armored, from a horse, while many of the opponents were on foot. Furthermore, Francis knew what "doing penance" meant. It was reparation for sins committed.

If he had killed anyone, Francis would have felt it deeply. He certainly would have felt that he had to do penance for the rest of his life for doing such a thing. He would have felt that he had to do something drastic like be the friend of lepers in order to make amends.

Furthermore, his fighting in the war with Perugia could be the background for Francis becoming the man of peace. Of course, the sources were written by men who were submerged in war, for the world of the Christian crusades against the Muslims was a world

---

37   The *Testament* of Francis is one of the most important parts of his *Writings*. We do not know who was the first compiler of his writings, but all of the lives of Francis quote from it. The earliest compilation available to us is Assisi Codex, MS. 338, now in the municipal library of Assisi. The great Franciscan scholar, Cajetan Esser believes it was compiled in the middle of the 1200's. Others say the compilation was done in the early part of the 1300's. Within this Codex is the Second Rule of Francis (fol. 12r-15v); the Testament (fol. 16r-18r; the Admonitions (Fol 18r-23v; the Letters (fol. 23v-32v); Letter to All the Faithful, to a General Chapter and to All Clerics, and Salutation of All the Virtues (fol. 32v-33r); Canticle of Brother Sun (fol. 33r-34r; Office of the Passion (fol. 34v-42r; Religious Life in a Hermitage (fol. 43) and the dubious Paraphrase of the Lord's Prayer (fol. 34r-34v). Other Codices are available.

desensitized to the problems of war and killing. Francis, on the other hand, was a sensitive man, in tune with human suffering.

At any rate, Francis was captured, and he was held prisoner for one year in a dank prison in Perugia. After the harsh skirmish, it was no easy tow to be a prisoner of war. It made no difference whether the person was a captured soldier or a captured citizen of a devastated town, male or female. The poor souls were placed in dank, stinking cisterns or other unimaginable places without heat or other facilities. During celebrations of the victory and other festivals in conquering cities or towns, the citizens brought the prisoners out of their hovels and humiliated them in any way that they desired. For example, to the delight of the conquering citizenry, captured soldiers in some Italian cities were made to spend the celebration day residing on all fours in pig pens while the citizenry laughed and threw garbage at them, or they made them move around a ring on all fours behind donkeys that were brought in for the celebration. Many other humiliations, which only the human imagination can conjure up, were imposed on the captives. In Forli, a city approximately a hundred miles directly north of Assisi on the road to Milan, the citizenry shod their hereditary enemies like mules to torture, mutilate, and humiliate them (Englebert, 1965, 44).

Although he kept up his spirits, as well as the spirits of the other prisoners, prison life was not easy on Francis. He had lived a pampered life until then. A full year of captivity under such conditions was a big chunk out of his life -- he only lived to the age of 45. He was released in November, 1203, because he grew ill in prison -- he was probably ransomed by his father (Englebert, 59, 424-425).[38]

---

[38] The great Franciscan scholar, Fortini, denies that Francis returned in November, 1202. A temporary truce was made between Assisi and Perugia in August, 1205. It was probably then that he returned home. The war between the two cities actually lasted until 1210.

When Francis was released from the prison in Perugia, he was a broken, sickly, young man. He spent many days in bed nursed by Pica, his mother, and then he was finally able to limp around in the fields on a cane. He learned to appreciate the birds, the butterflies, and the poppies that grew wild in the spring. After all he had been through, he became more sensitive to creation, something he appreciated for the rest of his life. All of nature began to open to him. During these days, he also became more sensitive to the poor and needy (I Celano, II, 3; II Celano, , II, 5; Bonaventure, I, 1).

CONVERSION

Going on a crusade remained in Francis mind. Pope Innocent III was trying to get rid of the remnants of Emperor Henry VI from cities in Apulia in southern Italy, and he was recruiting young men from everywhere. He promised them the same benefits that he gave the crusaders, which included "absolution" or complete forgiveness for killing people. Francis again donned his armor and mounted his horse to go on this military mission. When he reached the first town south of Assisi, Spoleto, he again grew ill, and then he had a dream. "'God said to him in the dream, "Francis, who can do more for you, a lord or his servant...." When Francis answered, "A lord could do more," he received the reply, "Then why are you abandoning the Lord to devote yourself to a servant."[39] Francis then said, "What will you have me do?" The Lord then said, "Go back to your own town, and I will let you know.'"

Dreams, ecstasies, and later, speaking crucifixes -- what we would call extraordinary phenomenon -- were not extraordinary

---

[39] When Francis went to see Pope Innocent a few years later in 1209, he probably did not tell the pope that he had a dream which said that he -- Innocent III -- was only a servant, not the lord, and that the pope did not speak for God. Francis always tried to avoid such controversies.

to people of Francis time. They were true spiritual phenomenon. Francis and others of his age expected such things to happen. Such experiences were doors to the human spirit through which the Spirit of God spoke to these human souls. The dreams were such a door to Francis's inner spirit. Francis then went back to Assisi overjoyed. He then expected God to provide for him: he increasingly relied on God to show him the future" (I Celano, II, 5; II Celano, II, 6; Bonaventure I, 3).

Francis, then, went frequently with a friend of his from Assisi to a grotto. The friend waited outside while Francis went in to pray. Francis became enflamed with a new ardor, the sources say. The companion said later that "one person seemed to have entered the grotto, and another came out" (I Celano, III, 6; See also II Celano, II, 6; Bonaventure I, 4).

The sources state that one day Francis was praying before a crucifix in a crumbled, fallen down church of San Damiano. The image on the crucifix in the church called Francis by name and said to him: "Francis, go, repair my house, which, as you see, is falling completely into ruin" (II Celano, VI, 10; Bonaventure, II, 1; Sacrum Commercium, 8-9[40]). Mistaking the message, he immediately set out to repair that church, which, after working hard, he actually accomplished (II Celano, VI, 11). Historians believe that he then repaired two or three other fallen down, poor churches in the area, including the future base of the Franciscan Order, the Portiuncula (Bonaventure, II:1).

But, as he was building, Francis gradually realized that building

---

40 The *Sacrum Commercium* is an allegorical work of early Franciscan origin. It is a classic of religious oratory. Six of the thirteen existing codices assign the year 1227 as the year of its composition. That is one year after Francis died. No evidence exists, either internal or external, to choose any other date. Outside of Francis's own writings, it is probably the earliest Franciscan document that we have. The author remains a mystery, but the style is much like Thomas of Celano's other works. Note one passage in particular, *Sacrum Commercium, 9* :"Francis asked: 'Tell me, where does Lady Poverty dwell...?" And the response is given "...we have often seen her pass by, for many have sought her, but often she returned alone and naked, adorned with no jewels, unescorted by any companions, clothed in no garments."

crumbled down churches by the wayside was not the object of his inspiration. Jesus was telling him that the whole Church was in shambles. Francis gradually got the message clear and straight, and he set out to reform the whole Church of Jesus Christ, which was truly and thoroughly devastated.

The message received at San Damiano clarified every step of Francis's life. It was then that his main purpose became to become like Jesus – to imitate him as closely as he could. He was no longer interested in special perks. He was not interested in an involved and intricate way of life for himself. He was interested only in emptying himself for the sake of Jesus Christ. In this he stood out in the Church in his age as someone different, and eventually as someone special. Little speaks of him in relation to the religious figures and groups of the eleventh and twelfth centuries: "The friars in a sense combined the successful ways of their forerunners into a coherent and workable spiritual program" (Little 1978:146).

But his real conversion, we are told in his *Testament*, came when he was able to look at the lepers. From then on, the lepers were always there, and Francis would show them "mercy." He saw in them a reflection of his own sinful soul. He ate with them, prepared food for them, and washed them. "Mercy" was a word taken from the other poverty movements of the time. These other groups had stepped in to care for these and other poor human beings (Vauchez, 2112, 23).

Peter Bernardone, Francis's father, was embarrassed by all this "nonsense," and he took Francis before the bishop, the only proper court to hear the case because Francis was insisting on clerical status. Francis stood before his father and everyone else and took off all his clothes. As he stood there naked, he gave his clothes back to his father and he said, " I no longer have a father, Peter Bernardone, but only a Father Who is in heaven." The bishop told his servant to give Francis a tunic to cover himself, and Francis walked off in that cloak. He was on his way to a new life, not knowing its content. The emptiness and loss inside him quickly filled with joy. But Francis felt the loss of his family. They had given him shelter and love since his birth. And he felt deeply the curses of his father whenever they met.

That night he was attacked by robbers. Because they found nothing on him to steal, they threw him into the deep snow in a ditch (I Celano, IV, 15-16; II Celano, VII 12; Bonaventure II, 4-5). But Francis did not care, he was on his way to imitate Jesus and to repair his Church. The Church was pompous, but Francis was persuasive, even with these pompous men. He learned much from the poverty movements that were condemned by the Church before him, and he was intent not to fall into the problems that waylaid them. Young men quickly came to join his movement. In 1209, he and his first twelve recruits went to see Innocent III and, surprisingly, got his new Franciscan life approved. Francis's gift of persuasion won the day.

Francis had intelligence and practicality. In order to exist, He knew that he had to live this poor Gospel life within the Church. Time and time again he told his friars to be obedient to the clergy, the bishop and the pope. His order, he knew from history, simply could not exist in his age unless it did so. He settled that issue first, then he was able to go on to essential matters. Such obedience won the approval of Innocent III and the other Popes who came later in Francis's life. He wrote in his Rule of 1223: "The Rule and life of the Friars Minor is this, namely, to observe the Holy Gospel of our Lord Jesus Christ by living in obedience, without property, and in chastity. Brother Francis promises obedience and reverence to his holiness Pope Honorius [the present Pope] and his lawfully elected successors to the Church of Rome. The other friars are bound to obey Brother Francis and his successors." (Francis, *Rule of 1223*, chapter I) Francis was not going to get himself in the position of opposing the only haven available to him. That would consume his energy and the whole pattern of his life. He had other work to do.

Francis was a genius in avoiding arguments. He never allowed himself to be concerned with questions of doctrine. The doctrines he held were a given for him – he found them all in the Gospels, especially in the Sermon on the Mount. If there was anything more, others could be concerned about those issues. Francis followed the Spirit throughout his life, and he systematically and carefully avoided polemics of any kind -- with Church people, with the crusaders, with the Sultan, or with anyone else. He showed positive regard for every person he met, and he knew his Gospel message. If anything was needed, the Gospel and the Sermon on the Mount would give him the answer.

For Francis, faith was a spiritual reality which began with a change of heart and developed into a heart consecrated to the poor Jesus who he now found in poor people whom he met in the world. He was a humble man, looking up to every beggar and every leper he met. He did not treat them differently than he treated kings and Popes. For Francis, neither monarch nor dignitary was any better than the poorest leper or beggar. Francis noted in his Testament:

> This is how God inspired me, Brother Francis, to embark upon a life of penance. When I was in sin, the sight of lepers nauseated me; but then God himself led me into their company, and I had pity on them. When I had once become acquainted with them, what had previously nauseated me became a source of spiritual and physical consolation for me. After that I did not wait long before I left

the world [his former life of killing others in war and frolicking in the world]. (Francis, *Testament*)

His main stress was on the Beatitudes and the Sermon on the Mount:

> And this is my advice, my counsel, and my earnest plea to my friars in our Lord Jesus Christ that, when they travel about in the world, they should not be quarrelsome or take part in disputes with words or criticize others; but they should be gentle, peaceful, and unassuming, courteous and humble, speaking respectfully to everyone, as is expected of them.... Whatever house they enter, they should first say, "Peace to this house..." (Francis, *Rule of 1223*, chapter 3).

In his Testament Francis wrote that the Lord revealed the greeting that he should give everyone: "The Lord give you his peace!" It was all he could give, and he gave it to the leper, the Sultan, his own brothers, and every other person. His prayer and his brilliant, practical mind, could not come up with anything better to say to anyone. He went on continuing with the theme of the Beatitudes: "With all my heart, I beg the friars in our Lord Jesus Christ to be on their guard against pride, boasting, envy and greed, against the cares and anxieties of this world, against detraction and complaining (Francis, *Rule of 1223*, chapter 10). Then he concluded: "And so, firmly established in the Catholic faith, we may live always according to the poverty, and the humility, and the Gospel of our Lord Jesus Christ, as we have solemnly promised" (Francis, *Rule of 1223*, chapter 12).

With a thorough Jesus thrust, a constant obedience to the Church, which insured his existence, and an absolute avoidance of polemics, Francis saw himself through the maze set by the Church for its poverty movements. He survived where others did not, and his spiritual genius made it happen.

THE LEPERS AND THE SULTAN

Many stories exist about St. Francis in the sources. But we will here stress the most important ones. The most important visits Francis made in his peace mission were to three very different types of people, the lepers, the Christian armies besieging Damietta, and the Sultan. The lepers, Francis gradually came to love and serve. They were Christ's poor in this world. He spent many hours and many days with them, and they loved him and appreciated him.

Francis himself was received well by the knights besieging Damietta, but his message was not. (II Celano, IV, 30) Francis had come to them with a message of peace, and that message was ridiculed. In Francis's presence the army went to battle despite Francis's warning that the battle would end in disaster. Francis, Celano wrote, "forbade the war and the reason for it" (II Celano, IV, 30). The crusade, in fact, did end in disaster as Francis foretold.

So Francis journeyed next to the Sultan's camp with the same message of peace. Most biographers of Francis are quick to say that Francis went to the Sultan during the fifth crusade in order to convert him to Christianity (Bonaventure, IX, 7-9; II Celano, IX, 8; Fioretti, 24), and/or to seek martyrdom (Bonaventure, IX, 7-9; II Celano IX, 7; Fioretti, 24[41]). But peace between Muslims and Christians was clearly the main thrust of his journey in 1219.[42]

---

41 The *Fioretti* was written by an Italian Franciscan who lived a hundred or so years after Francis died.
42 Vauchez seems to believe that Francis went to the Sultan to convert him. This is unlikely. Francis was always the man of peace. He undoubtedly went to Damietta and the Sultan to be a peacemaker -- peace was his mission to them.

As we have said, Francis wrote in his Testament "God revealed a form of greeting, telling me that we should say, 'God give you peace.'" For Francis the greeting was more than words spoken into the wind. Francis learned the greeting from the Beatitudes: "'Blessed are the peacemakers, for they shall be called the children of God' (Mt. 5:9). They are truly peacemakers who are able to preserve their peace of mind and heart for love of our Lord Jesus Christ, despite all that they suffer in this world (Francis, Admonitions, XV). Francis was grounded in peace.

Francis went to the Sultan as a listener as well as a speaker for peace. The exchange between the two men from two different cultures was deep and penetrating. Clearly, neither took a superior position. Clearly Francis was changed after he returned. We will give ample proof of that. We have reason to believe that so was the Sultan.

Martyrdom was not his intent, even though Francis knew he risked martyrdom by going to the Sultan's camp. He was willing to take that risk. "No matter where they are," he wrote in "The Rule of 1221" "the friars must always remember that they have given themselves up completely and handed over their whole selves to our Lord Jesus Christ, and so they should be prepared to expose themselves to every enemy visible and invisible, for love of him..." (Francis, Rule of 1221).

And any thought of converting the Sultan was ridiculous. Francis was smarter than to think such a thought. He said in "The Rule of 1221," Chapter 16, regarding missionaries among the Saracens and other unbelievers: "Our Lord told his apostles: 'Behold, I am sending you forth like sheep in the midst of wolves. Be therefore wise as serpents and guileless as doves' (Mt. 10:16) (Francis, "Rule of 1221"). And that is what Francis was when he entered the Sultan's camp: he approached the Sultan wisely and guilelessly. If missionaries to the Muslims should see that they can preach the Gospel of Jesus, they should do so, but if not, they should carry themselves as decent Christians, not quarreling with others but loving everyone as God's children (Francis, Rule of 1221).

It is also not true that Francis refused all the Sultan's gifts. Celano is clearly wrong (I Celano, 57). As a gift, he received from the Sultan an ivory ram horn that could be used to call people to prayer. The horn is preserved under the Basilica of St. Francis[43] next to the letter to Brother Leo, which we will speak about in a few paragraphs.

Francis had to stay a number of days, perhaps weeks, in the Sultan's camp -- more than the couple days that Salvatorelli indicated (Salvatorelli, 1928, 238). This is a reasonable assumption because Francis was obviously deeply impressed with the Sultan and the Muslim way of life. This was true in spite of the fact that he left his growing group of brothers behind, a group that sorely needed him in this period of growth. Francis had to believe that he could bring back to them something special, something that they needed. Nonetheless, his journey did cause him to return with fatigue and illness (Salvatorelli, 1928, 238).

After Francis came back from visiting the Sultan in 1219, he showed the Muslim influence on the latter part of his life in his "Letter to the Rulers of the People," written in 1220 or somewhat later.[44] He was obviously inspired by the *adhan*, the five times a day the Muslims turned to Mecca to pray. In this letter, he was not content to simply admire what the Muslims did. He wanted to bring the practice back to Christianity. Of course, Francis and his friars were no strangers to periodic prayer. But what was impressive

---

43 I was privileged to be permitted to see it.
44 The only copy of this letter in existence is the one Fr. Luke Wadding (1588-1657), an Irish Franciscan and historian, transcribed into Francis's collection of writings. But it is universally accepted as a true writing of Francis. The head of the Franciscans, Francis Gonzaga (1579-1587) said that the head of the Franciscans at an early period, John Parenti (1227-1232) brought it to Spain. Wadding translated it from the Spanish copy.

to him was the universality and public nature of the Muslim prayer. Every Muslim prayed at certain periods of the day. Not only was the practice essentially good, he felt, but it had the potential of linking Christianity with the Muslim community. It had a potential for promoting peace between Muslims and Christians: "...See to it that God is held in great reverence among your subjects," he told his friars and the clergy of his age, "every evening, at a signal given by a herald or in some other way, praise and thanks should be given to the Lord God almighty by all the people...." And again in the "Letter to All Superiors of the Friars Minor,"[45] he wrote"... When you are preaching, too, tell the people about the glory that is due Him, so that at every hour and when the bells are rung, praise and thanks may be offered to almighty God by everyone all over the world..." (Francis, Letter to All Superiors of the Friars Minor).

Also, there exists further evidence that the Sultan influenced Francis's spirituality. Somewhat later, Francis experienced an unusual spiritual experience when he was visiting Mount LaVerna, a large hill in a wooded area north of Assisi and east of Florence. Tradition states that he received the stigmata there, the wounds of the crucified Jesus on his hands, feet, and side. After this experience, Francis asked Brother Leo, one of his first companions, to bring him a pen and a piece of parchment so he could write out a prayer for him. He actually wrote two prayers, one on each side of the parchment, and some sketching on one side. After he wrote them, he gave them to Brother Leo and he told him to keep the prayers on his person as a remembrance of him. Brother Leo did just that.[46] The piece of parchment is preserved, now, under the Basilica of St. Francis in Assisi.

---

45 This work cannot be precisely dated, but obviously was written later in Francis's life. Wadding translated it from the Spanish version, the only copy he knew existed. Another version, from the 14th century, was edited by Paul Sabatier.

46 Not everyone is permitted to see the parchment because of maintenance and security reasons. The prayer itself is easier to read, but because Leo carried it on his person, the other side is smudged and blurry. The parchment I saw was the size of a small paperback book.

THE CONSUMING FORCE

The prayer Francis penned on one side is clearly legible. It closely resembles the Muslim prayer called the *Salat*, which is a meditation on the ninety-nine most beautiful names of God. Muslims pray it using a set of prayer beads. These ninety-nine names come from descriptions of God in the Qur'an: the Compassionate, the Merciful. the Sovereign, the Holy, the Peaceful, the Mighty, the Forgiver, the Generous. Francis did not mention all ninety-nine attributes of God, probably because he was running out of parchment space. He also added the Trinity to the prayer something a Muslim would not do, but it gave the prayer a Christian tone, something Francis, of course, wanted to do. Francis's prayer goes as follows:

You are holy, Lord, the only God, and your deeds are wonderful.
You are strong,
You are great,
You are the Most High,
You are almighty.
You, holy Father, are King of heaven and earth.
You are three and One, Lord God, all good.
You are good, all good, supreme good, Lord God, living and true.
You are love,
You are wisdom.
You are humility,
You are endurance.
You are rest,
You are peace.
You are joy and gladness.
You are justice and moderation.
You are all our riches, and you suffice for us.
You are beauty.

You are gentleness.
You are our protector,
You are our guardian and defender.
You are our haven and our hope.
You are our faith, our great consolation.
You are our eternal life, great and wonderful Lord, God almighty,
Merciful Saviour.

After writing the prayer, he turned it over and wrote the blessing for Brother Leo from the Book of Numbers 6: 24-26:

God bless you and keep you.
May God smile on you, and be merciful to you.
May God turn his face to you and give you peace.
May God bless you Brother Leo.

On the second side, Francis also drew the head of a man at the bottom of the parchment, as if the figure were lying down flat on the ground and looking straight up. And then he drew the letter *tau* rising from the figure's mouth. The *tau* was Francis's signature. He also wrote additional words and a sketch which appears on both sides of the vertical lines of the *tau*.

The meaning of the words vary according to whether the T sound is included. The phrase can be viewed as *fleo*, "I weep" or "*fleo te*" I weep for you. Some now unintelligible sketchings exist behind these images. Heavy on symbolism and light on explanation, the parchment, which was indeed kept on Brother Leo's person the rest of his life, became worn. Some say it was Francis's attempt to ease Brother Leo's sufferings by blessing him and drawing his picture or that of Jesus with a crown of thorns. But the man I saw in the picture clearly had a three-tiered turban on his head. The man, then, would be the Sultan Malik al-Kamil or a generalized Muslim figure.

Now, certainly, all this is not completely definitive. Francis was no artist, and Leo carried the parchment around on his person for many years, thus obscuring the image. But the person on the etching made by Francis looked more like a person with a three-tiered turban than a person with a crown of thorns, or a person with hair on his head, or more unlikely, a person with a bald head.

There are a couple of possible explanations for the etching, especially in light of Francis's secrecy about the matter. Other explanations have been given in the past. But two are possible and one of those two are more likely. Possibly Francis merely simply wished to share an intimate greeting with a dear friend -- a greeting which gave his friend an insight into his true spirituality. But even more probable is the second -- Francis knew that his new knowledge, gained from his relationship with the Muslim world, which he had learned to love, would be devastating to his new Franciscan community. Francis knew what had happened to the Humiliati, the Waldensians, and the people from the ancient Christian community in the Alps when they took positions contrary to the Papal mind. Now, the Sultan, an enemy of the Pope, had a great impact on Francis's spirituality. Francis felt it was of paramount importance that he keep this relationship with the Sultan and the Muslim community a secret. He was aware that the Pope, his brothers, and the Christian world would never understand the impact that the Sultan had on him. Nonetheless, Brother Leo would understand. So he did tell him about it.

Francis did not publicly reveal the full story of the communications he received on Mount La Verna. Nor did he ever explain to the public the letter that he secretly gave to Leo.

That day through the rest of his life, Francis was often found weeping. He was torn in two, and the early sources did not know why. Was it because Christianity and the Muslim community were so divided? Was it because he saw his brotherhood degenerating as it increased in numbers? Was it because of his own former sins? Or was it because he knew that he could not do more to perform his main mission -- to keep the church from falling into ruin? Probably it was all of the above.

Not much is necessary for a summary of the life of this great man. One point can be highlighted. After his conversion Francis was Jesus-driven. To the best of his ability, he never missed greeting any person he met along the path of his life. He attempted to greet and meet everyone, and everyone he met walked away in the glow of his simple presence.

FRANCISCAN GROWTH

Francis of Assisi died in 1226. He was made a saint by Pope Gregory IX, the former Cardinal Hugolino, two years later in 1228. He had always spoken to his friars about obedience to the Pope. Obedience to the Pope kept them in existence to our own day. Now that obedience became a weakness of the Order.

By 1250, approximately 30,000 Franciscans walked the earth. The group of twelve that started the Order in 1209, indeed Francis himself, could not have anticipated or understood such growth.

Naturally the members of the Franciscan community took on many various functions. The Order of Francis of Assisi became one gigantic administrative problem. Preachers found that people needed pastoral care, so they wanted to become pastors of parishes. University masters had a flood of young Franciscans entering their universities, but bishops were hesitant to allow them a foothold in any city, university cities included. Papal support was needed and was granted.

The growing community needed papal support to do any church work, and Popes were usually generous in giving that support. But Popes demanded a payback as friars became teachers in the universities, pastors, bishops and even cardinals.

Just where would Francis, if he were alive, have put his foot down and said "no!" to a pope. He certainly would have done so when the pope placed the burden of inquisitorial tasks on the Franciscan Order. According to his manner, he would have gone to the pope in a humble and personal manner, and then he would have talked the pope out of the necessity of performing these tasks. He would not have allowed the inquisition to touch his brotherhood.

Indeed, only a few years after the death and canonization of Francis, Gregory IX pressed the Franciscan Order into service as inquisitors. "It was the will of the pope," said the Franciscan administrators at the time, and Francis told them in his rule that they should always obey the pope. Consequently, the Franciscans entered the inquisitorial hell. Neither the friars who were called on to become inquisitors, nor their administrators had the spiritual acumen or the persuasive abilities of Francis. Francis had wished "peace" to everyone, and he encouraged his brothers to wish everyone the same. The willingness of his community to allow some to join the band of inquisitors undoubtedly made Francis's ears curl in his grave. The new positions gave the *Ordo fratrum minorum (the Order of little brothers)* power over others, something Francis did not desire. In fact, some of the Franciscan inquisitors relished the position, thinking that they were doing the Church a great service, but this did not justify what they were doing.

All in all, it is a standard Thomistic principle that the corruption of the best is the worst. The principle certainly holds true in the Franciscan movement during the Hugolino/Gregory IX papacy down through a number of other popes when Franciscan inquisitors became comfortable with their vocations. A tiny glitch existed in Francis's armor -- for indeed he did insist that "a true Franciscan always obeys the pope" -- which ended with Franciscans torturing men, women and children, and burning them at the stake.

The inquisitorial Franciscans did their work in Southern France, in Italy, and in Spain. The most infamous act of the Franciscan inquisitors that comes to our knowledge happened in 1426. The Franciscan inquisitors laid waste to the people of 31 villages in order to weed out a supposedly heretical group called the Fraticelli.

The Fraticelli were a group who continued in the footsteps of Angelo Clareno after his death. Angelo Clareno joined the Franciscans somewhere around 1280. He was convinced that the Franciscans were not living according to the will of Francis. Therefore, he and his followers lived a simple, poor religious life, often a hermit's life, as "spiritual Franciscans." Some of the Fraticelli were even married people or single people living in the world. They were all considered "heretics" at the time, and the brunt of the inquisition laid heavily not only on them, but on the men, women and children who lived around them.

Chapter 10

THOMAS AQUINAS, THE ANGELIC DOCTOR

In the University of Paris at the end of the 13th century, Thomas Aquinas brightened the skies of the church with intelligence greater than many who came before him. He was exalted by Popes, who sometimes made him a super saint, and by his avid followers, the "Thomists," some of whom imbibed his writings without any consideration of his historical context.

In response to many who were trying to use their own knowledge to dig into God's life, Thomas clearly said that knowledge of God is always problematic: we are never able to grasp what he is, but only what he is not. The words we use about him are also limited and problematic.[47]

He was eclectic, drawing heavily on the philosophy of Aristotle, and to a lesser degree Plato and the early fathers of the church. He seldom ever stood alone, but he was a genius at uniting the thought of others into an integral whole.

Although some Thomists might be surprised by the fact, he never taught anything but biblical theology in the universities of Europe. He never taught systematic theology nor philosophy, but he knew the scriptures cover to cover. Nonetheless, he was deficient in the knowledge of the Greek and Hebrew languages.

---

[47] Here Kenan B. Osborne quotes Rega Wood, "Individual Forms: Richard Rufus and John Duns Scotus," in Honnefelder, Wood, and Dreyer, *John Duns Scotus: Metaphysics and Ethics*, 271.

He was daring in his acceptance of pagan insights, even fawning in following Aristotle's philosophy. But he stood apart from Aristotle in faith-oriented issues and ethics, and his political/social works were exulted, even angelic, but certainly impractical in his age or ours.

So Thomas's academic resume was very good, but not flawless. If he would have never written his *Summa Theologiae* or his *Summa contra Gentiles,* he would have never been showered with the supreme accolades that he received. For the most part, his proofs for the existence of God are highly academic, and his just war theories are as dangerous as placing a loaded shotgun in a playroom filled with four year old boys.

BASIC ORIENTATION

According to James A. Weisheipl, O.P., from the Pontifical Institute of Mediaeval Studies in Toronto, Thomas learned Aristotle from adapted and corrected translations of two Muslim scholars, works which gradually worked their way into the West around the year 1217 in the translated works of Michael Scot, a writer and translator in Frederick II's court. (Weisheipl, 1983, 15). His schoolmasters, including Albert the Great, taught him the ins and outs of Aristotle's thought.

Thomas espoused Aristotle in dangerous times: the Crusaders were plundering the East, and public sentiments in the West toward anything Eastern was at a low ebb (See Lamb, 1966, 3). Thomas had to walk carefully with his Aristotelian baggage in a church that was thoroughly politically-oriented toward war and inquisition. For his part, he was strongly opposed to a political church and a political papacy (Thomas Aquinas, *Scriptum super Sententias II, dist. 44*). In his *Scriptum super Sententias,* Thomas stated that the pope is spiritual head of the church, nothing more and nothing less. All the pope's political and worldly accretions were what Thomas called "historical accidents, and they must be considered that, and nothing more" (Weisheipl, 1983, 8).

One of the reasons for Thomas's refusal to accept any position which involved him in politics or other temporal dealings was the fact that he was a solitary man. He neither accepted the position of abbot of Monte Casino, nor the archbishopric of Naples. When asked about being a cardinal, he said in effect, "Fine, but do not expect me to leave my friary just because I am wearing a cardinal's hat." He was simply an enclosed person. He wanted nothing to do with any social life. Nonetheless, political business and worldly accretions were the complete focus of Pope Innocent IV and ecclesiastics of Thomas's time. Thomas was intellectualizing and the world was moving on without him. This apparently was fine with him, with the popes, with the superiors in his Order, and with many around him who stood with the Pope in his wars and in his inquisitions.

At the same time, Thomas produced a social philosophy that was brilliant beyond compare, academically speaking, but impractical in the world in which we live. It was never recognized nor put into practice. But he did utilize Aristotle to make the literal interpretation of scripture more palatable in an age that was engrossed in Augustine's spiritual interpretations.

Knowing his noble background, Thomas could stand with a few others in the academic world around him who showed zest for novelty in an age that was suspicious of any new thought. He was a traditional Nicene, and noticeably, at appropriate times, when the eyes of suspicious clergy turned his way, he made it a point to become strongly and imminently Catholic in accord with the thinking of the church of his time. In this he was not the "innocent, angelic doctor of the church," as many have called him, but a discerning, even, at times, wily one in the academic field. In this he played his own game of politics. He always stayed in touch with the direction the hierarchical winds of the Church were blowing, and he knew, at any given point of time, just how far those winds would allow him to lean over the cliff to pick up other bits of knowledge and insight from non-Christian sources.

His works were not accepted by some at the time. At the same time, they would help fill an academic gap between East and West at a crucial time in history. With Thomas and his intellectual cohorts, East and West were united in common efforts of philosophy. Thomas found unity in thought with the East's great scholars and thinkers.

At first, Thomas, with others in his academic community, was attacked by many in the West. Sanctions were placed on his works by some bishops in his age. In the long run of history, though, his acceptance by the church was overwhelming.

PROBLEM WITH THE THOMISTS

The greatest weakness of Thomas's works down the ages was mainly not his problem, but the problem of other church scholars and churchmen who read Thomas without taking into consideration the age in which he lived. As James A. Weisheipl says: ideas must be considered in the context of the age in which they are developed (Weisheipl, 1983, 1)."Thomas's followers," not Thomas, was the main reason for the decline of academic Thomism in our own age (Weisheipl, 1983, 1). Thomas's followers ran with Thomas's ideas, which are stark, rigid, and sometimes arbitrary if not considered in the light that careful historians can place on them. Thomas was an intelligent man. He knew that time would bring in new ideas from new perspectives, just as he joined forces with ideas that preceded him. But many of his followers saw him as the final stage of all philosophy and theology.

Thomas was, for the most part, just doing the humble, but significant job he set out to do. Utilizing Aristotle as his basis, he recorded his own thoughts and his works from the perspective of his own age. He also left leeway in his works for future advancements.

Much later, church scholars and hierarchical supporters placed him on a pedestal that no philosopher or theologian should be placed, and they held in suspicion any other philosopher or theologian who said or wrote anything that did not agree with Thomistic views. The 19th and 20th century was especially noted for making Thomas the greatest philosopher and theologian that has ever come upon this earth. In the 19th and 20th century, official church theology and even philosophy became "Thomism." Works by writers with opposing opinions filled the locked sections of the libraries of Catholic universities and seminaries. Theologians and philosophers with varying, solid opinions were ridiculed and demoted.

LIFE AND LATER INFLUENCES

There is no documentary evidence on the day or even the year of Thomas's birth. Leonard E. Boyle and James A. Weisheipl both say 1224 or 1225 (Boyle, 1982, 2; Weisheipl, 1983, 351), which is two or three years after the death of St. Dominic, and a year or two before the death of Francis of Assisi. Others say 1227. Others say other various dates. Birth dates were not generally noticed in Thomas's age.

Thomas was born at the Aquino castle of Roccasecca, over 125 miles southeast of Rome, to a wealthy, influential family. His father was Lord Landulph d'Aquino (Tugwell, 1988, 201), and his mother was Donna Theodora d'Aquino. Thomas's father was judge for the district around Naples (Tugwell, 1988, 201).

Thomas's birth to influential nobility is significant because authorities had to think twice before attacking him. This, together with his own ability to discern the direction of church politics at any given moment, gave him leeway to maneuver when other innovators were squelched by the hierarchy.

Early in Thomas's life, a traumatic, tragic incident occurred which influenced his whole emotional life. Lightning struck one of the castle towers in which he lived, killing his little sister and some horses that the family owned. Thomas and his nurse were unharmed. From that time to the end of his life, Thomas had an intense fear of lightning storms (Weisheipl, 1983, 9-10).

Being the youngest of a large, noble family, inheritance became an Aquino family problem. Therefore, Thomas's parents always intended that he join religious life. It was his destiny. This was not unusual at the time among the youngest in noble families. If the youngest man became a religious, it lessened the inheritance burdens.(Tugwell, 1988, 202). A document dated May 3, 1231 stated, that in payment for Thomas's acceptance into the monastery school, Landulph, Thomas's father, gave funds to repair 2 mills on Monte Casino property, the profit from which was to fund a yearly grand banquet for the monks (Weisheipl, 1983, 11). Thomas began his education at the age of five at the Benedictine monastery of Monte Casino (Feser, 2009, 3).

What was unusual about his movement to Monte Casino was that a distant relative of Thomas, Landulph Sinibaldi, was abbot of Monte Casino (Weisheipl, 1983, 12). Did the two Landulph's and Theodora, Thomas's mother, connive to groom Thomas to become abbot of Monte Casino? Some think so, and it seems highly likely (Feser, 2009, 3; Tugwell, 1988, 202)). Thomas remained at Monte Casino, but only as a student, from 1231-1239.

In 1239, Monte Casino fell victim to the continual hostilities between Emperor Frederick II and Pope Gregory IX. Frederick was excommunicated. He then made Monte Casino his personal fortress. More and more monks were expelled to make room for Frederick II's military until only eight monks remained at the monastery. It was certainly not a good environment to educate any young person. Thomas moved home to Roccasecca during the spring and summer of 1239.

At the age of about 19 or 20, Thomas studied at the *studium generale* in Naples. He studied there from the years 1239-1244 (Tugwell, 1988, 202-203). Here Thomas first studied Aristotle. During those years he also got to learn about the Dominican Order. In April, 1244, despite great opposition from his family, who preferred that he join the Benedictines and become abbot of Monte Casino, Thomas became a member of the Dominican Order (Weisheipl, 1983, 27).

He did so against his parent's wishes. Therefore, his brother, Rinaldo, and soldiers of Frederick II kidnapped him. They brought him back to Aquino and held him prisoner for a year and a half, from 1244 to 1245. At one point, Rinaldo, his brother, played a practical joke on Thomas. He sent a scantily clothed young woman into his bedroom to lure him into sexual acts. Thomas violently resisted the advances of the woman.

In time, his mother relented. She sent Thomas off to the Dominicans with her blessings (Weisheipl, 1983, 32, 35).

Thomas was then sent by the Dominicans to the University of Paris where he met the great German scholar, Albert the Great (1200-1280). Albert spiked his interest in the works of Aristotle (384 BC-322 BC). Albert, we are told, purged Aristotelian philosophy from many of the errors still found in it (Garrigou-Lagrange, 1943, 4).

QUIRKS OF PERSONALITY

Looking at Thomas, we neither see an ascetic nor a handsome man. He was obese, tall and robust. (Tugwell, 1988, 259) He was not interested in special food, but he liked food in general. He was not keen on fasting.

Also, Thomas was not a vibrant person. He had a withdrawn personality throughout his life. He floundered in conversation and was characteristically silent when the gives and takes of conversation was expected. If he was lured into the parlor, he would escape as soon as possible. He was not good at small talk and he had little sense of humor (Tugwell, 1988, 261). He was unsocial, and his favorite recreation was walking around the cloister alone. This flaw in his personality even bordered on autism. Certainly, Thomas was eccentric. He kept to his own thoughts and insights to the point that he was embarrassingly unaware of the world around him. He made strange outbursts in public because of new insights he perceived with his thoughts. His mind would regularly drift away into some other world of his own thinking (Tugwell, 1988, 262).

One of his most obvious character traits was his distractedness with the regular events of life. He neither noticed the food that was in front of him nor did he notice when his plate was taken away. In conversation, he would suddenly not be present to the others, but he would be thinking of something else. He also made rude statements to and about others without realizing that he was hurting them. He was so clumsy and uncommunicative that other students at the university labeled him "the dumb ox." A staunch supporter of Thomas, Edward Feser, speaks of what he calls "a famous story" about him:

> ...while at dinner with King Louis IX of France he [Thomas] got thinking about the Manichaean

heresy, struck the table exclaiming "That settles the Manichees!" and called for his secretary to take down the argument that had just occurred to him. Suddenly realizing where he was, Aquinas apologized and explained to the other startled guests that he thought he was alone in his room (Feser, 2009, 6).

This great theologian, known for his logic, was not above utilizing negative rhetoric similar to that of earlier Roman scholars. In treating the wickedness of men, he wrote about Arius in the following terms: "Such were the teaching of that most wicked Arius whose abdomen burst asunder [at his death]" (Thomas Aquinas, *Commentary on Ephesians,* 4, 5). It was a poor attempt to link Arius with Judas who, according to Acts 1:18, died in a similar way. But Luke, in Acts, mentions the event concerning Judas as an unfortunate event which he was bewailing. Thomas used it as an instrument to try to show wickedness in Arius who died in a similar unfortunate manner. Using the unfortunate manner of a person's death to emphasize a person's supposed wickedness is and was gross.

Arius's death was an unfortunate incident which happened by accident or illness. It had nothing to do with any supposed wickedness in the man. It could have happened to the most virtuous person. Thomas should have known better.

CONTINUED ACADEMIC WORK

In 1248, Thomas followed Albert to Cologne. Albert admired Thomas, and he predicted that the bellowing of this ox would someday be heard throughout the whole world (Dyson, 2002, xvii). Yet, differences in Thomas and Albert are apparent. Albert was fascinated by the make-up and complexity of things; Thomas was profoundly uninterested in Albert's fascination with the complexity of the world around him. He was interested rather in ideas and truths. The relationship between Albert and Thomas was an interesting one. They approached reality from completely different positions.

Thomas was ordained a priest in 1251. Not much was mentioned concerning his ordination to the priesthood. The fact was taken as a matter of course in someone from a noble family.

In 1256, after Thomas wrote his thesis, *Scripta super libros sententiarum,* a treatise on the *Sentences* of Peter Lombard, he received his master's degree, his license to teach. He was immediately named regent master in the school of theology at Paris and began writing his *Summa contra Gentiles* (Weisheipl, 1983, 351). He then studied and taught at Paris, Naples, and Orvieto, where he completed this *Summa*. He was then assigned to Rome and Viterbo (Feser, 2009, 3). There he began to write his *Summa Theologiae* in 1266 (Weisheipl, 1983, 352). He was again assigned to Paris from 1269-1272 (Weisheipl, 1983, 352). He became regent in Naples in the fall of 1272 (Weisheipl, 1983, 352).

His productivity during only 49 years of life was admirable. During a final stint at the University of Paris between 1269 and 1272, he also wrote commentaries on Aristotle's works, works on *Ethics,* and his brilliant work on *Politics*. He dictated most of his works to secretaries given to him by the Dominican Order (Dyson, 2002, xvii). He would go from one room to another telling them what to write. He also wrote works on prayer, contemplation and religious life.

He worked on the *Summa Theologiae* from 1266 until ill health, a possible stroke waylaid him during the celebration of Mass. This illness forced him to stop writing in 1273. A stroke is probably more likely than "the mystical experience" that Feser and others say he had during Mass (See Feser, 2009, 6). A mystical experience does not leave one unable to continue ones work. A stroke, while it might come with a pseudo-spiritual high, might do just that. The *Summa* was unfinished at his death.

After he became ill while saying Mass, Thomas remained weak and unable to work for the rest of his life. In this light, his famous excuse for not working, spoken to a friend, Reginald of Peperno, seems lame: "Reginald, I cannot. After what I have seen, everything that I have written seems like straw." This is rather the statement of a very sick man who was just unable to do the thinking that he had once done.

Nonetheless, Thomas did manage to at least start his journey to the Second Council of Lyons in February of 1274. On the way, he hit his head on a low hanging tree branch (Feser, 2009, 6). Perhaps it was another stroke. He then became obviously and mortally ill, and he was taken to be cared for by Cistercian monks in the vicinity until his death. He died on March 7, 1274 (Dyson, 2002, xvii).

DOMINICAN AND PAPAL ACCLAMATION

In 1309, Thomism was made the official doctrine of the Dominican Order. This was followed by even stronger mandates in 1313, 1314, and 1315. No Dominican could be sent to the University of Paris without studying Thomas for at least three years (Tugwell, 1988, 243).

Pope John XXII made Thomas a saint of the church in 1323 in a ceremony celebrated by Pope John XXII (Dyson, 2002, xvii). There was one problem before he was made a saint. One cardinal of the church said that after his death he performed no miracles. "No miracles?" said another, as he picked up the *Summa's,* "Here are the miracles!" Later he was made a doctor of the church -- some say, the greatest doctor of them all.

Post-canonization papal accolades already began with Innocent VI (1352-1362) who in a Sermon on St. Thomas said:

> His teachings stand above that of others, the canons [of Canon Law] excepted. They possess such an elegance of phraseology, a manner of statement, and a soundness in their propositions, that those who hold to them are never found swerving from the path of truth, and he who dares to assail them will always be suspected of error (*Acta Innocentis VI;* Garrigou-Lagrange, 1943, 5).

So Thomas's fame as a scholar grew. His *Summa Theologiae* was placed on the altar next to the bible at the Council of Trent in 1545-1563. It was a symbolic action, showing the mind-set of the bishops attending the Council. His fame reached its zenith when Pope Leo XIII wrote his encyclical, *Aeterni patris,* on August 4, 1879. Leo XIII was consumed by concerns regarding the threat of liberalism. Leo XIII wrote in his encyclical:

> Let carefully chosen teachers strive to implant the doctrine of Thomas Aquinas in the minds of students, and set forth clearly his soundness and excellence over others. Let the universities ... illustrate and defend this doctrine, and use it for the refutation of prevailing errors (*Acta Leonis XIII,* 283-5, Rome, 1879).

This encyclical set the tone for teaching only Thomistic

philosophy and theology in Catholic universities and seminaries preparing candidates for the priesthood. Let us be fair. Leo XIII's words did not make Thomas the official theologian and philosopher of the church, but it might just as well have done so. That is exactly what happened. Thomas was thereafter the official Church theologian and philosopher until the 1960's and even beyond.

Not to be outdone, other Popes followed in rapid succession, adorning Thomas's works with praise. The world was becoming smaller with easier communication, and seminaries preparing students for the priesthood and Catholic Universities took the papal words to heart. Benedict XV in 1918 said: "Mental philosophy and theology must be taught according to the method, teaching and principles of the Angelic Doctor, to which professors should religiously adhere" (Garrigou-Lagrange, 1943, 8). Students thus became smothered in Thomism. Pius XII, in his *discourse to seminarians*, June 24, 1939, wrote: "By recommending the teaching of St. Thomas, eagerness for the discovery of truth, and the diffusion of it is not suppressed, but rather is stimulated and provided with a safe guide" (*Acta Apostolicae Sedis,* 31, 1939, p. 247).

In following the mandates of the Popes, students in Catholic universities and candidates for the priesthood in the 20th century suspected or knew that there were other views of philosophical and theological reality written which would fit better into the thinking of the times. There was, for example, Husserl (1859-1938), Heidegger (1889-1976), Merleau-Ponty (d. 1961), and Michel Foucault (1926-1984) whose works could be explored. But Thomism was taught to them. The hierarchy hindered the philosophic minds of teachers and students alike. Some wished to see progression of thought and wished to study and develop other insights into reality. Kenan B. Osborne is one of those who hinted that freedom to explore other views would benefit the church. He states in *Christian Sacraments in a Postmodern World*:

> In some areas of the Roman Catholic Church, contemporary philosophy as well as modern philosophy have been judged to be counter-productive. Those who take this negative stance generally operate from a standpoint that there is and has been within Roman Catholic circles a *philosophia perennis,* an eternal philosophy (Osborne, 1999, 16).

In his encyclical, *Fides et Ratio,* John Paul II, even though he was inclined to be a Thomist, finally opened the doors and windows when he stated, "the Church has no philosophy of her own nor does she canonize any one particular philosophy in preference to others" (John Paul II, *Fides et Ratio,* 49).

METAPHYSICS

Thomas utilized Aristotelian philosophy almost exclusively in his own philosophical writings. He did so because he was convinced that Aristotle had thought through basic natural reality as far as any person could. For the most part, what Aristotle lacked, as far as Thomas could see, was all the reality that Jesus and divine revelation added to the Aristotelian view of reality. Thomas's genius was in creating a synthesis for his age between the reasoning of the pagan Aristotle and revelation.

In spite of the fact that the Church has spent years heaping praise on his works, Thomas is over-rated as an original philosopher. Most of Thomas's philosophy was written by Aristotle 1800 years before Thomas came on the scene. While Thomas documented this in his work, many of his followers did not. Many teachers of "Thomistic" philosophy in the 20th century, and even earlier, rarely mention Aristotle. Teachers gave students the impression that Thomas was the genius behind the discovery of "potency and act," "matter and form," etc.[48]

Furthermore, when we consider Thomas's writings on Aristotle, which was translated by Avicenna (980-1037) and Averroes (1126-96), two Arabs, Thomas had to tread lightly because Aristotle was a pagan and Avicenna and Averroes were Muslims. Popes were engaged in Crusades against Arabs, and they were heavily pursuing inquisitions elsewhere, so they were sensitive to anything pagan. Dyson tells of some of the problems Thomas and his fellow students faced: "Repeated ecclesiastical censures culminated in 1270, when thirteen Aristotelian propositions were condemned as heretical by Bishop Etienne Tempier of Paris, a condemnation repeated and extended in 1277 [two years after Thomas's death]. Almost the whole of Thomas's professional life was therefore passed in an atmosphere of hostility towards Aristotle" (Dyson, 2002, xxiii-xxiv). Thomas was certainly no wimp in facing such opposition, but he felt that he had to be wily in order to see himself through it.

At the same time, Thomas was drenched in the Church's teaching. It was difficult for him personally to tear himself away from any Catholic belief. Philosophical and theological concepts that were taught to him from childhood were difficult to lay aside.

Theological leeway was non-existent. All theologians were wise and prudent to write here and there in their works that everyone from maidservant to kings must be subservient to the Pope. Thomas did so on spiritual matters. If he said the right things about the Pope enough times, he knew that he could avoid disaster. In his own age, Thomas was only prudently.

---

48 Some teachers of philosophy, of course, recognized this as a problem. Kenan B. Osborne (Osborne, 1999, 2) mentions "Aristotle and Thomas Aquinas" together.

Now let us look at Aristotle, the person Thomas so emulated. Where did Aristotle fit in the history of philosophy? Many years ago, pre-Aristotle, a Greek philosopher named Parmenides (c515-450 BC) denied that change was possible. If some being were to change, he stated, another would have to change it. The thing that changed would have to be something other than being, and that would be non-being, nothing. Well, we all know that nothing does not exist and cannot change anything. So, he said, change was impossible.

Parmenides was not able to get past his own thinking on the matter. He certainly must have known that he was wrong, but he could not see how he was wrong. True philosopher that he was, he followed his thought through to the end, and, of course, he ended in a dead end.

I am sitting here looking out the window at spring blossoming before me. The trees have turned green and the poppies are ready to burst forth. The deer are moving past my window with new-born fawns. Spring birds are moving in to feed. Change is obviously possible, but how can a person describe it. Thomas went back to Aristotle to find the answer for what is happening before my eyes.

- He said, quoting Aristotle's thought on the matter: "A being is sometimes only potentially a being, or as Aristotle would say, the being is "in potency," and sometimes that being is "in act." Aristotle states, in time, everything is in potency before it is in act. But what is in potency cannot raise its own self to be in act; it must be raised to act by something else that is already in act" (*Summa contra Gentiles*, I. 16. 3).
- Potency is controlled. It is inherent in the actual being as a possibility. The leaves on the trees have the potency

to grow only on the trees. Thomas said, also quoting the thought of Aristotle: "Further, just as each thing comes to actuality naturally, so it is naturally receptive to become something else which is within it to become" (*Summa contra Gentiles*, I. 16. 6). This piece of rubber which I call a rubber band could become a bouncing rubber ball.

- Furthermore, something in act must make the potency actual. For example, the sap must come up the trees and generate the leaves. Thomas said, again quoting the thought of Aristotle: "We see something in the world emerging from potency to act [like the spring-time]. Now, it cannot pick itself up by its own boot straps to move from potency to act, since potency cannot move on its own accord. Some prior being is therefore needed to draw it forth from potency to act. [like the sap] (*Summa contra Gentiles*, I. 16. 7)."
- There is no such thing as pure potency.
- God is pure act.

All of this is written in *Summa contra Gentiles*, I. 16, and many Thomistic teachers taught it as Thomas's without reference to Aristotle, even though it is completely and totally Aristotle's thought. Thomas merely copied it from the ancient philosopher. Credit should not be given to anyone for the thinking and work of another. Michelangelo should not be credited with stating that the earth goes around the sun. That is in fact Galileo's discovery. Everyone who has an education knows that Galileo should be credited with the discovery. Neither does Thomas Aquinas, or more precisely, the avid followers of Thomas, have any right to Aristotle's metaphysics regarding potency and act. Thomas was not the one who discovered the idea. Thomas recognized this better than anyone.

Thomistic writers and teachers right up to this very day often slip into a "second-handed plagiarism" when writing and teaching not only potency and act, but also matter and form, the 4 causes, material, formal, efficient and final, or the essence of the five natural proofs for the existence of God.

MATTER AND FORM AND THE 4 CAUSES

Everything that we know in this world is composed of matter and form, Aristotle first told us, and then Thomas repeated it. Matter and form make a thing capable of change. For example, we might melt the rubber down and make it into a ball. We can imagine the rubber band having no actuality at all, but we can only do so with our mind. This would be prime matter. Thomas stated:

> ...we should note that every generation from matter to form is from something to something. That from which generation arises is matter; that to which it proceeds is form (Thomas Aquinas, *De Principiis Naturae 2.15*).

That brings us headlong into the four causes, something Thomas was completely committed as metaphysical principles (Thomas Aquinas, *De Principiis Naturae, 3.20*). However, Aristotle said it first:

- the material cause -- that underlying material which make up the rubber band.
- the formal cause -- the structure exhibited by the rubber band.
- the efficient cause -- that which actualizes the rubber band and brings it into being.
- the final cause -- the goal or purpose of the rubber band

Now today in modern philosophical studies,, the return to the subject, the "I", or the efficient cause is stressed much more than the other causes.

The final cause of all things is, according to Aristotle, the great *Unmoved Mover, God*. Yet for Thomas and for Aristotle, the Unmoved Mover is somewhat a misnomer, because for them God is very active. He does not sit around collecting cobwebs. If he did, he would, all and all, be an unattractive God. Thomas was intimately involved with Aristotle's thought patterns.

ETHICS

Thomas's ethics is not a minor part of his total work. 1004 articles, approximately one third of the *Summa Theologiae* is devoted to the virtues and material related to the virtues (Pinsent, 2012, 2).

For the most part, Thomas departed from Aristotle when he developed his ethics. The parting was purposeful. Thomas felt that he had to part with his great teacher in order to be an authentic Catholic. He thus turned away from the *Nicomachaean Ethics* of Aristotle and returned to a more traditional, Catholic ethics. Thomas's largest account of the virtues is found in *Summa Theologiae*, IIaIIae, 1-170. Thomas dedicated himself to faith, hope and love. Even the accounts of prudence, justice, courage, and temperance, which did have counterparts in Aristotle's work, were structured differently than Aristotle structured them. Aquinas incorporated under these four virtues other virtues which Christian tradition exalts. For Thomas, patience was part of courage, and humility was part of temperance (Pinsent, 2012, 3).

Thomas called the Aristotelian virtues *acquired* virtues. Christian virtues were for him virtues *infused by God*. So Thomas's virtues, together with the gifts, the beatitudes, and the fruits that go along with them, were completely different from Aristotle's acquired virtues. For Thomas, Christian virtues have a specific goal -- that of eternal life. (Thomas Aquinas, *Quaestiones Disputatae de Virtutibus in Communi,* q.1, a.10) Augustine can be seen peeking around the corner as an influence on Thomas here. The hierarchy of the church of the time was a church that relied heavily on Augustine.

Then Thomas makes a defining statement on the infused virtues:

> It is clear that love, insofar as it orders man to his last end, is the principle of all good works to which the human person is ordained. Also, with love, all the moral virtues which perfect a man are infused into the person. So all infused moral virtues do not only have a connection with prudence, but also love. And whoever dismisses love through mortal sin, dismisses all the other infused moral virtues (Thomas Aquinas, *Summa Theologica,* IaIIae, q.65, a.3).

This, of course, was traditional Catholic thought. All goodness is destroyed in a person who commits one act against love -- infused faith, hope, the infused cardinal virtues of prudence, justice, courage, patience, temperance, asceticism, humility, magnanimity, the cognitive gifts of knowledge, wisdom, and counsel the appetitive gifts of courage, fear and piety, the beatitudes of poor in spirit, meekness, hungering and thirsting for justice, mercy, pure of heart, peacemaker, the fruits of long-suffering, love, joy, peace, goodness, benignity, patience, faith, modesty, continency and chastity -- all are gone.

There is something controlling about Thomas's ethics which

we must dig deeper to see. It is the church officials once more manifesting their appearance.

- First, what was a mortal sin which some poor peasant might commit? Certainly they included some of the things that Jesus also mentioned: murder, serious lying, infidelity, etc., which seriously were rejections of love. Some other sins mentioned were frightfully minute. Some of them were only laws of the Churchmen's own making to protect themselves and keep their flock in line. They included dubious heresies of many shapes and types, schisms of sometimes little merit, some of them insignificant, and excommunications. Some excommunications were hurled indiscriminately by threatened and angry popes and churchmen. They hurled them, sometimes in anger, at non-conforming people. The "guilty parties" did not always substantially reject love. As an example, Francis of Assisi, as a citizen of Assisi, was excommunicated by an angry Pope as a young man. Certainly, these were not rejections of love. An emperor might have been able to discern that a pope or bishop was just being stubborn, and the emperor committed no mortal sin, but could a poor peasant be as discerning?
- Second, the priest was in control. He had to give the poor peasant absolution for his or her mortal sin. So the priest was not only in control of giving absolution, but he was also in command of the infused virtues which were supposedly lost even in the bogus mortal sins.
- The priest was also in control of the gates of heaven. Upon receiving absolution, all the infused virtues came flowing back to the poor peasant. And, if he died, he could go to heaven. The priest was in control. He was a powerful man.

SACRAMENTS

Thomas taught that there were seven sacraments and seven sacraments alone. He generally entered notes of flexibility into his writings, and he does so here, allowing for following ages to change or clarify his words (Chauvet, 2001, xiv). But some Thomists turned the seven sacraments into stone.

Thomas, Luther, Calvin, and the bishops at the Council of Trent did not have at their fingertips the knowledge of history that we have today. We cannot give these men's writings on the sacraments the same normative weight which they once enjoyed within their respective churches. This is true regarding Thomas's dealing with the sacraments. (See Osborne, 1999, 6-8)

First of all, Jesus, in his life-time, did not institute seven sacraments. Because of new scholarship on the matter, the decisions of the Council of Trent must be re-thought. I say this in spite of the "let them be anathema" that the council hurled at those of us who say otherwise. Baptism and Eucharist can truly be traced back to Jesus, approximately in the year 27 CE. But the sacrament of reconciliation came into vogue around 150 CE. Holy orders, along with the anointing of the sick followed around 200 CE. Marriage was not made a sacrament until as early as 400 CE, maybe even as late as 1150 CE. Confirmation was separated from baptism as a separate rite around 1000 CE. (Osborne, 1999, 6-8)

Not that they are not all true sacraments. The seven sacraments are truly sacraments of God, but also, all of creation is charged with sacramentality for us to experience. (Osborne, 1999, 52) Each becomes a true sacrament for us when we are open in faith to the fullness which it holds. I speak of the beautiful sunrise and sunset, the trees in the fall, new life in the spring, a new friendship gained, a well-deserved vacation, the birth of a child, release from pain, a home to live in, food to give us strength, the harvest in the fall, the void caused by sickness in ourselves or in a loved one, or even the void caused by the death of one dear to us. All these can be sacraments and many more, but we must be open to them in faith.

Thomas followed Augustine in calling a sacrament "a sign of a sacred reality." However, in his writings, and exemplified especially and more rigidly, in the catechism of 1947 by the Thomists, the sacraments are proposed to us not so much as revelatory signs of God -- which they truly are --as they are foisted upon us as the operative means of salvation. Thomas goes on to favor what he calls an *ex opere operato* (roughly translated, "sacraments work simply because the rites happen") approach to the sacraments. This approach is clearly magic, and it has side issues, because it gives immense power to priests and bishops. In Thomas's writings, the priests and bishops are less pastors and ministers of the Gospel as they are sacred intermediaries (*sacerdos*) consecrated to build a bridge (*ponti-fex*) between God and humanity. In this, Thomas erred.

On top of this, the whole operation of administering sacraments is clearly individualistic in Thomas's writings. Thomas is speaking of a "Jesus and me" spirituality. Where is the community of faith in his writings? It is clearly missing. Sacraments are delivered by the priest or bishop for the benefit of the individual's spiritual life, as Augustine said, so he or she can get into heaven. The only required activity of the individual is an essential one -- that he or she place no obstacle (mortal sin, including church sanctions, forbidding access to the sacraments) in the way so the sacrament can "work." Later, Thomas tried to modify all this a bit so that sacraments for him were not machines. But the bulk of his work still stands as written.

For Thomas, God saves human beings through the sacraments. Seven sacraments are human beings' primary means of salvation. Turn it around and human beings can make every day a spiritual offering presented for the glory of God through the sacraments (Chauvet, 2001, xvi). For Thomas, this is individual spirituality from beginning to end. The sacraments bring us to the apex of spirituality (Chauvet, 2001, xvii).

This is not the way it happens. Take the last supper as an example of what Jesus was trying to signify by sacrament. At the last supper we do not have a group of holy people. All of the apostles who were there were weak; some would even soon betray Jesus. Only one, John, snuck around and showed up underneath the cross with some braver women followers. We can presume that some of these staunch women, maybe all of them, were present at the last supper. We are dealing with a community of faith who were more or less sinners, gathering with others who were definitely weak sinners for a meal with Jesus. Louis-Marie Chauvet, professor of sacramental theology at the *Institut Catholique* in Paris, a school that, in centuries past, was familiar to Thomas Aquinas, clarifies this for us:

> For Mass [Eucharist] is not meant to favor an intimate relation to God -- in that case it might be better to follow Mass on the television. It is a church of action. It is lived as a church, a church made up of men, women, and children who are sinners but who dare to acknowledge themselves as the "holy church" of God; a church made up of different members, often divided among themselves but, however, given to the world as "body of Christ"; a church made up of persons reluctant to commit themselves to conversion or mission but which dares to recognize itself in faith as the "temple of the Holy Spirit," the Spirit that renews

all things…. Here is both mystery and scandal….
(Chauvet, 2001, 38).

We know that we do not have a direct line to Christ. We know that we do not quite match up. But still… We are the faith community that continues onward. Everyone knows that she or he is not the most beautiful, the most intelligent, the strongest. Long ago, life inflicted this truth on each of us until down deep within us it has become a conviction. "But still…" (Chauvet, 2001, 39).

So what if we are not the most beautiful, the best, the most holy. We believe, and we do so in Jesus' community. Like the apostles of old, let us gather together in a faith community and recognize his presence among us -- even though he is not present physically, even though we are sinners. He has risen! He has truly risen! He still lives in our midst. Whether this leads us to eternal life or not, is not immediately the point. Probably it will -- Jesus said it will. But right now, the community of Christ and it's needs is the emphasis. We belong to Jesus' community, and we belong to the world with its needs.

It is the faith community that Thomas Aquinas forgot. It is the sign value of the water and wine made into his presence in the community that Thomas first recognized, then de-emphasized. It is the universal Christian sign of Baptism through which we enter into that community of Jesus.

5 NATURAL PROOFS FOR THE EXISTENCE OF GOD

Again, with help from Aristotle, Thomas did come up with the notion that the existence of God can be proven naturally in five different ways (Thomas Aquinas, *Summa Theologia, I.2.3)*: the proof from motion, the proof from the contingency of the world, the proof from causality, the proof from the grades of perfection, and the proof from finality. Thomas does not spend much time expounding on these proofs, but they are, nonetheless, the most famous proofs for the existence of God ever written. Their notoriety extends far and wide.

It might be unfair, in context, to emphasize these proofs as much as they have been emphasized. After all, one late afternoon just before Vespers, or just before lunch (who knows), Thomas dictated them and then left them, and went on to new thoughts the next day or that afternoon. Maybe we should not be too critical of such a fleeting action on Thomas's part. In defense of Thomas, the Thomists insist that Thomas enunciated the concepts of his 5 proofs throughout his *Summa's*. The truth of the matter is that Thomas was such a devoted disciple of Aristotle that he did constantly bring forth the Aristotelian concepts that supported the 5 natural proofs for the existence of God. However, it remains true that he only put together his 5 proofs for the existence of God one time in his writings.

- The first proof is the proof of Aristotle's Unmoved Mover. Thomas states that everything that moves in the universe is moved by another. But somewhere down the line, there must exist someone who moves other things, but is not moved by anything else. This is the Unmoved Mover, or God. Edward Feser has spent over 15 pages (Feser, 2009, 65-81) defending Thomas and Aristotle's first proof from motion or change.
- The second proof is Aristotle's proof from causality. We have a beautiful world in which we live. Something must have caused it, brought it into existence. For many ordinary persons, the proof from causality might be the most understandable and the most convincing of his arguments.

The burst into spring after a long winter is a proof of value for some. The fact that we exist here as intelligent beings on earth, beneath the sun, is another. There must, then, be a God who made it. No profound further explanation is needed. This proof is truly sacramental in nature. It belongs to what Thomas would call infused. It thereby is not natural at all, but it belongs to the God-given, revealed portion of Thomas's theology.

- The third proof is the proof from contingency. What exists depends on something to hold it in existence. We do not hold ourselves or our world in existence. Therefore, a God must exist, holding everything in a beautiful order. This, too, takes Feser 10 pages (Feser, 2009, 90-99) to define, and a few people do understand it. It tends to be found only in a philosopher's bag of groceries.
- The proof of the grades of perfection is simply baffling to the natural human being striving to eke out a living on this planet. There exists many created things around us, and they have varying degrees of perfection. Some humans are more virtuous than others. Plants are higher than rocks in perfection. Humans are more perfect than plants or animals which cannot think and will like humans can. Therefore, there must exist someone who is most perfect of all on the perfection scale, God. It takes 10 pages (Feser, 2009, 99-109) for Feser, who is usually an excellent explainer, to expound its meaning and debunk objections to it.
- Finally, the proof from finality (the teleological argument) states that all is made with an end in mind. If I make a tool case, it is to hold my tools and keep them safe; if we build a bridge, it is to travel from one side of the river to the other. If creation and human beings are made, they

must be made by God for his own reasons -- so we might enjoy life with Him in heaven. Therefore, a God must exist to do such planning. This is another proof that is confusing, and it presumes a lot. The human brain gets lost somewhere between the tool case, going over the bridge, and the God who must exist to make a plan to get us to heaven. It also takes Feser 11 pages to delineate (Feser, 2009). Some philosophers think it an excellent argument.

Thomas probably did not spend much time evaluating these proofs before enunciating them. He knew what Aristotle had said on the matter, and one day, for some reason, he decided to summarize those thoughts But since that time, Thomistic philosophers have cherished them: other philosophers, especially in our day, have trouble swallowing them , and common people have trouble comprehending them. James A. Weisheipl states his reason for the proofs' non-acceptance: "Whether any one of these proofs can convince a non-believer, an atheist, or a skeptic is another matter," he states, "for emotions easily get into the way of logic" (Weisheipl, 1983, 228). Emotions have nothing to do with many of the proofs' non-acceptance. The proofs are simply difficult to understand, highly intellectualized, and, for many, do not have within them the convincing power necessary to be accepted. Furthermore, one of the proofs is not a natural, philosophical proof at all, but it is theological and sacramental in nature.

Not that most of these philosophers and most of the people of the world do not believe in a God. They have their own reasons for doing so. Perhaps one of those reasons is one of those mentioned by Thomas, perhaps number 2, on causality. Perhaps they rely on revelation, the bible. Perhaps they have other reasons. Nonetheless, everyone, except the Thomists, have trouble with the bulk of his natural arguments, which means that they are not very good *natural* arguments to begin with. They are nonetheless, the arguments of a superior human mind, so we handle them with respect.

The impression given, as Bertrand Russell mentions, is that Thomas first believed in the existence of God from faith and revelation, and then he set out to prove it with his own mind. It was Thomas's way. If he found rational arguments which supported revelation, so much the better. If not, he fell back on revelation. This, Russell states, is not a legitimate philosophic procedure. A true philosopher, like Parmenides, goes wherever his own conclusions lead him no matter the consequences. Thomas was not being a good philosopher if he came up with his 5 proofs for God's existence because he knew God existed from revelation. Thomas was working as a theologian posing as a philosopher. So we handle Thomas's natural arguments for God's existence with mixed feelings. And we recognize that Bertrand Russell might have a point when he writes that Thomas was not on the level of the great philosophers, ancient or modern.

IMMORTALITY OF THE SOUL

The Aristotelian held that substance could only be known through its sensible manifestations. As Beryl Smalley said in *The Study of the Bible in the Middle Ages*:

> In adapting Aristotle to Christianity, St. Thomas united soul and body much more closely than the Augustinians had done. The soul is the form of the body, present in all its parts, acquiring knowledge through the senses, not through innate ideas. Its dependence on body ceases to be a penance or hard necessity, and becomes "proper" to it. Intelligence

and physical sensitiveness go together... (Smalley, 1952, 293).

At death, Thomas said, the soul is temporarily separated from the body. Thomas regarded that the human soul is immortal. However, when it leaves the body at death, it is an incomplete substance, a substance that longs to be united with a body (Thomas Aquinas, *Summa Theologia* I.75.2; *Quaestiones Disputatae de Animo*, 1). Thomas adds: the existence of the soul after death places it in a state where a person longs for the resurrection, when the soul is again united with the body. Nonetheless, Thomas said that the separated soul rejoices immediately in the joys of redemption. The essence of happiness in heaven consists in the vision of God, for which the soul does not need the body.

Elisabeth Kubler-Ross who has had much experience in dealing with the dying, and has written many books on the subject, adds a psychological proof based on her own observations. She writes that her experience of being with dying patients makes her convinced that there is an after-life, and that our inner conviction that we will not die is proof in itself that we will live on and that there is a God. She states: "I believe that the soul or the spirit continues to live, and it is conceivable that this is the reason why it is so difficult for us to conceive of our own death" (Kubler-Ross, 1974, 155). Now, if anyone is looking for a natural proof for an afterlife, here is one. In her works there is only one further explanation of this statement that I could find. It is in her book *Death: The Final Stage of Growth:* "Death is the final stage of growth in this life. There is no total death. Only the body dies. The self or spirit, or whatever you may wish to label it, is eternal. You may interpret this in any way that makes you comfortable" (Kubler-Ross, 1975, 166).

Some of us, of course, even though we understand her observation, will reject Kubler-Ross's statement on the immortality of the soul just as some of us reject the statement of Thomas Aquinas. In fact, leaving Thomas aside for a moment, let us go one further step and make a bold statement: some agnosticism and doubts about our immortality exist even in the most devote believer of faith and revelation among us.

THE LITERAL SENSE OF THE BIBLE

Almost 30% of Thomas's extant work is commentaries on scripture. (Kennedy, 1985, 3) This might be surprising to many scholars, because so little attention has been given to Thomas's scriptural analyses and commentaries. Thomas never taught anything but scripture. His *Summa Contra Gentiles* and *Summa Theologiae* were done on the side -- as serious hobbies.

Thomas did much to explain the why's and wherefore's for the necessity and the superiority of the literal sense of scripture. The spirit of the scripture is always expressed by the text itself, by its literal sense (Smalley, 1952, 293). Aristotle first stated, we cannot disembody a person to investigate the person's soul. Thomas took the same approach with scripture. We cannot understand the scripture by disembodying it, distinguishing its letter from its spirit (Smalley, 1952, 293).

Thomas defines the literal sense as that meaning which is signified by the words themselves. As he explains it, it becomes clear that the *verbum* that he speaks of is the inner word in the author's mind which can be spoken (*per voces*). (Kennedy, 1985, 7; 175).

Matthew L. Lamb goes too far when he credits Thomas alone for illuminating the literal sense for the church. He discredits all of the theologians who insisted on the literal sense in history preceding Thomas. Lamb wrote: "Yet none of the

Fathers who were to influence medieval exegesis declared the sufficiency of the literal sense; nor did any of the commentators or theologians prior to Thomas" (Lamb, 1966, 11)." As Robert George Kennedy in his doctoral dissertation states: "... Thomas' doctrine is shown ... not to be so original as has been previously thought" (Kennedy, 1985, prelude). Kennedy states that every major element of Thomas's thought on Scripture was taught by one of his predecessors (Kennedy, 1985, 6). One way of teaching, according to Thomas, is by example -- generally using the literal sense in writings and in homilies. Certainly we showed in volume one of this work that Marcion, back in the early part of the second century, insisted on using the literal sense. The second volume shows that so did John Chrysostom. Through a brief survey of the fourth and the beginning of the fifth century, Lamb, contradicts himself by mentioning that Clement of Alexandria and Origen "initiated a cycle of liberal and scientific studies to provide the Christian interpreter with an accurate grasp of the text and its historical meaning" (Lamb, 1966, 11).

Nonetheless, when Thomas discovered Aristotle, he was able to add an element concerning the literal sense that was not present in the world of biblical theology up to his day. Lamb makes Thomas's contribution clear. Before Thomas, under Augustinianism, the visible world and human history were symbols of spiritual realities to come, known only through illumination (Lamb, 1966, 6). Thomas's relationship with Aristotle showed him that the visible world and history take on their own value; they are not just symbols of a higher realm. Aristotle caused Thomas to see Scriptures as fresh and as vulnerable as he saw creation (Lamb, 1966, 6).

In the Augustinian world, there was little need to analyze the human and divine authors of scripture; there was little need to analyze how God and man could author the same books of scripture (Lamb, 1966, 6). Lamb continues brilliantly and simply:

- Athenagoras saw the human author as harp strings played by the Holy Spirit.
- Origen, when all was said and done, said that the bible had deep spiritual meaning. For him, to accept a literal meaning was to deny divine revelation.
- Even though St. Jerome was fond of portraying the human personalities of the prophets, he hemmed and hawed when he tried to explain how this harmonized with his idea that the prophets were the pen used by God.
- St. Gregory simply said that God was the author of the books of scripture.
- Augustine simply saw scriptures as a letter from heaven (Lamb, 1966, 8-9).

Thomas said that Scriptures aids us to return to God. God did not write the books, but God was, in Aristotelian terms, scripture's first mover, its first author. God disposed humans to write as they did. For Thomas, human beings wrote the books -- they are responsible for the contents. The human author is in no way superfluous. The literal sense of each one's writings was understood to be its content. Those trained in bible studies could now be confident that they were not being trained for anything but the literal understanding of the bible. Thomas said in his *Scriptum super Libros Sententiarum*, the *Sentences*, that it is through the literal sense alone that the truths of the faith are received (Kennedy, 1985, 108).

In Thomas's understanding of inspiration, man's apprehension of truth progressed through the Old Testament into the New

(Lamb, 1966, 9-10). The human authors gradually, one after the other, came to understand God's message more and more clearly. God, as first author, got his message through to humanity, but he did so by taking humanity's weaknesses into account. He did so slowly.

JUST WAR

Thomas was born more than a hundred years after the First Crusade burned Jews alive and massacred Muslims by the thousands when taking Jerusalem. The whole of the Crusade was hideous, inexcusable and useless. Furthermore, it is quite clear from Jesus' words that he would have not have had anything to do with any so-called just war, nor would he have let his followers have anything to do with it. Nonetheless, medieval Christians donned the cross, and warfare became a part of life.

In this they are no different than we are. We have not grown one inch from the medieval mentality. Only our weapons have increased in killing-power. We no longer throw spears at one another; we no longer use swords; we no longer throw catapults. Today, we use nuclear warheads, and we send them off in manless drones.

As we amass weapons for the next war, we do so at the expense of robbing the poor of their ability to lead decent lives; we do so at the expense of denying people the right to decent universal health care, and comfortable living in their old age. But, we do have power in abundance -- enough to blow the whole planet to kingdom come. Now our military is undoubtedly looking for the next nation or island where we have an excuse to test all this military apparatus. For we feel that we have to keep it all in good working order to defend our nation should it ever be attacked.

Thomas clearly drew from Augustine, or rather the thinking

of the Augustinian church hierarchy at his time, to answer the question of whether there can be a just war. He starts by saying that if the matter is analyzed superficially, war is an apparent sin from any Christian perspective. But he lacked the courage to take that stand on the matter. After this statement, he turns and says the opposite. He completely caves into the *mores* at the time and comes up with conditions for a just war.

- Sovereign authority must make the decision to go to war. Obviously, this means the Popes, bishops and kings of the time. It was a pat on the back for those who were fighting the crusade against the Muslims.
- It must be a "just war," whatever that means, but obviously it was the job of the Pope, bishops, or kings to decide the matter.
- There must be an intention to promote good, not evil. We have to ask ourselves "how is this possible. Somehow, "war" and "promoting good" are an oxymoron.
- War must be carefully regulated toward the goal of peace, with a love for one's enemies, attending to mercy, charity, and forgiveness. Here are other oxymorons.
- He insists that toleration for the Jews is necessary. Thank God, he said that.
- He insists that, in some circumstances, killing for the common good is an act of love toward an unwilling victim.

We are forced to think, "Thomas, you were a bright person. The brightest, perhaps, of your age. How could you fumble around with these empty words. If you would have argued so inanely when you were attending the University of Paris, other scholars would have ripped your arguments to shreds in debate."

Obviously, Thomas never was involved in war. But certainly

his brothers were. Thomas was not as innocent as he is made out to be by some. He was a wily man, who was able to determine with his mind just how far he could go. He went that far and no further. Thomas was appeasing the hierarchy and kings of his day. He was not about to get tied to a stake and burned. He was here being "the good boy," saying exactly what the hierarchy and kings wanted to hear.

POLITICAL/SOCIAL WRITINGS

One area in which Thomas was able to continuously show his own brilliance unencumbered by the theological, papal/bishop yokes about his neck, was his political/social writings. Utilizing Aristotle as his base, he advanced political theory over the prevalent Platonistic, Augustinian theories of the day. As Dyson states: "St. Thomas's remarks may be taken as a turning point in the history of political thought" (Dyson, 2002, xxv). This is not whittling Thomas down to slivers although Thomists might think so. It is saying much about the man, although it also shows him as naive according to present day thinking. His contribution to an exemplary society in his political writings is considerable.

Augustine had been a plague on politics:

> For St. Augustine ... earthly politics is on the whole a regrettable and squalid business. At best, it is a necessary evil. Political arrangements are inseparable from the sinful condition of fallen man. Government would not have come into existence at all had the Fall not occurred. It originates in human greed and in the desire which men have to dominate one another. Its redeeming feature is that it functions to limit and control man's destructive

impulses, to punish the sinful and to test the faith of the righteous. Earthly peace and justice are uneasy, transient and unstable. They are pale copies of the true peace and justice laid up in heaven, which will be realised only after the end of earthly history, when the City of God enters into its inheritance of eternal bliss (Dyson, 2002, xxiv).

A HUMANE, WELL-ORDERED WORLD

Thomas, on the other hand, taking Aristotle's lead, (Aristotle, *Ethics 1:7 1098a5)* finds no problem with a humane and well-ordered world. Well-being for humans as social, political beings on earth, with lives moving in a common good order toward heaven, he thought, was possible and desirable (*De Regimine principum*, I, 1). Not that a certain amount of privacy and self-sufficiency was not desirable and necessary. It was especially needed in the family for the natural activities of procreation, nourishment, recreation and discipline. But self-sufficiency must give way to communality in the sharing of trades and the forming of a city (Thomas Aquinas, *De Regimine*, I, 2). Therefore, in the same light, humans are bound to obey secular powers (Thomas Aquinas, *Summa Theologiae* IIaIIae 104, 6, *responsio*).

Thomas believed that a kingship is the most desired form of government, something that we might expect from a man with his noble heritage. After all, he belonged to a powerful and noble family whose life revolved around kings (See Thomas Aquinas, *De Regimine principum*, Preface *et. al.*). But the well-being of a community, no matter what form of government was governing a country, lay in the preservation of unity or peace (Thomas Aquinas, *De Regimine*, I, 3).

But then Thomas began to show a difference between his position and any other position on the matter. Regardless of the form of government that was established in a place, all citizens should have some share in the government. Such an arrangement would secure the peace of the people (*Summa Theologiae*, IaIIae 105.1, *responsio*).

PRIVATE PROPERTY

And then hidden in his writings we find blockbuster, revolutionary statements as Thomas dealt with private property. His writings were more in line with Jesus' life and teaching than others up to his age. They also differ from the thinking of our present day, although some primitive societies, including the Native Americans, had the same ideas as Thomas.

Thomas believed that property was given to us from nature, and must be managed responsibly. "The rich man is reproached for supposing that external things belong to him principally: that is, as though he had not received them from another: that is, from God" (IIaIIae 66 1 ad 2). As Aristotle said in *Politics* 1:3 (1256b7): "… the possession of external things is natural to man." Thomas agreed. But no one has the exclusive right to own property. Thomas made a distinction between *ownership* and *use*. We are certainly entitled to use as much property as we need to enable us to meet our earthly needs comfortably. Then, anything that is deemed excess property we owe as a moral duty to the poor.

This certainly differs from the general view of private property in Thomas's day up to our own day. No matter where humans received their property, goods, or their money, humans have considered it their very own possession. It might be that they received it by inheritance, by hard work, by financial decisions intelligently made, by manipulation of their money through the stock market, or by good luck in gambling. It makes no difference. For Thomas, that money or that property is allotted for the use of all of humanity. We do not own it. It lays at our door, it is true, but it is given for the benefit of all.

In the event of an emergency where help is needed immediately, Thomas makes his point clear:

> … For example, if a person is in immediate danger and no other help is available – – anyone can then lawfully supply his own need from the property of another by taking it either openly or in secret; nor, properly speaking, does this have the character of theft or robbery.….Properly speaking, to take and use another's property secretly in a case of extreme necessity does not have the character of theft, because that which someone takes in order to support his own life becomes his own by reason of that necessity (IIaIIae 66:7 *responsio* & ad 2).

Certain Native Americans have made the same wise statement. One of the best recent expositions of Thomas's principle is given in a book of fiction, George R. R. Martin's, *Game of Thrones: A Storm of Swords*. In it, Ygritte, a young spearwife, says simply, "And men can't own the land no more'n they can own the sea or the sky (Bantam Books, 2011, 559)."

What does this mean in practice? If we do not want our property to be taken by force from us by the poor and needy, it is our responsibility to use our money for the benefit of others. Otherwise, the poor have the right to take it from us. This information regarding Thomas Aquinas's thought has to make the hair stand up on the neck of the conservative rich who think Thomas

Aquinas is so great. He is clearly standing for the poor and the needy.

Certainly we would need to see that everyone's basic needs are taken care of. After all, we do not want people coming around and taking things from us because they are needy. This would make a more peaceful world as well. It would mean not marching around the world to fight wars, because, if we did, we would not have the resources to take care of everyone's basic needs. We would have to take care of the environment. We could go on and on. I am sure this is something the rich, intelligent Thomists either never find or ignore in Thomas's writings.

What Thomas plainly says about private property is bold. But it is more in touch with Jesus' teaching than many modern and ancient theories. "You, yourselves give them something to eat," Jesus said.

LAW

Law is, for Thomas, the rule and measure of reason. A relationship between the superior and inferior involves a picture in the mind of the superior of what the inferior should do or be (Thomas Aquinas, *Summa Theologiae*, IaIIae 91).

Natural law tells us to do good and avoid evil. It tells us to live at peace with our neighbors. We do not have to learn about these things or have them legislated for us. To all human beings, they stand to reason. We certainly know that we are to do good and avoid evil, but we do not necessarily know what is good or evil in some specific circumstances, nor do we know what to do with people who do evil. Because of this gap we have human laws.

Human laws can be changed or dispensed with from time to time in order to suit changing times or exceptional circumstances. If human laws should be unjust, they are not really laws at all, and we are not bound to obey them (*Summa Theologiae,* IaIIae 96 4 *responsio*). But if the consequences of disobedience should be worse than any good which disobedience might secure, we should obey the law (*Summa Theologiae, IaIIae* 96 4 *responsio*).

Eternal law is God's law, the law that is in God's mind. To it everything in the created universe is subject. It directs all the actions and motions of the universe.

The final kind of law is divine law. It is the law of revelation, made accessible to us from Scripture and the Church.

STATUS, WEALTH AND SAINTHOOD

Persons with wealthy families, regal pedigree or papal friends were the ones who were able to become saints of the church during the eleventh to the fourteenth century.

- Charlemagne (742-814), of all people to be made a saint, was a Roman Emperor (canonized a saint in 1165; then demoted to Blessed in the 18th century by Pope Benedict XIV);
- Edward the Confessor (1003-1066) was King of England (canonized a saint in 1161);
- Thomas a Becket (1118-1170) was Archbishop of Canterbury;
- Francis of Assisi was a very poor man of the people, but he was a close friend of his cardinal mentor, Cardinal Hugolino, who became Pope Gregory IX, and proclaimed Francis a saint on July 16, 1228, a year and 10 months after his death on October 3, 1226;
- Anthony of Padua (1195-1231) was born to a wealthy family in Lisbon, Portugal and was canonized only one year after his death in 1232;

- Louis IX (1214-1270) was the crusading King of France;
- Thomas Aquinas had an intense noble background. He was made a saint in 1323.

On the other hand, persons who were not connected, or obnoxious to Popes, hierarchy or kings, even though they were saintly and wise human beings, never made the hallowed list: Marcion, the Montanist women, Tertullian, and others.

The Pope and bishops were and continue to make saints of their own liking. If the bishops and pope had to chisel on the personalities of their saints a bit to make them into the persons that they wanted them to be, they were not above doing just that.

SUMMARY AND ANALYSIS

The writings of Thomas Aquinas became, like scripture, a closed canon. Like the closing of inspired scripture at the moment John finished the Book of Revelations, true theological and philosophical knowledge ended for many at the moment Thomas had his stroke and finished writing the *Summa Theologiae*.

This is pre-eminently not true. Philosophy and theology has continued onward, and those philosophers and theologians who were oppressed for differing with Thomas Aquinas are truly martyrs for pursuing further truth. Theology and philosophy must adapt to accommodate other intelligent thinkers. Thomas would have agreed that this is true.

Our impression of Thomas Aquinas is, then, mixed. In some ways, he has done a great service to humanity. In other ways he did not do the great things that some in recent years insist that he did. However, we must realize that he never intended to be the superman of thought that others have tried to make him.

Thomas has been overrated as a philosopher. The church has established him beyond criticism for the best part of a century, a position that he would agree was ridiculous. But he is no longer above criticism, so frank acknowledgment of his faults is now possible. Thomas would readily admit that he had faults. Some of his works were superficial. His literary style was often difficult: he got himself involved in elaborate and distracting side issues, interesting to him, but not to anyone else. His arguments were often clouded by subtle and trivial distinctions. He was, at times, intellectually dishonest because he was, in advance, committed to a closed system of religious and moral values that was highly judgmental, and he was intensely committed to supporting and confirming those beliefs and upholding those judgments. Undoubtedly, it was the only way Thomas could survive in his period of history.

All in all, in the final analysis, if Aristotle and faith are stricken from Thomas's philosophy, there is little left. We sit here with the *Summa's* in our hand and wonder, "Where is the philosophical beef?" Thomas Aquinas relied almost exclusively on Aristotle for his philosophy. When faith enters the picture, we speak about Thomas's theology.

His work on scripture, utilizing Aristotle as an aid, was significant. After all, whenever he taught in his lifetime, he taught only scripture. His work on the literal sense of scripture made the need for the literal sense more understandable.

In his work on the sacraments, Thomas firmly believed that only seven existed, and these worked *ex opere operato* to get as many of us as possible individually into heaven. Community sacramentality is clearly downplayed in his writings. This is an error of great magnitude which influenced the church throughout the ages.

In his theological works Thomas was heavy on dogma. It is understandable in his age, but it was even an aberration in his age.

It led to the inquisitions and the reformation. It is our duty to learn from the past. In our own age dogma must give way to community love and care in Jesus. Christian baptism is the element that all Christians hold in common: all Christian groups recognize the baptism of every other Christian group. (Smits, 2008, 1) The world needs Jesus too much for us to continue walking around as though our group is superior to your group. Today, any Christian walking around with his or her nose in the air as though he or she is superior to other Christians is hindering the growth of Christianity in the world. Jesus never took such a stance: he prayed for the unity of us all.

In his political work, Thomas was by far the ablest and most active of anyone in the Latin West in his day. Here he did excel, but this part of his excellence has been kept carefully hidden from us, and it never influenced the world. He helped to make normative political theory possible and reasonable according to the words of Jesus. At the same time, something would have to change in modern society to make his words acceptable in our world as it caters to the rich. It is the rich in spirit in our modern world who find his words impossible and unreasonable. The present world will have to turn upside down to make his thinking on the matter practical. Nonetheless, if we would follow Thomas's teachings on the matter, the world would be a better place for all. This and this alone would make Thomas Aquinas a great teacher of theology.

It is unfortunate that he could not take the stance of a brave man when it came to writing about war. He truly became weak-kneed on this issue, and his arguments were superficial and empty.

So, Thomas's writings are sometimes excellent, and at other times they are hard to digest. Most of the time, Aristotle is leaning over Thomas's broad shoulders, whispering in his ears. At other times Augustine is near at hand influencing him.

Finally, we get the impression that Thomas, as intellectual as he was, was not in touch with the world he lived in. Kings and popes were fighting. So-called heretics were burned at the stake. Meanwhile, Thomas was in a room forming theoretical concepts. For example, he might have done better to deal with the issues of the day than with the Manichaeans, who lived many years before him. Aristotle, also, thought many thoughts about reality rather than investigating them. For example, he was convinced that a larger stone would fall faster than a smaller one from some high place. This is totally not true. They both fall to the ground at the same rate of speed. Aristotle erred because he never investigated the matter, but he only thought about it. This also was Thomas's problem. He was a great thinker, but he did not often investigate his data.

Chapter 11

THE INQUISITIONS IN GENERAL

The inquisitions were initiated originally to protect a commendable human reality, truth. But often it was "true concepts" alone that they were talking about. They were not so much interested in true Christianity. They were not even interested in true humanity or correct living. After Justin Martyr coined the word "heresy," the church jumped on the word, for it fit nicely into its stringent but watered down version of Christianity. In a perversion of Jesus' message, the Church canonized its own version of truth, and in doing so, it condemned everyone who disagreed with them.

Thereafter, from their lofty, rich, even perverted perspectives, anything that sounded weird or looked weird from the viewpoint of these churchmen or emperors was suspect, possibly initiated by the devil. Popes, bishops, secular rulers and clerics emphatically canonized concepts that did not hinder their own lifestyles. In this way, they used the Church to extend their own means and purposes.

After all excuses are recorded and sifted through, the inquisitions became blatant power plays by Church people and political leaders. They proclaimed their own version of "the Christian light of truth," convicting others who did not conform to their version of Christianity.

Even in the first two centuries, certain Christians, Marcion and the Montanist women are good examples, were victims of inquisitions of a certain sort, but not one of the early fathers who called out "heretic!" was yet able or willing to become an inquisitor by vocation. In fact, in the early years up to Constantine, they often were the ones persecuted. After that, up to the year 430 C.E., they had to rely on secular authorities to do their persecuting for them.

From 597 C.E. to approximately 1022 C.E., a period of 435 years, the Church authorities did not kill anyone.[49] To gain some perspective, 435 years backward from our present date would take us to the 1570's C.E., the birth of Michelangelo. It is a long period of time.

After 1022, people, even saintly people, were formally tortured, humiliated, intimidated, and imprisoned by the inquisitions – all in the name of Jesus. Many who suffered were true martyrs to Jesus' message and Jesus' cause.

Some inquisition historians who lived and wrote in the period between the two world wars easily shook off the inquisitions as part of man's evolutionary process. It was a barbarian period in history, they wrote, that humanity had to go through and now have outgrown.[50]

Recent history has proven these men wrong. During the Second World War, six million Jews were mercilessly murdered. Official Church silence was noticeable. On top of that, as a continuation of the inquisitions, the recent "shock and awe" invasion of Iraq and Afghanistan with the imprisonments and tortures of El Qaida members and anyone who looked like an El Qaida member, reverberates even today around the globe. Again, official Church silence and the silence of most Christians

---

[49] R. I. Moore (*The Formation of a Persecuting Society: Authority and Deviance in Western Europe 950-1250* (Second Edition) Oxford, Blackwell, 2007) indicates that the Church went this long period of time without killing people.

[50] R. I. Moore (2007) cites Henry Charles Lea and J. B. Bury as holding such opinions.

is evident. All told, crass human activities and Church related silence have lain to rest the excuse of the "evolutionary theory" of the inquisitions.

Other historians take the clergy and the civil officials off the hook by saying that they were not free agents in the inquisitions. In true Augustinian fashion they say that it was sinful people who were its initiators. Sinful society forced the hands of the authorities of the Church. The clergy themselves were not prone to violence.[51]

The common citizenry did, at times play its part. "Kangaroo courts" and mob pressures certainly were part of the inquisitions. But the kangaroo courts and the mobs were mostly instigated by their clergy and political leaders. The common citizenry did not have the theological background or the political prowess to promote an inquisition. If the common citizenry had any fault in the matter it was that they caved into pressures of the powers of the day by either letting themselves be stirred to anger, or by sitting passively on their hands in their homes while, on their doorsteps, the clergy and politicians actively pursued the inquisitions.

The fact is, the clergy and civil authorities played the leading role in the inquisitions which started at the millennium and endured to some degree for the next six or seven hundred years. Only at times did the common citizens stand up, protest and even die with their "heretic" neighbors. A prime example was the Christian people of Beziers, true saints and martyrs, who died in their attempts at brotherly and sisterly love.

PRE-LATERAN IV PERSECUTIONS

The IV Lateran Council of 1215 was a pivotal point in history – that point in history when all the junk which had piled

---

51 R. I. Moore (2007) mentions Sir Richard Southern and Bernard Hamilton as holding this position.

up earlier in the church made worshipping in it difficult. Earlier chapters in this book have shown us a few of the precedents which encouraged the members of the Council of 1215. I. M. Moore and Norman Cohn especially, have done valuable research on this matter of precedents to the IV Lateran Council1215:

- In 1022 Robert I of France burned heretics at the stake (Moore 2007, 8).
- In 1025 Gerard, bishop of Cambria, had a group of heretics tortured, and then upon repentance, reconciled the group with the Church (Cohn 1975, 22).
- In 1028 the magnates of the city of Milan ordered the burning of certain heretics (Moore 2007, 8).
- In 1035 Heribert, archbishop of Milan had some heretics burned (Cohn 1975, 22).
- In 1052, even though churchmen resisted, Henry III hanged heretics at Goslar (Moore 2007, 8).
- In 1077, Gerard II, bishop of Cambria burned a heretic by the name of Rhamird (Cohn 1975, 22).
- In 1166 Henry II issued the Assize of Clarendon. Chapter 21 of the Assize is the first secular legislative attack on heresy. It forbade any help or aid to be given those whom he had condemned as heretics at Oxford. Reflections of this Assize are certainly found in the Fourth Lateran Council (Moore 2007, 8).
- In 1184, at the synod of Verona, the Church foamed at the mouth with inquisitorial convulsions when Pope Lucius III joined with Emperor Frederick Barbarossa to issue the papal letter, *ad abolendum*. *Ad abolendum* was the first true European-wide attack on heretics (Moore, p. 8). The unrepentant were given over to the secular powers for punishment (Cohn 1975, 23).

- In 1194 Alphonso II of Aragon ordered convicted heretics to be expelled from his kingdom.
- In 1197 his successor Pedro II ordered that heretics should be burned at the stake (Moore 2997, 8).
- In 1199 Pope Innocent III issued a letter, *Vergentis in Senium,* which declared that heretics were liable to the same procedures as those convicted of treason (Moore 2007, 8).
- In 1208, the Albigensian Crusade took place in Languedoc in the southern part of France (Moore 2007, 9). Horrendous as it was, it was followed by its own inquisition. (This book treats of the matter in an earlier chapter.)

The actions of the IV Lateran Council in 1215 set the tone for the Church for the next 300 to 500 years, and to some extent to our own day. What were the fears of Churchmen and civil authorities?" Why did they see heretics as such a threat?

The popes, bishops, and civil authorities saw that other influential people had different religious principles than they had. Quite simply, this was the threat to them. It threatened the hold that they had on their people, their base of operation, and their good life.

The problem began with Marcion, who was effectively squelched. It became a frightening reality in Augustine's day with the so-called "Manichaeans." John H. Arnold writes about it in *Inquisition and Power: Catharism and the Confessing Subject in Medieval Languedoc*: "The true Manichaeans – a dualist sect founded in Persia by a man called Mani in the third century C. E. – died out in the West in the sixth century. They had however left an "after image" for the Middle Ages. (Arnold 2001, 21)." In other words, the Manichaeans lived again every time a heresy arose in the midst of churchmen.

Arnold uses an example to bring out his point:

> The chronicler of the bishops of Liege tells us that around 1048 the bishops of Chalons-sur-Marne wrote to Bishop Wazo of Liege, asking advice on how to deal with heretics in his diocese. The bishop told Wazo that "there were some country folk who eagerly followed the evil teachings of Manichaeans and frequented their secret conventicles, in which they engaged in I know not what filthy acts, shameful to mention, in a certain religious rite." These "Manichaeans" avoided meat, abhorred marriage, and forbade killing any living thing. The bishop was not concerned with the salvation of the "Manichaeans" themselves; he was more troubled by the effect they were having on the general populace. Thus, he asked Wazo, should he use lethal force against them, "lest, were they not exterminated, the whole lump be corrupted by a little leaven"? Wazo counseled toleration, in part because he felt that heresy was perhaps a cross that good Christians had to bear, and in part because he was worried about reports that certain people were executing as heretics anyone who had a pallid complexion (presumably because pallor indicated fasting, which might mistakenly indicate heretical asceticism) (Arnold 2001, 19).

So, in these early days after Augustine, fear systems, not firm knowledge, came into play within the churchmen who saw differences of opinion in their people. Some of their people were following what the bishop called the evil ways of the Manichaeans, and those people attended Manichaean secret conventicles, engaging in they knew not what filthy acts. The clergy were running scared. "Manichaeans," led by Mani, had died out centuries before, but that was the model which came first to their fear-filled minds for the "heresies," which were often simple differences of opinion, in their midst. Arnold relates that the concern in the Middle Ages was with the few dangerous heretics (perhaps led by an individual heresiarch), and their easily corrupted laity (Arnold 2001, 20-21). In this period before the Lateran Council, the Church saw heresy as just that: a demon heresiarch shepherd leading astray the Church's *idiota* sheep. The Church was intent on finding the demon, the heresiarch shepherd, get rid of him, and then instruct the dull sheep.

The Fourth Lateran Council changed the manner of dealing with heretics. The churchmen thought that the Council had laid out in detail to all the faithful just what was expected of them. Tactics then changed radically, and the process of inquisition involving all citizens gradually became the main instruments by *Tweedledee* churchmen to make sure that everyone else was a veritable *Tweedledum*.

LATERAN COUNCIL IV OF 1215

The role of the clergy in the inquisition is well documented. The Lateran Council IV, which was called by Pope Innocent III in 1215 is pivotal. Conceptually, it is the apex of much that went wrong with the Church since the time of the apostles.

The Council dealt with many internal ecclesiastical matters (Canons 4-70), which for the most part fell into the realm of expected material for a Church Council of Bishops. Getting the Church in order was important, and complicated issues arose. But these internal matters were only appendices to the matter at hand. The main reason for the Council was the demolition of all dissent within the Church. The Council, led by Pope Innocent III, did not waste time in getting to the crux of the matter:

Canon 1 of the Council was a doctrinal statement – something also considered normal and expected whenever bishops gathered in formal council. But here was doctrine with a bite, with ecclesiastical teeth in it. The bishops in Canon 1-3 attacked "heretics," creating their straight-line view of Christianity. It set up doctrines which all Christians were expected to accept without question.

The Council fathers saw in their explanation of theology a 1200 year advancement over the Gospel's description of Jesus. But a further relevant question would be: would Jesus even have recognized his own self in the truncated description which the Council gives of him? The Council's description of Jesus reads as follows:

> ...and finally, Jesus Christ, the only begotten Son of God, who was made flesh by the action of the entire Trinity in common, and through the co-operation of the Holy Spirit. He was conceived by Mary, who remained ever a Virgin. He was true man, composed of a rational soul and human flesh, one person with two natures. He came among us to point out more clearly to us the way of life. In his divinity he was immortal and unable to suffer; in his humanity, he was capable of suffering and dying. In fact, he did suffer and die on the cross for the salvation of the human race. He descended into hell, rose from the dead, and ascended into heaven. He descended into hell through his soul, rose from the dead through his

flesh, and ascended in both his soul and his flesh. He will again come at the end of time to judge the living and the dead. At that time, he will render judgment on everyone according to works done, both to those who did evil and to those who did good deeds. All will arise with the bodies they now have so that they might receive proper judgment according to their merits, whether these be good or evil. The evil will go to eternal punishment with the devil. The chosen will enter eternal glory with Christ (*The Twelfth Ecumenical Council: Lateran IV,* Canon 1).

The doctrine of the IV Lateran Council regarding Jesus could benefit from some tuning, or at least some further explanation. The Council fathers utilized the Greek/Roman classical description utilized by the fathers of the Church to describe Jesus. This is fine. But even in this context, concerns exist.

1) Jesus is divided into so many parts that his own dignity is infringed upon. In true Roman, not Greek, fashion, he is called a person. He is described as true man, that is, one person with a rational soul and human flesh, with two natures, human and divine. In his divinity he is immortal and could not suffer. In his humanity he was created mortal and could and did suffer and die. He went to hell in his soul, rose in his body, and ascended in his body and his soul. This needs considerable explanation which is never given. Without explanation or further insight, we see Jesus as hamburger just ground.

2) The Holy Spirit is then given another role separated in some way from the Trinity working in common. The Council drops Mary almost incidentally into the midst of all the activity of the Holy Spirit who was busy creating the man, Jesus. The impression is given that it is an ill-thought out, rote, uninspired and uninspiring formula of the time. Also, some more respectful care might have been taken to describe Mary's role as the mother of God. That important role is never mentioned. Dignity of the person is not considered important here. Bishop-accepted truth is.

It is clear from the so-called doctrinal section that doctrine was not the stress of the Council. Later it became obvious that condemning heresy was the Council's stress. Doctrine was utilized to counteract and corner the perceived heretics. This would explain the flippant, impersonal, and even disrespectful manner in which dogma was treated at the council. The Council took the doctrine which they enunciated, journeyed hither and thither with it, and destroyed with fire those who contradicted it (*The Twelfth Ecumenical Council: Lateran IV, Canon 1*).

Immediately, Canon 2 condemned a "heresy" of particular and immediate concern, the teachings of Joachim of Fiore, a well-known Christian prophet. Joachim recanted, but the Counsel feared that the Joachimites, his followers, might not do so. Canon 2 also regarded the teachings of Amaury de Bene as not only heretical, but "insane" (*The Twelfth Ecumenical Council: Lateran IV, Canon 2*).

Amaury de Bene, a cleric and a professor at the University of Paris, maintained that God and the universe are one: God is everything and everything is God. The knowledge the spiritualized received in this new life was paradise for them. Those who were completely filled with the Spirit of God were called "the spiritualized," and they were already enjoying the life of the Resurrection. Amaury de Bene found followers among many priests and clerics, and for some time they propagated his teaching without detection by the ecclesiastical authorities. Amongst other errors perceived in this doctrine, the bishops saw this doctrine as a watering down of morality, since any sinful act committed is not only an act of man, but an act of God as well. Amaury de Bene never said this – the bishops came up with this corollary on their own in order to further condemn Amaury de Bene. In 1210 a council of bishops and doctors of the University of Paris took measures to punish Amaury de Bene and his followers. Ignorant converts were pardoned. Four were condemned to prison for life. Ten priests and clerics, who were obstinate, were publicly degraded, handed over to the civil authorities and were burned at the stake. Amaury de Bene was already dead, so they could not do much to him. He was condemned and excommunicated *in absentia*. His bones were then exhumed and cast into unconsecrated ground (*The Twelfth* Ecumenical Council: Lateran IV, Canon 2) (For the translation, see Catholic Encyclopedia).

Canon 3 showed the bitterness with which Pope Innocent III and the bishops dealt with the heretics. The transcript of the council reads:

> We excommunicate and anathematize every heretic who might arise who teach various doctrines opposed to the teachings of the holy, orthodox and Catholic faith. These heretics have different faces, but they are all joined at the tails by their vanity. Those who are condemned of heresy must be handed over to the bailiff of the secular authorities to

be punished with appropriate justice Furthermore, their property must be confiscated. If they be clerics, they will first be expelled from their orders, and the property of their Churches will be confiscated (*Twelfth Ecumenical Council: Lateran IV,* Canon 3).

But the council fathers did not stop there. If they would have their way, everyone who even was suspected of digressing in any way from their view of Christian truth was to be personally degraded:

> If a person is even suspected of heresy, unless he quickly proves his innocence by an appropriate defense, he must be anathematized and avoided by all.

Also, secular authorities would have to put their full weight behind the Council decrees:

> Secular authorities ... must, to the best of their abilities, exterminate all heretics in their territories.... If a temporal ruler refuses to cleanse his territory of heretical foulness, let him be excommunicated... (*The Twelfth Ecumenical Council, Canon 3).*

Finally, anyone who supported a heretic in any way was to be considered a heretic himself/herself. The council makes it clear in the following statement that it meant to annihilate the person of any heretic or heretic sympathizer. He or she was to be considered a non-entity, a non-person:

We also excommunicate anyone who gives any semblance of credence to the teachings of a heretics, anyone who gives him safe harbor, defends or supports him in any way. Such a one has one year to change. If he does not do so, he will become by law a non-person: he will not be able to hold public office or join in any official deliberations; he will not be able to vote or give testimony in court; he will not be able to make a will or receive an inheritance; he can expect others to give him no justice, but others can take anything from him. If he is a judge, his decisions will have no binding force.... If he is an advocate, no assistance shall be sought from him. If he is a notary, the doctrines he notarizes are invalid. For if the author is condemned, so is the reader or anyone who shows the author sympathy. If anyone refuses to snub a heretic, he also shall be ostracized from the Church until he makes suitable satisfaction. Clerics shall not give heretics the sacraments or give them Christian burial. They shall even refuse any alms they should offer them. If they do any of these things, they will be deprived of their office until they receive a special indult from the Apostolic See (*The Twelfth Ecumenical Council, , Canon 3*).

The council was bitter and defensive. Individual thought out-of-step with the linear thought of pope and bishops was considered not only an attack on the Church, but an attack on them personally. If the bishops at the Council had their say, and they did, repercussions were dire in the extreme. They felt that they had legitimate power as God's representative to destroy even the God-given person of anyone who dared to disagree.

INNOCENT III

At the same time, sad to say, Innocent III and many of those who stood behind his throne led pompous lives. They felt that the life of pomp and ceremony which they lived was the life due to the representative of Christ on earth. Also, Innocent III, besides being a religious leader, maintained an active political life.

But what does this tell us about Innocent III and his knowledge of Jesus? As Jesus and the devil stood looking at the known world from a very high mountain in the desert, Jesus was tempted by the devil. "I will give you all this power and the glory of these kingdoms," the devil told Jesus, "if you prostrate yourself before me." And Jesus told the devil, "You shall do homage to the Lord your God, him alone shall you adore" (Luke 4:5-8). Innocent III accepted the power and the glory of the world as his own; Jesus did not.

Innocent III and his bishops were convinced that their political bent, their attacking heretics, destroying them, even to the point of making them non-persons in society, was virtuous and supposedly protective of Jesus own mission. This in spite of the fact that Jesus' mission included the protection of the dignity of persons he met, including society's dregs: Matthew, the tax collector, Mary Magdalene, the soldier in the garden, the leper who was told to go and sin no more, the good thief, and even the Pharisees. Could the Pope or Church administrators, then, call themselves Christian and do anything less? Would it have been better to use a little compassion, as Jesus did, instead of humiliating the poor "heretics" as much as possible, and then, when they were completely devastated, hoisting some of them onto tarred branches, and torching them?

FOLLOW-UP TO LATERAN COUNCIL IV

Did the people who faced the inquisitors even have a chance? The inquisitors' words and the writings of the court secretaries help us to answer this question. The question is: would anything the defendants had to say have influenced their inquisitors. Arnold quotes a Franciscan friar, Bernard of Deicieux, who was tried by an inquisition in the fourteenth century as stating that St. Peter and St. Paul would have been found guilty if they were tried by his inquisitors (Arnold 2001, 5). Jesus himself would not have been exempt.

Arnold goes on to say that the inquisitions themselves existed in a Manichaean divide between the "true" and the "false." The conception of reality of the inquisitors was not only *their* reality, but it was a reality that they imposed on others..."(Arnold 2001, 7). In other words, the inquisitions were manipulative activities; they were, as we have already stated, power plays (Arnold 2001, 8). As Jean Dunbabin states in *Captivity and Imprisonment in Medieval Europe, 1000-1300* (New York, 2002) prisons became essential, "because they and only they offered the necessary space and privacy within which men's spirits could be broken" (Dunbabin 2002, 126).

Inquisitors set up the categories of inquisitorial transgressions and they controlled the language and discourse of the inquisitorial proceedings. The accused was seldom allowed his or her own voice. Reality was the inquisitor's reality and the person was only asked questions according to the mind-set of the inquisitor. The person could not offer any defense of his own because everything was already set in stone. The person was forced and manipulated into identifying any accomplices (Arnold, 2001, 9-15).

Some individuals pleaded guilty to obviously fictional crimes of heresy and witchcraft. Some of them were even burned at the stake after pleading guilty to preposterous, impossible "crimes" (Arnold, 2001, 9).

For the most part, up to the time of the inquisitions, accusatory court procedures had always begun with private individuals bringing charges against another. In the inquisitorial procedures, things changed. The church authorities were the agents of accusation. They were in charge of gathering evidence from various individuals. When they had enough information from such denunciations, the person was considered guilty. The judge in the case proceeded to an interrogation, an inquisition of the suspect. The person was ordered to plead guilty to not only a crime, but to the precise crime which existed secretly in the mind of the inquisitor who had already decided on the person's guilt. "Power" was written on the pages of the proceedings. The accused did not have a chance. In fact, the accused person often did not even know the crime which existed only in the mind of the inquisitors -- the crime to which he or she was supposed to enunciate and to which he or she was to plead guilty. And the inquisitors were not about to help him or her to discern his mind concerning the crime.

So-called "Christian" inquisitions were used to demand the acceptance of Catholic religious agendas. But they were not only utilized to diminish perceived errors in the Church proper, but also to diminish the wayward fears of certain popes, bishops, and sometimes those of the populace. They were also utilized to further programs of revenge, to fund wars, and to degrade and eliminate opponents and enemies of clergy and politicians. Pseudo-Christian facades were added to salve and soothe the consciences and continually prop up the consciences of the accusers and prosecutors and those making the denunciations.

In response to Lateran Council IV in 1215, various rulers of Europe decreed the death penalty for unrepentant heresy (Cohn

1970, 23). The Humiliati, the Waldensians, the Fraticelli, and the Cathars were groups who fell into the hands of Church inquisitors and felt the burden of church authorities.

Looking at the inquisitions in another way, they were part of the on-going dissolution caused by structures within the Christian Church which put emphasis on the so-called truths held by the reigning hierarchy over Jesus' teachings and everything else. The supposed truths of the hierarchy were often influenced by personal or group fears, idiosyncrasies, and even psychopathologies. They were also sometimes twisted and deformed to be utilized as tools to meet the personal power desires of the authorities. Hierarchical, sometimes perverted or ill-defined, human "truths" were used for a multitude of varying purposes to keep the lay people in line. Sexual perversion and misogyny are also reason for some inquisitorial questionings and convictions.

INQUISITIONS AND JESUS' TEACHINGS

The person who believed that the inquisitorial process was legitimately sanctioned in any way, shape, or form by this or that passage of Jesus was clearly reading a sparse Gospel. Whatever passages of the Gospel he was reading was certainly avalanched by hundreds of others that were opposed to those inquisitorial activities.

Certainly, human truth, sincere and humble, was something that true Christians have constantly sought throughout history. It is the reality behind the words of Jesus to Thomas: "I am the way, the truth and the life" (John 14: 6). By these words, Bruce Vawter, C.M., tells us that Jesus was indicating to Thomas the Christian way through himself to the Father (*Jerome Biblical Commentary*, vol. II, 1968, p. 453).

In imitation of Jesus each true Christian and each Christian community walked, seeking truth in Jesus. But, any Christian in history who thought he or she had the truth, total and complete, had missed it, because Jesus and the Father were always much bigger than any human estimation. Words spoken by the mouth and written in books and documents were incapable of totally holding Christian truth. Yet such words spoken and penned by humans, supposedly Christian and spiritual words, were the material utilized by inquisitors to burn and torture others.

THE POPES AND THE INQUISITIONS

Popes Innocent III and Pope Gregory IX, among others, were notorious in their attempts to establish their spiritual empires on earth. In doing so, they searched incessantly for anyone who would not bow to their spiritual power. They considered such people to be "heretics."

'Verity Murphy in a presentation in BBC Online (June 15, 2004) reports on an 800 page Vatican report which plays down the brutality of the Inquisitions. The report says that "in fact the much feared judges of heresy were not as brutal as previously believed." Murphy goes on to say that the Middle Ages did not use execution or torture as much as was previously thought.

In writing these words, Murphy maneuvers the court of popular opinion ineptly, assuring that the church will lose. One act of torture performed by the Church of Jesus is unbelievable. 40,000 to 50,000 deaths and many more acts of torture – which are documented by primary historical record -- are catastrophes of mammoth proportions. If the Church now feels relief that it can admit to 50,000 murders instead of 9 million, it is sad indeed. The Church would have done itself a service by saying nothing at all.

The report does not mention the details. What about the acts of torture and the confiscations of property which destroyed human lives? For the rest of their days, many of those tortured were not able to move their arms and legs, but had to drag themselves through the streets as non-persons, with their yellow *sanbenito* on their bodies, begging the garbage from the tables of the real citizens. What of the imprisonments in the cold, dark, dank, rat-infested holes, where speaking a word to a prison guard was a major offense, causing the prisoner to be brought into the exquisite torture chamber of the prison? What about the galleys, where a person was likely to be whipped and die on the ships? What about the severe whippings?

It is abundantly clear that the Church was involved in these inquisitions. Pope Gregory IX actually set norms for the interrogations. He "adapted certain elements of Roman legal procedure and charged appointed clergymen to employ them in order to preserve orthodox religious beliefs from the attacks of heretics."

INQUISITION, POLITICS, THE LOCAL CHURCH AND THE POPULACE

But the medieval Church consisted not only of those members who stood piously behind the papal throne. Furthermore the inquisition was not always merely a Church matter. Gary Macy made this clear in his insightful work, "Nicolas Eymeric and the Condemnation of Orthodoxy." Macy states that the medieval Church pulsed with ebbs and flows of papal influences, but Europe and the local Churches never revolved solely around the pope (Macy 1998, 369). Papal words had to reach the borders or the shores of the local Churches and countries. Then significant persons in the local Churches, among the local politicians, or among the populace had to show some accord with those words. All in all, when the Pope was concerned, secular politics and the local Church had to play its part in the executing of any papal decree. The local churches carried out these decrees as they saw fit. Each church, for better or for worse, carried them out in their own particular fashion.

Macy makes a strong statement in his work. He says that any medieval historian who sees the medieval Church as a papal monolith flies in the face of reality and could be suspect of taking a prejudiced position in order "to buttress modern agendas" (Macy 1998, 369).

It would be a mistake, then, Macy insisted, to see the inquisition as some monolithic, totalitarian procedure ruled by the Pope. Sometimes, with a nudge from a pope, local politicians or the populace initiated the procedures. But the manuals given by the Popes and others were often guidelines rather than rules.

Therefore, most today agree that there was not one "Inquisition" (with a capital "I") but "rather a series of local inquisitions (with a small 'i')," all separate entities from one another. Ironically, it is a fact that it was the simple lay person who suffered the most from these inquisitions, not the theologians. Macy elaborates:

> Theologians were often accused of heresy, but few ever suffered much because of it. In my studies of theologians accused of Eucharistic heresy, I have found only one example of a theologian who was burned due at least in part because of his teaching on the Eucharist. John Wyclif seemed not to have objected, however, since he had already died of natural causes some twenty years earlier. [He was burned *post mortem* and *in absentiam.*] In order to preach complex theological opinions which could be construed as heresy, one needed to be educated and if one were educated, one usually had the

political connections necessary to survive accusations of heresy (Macy 1998, 370-381).

The inquisitions did hand their heretics over to secular authorities to be put to death. When it did, it felt it had scripture to justify its actions:

> If your brother, sister or your father or your mother, or your son or daughter, or the wife you cherish, or the friend with whom you share your life, if one of these secretly tries to entice you, saying, 'Come, let us serve other gods,'...you must not give way to him, you must not conceal his guilt. No, you must kill him; your hand is to be the first raised against him in putting him to death, the hand of all the people will come next (Deuteronomy 13: 7-11).

And if someone needed a text from the Gospel, they had another verse handy:

> Anyone who does not remain in me is like a branch that has been thrown away -- he withers; these branches are collected and thrown into the fire, and they are burned (John 15:6).

The inquisitions took this Gospel passage literally. They gathered Cathars in Languedoc, the Waldensians, worshippers of the Old Religion, others who they considered heretics in Spain, Rome, and elsewhere and they treated them like "withered branches." They threw them into the fire. They did so simply because the established Church, usually in league with the political forces, believed that anyone who believed anything but "normal doctrine" was in league with the devil, or was "outside the true faith" of Jesus Christ. The procedures of local inquisitions became a blot on Christianity. The Church was often heavily supportive or actively involved in each inquisition.

INQUISITION OF THE THEOLOGIANS

Later, in 1542, Pope Paul III actually started a permanent inquisition, a congregation in the Roman Catholic Church whose task would be "to maintain and defend the integrity of the faith, and to examine and proscribe errors and false doctrines."[52] Even though, in our day, the congregation no longer fingers people to be burned at the stake, it continues the work of what it calls "The Congregation for the Doctrine of the Faith," chaired by a Cardinal. Learned theologians have suffered more from this office than did theologians from the inquisitions of the Middle Ages. Before becoming Pope, Pope Benedict XVI was head of this congregation, and he, is responsible for causing limitless damage to the reputations of great theologians. *National Catholic Reporter* gives a list of some of the individual theologians:

- Jacques Pohier was disciplined by Pope John Paul II for his views on Christ's resurrection. He left the Dominicans in 1984.
- Hans Kung lost his license to teach Catholic theology

---

52 The Congregation of the Holy Office has made some embarrassing decisions in its history. In 1616 it decided that the sun was not the center of the solar system, and that the earth does not move around it. The first statement was considered "heretical" and the second "against the common teachings of the faith." Both scientific findings were considered absurd by the Congregation. Thus, the Congregation condemned Copernicus. In 1633 they put Galileo Galilei on trial for his Copernican tendencies, convicted him of heresy, and demolished this great man. The Office continues to this day under a different name, The Congregation for the Doctrine of the Faith. Pope Benedict XVI was the Cardinal who headed the Congregation before his election as Pope.

because the "Vatican investigation" begun in 1975 found fault with his views on papal infallibility.
- Edward Schillebeeckx was the theologian of the Dutch bishops at the Second Vatican Council (1962-65). He has been constantly harassed by the Congregation of the Doctrine of the Faith since then. In 1979, a trial or procedure was convened to investigate his Christology. An international uproar caused the Congregation to drop the matter in 1980. Since then, he has received several "notifications" from the congregation that his writings remain in conflict with church teachings.
- Charles Curran was once a professor of moral theology at the Catholic University of America. He lost his license to teach theology in 1986 because the Congregation did not approve his views on sexuality and medical ethics. He then accepted a position at Southern Methodist University.
- Leonardo Boff is one of the most famous "liberation theologians." The Congregation investigated him in 1981 and objected to his Christology and his views on the structure of the Church. He was silenced in 1985. Cardinal Lorscheider and Arns came to his rescue, but he was silenced again in 1991. In 1992, he left the priesthood.
- Gustavo Gutierrez is often called the "father of liberation theology." In 1984 and 1986 the congregation criticized aspects of liberation theology. In 1988 they again investigated Gutierrez. Although nothing came of it, all these investigations had an influence on the man's life.
- Karl Rahner, probably the most influential theologian of the 20th century, spent most of his life under Vatican scrutiny. Pope John XXIII had him silenced and that Pope was extremely critical of his writings. Pope Paul VI called him forth again, and Rahner was one of the great lights

of Vatican Council II. After his death the Congregation proclaimed him "an orthodox theologian."
- Matthew Fox was questioned by the Congregation in 1983 concerning his views on sexuality, original sin and pantheism. He was silenced by the Congregation. He eventually joined the Episcopal Church in 1994.
- Bishop Jacques Gaillot was removed from his position as bishop of Evreux, France, because his identification with the poor and his advocacy for homosexuals and contraception was considered too unorthodox for a bishop.
- Jon Sobrino, a liberation theologian and former theological advisor to Archbishop Oscar Romero in El Salvador, was censured for his writings, which were deemed "erroneous or dangerous." Sobrino rejected the Congregation's rulings, and the Congregation did not act in his regard.

Chapter 12

THE INQUISITION OF THE "WITCHES"

Inquisitions threw Christianity onto the rack when it sought out the witches, whose ways were grossly misunderstood by most people at the time. From 1300 to 1782 approximately 40, 000 to 50, 000 so called "witches" were executed in Europe. Many of them were burned. In England they were hung (Purkiss 1996, p. 17). Others died in other ways. 75% to 80% of them were women and girls.[53] Approximately 20% to 25% of them were men and boys.

THE OLD RELIGION AND THEIR DEEPER KNOWLEDGE

First, we will deal with the fact that the old religions and deeper knowledge of humanity had nothing to do with the witches as we know it. Some historians of the past, notably Margaret Alice Murray, followed an apparently obvious lead. Murray and others were convinced that members of the old religions were the most obvious victims of the "burning times."

---

[53] Gibbons, Jenny, "Recent Developments in the Study of the Great European Witch Hunt," found in the book *The Virtual Pomegranate,* and Starhawk's *The Spiral Dance,* p. 5, say 9 million people died. She follows in a pre-1975 group of scholars who based their information on the historical fiction of Etienne Leon de Lamothe-Langon's *Histoire de l'Inquisition en France,* written in 1829. Modern scholarship opts for the more realistic figure of 40,000 to 50,000 – still a horrifying number.

The old religions began innocently and naturally enough tens of thousands of years ago. Ancient peoples who lived on earth even before Abraham struggled to understand and relate to their gods and goddesses. With creation around them as their revelation, they ventured forth. Their rites and religious practices contained much insight and wisdom. They learned that the human body and other living beings contained power which emanated from it. They learned that the human touch and certain herbs could heal.

The history of the old religions went back at least 35 thousand years -- among our early ancestors who lived on the rich tundra of Europe and Asia. The people were hunters mainly, following wooly mammoth, deer, bison, and other animals across the plains and into the rich forests of the time. They were a religious people. Their religion was formed around nature, the world their gods gave them. They were not much different than we are. They found their world both beautiful and threatening.

They found among their members individuals who had a deeper insight into nature and the gods who gave them their power. Some of their groups were exceptionally able. These individuals were the mediators with their gods. They were the priests, the priestesses, and the shamans who piqued the imagination of the people, told them the stories about realities that they could not see. They interpreted meaning for their people and helped them understand the storms, the deaths, and the new life that birthed around them. They brought a sense of wonder to the people.

Some people in Europe and Asia continued to believe in the old religion into the Christian era. Small groups of these early peoples gradually grew into settlements, settlements grew into villages, and villages grew into towns and cities. Many, but not all of these religions were eventually Christianized. Native Americans as well and other like-spirited religions in ancient Greece, Rome, and Africa naturally followed a similar development.

Certainly, early Christianity looked down on such "pagan" religions and saw them in need of conversion. However, surprisingly, after much research on real case histories, we know that these people were not those convicted during the witch craze.

THE NEIGHBORHOOD OF THE IMPOVERISHED WITCHES

Case studies of the witch trials indicate that, for the most part, the convicted witch was a person who belonged to a low social class of society (Purkiss 1996, 242). The lines between fact and fiction are blurry in court case studies of the witches and their accusers. While it is unbelievable that witches with satanic powers existed, historians are baffled by the fact that across Europe the profile of the witch did not basically vary. Witnesses and convicted witches told the same stories in Germany, Spain, France, Italy and in the far north. Why was this so? Is it possible that, like the old religions, a group of people, who we now historically call witches, gained a deeper insight into humanity, which scared a more ignorant, unknowing population? Or was it a case of the ascendance of the common lower unconscious of humanity creeping into consciousness among acceptable people, which was tapped in more acceptable ways by Jakob Grimm and Mircea Eliade?

The fears of witches arose sporadically among the people. They were not a constant in the life of the population. Periodically the people felt the fears and then went into a period of frenzy. After the frenzy was over, they went back to life as usual. Witch crazes were on again, off again realities in the lives of the people of Europe. As Gustav Henningsen says, it was a case of collective fears and delusions. He continues to explain:

> The content of collective delusions may vary ... but the underlying human feeling seem to be quite constant. One could also reverse the situation and say that unless we understand in advance that human nature is unvarying and that only conditions change, historical research would be meaningless; for if we do not consider man as one of us, as an equal, how can we then ever hope to understand him or put ourselves in his place? The most precious tool of research is ourselves, and like the anthropologist we must persevere until we can identify with the people we are studying, speak their language, and experience the world in their way. With this attitude history becomes something other than a mere study of past events; it turns into a journey of exploration backwards in time to a series of historical societies which tell us something new (and old) of man and his possibilities, under changing conditions (Henningsen 1980, xxvi).

In order to understand the witch stories it would be easy for historians to remain objective computers, robots collecting data. But this would not do justice to either the witches or their accusers. On the other hand, the historians could humbly look into their own human hearts in order to see the myths and delusions of human nature standing there. Only then could they appreciate the stories that the witches and their accusers told us. The neighborhood that birthed the witches in the witch crazes gives historians a deep insight into the witches themselves as well as our own selves. Robin Briggs writes:

> We are writing here about a specific social situation,

that of the early village. Normally this constituted a grouping of a few hundred people who lived in conditions we are not used to even imagining. There existed no shops in which they could buy goods, no paved roads, or public services of any kind. This was a world of peddlers, of dirt paths, wells of varying quality, privies of varying quality, and outside fires or candlelight. Houses were smelly and uncomfortable, sheltering animals alongside people. Neighbors were forced to interact daily, giving one another goods and services. They either did this or they or their neighbors died. The system of exchange was objectively unquantified, but certainly everyone kept track to see that it was balanced. (Briggs 1996, 139).

Such a system was ripe for what was to come. Social relationships were constant, and the benefits a person hoped to gain from such relationships far exceeded what was possible. A charity given today was expected to be returned in some way tomorrow while all were expected to do their best to contribute to the aid of the total loser, the sick and the elderly. Then famine and disease also entered the picture, and some of them, even children, began to die.

In such conditions, where everyone was struggling to "make an existence in this world," animosities grew. Some were considered "slackers." They were perceived as not doing their part. It was not only one incident, but incident after incident that grew to an infinite amount of "overdue bills." This perceived breach of neighborly duty was considered an aggressive act, causing members of one's own family to die because of it. Certainly, the "slackers" were to blame. Some of those considered to be slackers did not think that they were. They were doing their part as best as they could, maybe even beyond what anyone could imagine. Yet animosities grew to the boiling point.

At a distance, the Church, too, was involved to some degree in village life, but it had its own problems. It was busy with its own agendas.

Then the stories, the myths of the time, took over to fill the religious gap among common folk. Stories of witches circulated among the villagers: sabbats, covens, devils, draining the blood out of children and eating them. These were perfect stories for people who were beginning to despise one another. Robin Briggs states that, in reading the witch trials, unmotivated malignancies are almost never mentioned in the accusations or the confessions.

Witches saw the happenings from their own, oppressed point of view. They were essentially reactive, responding to acts of aggression or hostility from others. They had to be provoked before they fought back. But it was their perceived failures of charity and communal unity which caused people to charge them with witchcraft in the first place (Briggs 1996, 137).

Those convicted told folk fairy-tales much like those told by every human society. But in the case of the witches, their lashing out, the delusions they were under, and the myths they lived led to their destruction.

THE STEREOTYPICAL WITCH

No matter where or when we find them, the stories and folklore of the witch is clear, blatantly detailed and the same. The story goes as follows: "The witch was a human being – usually a woman but sometimes a man or even a child – who was bound to the devil as the devil's servant and assistant" (Cohn 1975, 99).

THE INQUISITION OF THE "WITCHES"

Well into the fifteenth century the folklore of the witch became clear. The devil, the story goes, approached the person at a time of desperation, making promises of prosperity if the person renounced Christianity. The prosperity promised was a deception. It never happened. But the witch and everyone else believed that the devil gave the witch something else -- the ability to lash out and harm anyone she or he pleased (Cohn 1975, 100). Not only did the witch have the power to harm, but, the story goes, the devil insisted that he or she use the power liberally.

The story, then, gets more and more bazaar. At times the witches would get together in a sabbat, a meeting with the devil. Such meetings kept the witches in line, and let the witches know that the devil alone was in charge. The various accounts of the sabbat differ only in minor details. The devil was visible as a half man, half goat. His eyes spouted flames as he sat on an ebony throne. He punished those witches who did not do enough evil in the interim, usually by a severe flogging. The witches kissed him on his left goat's foot, or on his genitals or anus. A revolting banquet, sometimes of murdered children or men, was then shared. A sexual orgy followed. The devil then gave a rousing speech and dismissed them, telling them that if they did not do even more evil than before, they would be severely punished at the next sabbat (Cohn 1975, 101-102).

Witches, as the story was told, were grouped in numbers of thirteen called a coven. One of the group was the leader and brought messages from the devil to the coven. But the coven was not a constant. "In some regions of Europe," Henningsen states, "the witches were expected to operate single-handedly" (Henningsen 1980, 11). During the periods of the witch crazes, witches were considered the worst of the worst on this earth.

THE FEARS GENERATED BY THE "WITCHES"

Henningsen goes on to state the type of mental activities which generated a witch craze:

> There was no need to take any notice of what was said when ordinary people quarreled and hurled imprecations at each other, for that was perfectly commonplace. But sooner or later a curse was bound to come true; it might not happen for a long time, and it was only when a misfortune, especially one that was predicted in an imprecation, had finally occurred that one realized he had been cursed. (The argument was sometimes enforced from the opposite angle: after the damage was done people began to speculate about whom they had been on bad terms with; and when that person who hurled the words at another, was brought to court, that all her neighbors racked their brains to remember other "mysterious incidents" (Henningsen 1980, 11).

The law of averages existed in the witch crazes. Sooner or later, one curse or the other spoken in a fit of anger would come true. When it did, the person who hurled it was suspect of witchcraft. Then if anything seemingly unexplainable happened – if a drought came, if a flood came, if the sun did not shine for two weeks, if a child died, if the plague came, the one who made the curse was questioned about that as well. The witch accused saw the inevitable coming and might play the role for all it was worth. After all, here was power; here was notoriety which the accused witch never knew her or his whole life.

The origins of imagined satanic cults are found within human nature. They are the product of the fears and omissions of human life. They show us the power myths can have over our lives.

THE PROBLEM OF THE INTELLIGENTSIA AND WITCHCRAFT

Interestingly enough, the first years of a witch hunt mainly took place among the intelligentsia. Kings charged someone with witchcraft when they felt threatened. Noblemen did the same.

Many among the intelligentsia were taken in by witch phobias. Fabian Alejandro Campagne asks the question, "How could some brilliant intellectuals of the Renaissance have believed in witches?" ("Witchcraft and the Sense-of-the-Impossible in Early Modern Spain: Some Reflections Based on the Literature of Superstition (ca 1500-1800)" (Campagne 1996, 2003, 96, 1).

> How could Jean Bodin reconcile the publication of his *Six Books of the Commonwealth* with the ridiculous witchcraft stories included in his *Demonomanie des Sorciers*....In 1530, Pedro Cireulo published in Alcala de Henares his *Reprobacion de Supersticiones y hechizerias*. Throughout the book, the Spanish theologian condemns a great number of beliefs and practices: belief in the evil eye, the use of amulets, reliance of horoscopes, healing by spells, and rainmaking. In this same treatise, however, Cireulo defends the reality of the sabbat and the flight of witches. This apparent arbitrariness appears also in medical literature. In 1580, Francisco Nunez published in Alcala de Henares his *libro del parto humano*. The book describes the most usual ailments

affecting the newborns. But, surprisingly, the thirty-first heading is, "Of the cures against witches and against all kinds of vermin that offend children (Campagne 1996, 25-26).

Cireulo and Nunez were professors of theology and medicine at the Universidad de Alcala de Henares. Campagne concludes:" There can be no doubt: a wide cultural distance separates us from a vision of the world that we ceased to share centuries ago" (Campagne 1996, 2003, 26).

Should Bodin, Cireulo and Nunez have known better? We can make a case for it. After all, Julio Caro Baroja in his work "Witchcraft and Catholic Theology," states that Spanish classical writers of the Golden Age, Cervantes, Lope de Vega, and Francisco de Quevedo (1500 to early 1600's) all refer to the witch with a touch of irony or skepticism (Campagne 1996, 2003,21). In fact, Lope de Vega in his *La Dorotea,* in which erotic witchcraft plays a constant theme, makes a significant statement: "It is with lovers as with witches, who believe that they are carried bodily to the place whither their imagination takes them" (Baroja 1990, 21).

Nonetheless, Bodin, Cireulo and Nunez were a product of an age when the most wonderful and the most fearful things imaginable, including witches, could happen at any turn. The sense that "everything is possible" was overwhelming among humans in this period. It was believed by the intelligentsia of the age, including the popes and bishops, as well as the common folk. Education played little part in allaying the fear of witches.

When Bodin was facing a person who was wondrous, evil, or different, he called that person a "witch." It was the appropriate word at hand for him. The bewildering word "witch," together with "melancholia," was acceptable, at times, even in learned writings. Ginzburg's documentation shows that after 1500, "scholarly and popular elements were by now inextricably merged" (Ginzburg 1991, 6). By this time, many of the elements of witchcraft, including the sabbat were rooted in popular culture – from the back alleys to the university. This is not so strange in human society.

Campagne quotes Wittgenstein as observing:

> The limits of one's language mark the limits of one's world. The institution of society is, at any given time, the product of the intersection of a great number of social imaginary significations. Consequently, nothing can belong to society if it does not refer to the network of significations" (Campagne 2003, 27).

THE STORIES OF THE WITCHES IN THEIR OWN AGE

Ginzburg tells us about the general folklore of the age which included the Sabbat:

> There exists, for example, a rich series of testimonies concerning night flying in which a number of women claimed they participated in ecstasy, in the retinue of a mysterious female divinity who had several names depending on the place (Diana, Perchta, Holda, Abundia, Madonna Oriente, etc.) .... Here it is a matter neither of late folkloric tradition, nor of a literary text, nor of beliefs considered alien to witchcraft (Ginzburg 1991, 10).

We come back to the reality that all the witches and witnesses from about 1430 onward told the same story of the sabbat. Ginzburg concludes that the answer has to be found in the myths, the stories which were being told among the populace. We are in the realm here of something akin to Jakob Grimm, told not by the persons themselves, but interpreted by hostile testimonies. Ginzburg states:

> On witchcraft (this is quite obvious, but it does not hurt to repeat it) we possess only hostile testimonies, originating from or filtered by the demonologists, inquisitors, and judges. The voice of the accused reach us strangled, altered, distorted; in many cases they haven't reached us at all. Hence – for anyone unresigned to writing history for the nth time from the standpoint of the victors – the importance of the anomalies, the cracks that occasionally (albeit very rarely) appear in the documentation, undermining its coherence. From the disparity between the ...stereotypes of the inquisitors there emerges a deep stratum of peasant myths lived with extraordinary intensity. Little by little, by the gradual introjection of a hostile cultural model, it was transformed into the Sabbat (Ginzburg 1991,10-11).

Ginzburg tells us stories which come to us from different periods of time and different places:

> In 1319 a sacristan in a small village in the Pyrenees told an inquisitor that he was "an *armier*, someone

THE INQUISITION OF THE "WITCHES"

who had the power of seeing souls and talking to them." He said that the dead drank good wine in any house they went into, but the wine was never diminished "because it is the dead who drink it" (Ginzburg 1991, 89).

Then in 1575, at the opposite end of the Alpine arc, Troiano de Attimis, attested concerning the town crier:

> At night, especially on Thursday, he goes with the others, and they repair to certain locations to perform marriages, to dance and eat and drink; and on the way home they go into cellars to drink and then urinate in the casks. (Ginzburg 1991, 89).

Ginzburg spends the whole book (*Ecstasies: Deciphering the Witches' Sabbath*) telling such vulgar and even obscene stories, drawing from them the fantasies and myths of the people of the time. His conclusion is that the stories are truly myths, and no inquisitor, ecclesiastical or civil court should have put much stress on them. Certainly they misunderstood the peasant culture as well as their own when they went so far as to convict these poor souls of witchcraft and even to put them to death.

WHO WERE CALLED WITCHES?

From the records of trials, Henningsen tells us, the suspects in the witch hunts were the following:

> One group consisted of the weaker members of the community: beggars, cripples, widows, the very old, and orphans; in short, all those who could be

accused without risk. The other group consisted of those who had rejected the moral order of society: fawning, envious, thieving, aggressive, spiteful, promiscuous, and odd people; in fact, all who were in any way unattractive (Henningsen 1980, 12).

Today scholars agree that the group persecuted as witches were simply different, misunderstood, and rejected people of their age. The main accusers were members of the populace who firmly believed that "the evil impossible" was living in their midst. Hutton states that the tragedy of the witch hunt in Europe was that the victim's crimes had no existence outside the imagination.... Their offenses were illusory, their punishments very real" (Hutton 1991, 307).

Hutton goes on to say: "What urgently requires further investigation is that world of dreams and fantasies ... could have such dreadful consequences" (Hutton 1991, 307).

As we have already stated, pre-Christian peoples had their own way of dealing with their gods through the sensitive people who became their mediators.

The early books of the Old Testament even did not take exception to the perceived presence of witches among them, and these books inflicted capital punishment on any such witch. The Book of Exodus reads: "You shall not let a witch [a sorceress] live" (22:27). The Book of Leviticus reads: "A man or a woman who acts as a medium or fortuneteller, shall be put to death by stoning: they have no one but themselves to blame for their death" (20:27). The Book of Deuteronomy reads: "Though the nations whom you are to dispossess listen to their soothsayers and fortunetellers, the Lord, your God, will not permit you to do so" (18:13).

Greek antiquity also had archetypes of the witches. Medea

was a tragic heroine, given to magic arts (Baroja 1990, 22). Often female figures were allied or associated with and protected by feminine, nocturnal deities: Selene, Diana, the moon, or the horrible Hecate (Baroja 1990, 23).

Entering the Christian era, the Greek philosophers, well-versed in the literature of the Greeks, soon came to the fore. Often bypassing Jesus and his teachings, they were only able to touch up a bit the inheritance received from the Old Testament. Baroja sums up the situation well:

> Officially, the triumph of Christianity left little room for any conception other than that inherited from Hebrew monotheism, according to which there are only two spheres of action in human life: the Good, pursued by those who submit to the law of God, and the Evil, inhabited by followers of the devil and demons. In Christian ethics, all that is morally wrong – beliefs, vices, violent passions – is of diabolical origin, and the ancient divinities are nothing but representations of the devil, by whom, according to Christian belief, the whole of humanity was plunged into error until the advent of the Messiah (Baroja 1990, 23).

Again, Augustine seals the issue for Christianity. His relevant text is his personal experience: on the authority of unnamed, "trustworthy" (of course), persons, he also relates other dreams with strange effects. He then mentions in his *City of God,* lviii, 18, that, by divine permission, the demons of paganism could do other deceptions as well. Regarding witches and the devil, Augustine has given us stories, he has given us hear-say, but has he pierced the depths of intelligence to give us basic reality as well? The answer is obviously "no." Nonetheless, his stories carried the day.

Augustine was moving further and further from the idealized Christian, and closer and closer to pagan society when he wrote about "the dutiful judge" in his *The City of God*:

> [The witness or defendant who is tortured] suffers for a doubtful crime ... and not because he committed it.... For the wise man does not judge in this way to do harm, but because ignorance is unavoidable – and yet the needs of human society make judgment [to torture] unavoidable (Augustine, *The City of God*, XIX, 6).

Throughout the Middle Ages, Augustine's thesis was adopted by Catholic theologians.

Another text mentioned by Baroja had great influence on early Catholic theologians and canon lawyers from the 10th to the 13th century. It was also quoted in certain councils in the fourteenth century. It was called the *Canon Episcopi* supposedly promulgated by a council at Ancyra in the year 314, a council which never took place. It was quoted by Regino, Abbot of Preem in Germany, who died in 915. Its intent was to put some sanity into the dealings with witches, but it clearly did not:

> ...uproot from parishes all kinds of sorcery and magic, which are pernicious inventions of the Devil. ... Nor should any credence be given to what follows: viz. that certain women, perverted and dedicated to Satan ... believe and profess that they ride at night-time with Diana, goddess of the

pagans, and with Herodias, astride certain beasts, in a company of innumerable other women, traversing immense spaces and obeying Diana's orders like those of a mistress who convokes them on certain nights. Great throngs ... believe in all these lies and thus fall back into pagan error. It is Satan who ... having gained possession of the soul of an unfortunate woman ... takes on the appearance of divers persons and deceives the spirit of the one in his power, by showing her unknown persons or guiding her on strange voyages. The soul that has abandoned itself to him imagines that it is accomplishing in the body things that take place only in the mind.... those who believe such things have lost the faith and no longer belong to God, but only to him in whom they believe, that is the Devil (Regino, Abbott of Preem; Baroja 1990, 26).

Christian historians point to the fact that many sane and sensitive early Christian missionaries took exception to the Old Testament and encouraged newly converted kingdoms to pass laws protecting these men and women. Jenny Gibbons tells us that in the 5th century the Synod of St. Patrick ruled that "A Christian who believes that there is a vampire in the world, that is to say, a witch, is to be anathematized..." (Gibbons, 3). A capitulary from Saxony (775-790 CE) states: "If anyone, deceived by the Devil, believes after the manner of the pagans that any man or woman is a witch and eats men, and if on this account he burns [the alleged witch] ... he shall be punished by capital sentence" (Gibbons 2, 6). In 1258 Pope Alexander IV explicitly refused to allow investigations of witchcraft unless manifest heresy was involved:

C. L'Estrange Ewen states that the Church followed the Old Testament lead in its persecution of witches: "The Church blindly following [Old Testament] biblical texts believed that the slaughter of wizards and witches was in accordance with the wishes of the Almighty" (L'Estrange 1929, 1).

Traditional attitudes toward witchcraft grew from the hysteria of a Church and a people who did not have the vocabulary to deal with realities around them. It swept across Germany, Switzerland, eastern France, England and Scotland. The perceived threat was enhanced by disease, famine, invasions, other natural disasters, and eventually the stresses which came after the period of the Reformation:

> Witchcraft cases increased slowly but steadily from the 14th-15th century. The first mass trials appeared in the 15th century. At the beginning of the 16th century, as the first shock-waves from the Reformation hit, the number of witch trials actually dropped. Then, around 1550, the persecution skyrocketed. What we think of as "the Burning Times" – the crazes, panics, and mass hysteria – largely occurred in one century, from 1550-1650. In the 17th century, the Great Hunt passed nearly as suddenly as it had arisen. Trials dropped sharply after 1650 and disappeared completely by the end of the 18th century (Gibbons 2, p. 6).

The worst horrors occurred in fringe areas or in areas where central Church and civil authority had broken down. In those areas local church and local civil governments were in disarray, and the common fears and weird imaginations of the populace ruled.

Even though the duration of the main part of the witch hunts was about one century, they did start much earlier than that, as the Synod of St. Patrick indicates, and it lingered in some areas. Henningsen states:

> It is significant that witch-hunting did not really acquire momentum until after the Council of Trent in 1563 had initiated the Catholic Counter-Reformation. In the same year in England a statute enacted by Elizabeth created legislation necessary to allow witch persecution. In Germany witch trials were not general until after 1570. Over the greater part of western Europe the persecutions culminated in the period between 1575 and 1650... (Henningsen 1980, 15).

Even when the persecutions were in full swing, they tended to take place in certain places and not in others. In Germany 26,000 witches were put to death, but in Ireland only four. Some of the most intense persecutions occurred next to areas that had virtually none at all (Gibbons 2, 7, quoting Robin Briggs, *Witches and Neighbors*).

In some places, Ewen tells us, professional witch-finders were utilized and made a good living doing it (Ewen 1929, 69). Through their dirty work, many witches lost their lives.

Notably, some of the acquaintances of Dame Alice Kyleter in Ireland were condemned, but Dame Alice was saved, probably because of her rank. The "Maid of Orleans," Saint Joan of Arc was burned at the stake as a witch. Ewen tells us that in Wakefield, England, a woman suspected of witchcraft was "actually killed by the populace" (Ewen 1929, 52).[54] He also tells us: "One of

---

54 Ewen quotes *Life of Oliver Heywood*, by Rev. J. Hunter, p. 168 n.

the three charges against Christiana Stokes, who was hanged [in England] in 1606, was that she had bewitched a man to death in 1593" (Ewen 1929, 53).

THE CHURCH, CLERGY, TORTURE AND EXECUTION OF WITCHES

Unfortunately, the official Church was not innocent in the torture and executions of witches. In 1326, the Church allowed the Inquisition to investigate witchcraft. Richard Kieckhofer in *European Witch Trials: Their Foundations and Popular and Learned Culture, 1300-1500* states that only 702 definite executions of witches took place in all of Europe from 1300-1500; of these, 137 came from inquisitorial or church courts (Kieckhofer 1998, 106-153).

Clerics often played an inciting role in the midst of the raving, fearful community. Kieckhofer in "Avenging the Blood of Children: Anxiety over Child Victims and the Origins of the European Witch Trials," p. 94 states that in the 1420's St. Bernardine of Siena preached enflaming sermons to the people of Siena. In one of them he told about a recent prosecution for witchcraft which he initiated in Rome. He then insisted that anyone who failed to come forward to accuse a witch was just as guilty as the witch herself. People did come forward with many accusations against their neighbors, and at the Pope's insistence the accused were taken into custody and were convicted.

Not only Church preachers, but Church authorities were clearly responsible. Certain guidebooks or manuals were drawn up to aid the inquisitors, the ecclesiastical and the civil courts.

In 1484 Pope Innocent VIII, who himself enjoyed the "good life," wrote *Summis desiderantes effectibus,* addressed to two Dominican priests, Henry Kramer and James Sprenger. Kramer and Sprenger were contemporaries of Leonardo Da Vinci in an age of geniuses. They, too, were men of intelligence who could have put that intelligence to many areas of expertise they pleased, but they chose to persecute "witches." The Pope gave to them the "office of inquisition, correcting, imprisoning, punishing and chastising, according to their deserts, those persons whom they shall find guilty..." (*Bullarium Romanum, Taurinensis Editio*). Word spread abroad, and panic grew.

In 1486 Kramer wrote *Malleus Mallificarum*, a "judicial casebook for the detection and persecution of witches, specifying rules of evidence and the canonical procedures by which suspected witches were tortured and put to death." The case-book is cold and calculating, a systematic, step by step, procedure for dealing with anyone charged with witchcraft.

Because Kramer and Sprenger had in hand the Papal Bull of Innocent VIII, they wielded papal authority. Kramer did a second revision of the work, which included the work of a certain man by the name of Nider and others. This work was called *Malleus Maleficorum* and it did not have papal approval, but his work became the Church's position on witchcraft for some communities in the fringe areas.

Kramer's works are filled with stunning sexual preoccupations. He makes this stark statement in his manual:

> All wickedness is but little to the wickedness of a woman....What else is woman but a foe to friendship, an inescapable punishment, a necessary evil, a natural temptation, a desirable calamity, a domestic danger, a delectable detriment, an evil nature, painted with fair colors.... Women are by nature instruments of Satan – they are by nature carnal, a structural defect rooted in the original creation (Kramer, 9).

By his very words, Kramer was a perverted judge, unfit to try any woman. Any magistrate who considered his *Malleus* as the correct book for such procedures had to be perverted as well. As Baroja states:

> ...it has been described as a 'stupid book.' Books that are merely stupid, however, do not have the unusual destiny of this one, which inspired the publication of others as late as the seventeenth century, and witch-hunts that continued in Protestant countries after the Reformation (Baroja 1990, 31).

Some inquisitions had the sanity to recognize that Kramer had a problem, and it was reflected in his writings, and immediately reprimanded and censured him. They also rejected the legal procedures the *Malleus* recommended. Thereafter, the *Malleus* was not the official manual utilized by the Church against the witches. To say so would be an exaggeration.

But the work had already been disseminated throughout Europe and the damage had been done. It would also be a gross exaggeration to say that the *Malleus* had no significant influence on the acceleration of witch trials after it was rejected by inquisitions (Kieckhofer, 1998, 23). A century and a half later, Stuart Clark states, Benedikt Carpzov, professor of law at Leipzig University, utilized it as one of his principal sources in codifying procedures in the German courts (Kieckhofer 1998, 53). Other local courts, attuned to the hysterias of the people, continued to use it or manuals much like it.

According to the translator of the 1928 edition of the *Malleus Mallificarum*, "the *Malleus* serves as a horrible warning about what happens when intolerance takes over a society" (Summers 1928).

THE INQUISITION OF THE WITCHES – IN PRACTICE

At times, the terror of the witch-hunts was indiscriminate and indescribable. The accusation of two or three witnesses was all that was necessary. Once denounced, a person was guilty until proven innocent. (Summers) If the person did not confess, her or his house was completely searched. Servants and companions were imprisoned for as many as several years "in case perhaps, being depressed after a year of the squalor of prison, they may confess her crimes" (Kramer, Part I, Question 6).

Dire practices were used in many cases – usually in the "outback," the border areas, and in the civil courts where the established authority, Church and civil, had broken down. If they utilized the *Malleus*, they stripped the person and shaved the person's body to find "devil's marks" (Kramer, Part III, Question 7). Certainly they found only the usual birthmarks, moles, freckles and extra nipples found on any human body.[55] In the belief that the parts of the body the devil touched would feel no pain, they stabbed various parts of the body with needles. They used sleep deprivation, and starvation with a meager diet of bread and water, thumbscrews, and "boots" which broke and crushed the legs (Kramer, Part I, Question 6). Who can say that all this was free from sexual perversion? It is quite obvious that sexual perversion was involved.

Obviously most of these poor victims confessed that they

---

[55] Ewen tells us about the offensive nature of one stripping and searching. He writes: "...they began at her head, and so stripped her naked, and in the lower part of her belly they found a thing like a teat of an inch long, they questioned her about it, and she said that she had got a strain by carrying water which caused that excrescence. But upon narrower search, they found in her privy parts three more excrescences or teats, but smaller than the former: This examiner further said that in the long teat at the end thereof was a little hole, and it appeared unto them as if it had lately been sucked, and upon the straining of it there issued out white milkie matter" (*A Tryal of Witches at Bury St. Edmunds, 1664*, p. 16). Ewen goes on to write that this form of examination was not adopted to any extent officially in England, but it was common procedure in Scotland. The whole examination was disgusting, and showed no understanding of the human body at all.

consorted with Satan and that they had committed whatever dark and obscene practices the torturers could conjure up in their imaginations.

Thinking that the ordeal was finally over, the victim, now completely humiliated, was thrown into a cold prison cell only to find out that the tortures would now be increased. They were now admitted witches, so the torturers went to stage two. The condemned was now forced to come up with the names of the twelve others who made up her or his coven. Of course, at that point the person was so broken that names easily flowed from the mouth. Those poor implicated individuals were then brought into the torture chambers and the procedures were continued.

Confessions brought a "merciful" death -- strangulation at the stake before the body was burned or hung. Those who endured all and admitted nothing were executed alive (Kramer, Part III, Question 7).[56]

Why did the persons who were condemned as witches act as witches? They were convicted; they lost all their earthly goods; they were imprisoned; they were interrogated with the assumption that they were witches; their bodies were abused by being stripped so that even the clothes on their bodies were no longer their own; their bodily hair was shaved off so that even the hairs on the body were no longer their own; they then had their nude and hairless bodies examined closely for suspicious marks so that not even their bodies could be properly called their own; they

---

[56] Some in the age adapted a critical attitude to what was happening around them. The most famous case, according to Julio Caro Baroja, p. 41, was Friedrich von Spee, who had direct experience of the witch hunt. Von Spee published his work anonymously. It was called *Cautio criminalis seu de processibus contra sagas liber*. "He examines the circumstances in which people were accused of sorcery, and the variety of accusations supported by more than doubtful testimony. He refers to the influence of preachers, and to the fact that lawyers and inquisitors were remunerated in proportion to the number of convictions. He describes the forms of detention, interrogation, and inspection; the obtaining of confessions by torture, the passing of sentence, accusations of complicity, and retraction *in extremis*. The whole system was permeated by deception and prejudice. Men and women were inexorably condemned to death in accordance with a stereotyped image of their crime or crimes."

were then brutally tortured. It is no wonder that many of them fell into a psychosis and actually believed that they were witches. Or, if they were psychologically strong, it is no wonder that they threw everything to the wind and decided to act like witches -- after all, it was the only power which society would allow them.

Then, when the interrogators had them tortured again in order to discover their coven, it became payback time. They endured the torture for a while, and then leaked this name, then that name, until they leaked all those from their small village who had them brought in as witches in the first place. All of these were then brought into jail to endure everything that our "witches" endured. All this is not difficult to understand.

According to Starhawk the last official trial and execution for witchcraft in Western Europe was that of Anna Goeldi, who was hanged at Glaris in Switzerland on June 17, 1782.

Henningsen puts a concluding remark on the witch-hunts:

> The peculiarity of the witch classification is that the group is fictitious, nobody belongs to it, but individuals who deviate from the norms of their society are the first to be supposed to be members of this secret confederation, where all virtues of the society are inverted. The European witch craze is now history, but in principle it continues to repeat itself. Indeed, a characteristic of this kind of myth-making is that it continually returns in a new and plausible disguise. We shall always need men with courage enough to tear away the mask... (Henningsen 1980, 393).

Some historians blamed the Church for the witch-hunt. Sometimes the accusation was true. At times, the Christian

Church involved itself not so much in the Gospel of Jesus but in the torturing and killing of witches. It should have known better. If truth was of paramount importance to the Church of the time, the church's role in the persecution of witches was inexcusable. It certainly was not Jesus' idea.

CONCLUSION

Ginzburg prefers to look at the myths that surrounded the witches. He states: "All of them work a common theme: going into the beyond, returning from the beyond. This elementary narrative nucleus has accompanied humanity for thousands of years.... In participation in the world of the living and of the dead, in the sphere of the visible and of the invisible, we have already recognized a distinctive trait of the human species" (Ginzburg 1991, 307). Undoubtedly, the so-called witches gave the theme a particularly vulgar and profane touch, but as Ginzburg further states: "... here is not one narrative among many, but the matrix of all possible narratives" (Ginzburg 1991, 307).

Christianity was meant to aid people in the quest for this "matrix of all possible narratives." But Christian clerics from the time of the Greek fathers of the Church to the 18th century were too busy fighting over the truths of Christianity to nurture the life of the common Christian. It is not surprising that groups of people were forced to bear the label "witches" in order to fill that very human need for transcendence.

Our world is still dominated by fears, often fears beyond control. But they are, for the most part, not the fears that initiated the witch-hunts. For the most part, our world considers that witches are impossible, simply fairy-tales. We have gained a "sense of the impossible." We live in an age which gives us other tools and words to discern the activities of such different people, for example, the passive aggressive personality, the depressive personality, persons with psychotic breaks, the savants, persons with seizures, etc. But in our age, also, the word "terrorist" has taken on mythological proportions, not only among common folk, but among the elite of academia as well. Where Bodin saw witches, we see "terrorists" and Muslims under our rugs.

Chapter 13

THE SPANISH INQUISITION

If we were Pollyanna, we would say that the Spanish Inquisition was an attempt by good Christians in positions of authority to preserve the integrity of Christian religious truth and practice in Spain and elsewhere, and thus save the immortal souls of those heretics who had gone astray. Augustine would have said that. Perhaps in a straining attempt to be objective, this is the attitude which Henry Charles Lea also took in his volume 3 of *A History of the Inquisition of Spain*. In the beginning of Chapter 7 on "Torture," he tried to defend the Spanish Inquisition:

> To the modern mind the judicial use of torture, as a means of ascertaining truth, is so repellant and illogical that we are apt to forget that it has, from the most ancient times, been practised by nearly all civilized nations. With us the device of the jury has relieved the judge of the responsibility resting upon him in other systems of jurisprudence. That responsibility had to be met; a decision had to be reached, even in the most doubtful cases and, where evidence was defective and conflicting, the use of torture as an expedient to obtain a confession, or by its endurance, to indicate innocence, has seemed, until modern times, after the disuse

of compurgation and the judgements of God, to be the only means of relieving the judicial conscience. It was admitted to be dangerous and fallacious, to be employed only with circumspection, but there was nothing to take its place (Lea, 3, 6, 7, 1888-1906).

Lea states that torture was necessary until the jury system evolved. After a century has intervened since Lea wrote his monumental work on the Inquisition in Spain we have seen that Lea's justification of the use of torture has proven itself false. The judicial jury system came in and has been refined. Yet some continue to torture humans, as we see clearly in the holocaust, Abu-Graibe and Guantanamo. These happenings in the 20th and early 21st century are written in indelible ink in history. But this is not precisely our point. Even if torture would have been practiced by nearly all civilized nations from the most ancient times, a point disputed by most, and even if it continues to be practiced by some, it is still contrary to the way of Jesus. True Christians would do best to join the majority of the world in abhorring its use. Today, most nations have realized its degradation of humanity, as well as its futility in the judicial system.[57]

Lea finds excuses for the inexcusable. He lets the perpetrators of the Spanish Inquisition off the hook. He continues: "That it [torture] should be used by the Inquisition was a matter of course, for the crime of heresy was often one peculiarly difficult to prove..."(Lea, 3, 6, 7, 1888-1906).

---

57 The United Nations has passed a document that prohibits torture. The text of that document states that nations will take effective measures to prevent torture within their borders. It also forbids nations from transporting people to some other country where there is reason to believe that they will be tortured. This document was adopted by the United Nations General Assembly on December 10, 1984. It was ratified by the 20th nation, making it international law, on June 26, 1987. As of September, 2013, all nations of the Western Hemisphere and 154 nations of the world have ratified it.

Sadly, the Spanish Inquisition was only one of the offenses against humanity and the Jesus Community in the history of Christianity. We have already noted a number of others. Taking into consideration those movements of history, coupled with contemporary trends, we have to pessimistically admit that, unless Christians change to a Jesus-centered Christianity, there are probably more to follow.

The Spanish Inquisition was a major infringement. It lasted for 3 and a half centuries, from 1478 to 1834. In the process, it exported its terror to neighboring Portugal. It also managed to poison the "new world" through the hubris and catastrophic actions of Columbus, the conquistadors, and other invaders of the Americas. Columbus and the others would have done much better to consider themselves visitors to America instead of invaders.[58]

By the time of the inquisition, torture had become a common practice. The person who believed something different than the Grand Master of the Inquisition--Jesus' teachings was not the issue--was considered to be a person who deserved to be tortured and even, at times, burned at the stake.

Catholics and Christians everywhere must face the reality -- the Inquisition in Spain committed crimes against humanity. It certainly had nothing to do with Jesus who had respect for all, Jew and Gentile, and participated wholeheartedly in Jewish life and ceremonies. If Jesus would have lived his life-style in Spain during Torquemada's inquisition, as Dostoevski suggests, he would have been tortured and burned at the stake. The Spaniards who

---

58 Of course, America was "new" only to those who were excited about "discovering" it after 1492. It was not new certainly to those who had inhabited it for years, nor was it new to other explorers and some educated people who knew of its existence before Columbus. Indeed, it was and it remains the homeland of a huge, Native American population, even though they underwent genocide when the Spaniards and others entered the land. Those of us who came later are the strangers in the land, the "wetbacks," the migrants. Those who say, "It is okay for migrants to enter our country as long as they speak the language of the land are saying without knowing it, "All of us who speak English or Spanish should really be speaking Chippewa, Iroquois, Sioux, Crow, or Apache. We are the immigrants living in their land."

perpetrated their inquisition and their lackeys were clearly guilty of genocide.

The Spanish Inquisition, when all is said and done, was a Machiavellian machine utilized by the Church and state of the time to control the populace, gain revenues, and unleash personal vendettas against Jews, Protestants and other enemies of the king, queen, and clergy. As Michel Foucault stated, Christian truth was not the issue and was not preserved, but it was trampled upon and used as a cover to gratify base desires of church and state control.

They said that the issue was saving immortal souls. This was the sham initiated by Ambrose and Augustine. The intent of the inquisition was not in any way, shape, or form the preservation of veritable truths of Jesus or the salvation of souls. It was simply utilitarian and perverse.

LEAD UP TO THE SPANISH INQUISITION

Henry Charles Lea, in his monumental eight volume work *A History of the Spanish Inquisition,* written at the end of the nineteenth century, goes into detail in describing cases brought before the inquisition. His works paint a much different picture than the first two paragraphs of his chapter on "Torture" would indicate. Also, Edward Peters work *Inquisition* is excellent, as is many other works which bear out the gruesome elements of real cases of the Spanish Inquisition, placing the inquisition in its true perspective in history. Exaggeration is not necessary. The reality of the inquisition is gruesome enough.

KINGPINS OF THE EARLY INQUISITION IN SPAIN

An early example of the church people of the time who promoted the Inquisition in Spain was the Archbishop of Toledo,

Alonso Carrillo who was *ex officio* chancellor of the realm when Isabella became queen. He was a very rich man. He received revenues of eighty to a hundred thousand ducats a year, with patronages amounting to another hundred thousand more. But he wanted even more. His desire for riches and power was written all over his activities. Hernando del Pulgar wrote the following letter to him:

> The people look to you as their bishop and find in you their enemy; they groan and complain that you use your authority not for their benefit and reformation but for their destruction; not as an exemplar of kindness and peace but for corruption, scandal and disturbance (Lea, Book I, Chap. 1, 1906, p. 9).

His successor to the Archbishopric, Cardinal Ximenes, was of the same ilk. He was an appointee of Isabella. He, too, did everything to attain riches and power. During his youthful sojourn in Rome, Ximenes manipulated church officials in that city until they gave him papal "expectative letters" to the first Bishopric that should fall vacant in the archdiocese of Toledo. The position of archpriest of Uceda became vacant, so Ximenes went to fill it. However, Archbishop Carrillo had already filled it with one of his lackeys. Ximenes was unrelenting, so he was thrown into the hellish dungeon used for clerical malefactors. The living conditions there were far worse than they were in the ordinary Toledo prison. Ximenes remained there for six years. When released, he maneuvered himself into position to gain the bishopric of Toledo (Lea, 1906, p. 13), and from there he became a key figure in the inquisition.

In Spain, contrary to what we might think, little respect was shown the pope by the higher clergy and by the King and Queen. The popes of the time were only token heads of the Spanish Church. The power remained in the hands of Spain's royalty.

However, it will become as apparent as the pollution of the atmosphere that neither the popes in Rome at the time, nor the king and queen, nor the "high priests" of the inquisition were studied followers of Jesus. To attain their positions in the church or government, they had only to be astute and greedy politicians who out-maneuvered everyone else.

Another example occurred in 1482. The See of Cuenca became vacant and Pope Sixtus IV at first appointed one of his Genoese cousins to the position. King Ferdinand and Queen Isabella took the pope to task, demanding that only Spaniards should fill Spanish bishoprics. The King and Queen insisted that no matter what "might be the papal rights in other countries, in Spain the patronage of all benefices belonged to the crown because they and their predecessors had wrested the land from the infidel." Sixtus IV whined a bit about the power being the pope's by divine right, but he eventually caved in, and granted the King and Queen's demands (Lea, 1906, p. 15).

THE JEWS AND THE INQUISITION IN SPAIN

The inquisition in Spain, was unleashed mainly against the *conversos*, the Jewish converts to Christianity. Henry Charles Lea generalizes on the treatment of the Jews in Europe:

> Under the canon law the Jew was a being who had scarce the right of existence and could only enjoy it under conditions of virtual slavery. When Paramo, about the same period, sought to justify the expulsion of the Jews from Spain in 1492, he had no

difficulty in citing canons to prove that Ferdinand and Isabella could righteously have seized all their property and have sold their bodies into slavery. Man is ready enough to oppress and despoil his fellows and, when taught by his religious guides that justice and humanity are not a sin against God, spoliation and oppression become the easiest of duties. It is not too much to say that for the infinite wrongs committed on the Jews during the Middle Ages, and for the prejudices that are even yet rife in many quarters, the Church is mainly if not wholly responsible (Lea: 1906,I, 2, 1906, p. 35).

This was not always true in Spanish history. In early times, cordiality and a sense of equality existed between Christian and Jew. The change began early in the fourth century when the Council of Elvira forbade marriage between Christians and Jews "because there should be no society common to the faithful and the infidel." Even the mild mannered St. Isidore of Seville said that the Jews were condemned for their fathers' sins (*De Fide Cathol. Contra Judaeos*, I, 28, II, 5 &9).

The history of oppression against the Jews then quickly became the norm. At the Council of Toledo in 694, King Egiza appealed to the prelates to wipe out the Jews. If that was not possible, all the possessions of the Jews were to be confiscated. In response, the Catholic religious leaders decreed that all Jews, with their wives, children, and posterity be reduced to slavery and all their property be confiscated (Lea, p. 43). Right up to the time of Ferdinand and Isabella, and into their reign, the Christian continued to lay a heavy hand on the Jewish population. The Muslim, too, was treated with disdain. None of them were true human beings to Christians.

Between 700 to 710, when the Muslims conquered great parts of Spain, and in other periods when the Muslim held smaller parts of the country, the Muslims respected the religions of their fellow compatriots, Christian and Jew alike. The same was not true of the Christians whenever they took over the administration of the country.

THE BEGINNINGS OF THE INQUISITION IN SPAIN

Cecil Roth goes into much detail when he treats the beginnings of the Spanish inquisition. In 1378, an archdeacon by the name of Ferran Martinez stirred the citizenry of Spain against the Jewish citizens in their midst. On Ash Wednesday, 1391, he was particularly effective, motivating a mob to move murderously toward the Jewish quarter. The civil authorities were alarmed by the scene, and they had two members of the mob publicly flogged. This did nothing more than make them popular heroes. On June 6 of that same year, the mob actually invaded the Jewish quarter of Seville, killing hundreds of Jews.

The mob violence then spread from city to city in Spain until the total number of murdered Jews numbered approximately 50,000 (Roth, 1964, pp. 17-27). The Jews were given a choice, "convert or die." Customarily in such situations, Jews unflinchingly chose death rather than apostasy. This time in their long history, Roth says , many Jews gave into the pressure. Hundreds of thousands chose to become *conversos* to the Church in order to forestall further trouble for themselves. Of course, many remained Jewish at heart and practiced their former, sacred religion in secret while conforming to the mechanics of the Church.

THE MARRIAGE OF FERDINAND AND ISABELLA

Soon thereafter, on October 19, 1469, Princess Isabella of Castile married Prince Ferdinand of Aragon, uniting Aragon and Castile. Even though all the coffers were empty, the prince and princess went all out for the celebration. It was an expensive and solemn occasion, celebrated with borrowed money (Plaidy, Jean, 1967, p. 99). Isabella acceded to the throne of Castile in 1474, and Ferdinand took the throne of Aragon in 1479 (Kamen, Henry, 1965, p. 1).

At that point in time, Spain was virtually united. Only two political problems remained. The Muslims still held Granada, and, if they should call their armies to drive the Muslims off the Spanish peninsula, neither ruler was certain of the support of the Jews. Certainly, the financial help of the Jews was needed. Isabella and Ferdinand were unresponsive to letters from the Pope, who at times tried to dampen their zeal for unifying the country. They were content to use rather than adhere to papal directives and decrees (Lea, Vol. 1, Book 1, 1906, p. 154).

In 1455, when he was thirty five years old, a man by the name of Torquemada became prior of the Dominican friary of Santa Cruz in Segovia. In that year and years immediately following, he lived a quiet life in his friary. He put all his energies into a building project, supervising the beginnings of one of the most beautiful architectural monuments in Europe – the Dominican friary of Segovia.

After Isabella became Queen of Castile in 1474, Torquemada became her spiritual director. Isabella was twenty-three years old at the time. She was, by all external standards, a fervent Christian woman with some apparent nun-like qualities.

Along side of and in contrast to her visible religious bent,

Queen Isabella used capital punishment as an easy tool to restore order in Castile. She was strong, manly, unforgiving, and rigidly tenacious of her royal dignity. Even though Walsh is naïve about the supposed "peaceful" results of her ventures, he otherwise paints the picture for us:

> Evidently this fair young woman, who had time, with all her military and judicial activities, to bear five children in the course of some sixteen years, who heard Mass and read her breviary daily like any nun, never so much as flickered one of her auburn eyelashes as she rode away on her white horse, after saying crisply, in effect, "Off with his head!" Stolen goods were restored; criminals feared to shed blood, decent people slept soundly once more in their beds. In Sevilla, a notorious centre of crime, she had malefactors executed in such numbers that the aged Archbishop finally pleaded with her not to let justice forget mercy (Walsh, 1940, p. 137).

Torquemada was not yet politically involved. He was content with his prayers, his community and his building project.

PLANS FOR INQUISITION AND ELIMINATION OF MUSLIMS FROM SPAIN

As for Isabella and Ferdinand, the more they discussed the matter, the more intent they became on driving the Muslims from Granada. But they had few financial resources and they knew it would be all out "total war," long and costly.

Granada, the object of their concern, had been under Muslim

control since the eighth century. During that time, close contact between Muslim, Jews, and Christians had led to tolerance, if not mutual acceptance of one another. With war, that tolerance came to an end (Kamen,, 1965, p. 2).

Furthermore, Isabel and Ferdinand knew that they could not go to war against the Muslims in Granada unless they could rely on the revenues of the Jewish *conversos*. They did not need Jewish moral support, but they did need their finances. At the same time, they were certain that they could not endure the opposition of these Jewish citizens.

They speculated that they needed an inquisition to deal with the *conversos*, an inquisition in which the judges would be trustworthy Dominican friars who would be beyond the reach of intimidation and bribery (Peters, 1988, p. 84).

The King and the Queen commissioned Cardinal Pedro Gonzales de Mendoza, the future patron of Columbus, and Torquemada to write a petition to the Pope asking for the authority to set up the inquisition in Spanish territories. On November 1, 1478, with the customary diplomatic polish which had become customary in such matters, Pope Sixtus IV responded:

> The genuine devotion and sound faith manifested in your reverence for us and the Roman Church requires that as far as we can in the sight of God, grant your requests, particularly those which concern the exaltation of the Catholic Faith and the salvation of souls. From your letter ... we learn that in various cities, sections and regions of the Spanish Kingdoms, many of those who of their own accord were born anew in Christ in the waters of baptism, while continuing to comport themselves externally as Christians, yet have secretly adopted or returned

to the religious observances and customs of the Jews.... And not only do they themselves persist in their blindness, but they also infect with their blindness those born of them, or having communication with them, and their numbers increase not a little....Rejoicing in God over your praiseworthy zeal ... and hoping that you will not only drive out this falsehood from your realms, but that, also in our times, you will reduce to your rule the Kingdom of Granada ... and through the divine mercy will convert the infidels to the true faith ... we, therefore, grant your supplications... (*Boletin de la real academia de la historia,* vol. IX, p. 172).

Isabella and Ferdinand delayed for two years, a delay which historians strain to explain. Then, on August 26th, 1480, they published a decree initiating the inquisition in Spain. Cardinal Mendoza was placed in charge of the operation. Two Dominican friars, Miguel de Morillo and Juan de San Martin were given the jobs of inquisitors. Torquemada was the consulting expert (Peters, 1988, p. 84).

FERDINAND AND ISABELLA'S INQUISITION

In October, the inquirers turned their attention to the almost totally Jewish city of Seville. Three edicts of grace were published, starting in January, 1481. The third warned all good Christians to avoid associating with those who promoted Judaism (Peters, p. 151). The beginnings of the persecution were brutal.

Upon hearing the plans against the Jews, Diego de Susan, a very wealthy man, had organized an underground group who decided to gather weapons. One hundred guns were secretly collected and stored in the home of Pedro Fernandez Benadeba. The group agreed that the first Jewish arrest by the inquisition would be the sign for the group to rise up and kill the inquisitors, effectively stopping the impending inquisitorial nonsense. The plot would have succeeded if it were not for the beautiful daughter of Diego de Susan who confided in her boyfriend. The boyfriend went immediately to the inquisition with the knowledge (Lea, 1906, p. 162).

An *auto de fe* (a supposed "public act of faith" which was really an instrument of the inquisition, and had no "public act of faith" about it) was called for February 6th with a Mass in the Cathedral. Some who confessed were given penances and were reconciled. Six of the chief conspirators, all influential men of the city, were handed over to the civil authorities and were burned outside the walls of the city. Their property and goods were confiscated. Some of the men involved got wind of the impending inquisition and fled.

But a few days later three of the richest leaders of the city, Diego de Susan, Manuel Sauli, and Bartolome de Torralva, together with Pedro Fernandez Benadeba and Juan Fernandez Abolasia, a great lawyer, and many other rich and leading citizens were also burned outside the walls of the city (Kamen, 1969, p. 37).

The citizens of Seville, but especially the Jews of the city, were in panic. The very next summer, because of the weakened resistance of the people who were doing their best to adapt to the tragedies, the sickness called the plague invaded the city, killing 15,000. The people of the city requested the inquisition for permission to leave the city until the epidemic was over. The inquisitors granted this permission, and, of course, most of those who left never returned.

For those who stayed in Seville, another edict of grace of two months was given. In the midst of the plague, 17,000 confessed and were absolved, but their goods were confiscated. (Peters. P. 159). Some actively resisted the arm of the inquisition, and they were subjected to all the customary tortures common in Spain. All their goods were confiscated.

Detailed scrutiny of the inquisition by historians shows that, at times, false accusations were made. The procedures were ready opportunities for vengeance, anti-Semitism and sexism. Also, any indication of conformity to the traditions of Judaism was immediately pounced upon by the inquisitors. Family traditions, some of them incidental, which went back many years within the Jewish tradition, were not respected.

Pope Sixtus IV heard of the horror stories and undoubtedly felt responsible. Some good Christians of Jewish descent had been tortured. Also richer Jewish travelers to Rome said that Isabella and Ferdinand, intent on financing their war with the Muslims, were using the inquisition to financially plunder the Jews.

The pope wrote a letter, dated August 2, 1483, to the Queen and King. He told them that he was not happy with the inquisitorial activities of Morillo and San Martin. He censured the inquisitors for indiscretion and unjust conduct in Seville. In particular, he said:

1.) Cases before the archbishop were delayed unnecessarily.

2.) Methods of inquiry exceeded the moderation of law.

3.) Some were prevented from quick access to the court of appeals.

4.) Some pardoned in Rome had been unjustly burned in absentia.

5.) True Christians of Jewish descent could not live free from fear.

6.) Shame of public correction led the erring into despair.

7.) Not all penitents were forgiven and reinstated, free from molestation.

8.) Jewish Christians with cases pending in Rome were not treated as Catholics (Bull, Pope Sixtus IV, "Ad Futuram Rei Memoriam").

But he said nothing about the injustice of persecuting sincere Jews simply because they were firm and sincere believers in the Jewish religion. He said nothing about the fact that Jesus was a Jewish believer, and that there was integrity in that religion, even though it was different than Catholicism.

Because of his reservations, inadequate though they were, the pope at first refused an extension of the inquisition into Aragon. But in February, 1482, he changed his mind and agreed to it, but with one qualification – he insisted on taking the administration of the inquisition into his own hands. He appointed eight inquisitors for Castile and Leon. Torquemada was one of the eight (Kamen, 1965, p. 154).

THE INQUISITION OF TORQUEMADA

In October, 1482, Sixtus IV gave Torquemada, now 63 years old, control of the whole inquisition. At the same time, in a political countermove that insured the control of the queen and king, Isabella and Ferdinand made Torquemada a member of their own royal council (Kamen, 1965, p. 154). Morillo and San Martin were forced to take the fall, and they were counted out. Torquemada had carefully watched their failings, and he learned from their mistakes.

Isabella continued to make known her expectations to Torquemada. We have already seen that she, for all her charm, could be ruthless. The pope also carefully explained to Torquemada what he expected. Torquemada was no fool. He could walk that walk. He could please them both.

Torquemada did some antiseptic grooming to please the pope.

He was a builder, so he did some apparent improvement on the prisons. He also apparently improved the prison food and the usual procedures of the inquisition. The pope was happy. He did not know that Torquemada also maintained another "basement prison," where solitary confinement reigned and a torture chamber was a handy add-on.

If the old inquisition was gone, a new one took its place, and it was Torquemada's alone. He was able to do more than any of his predecessors to establish the power and authority of the inquisition in Spain.

While Rome tried to be watchful, Torquemada relied on stealth. Isabella's needs were constantly before his eyes. He knew that at times he had to introduce torture. He also had to introduce political revenge and terror. But most of all, he had to fund the war against the Muslims. If he kept the apparent beyond reproach, if his public image was charming, he could give the queen everything she wanted. And that is what he did. When the queen was breathing down his neck, he would snatch some carefully picked individual whom the queen detested, and, in secret, do to him or her everything that he and the queen wanted him to do, and that included appropriating all the property and riches of the person, horrible tortures, terrible incarcerations, slavery on the galleys, the insisting on the person wearing the *sanbenito*, the yellow garb with intense social stigma, for life and other penalties. Both pope and queen were happy.

All citizens of Spain who knew the reality of the situation kept their mouths shut. No one ran to Rome. We are not sure why no one stormed Rome. Perhaps everyone, especially the Jews, felt it was futile to do so. Certainly, it is clear that the non-Jewish citizenry, strongly encouraged by their priests and bishops, were happy with the inquisition (Henningsen, p. 46). As David Koeller wrote, the pope was never able "to wrench this extremely useful political tool from the hands of the Spanish rulers" (Koeller, 2001).

On the other hand, Torquemada knew he now had the control to add another dimension to the inquisition, the dimension closest to the hearts of Isabella and Ferdinand. He decreed that confiscated property of Jews would be used to defray expenses of the war against the Muslims. Many of those condemned were rich. Torquemada knew that, as far as the king and queen were concerned, the right to confiscate the property of violators was an important part of the inquisition (Plaidy, 1965, p. 122).

The extension of the inquisition to Aragon and beyond stirred some special difficulties. The greatest sign of opposition was the murder of the inquisitor, Peter Arbues, as he prayed in Church. But the inquisition survived even this.

Some say that 100,000 came before Torquemada's tribunal. Walsh quotes a reliable source, the secretary of Isabella, who said that in her whole reign 2,000 were put to death. If that is true, Walsh surmises, approximately 1,000 to 1,500 were put to death at the hands of Torquemada (Walsh, 1940, p. 174). Other estimates say that Torquemada was responsible for 8,800 deaths. Another group says that 5,000 to 15,000 were sentenced to prison, the galleys, and a life of certain poverty. Torquemada, if anyone, was the only one who ever knew the true number, and he was not admitting any numbers to anyone.

THE PROCEEDINGS OF THE INQUISITION

The miscellaneous offenses charged by the inquisition were eventually grouped under the general term of *propositions*. The propositions were the following: heresy, error, savoring of heresy, ill-sounding words, rash words, and words that were scandalous or offensive to pious ears, schism, insults and blasphemy. Some of the crimes indicated were meager -- things any normal citizen did every day. Thus the inquisition could prosecute anyone it pleased.

But the actual inquisition went even much further than these propositions indicate. It truly became an oppressive operation. In its procedures, the inquisition used torture when the victim denied the accusation and it believed that it had a solid case against the accused, but it was also used, at times, when the case was not clearly substantiated and was inconsequential.

The Supreme Council was the over-seer of the proceedings, and the law of the proceedings was clear. Before torturing anyone, the approval of the bishop of the diocese was necessary. The bishop or his vicar, the inquisitorial tribunal, a doctor, and a notary or secretary had to be present. The doctor could stop the proceedings at any point.

As we look over the cases which history has provided us, we notice that the inquisitors made many obvious exceptions to the rule – exceptions always favored the inquisition. Both men and women were tortured. Both sexes were stripped of their clothes and left completely naked. After this humiliation, the doctor examined the victim in front of all who were present. Then, at times, the person was given a pair of abbreviated underpants, similar to today's bikini bathing trunks, to cover themselves.

The inquisition knew no age limit for victims. To give us some idea of the importance placed on the Inquisition, and the zeal of the inquisitors, old people, even women, between seventy and ninety were tortured.

- Leonor Perez, a woman 70 years old, would have been tortured but she confessed after being stripped (Lea, 3, 6, 7, 6-7).[59]

---

59 Lea used the following documentation. When stripped, on May 10, 1634, the executioner reported marks of previous torture, so the proceedings were suspended. On June 14th, the sentence to torture her was again executed. She was again stripped. She then confessed to some Jewish beliefs and then she fainted. A postponement was necessary. Two days later she revoked her confession. On August, 1637 she was condemned to six years of exile and given a fine of two hundred ducats. Nonetheless, we still hear of her as in prison in 1639 (*Archivo de Simancas*,

THE CONSUMING FORCE

- A woman 90 years old was tortured at Cuenca (Lea, 3, 6, 7, 13).[60]
- Isabel Ganese, a woman 78 years old, would have been tortured, but she confessed (Lea, 3, 6, 7, 13-14).
- Isabel de Jaen, a woman 80 years old, endured five turns of the cords before fainting. Five turns of the sharp cords that were customarily used meant that the cords penetrated her skin and some muscles and nerves were damaged. Isabel was revived with difficulty (Lea 3, 6, 7, 14).[61]
- Jaime Chuleyla, a man 76 years old, was tortured.

Young boys and girls were also fair game to be jailed, stripped and tortured before the eyes of men of the tribunal.

- Isabel Madalena, a girl 13 years old, was accused of vague Moorish practices at Valencia in 1607. She was stripped and tortured and then was stripped again and given a severe penance of 100 lashes.
- A boy 15 years old was tortured.
- Ana Gutierrez, a ten year old girl, was arrested and exposed to imprisonment and the eyes and laughter of the jailors for one to two years without a charge against her (Lea, 1906, Book VI, Chapter 3, pp. 493; Chapter 7, pp. 13 & 16; Book 8, Chapter 7, p. 139).
- Joan de Heredia, a boy 10 years old was accused of going to a house where Moorish doctrines were taught. He was stripped and tortured, but he persisted in asserting his innocence and the case was dismissed.

Imprisonment in the "secret prison," the prison for heretics,

---

Inquisicion, Leg. 552, fol. 17, 22, 23).
60 Lea used the following documentation: *Llorente, Hist. crit.* Cap. XVII, Art. 1, n. 24.
61 Lea used the following documentation: *Mss. of Library of Univ. of Halle, Yc,* 20, T. I.

often involved solitary confinement. If a person ended up in this prison, he or she was to speak to no one, and no one was to speak to the individual who was confined. If the prisoner tried to talk to a prison guard, he or she was severely punished, usually with the lash.

As a general rule, no distinctive tortures were used by the inquisition. By this we mean that for the most part, but not exclusively, it used the same intense tortures used by the secular courts of Spain: the *toca*, the *garrucha*, and the *potro* (Kamen, 1997, p. 174; Walsh, 1940, 169).

The *toca*, or *aselli*, the water torture, or water boarding, was an involved affair, but it was one of the favorites of the inquisition.

THE CASE OF ELVIRA DEL CAMPO[62]

The case of Elvira del Campo, tried in 1567 is one example highlighted by Henry Charles Lea of the many horror stories of

---

[62] The historical facts related to Elvira del Compo's interrogation and torture read much like the morbid fiction stories written by Edgar Allen Poe. Further complicating the matter, many myths have followed the historical facts related to Elvira del Compo. One of those, for example, is that she was 65 years old when she was tortured. This is undoubtedly not true since Elvira bore a child in prison seven months before she was tortured. Elvira was undoubtedly a much younger woman. Almost unbelievably *Archivo hist. national*, Leg. 128, the document written originally by the exceptional notary, who was present at the interrogation and torture, is an accepted document, recognized by historians. Elvira del Compo was truly interrogated and tortured and this is undoubtedly how it happened. In a book edited by Yael Halevi-Wise, *Separdism: Spanish Jewish History and the Modern Literary Imagination*, Stanford University Press, 2012, Elaine Feinstein writes about the torture of Elvira del Compo: the passage is found originally in Feinstein's book, *Talking to the Dead*, Manchester, Carcanet, 2007. Feinstein writes: "Elvira del Campo was arrested in Toledo in 1567 on suspicion of Judaizing because she refused to eat pork; her story is related in Henry Charles Lea, A History of the Inquisition in Spain, vol. 3 (New York: Macmillan, 1922), 24-26." Also, Ariel Glucklich in *Sacred Pain: Hurting the Body for the Sake of the Soul*, Oxford University Press, 2001 records essentially the same story as Lea on page 153, and then writes: "The historiography of the Inquisition has been greatly enriched by the exquisite detail and detachment with which officials of the Church witnessed and recorded such interrogations and tortures." Glucklich goes on to recall Michel Foucault's elaborate claims that the state exerts power over its subjects. On page 170, Glucklich continues with the story of the interrogation of Elvira del Compo, and then states: "Elvira had no idea what the inquisitors knew ... and how much they wanted her to acknowledge." Abel A. Alves in his book, *Brutality and Benevolence: Human Ethology, Culture, and the Birth of Mexico*, Greenwood Press, 1996, on page 27, quotes some of Lea's recording of history concerning Elvira del Compo. And also, Renee Levine, in the book *Melammed Heretics and Daughters of Israel? The Crypto-Jewish Women of Castile*. Oxford University Press, on pages 56-57, further identifies Elvira del Compo as "Elvira of Ahnodonar del Compo, who lived southeast of Chillon."

the inquisition in Spain. We have the full story because the notary at the torture proceedings was excellent. He gave to history detailed notes of the whole proceedings. We give it here to show the ugliness, the arbitrariness, the shamefulness, the sexism, and the anti-Semitism of the Inquisition in Spain.

Elvira del Campo was a Christian of Jewish descent. She was married to Alonso de Moya, a scribe or notary of Madridejos. Twelve witnesses, including neighbors and ecclesiastics, said that she was a good Christian, attentive and regular in her religious duties, and that she was kind and charitable. They said that she went to Mass and confession regularly.

But two of her husband's employees, men who lived in the house, testified in great detail against Elvira. At the same time, her husband was notably absent throughout the proceedings. Elvira said in the proceedings that she feared him and her own father. Both the testifying of the employees and the absence of the husband undoubtedly show the fear of the inquisition and the power which it exerted over the people of Spain.

Elvira was arrested early in July, 1567. She was pregnant at the time of her arrest so she had to wait in the cold, dank prison for three months until she gave birth to her child. The prison did not have sufficient heat to warm her body, food to eat or even water to drink. She never saw her child after the birthing. She never did know what happened to her baby.

Prison was, then, a difficult time, a torture all its own. Elvira was used to a good life. She was not permitted to have books, pencil or paper. She was not able to work on hobbies or do any familiar tasks . She could talk to nobody. She had nothing to do but sit on a plank, which she used for a bed. She sat there with her own fears.

Furthermore, the charges against her were meager, embarrassing, and tragic. They clearly show in a clear concrete case the extent of the intense anti-Semitism, the macho insanity, as well as the sexual perversion that had become part of the legal structure. It was simply unbelievable that she was charged only with never eating pork and with changing her underclothes on Saturdays. She, however, did not know that this was the total case against her.

Yet these two incidentals somehow proved to the inquisitors that Elvira was a secret Jewess. She willingly admitted the acts. She did not eat pork, and she did, if anyone should care, change her underwear on Saturday. But she vehemently denied heretical intent. She did the deeds without any consideration that they were Jewish in nature. She did not like pork, and quite frankly, she did not understand how anyone else could like it. Regarding the changing of her underwear on Saturday, she was amazed that such a thing should be of any concern to anyone. When she was a young girl, she was taught to change her underclothes once a week by her mother. She thought that Saturday was a good day for her to remember to do it. The inquisition was not convinced that her explanation did not prove that she was Jewess, a heretic.

On April 6, 1568, after surviving squalid prison conditions for three months until the birth of her child, and then another lingering seven months of prison, Elvira was carried out of her prison cell to stand alone in the torture chamber before the bishop's vicar, the inquisitorial tribunal, the notary, the doctor, and the torturers. All of them were men. The plight of Elvira at her trial was transmitted to history by the thorough, precise, and detailed notary. He obviously missed no details. The trial is found in *Archivo hist. national,* Leg. 128. For illustration of the trivial evidence which justified prosecution for Judaism (see Lea, Volume II, p. 566).

At the beginning of the procedure, Elvira was told only that she should "tell the truth." She said that she had nothing further to say. She had already told them everything.

Elvira, the young woman, was then stripped naked. When stripped before all those men, "she said, 'Senores, I have done all that is said of me and I now must bear false witness against myself, for I do not want to see myself in such trouble; please, God, I have done nothing.' She was told not to bring false witness against herself but to tell the truth." As usual, a doctor gave her a complete physical in front of all present. This, in itself, was a tremendous embarrassment.

After the physical, the inquisitors usually gave the person to be tortured a pair of very brief underpants, similar to the bikini, to put on. However, the detailed record mentions nothing about the underpants in Elvira's case. Because of the otherwise very detailed report given by the notary, she probably received none. If she indeed received none, we do not know who decided, or why he or they decided that she should remain naked throughout the tortures. Why they thought Elvira's case was so exceptional is a mystery to historians.

Her arms were tied in the *garrotes* of the upper arms. One cord which cut into the skin was tied tightly around each upper arm -- probably behind her back -- in noose-like fashion -- attached to an elaborate system of gears and ropes, thus squeezing each arm more and more, and forcing the arms closer and closer upon each turn of a wheel, penetrating the skin in her upper arms. After twisting the cord one turn, there was a pause, giving Elvira time to consider whether she wanted to "confess." The cord was tightened, one turn at a time, slowly. Elvira screamed more and more intensely from pain throughout the *garrotes*:

> 'Take me from here and tell me what I have to say -- they hurt me -- Oh, my arms, my arms!' which she repeated many times and went on 'I don't remember -- tell me what to say -- Oh, wretched me!

-- I will tell all that is wanted, Senores -- they are breaking my arms -- loosen me a little -- I did everything that is said of me.'

Elvira's pain was unbelievable. As the procedure continued the cord tightened very tightly, until it started to cut into her muscles. The tribunal insisted that a period of time elapse after each twist to allow Elvira to feel the pain fully. Elvira was in agony. At one point, she cried through the pain, "I have told the truth," she pleaded. "Tell me what else you want me to say, and I will say it, for I don't know what more to tell you." More and more turns, were ordered. The cord cut into nerves to the bone. Then she was told the number of turns. There were sixteen complete turns of the wood. This was exceptional; this was unbelievable. Usually a grown man could withstand only five turns of the cutting cord. On giving the order for the seventeenth turn, the cord actually broke.

Her cries did not satisfy the inquisition. They released the cords temporarily and transferred her next to the *potro,* the iron bed with multiple spikes protruding out of it. She was made to lie against the bed with her bare back, and the spikes immediately began to dig into her flesh. The torturers spread her body full length on the *potro*. She was tied tightly to it with the *potro's* attached sharp cords with a turning wheel attached to each – just like those that were on the *garrotes*. They placed the cutting cords around her upper arms which were already demolished and around her thighs. Each was tightened so it penetrated the skin so Elvira could not move.

Her head was held ridged by an iron helmet. Her nostrils were plugged securely, and her mouth was forced wide open with another simple iron machine. Then the table was tilted back so her feet were above her head. She was now on the water board. The *garrotes,* were tightened on her upper arms again. So were the thighs: one turn, then two turns, then three turns. She shrieked, "If I knew what to say, I would say it!" as clearly as she could from her throat alone, as much as anyone with their mouth forced wide open is able to do.

A large piece of thick linen was then cupped in the middle of her mouth. Slowly water , was poured from a large liter jar onto the linen in her mouth. She had to struggle to swallow the water. She gasped frantically. As she tried to squirm loose, the cords were tightened more. The linen was forced into her mouth and down her throat by the water . She felt an ugly combination of pain and fear. Her stomach was distended from the water which was filling it. Her face grew red, then as blue as her arms and her legs. The veins in her whole body stood out from lack of oxygen. She felt that she was dying of suffocation, that she was drowning. Yet the water was still poured into her gaping mouth. After a while which seemed like an eternity, the *toca,* the linen cloth was ordered to be removed. It was taken out of her stomach and throat and the *garrotes* were finally released.

The torture was suspended and she was carried, now bleeding, once more into solitary confinement. After four days, the muscles tightened and became intensely sore, and her back and arms were now either beginning to heal or becoming infected . Elvira was again carried to the torture chamber to undergo the same tortures. While being stripped, she broke down completely, confessed to all her 'Jewish' habits, and begged clothing to cover herself. She then broke into meaningless babble.

Thankfully, Elvira was not subjected to the *garrucha*. She had suffered much too much already. In the torture of the *garrucha* the victim's wrists were tied behind her back and the attached rope was looped through a pulley on the ceiling. Weights were at times attached to the victim's feet. The victim was raised slowly from the floor, letting the victim struggle on tip-toes for a time. Then the poor soul was raised off the floor. Without notice, the person was suddenly allowed to fall a distance and stopped with a jerk, a procedure that wrenched every part of the body and often dislocated the shoulders, the hips and the legs. This process was often repeated again and again but not for more than an hour (Kamen, 1997, p. 170).

Elvira, in her confession said that, when she was eleven years old, the year her mother died, her mother had told her that she should not eat pork and that she should respect the Sabbath by changing her underwear on that day. Perhaps it was all true, but it still did not mean that she wasn't a true Christian.

She was sentenced at an *auto da fe* on June 13, 1568, The inquisition "reconciled" Elvira, but all her goods were confiscated, and she was sentenced to three years in prison. After the three years, she was condemned to wearing the *sanbenito,* a yellow garment with a cross on it which had to be worn at all times as a sign of infamy . She had to wear it for the rest of her life. The tortures had incapacitated Alvira. The muscles and nerves in her arms were useless to her. She could not effectively use her arms, and undoubtedly her legs no longer had any feeling -- they were undoubtedly numb for the rest of her life.

As it turned out, after a little more than six months in prison, imprisonment was commuted to "spiritual penances." Elvira ended up a beggar, ruined for life. She hobbled around in her *sanbenito*, eating the garbage that others threw her way after they were finished with their meals. Her total life was ruined. She was treated like a non-person for the rest of her life -- all because she did not like pork and because she changed her underwear every Saturday. The officials of the church can never be too careful (Lea, Henry Charles, 1907, Book VI, p. 24-33 & Book VIII, p. 233-234).

THE CONSUMING FORCE

This episode is written solely for the purposes of exposing the Spanish Inquisition. It clearly says it all. It exposes the sexism, the anti-Semitism and the anti-feminism which was an integral part of that inquisition. The world has already seen the Nazi catastrophe, which wiped out six million Jews and also degraded women. May this be the end of such nonsense within the group that considers itself the followers of Jesus.

Mary E. Giles states that ultimately all the historical records of women subject to incarceration, interrogation, and sentencing raise the specter of a special form of sexual sadism. Taken from jail, she is brought to the torture chamber. Everywhere she looks she sees men: the bishop or his representative, inquisitors, an attorney, jailers, a notary, torturers. All of them are looking at her. Imagine for a moment Alvira del Campo -- or a girl of thirteen, just coming to awareness of her sexuality --brought into a chamber where torture is administered. She is then stripped naked, and she is surrounded by men whose eyes are fixed on her body. Somehow the word *pornography* seems appropriate to a scene in which men masked as respectable Christian judges look at her body as it is examined by a male doctor, then tortured. Her naked body is fastened to the rack and the cords are gradually tightened and pitchers of water are slowly poured down her throat. Other horrible tortures are also administered. She is tortured until she moans and screams, and then begs for mercy.

Of course, sexual sadism is also a good description of the same tortures endured by men and boys.---And that is just the beginning. Some endure being burned to death, emprisonment, the galleys, whippings, losing all their property, and the infamy of wearing the *sanbenito* for life.

The judgment is easily made that the wrong people are being convicted. Many men should have been held accountable for these vicious acts.

THE INQUISITION AND THE SPANISH PEOPLE

Remarkably, the majority of Spanish people continued their complete support of the Inquisition. This is a stunning fact which no historian will deny and no one is able to explain. The public relations was exceptionally well done -- considering the fact that people were being burnt to death and tortured near their churches and homes. As far as we can tell, no one in Spanish society objected. This offense to humanity has to be charged to the apathy of the citizenry who stand by while their nation does unbelievable things to their neighbors and people of other nations.

Of course, Elvira confessed her own "crimes," and no living accomplice was involved in her case, because she did it alone. Only her dead mother was involved in any way. If there would have been others involved and she did not indict them, she would have been denounced publicly in a humiliating and large ceremony. Then she would have been publicly burned or received some other severe sentence. Elvira's prison term, of course, was severe enough. Prisons, as we stated above, were cold, and solitary confinement was inhuman for any social human being.

In other cases, the Inquisition was devastating to those who came before it. Reconciliation did free the accused from burning, but often with severe consequences. The person had to wear the *sanbenito* with a cross on it or participate as a penitent at liturgical ceremonies. Their property was confiscated, or the person was imprisoned, sometimes for life, or exiled, scourged, or forced to serve as a slave in the galleys of Spanish ships.

Upon release, the person always faced a life of poverty. If their possessions were not confiscated outright, the person would have to sell them to pay for prison room and board. The person's existence continued, then as a shameful one. After death, Peters writes, the *sanbenito*, with the person's name on it, was placed in the parish church, reminding all of the shame of the person.

To be brief, because the story in Spain has been essentially told, the Inquisition in Spain was extended to Portugal, where it was nearly as ugly as it was in Spain.

COLUMBUS AND THE ARAWAK INDIANS

The spirit of the inquisition was devastating and it spread to the new world as well. Howard Zinn in his *A People's History of the United States* wrote that in 1492, the same year that all Jews were expelled from Spain, Christopher Columbus sailed in three boats, the *Nina*, the *Pinta*, and the *Santa Maria* from the court of Isabella and Ferdinand toward the Arawak Indians in the Americas. As he approached the Bahamas, the naked Arawak men and women ran to greet him with food, water, and gifts. Instead of greeting them in return with gratitude, Zinn informs us that Columbus wrote in his log: "They would make fine servants.... With fifty men we could subjugate them all and make them do whatever we want" (Zinn 1980, 1).

The generosity of the Arawak was similar to that of the indigenous people of all of North, South, and Central America. They were all vulnerable to the conquest of ruthless, Christian men. Columbus, in his search for gold, devastated and eventually annihilated the indigenous people of the Bahamas. Zinn continues: "What Columbus did to the Arawak of the Bahamas, Cortes did to the Aztecs of Mexico, Pizarro to the Incas of Peru, and the English settlers of Virginia and Massachusetts to the Powhatans and the Pequots" (Zinn 1980, 11).

In 1535-1543, "the Franciscan bishop of Mexico, Francisco de Zumarraga, undertook the prosecution of Indian converts to Christianity who were thought to remain crypto-believers in their old religion." In this he followed the example of the Spanish treatment of the Jews (Zinn, 1980, 1-22).

In the early 17th century, the Puritans in what is now Connecticut and Rhode Island, in the land of the Pequot, appealed to Psalms 2:8: "Ask of me, and I shall give thee, the heathen for thine inheritance, and the uttermost parts of the earth for thy possession" (Zinn, 1980, 14).

This was just the beginning. Noam Chomsky writes in *The Chomsky Reader*:

> ...there may have been about 80 million Native Americans in Latin America when Columbus 'discovered' the continent – as we say – and about 12 to 15 million more north of the Rio Grande. By 1650, about 95 percent of the population of Latin America had been wiped out, and by the time the continental borders of the United States had been established, some 200,000 were left of the indigenous population, in short, mass genocide, on a colossal scale, which we celebrate each October when we honor Columbus – a notable mass murderer himself on Columbus Day (Chomsky 1987, 121-122).

DOSTOYEVSKY, JESUS, AND THE SPANISH INQUISITION

Fyodor Dostoyevsky in *Brothers Karamazov* has a section where he deals with the Spanish Inquisition and the Grand Inquisitor. He begins: "My story is laid in Spain, in Seville, in the most terrible time of the Inquisition, when fires were lighted every day 'to the glory of God,' and in the splendid *auto da fe* the wicked heretics were burnt." In that setting Jesus came down to earth once again to what Dostoyevsky called "the hot pavement" of that southern town where the day before "almost a hundred heretics had *ad majorem gloriam Dei* been burnt by the Cardinal, the Grand Inquisitor...." Jesus worked miracles there --even raised a small girl from the dead. Dostoyevsky continues: "... at that moment the Cardinal himself, the Grand Inquisitor, passes by the Cathedral. He is wearing his coarse, old monk's cassock. ...He sees everything ... and his face darkens. He holds out his finger and bids the guards take Him [Jesus]." The people were so cowed that they gave way to the guards and allowed them to act. The guards led him away to the Inquisition prison, and the crowd bowed to the Inquisitor. Immediately the Inquisitor went to see Him.

> 'Is it Thou? Thou?' But receiving no answer, he adds at once, 'Don't answer, be silent. What canst Thou say indeed...? Thou hast no right to add anything to what Thou hadst said of old. Why, then, art Thou here to hinder us...? Tomorrow I shall condemn Thee and burn Thee at the stake as the worst of heretics. And the very people who have today kissed Thy feet, tomorrow at the faintest sign from me will rush to heap up the embers of Thy fire.'

Then the Grand Inquisitor told Jesus that his biggest mistake was his decisions at the temptations in the desert when mystery, miracle, and authority were offered him. Jesus would have done best, the Inquisitor said, if he had accepted all of them.

He should have been the one who turned rocks into bread; he

should have, in the sight of all, thrown himself off the pinnacle of the temple and let the angels take care of him. He should have taken to himself the nations of the world. For people longed for someone to feed them. They longed for miracles in their midst. And first and foremost, they longed to lay their freedom before someone who would rule them.

The Inquisition was the complete reversal of the temptations of Jesus. It did what Jesus should have done. The Inquisition ruled the people of Jesus: "Didst Thou not often say then, 'I will make you free...?' For fifteen centuries we have been wrestling with Thy freedom, but now it is ended and over for good.... They have brought their freedom to us and laid it humbly at our feet.... Thou hast promised ... Thou hast given us the right to bind and to unbind, and now, of course, Thou canst not think of taking it away.

The Grand Inquisitor said to Jesus, "You have given to your people something they cannot understand, let alone put into practice. They are so tormented by freedom that they frantically search to find someone who will take it from them."

The Grand Inquisitor goes to the door of the prison and says to Jesus: "Go and come no more.... Come not at all, never, never!' And the Prisoner went away (Dostoyevsky, *Brothers Karamazov*, 5, 5). And the Spanish Inquisition's reign of terror lasted until 1834. With great pain most Christians review the Inquisitions. Freedom is an important part of Christianity. Love is essential. Coercion plays no role. Was the Grand Inquisitor wiser than Jesus? If so, then humanity needed an Inquisition. If Jesus was wiser, then true freedom, love and compassion are to reign.

Timothy in the New Testament mentions Hymenaeus and Alexander, who "have made a shipwreck of their faith .... These I have turned over to Satan so that they may learn not to blaspheme" (I Timothy 1:19-20). Handing over to Satan was a term used for simple excommunication, nothing more. Certainly no "water boarding" was involved, no rack. Also the Book of Titus mentions, "Warn a heretic once and then a second time: after that, have nothing to do with him" (Titus 3:10). Again, excommunication is the punishment, nothing more. The Gospel of Matthew has a parallel text:

> If your brother commits an offense, go and take the matter up with him, strictly between yourselves, and if he listens to you, you have won your brother over. If he will not listen, take one or two others with you, so that all facts may be duly established on the evidence of two or three witnesses. If he refuses to listen to them, report the matter to the whole congregation; and if he will not listen even to the congregation, you must then treat him as you would a pagan or a tax-gatherer (Matthew 18:15).

Little more is said in the New Testament about such matters. Clearly, the community paid heed to the wise among them, to the elders who held the community together in the recollections of Jesus which had come down to them from the previous generation. They listened to the stories of Jesus as believers in Jesus not as his slaves.

Some of the fathers of the first three centuries spoke against any coercion in religion. Tertullian mentions that individual conscience must be followed in regard to religion -- in religion, especially Christianity, free will is essential. Coercion is completely contradictory to the essence of Christianity (Tertullian, *Ad. Scapulam, c, ii*). Origen mentions that the law given the Christians in the Sermon on the Mount is different than the law given the Jews. Christians are no longer at liberty to kill their enemies or to burn and stone violators of the Christian law (Origen, *c. Celsus, VII, 26*). Lactantius, in 308 A. D. says it best:.

> Religion being a matter of the will, it cannot be forced on anyone; in this matter it is better to employ words than blows. Of what use is cruelty? What has the rack to do with piety? Surely there is no connection between truth and violence, between justice and cruelty.... It is true that nothing is so important as religion, and one must defend it at any cost....It is true that it must be protected, but by dying for it, not by killing others.... For nothing is so intrinsically a matter of free will as religion (Lactantius, *Divine Institutes v: 20*).

Cyprian of Carthage wrote similar words (*Ep. lxxii, ad Pompon, n. 4*)). Hilary of Potiers (*Liber contra Auzentium*) also rejected the use of such force.

It is a fact that up to Ambrose of Milan and Augustine of Hippo no father of the Church defended any punishment for heresy except excommunication. Political and post-Augustinian religious leaders initiated such penalties, and they did so mainly to solidify their own wealth or political power and influence. Augustine of Hippo's view of human nature as corrupt certainly also was an impetus to such activities.

Constantine and his successors took Christianity under its wings. Protection from the political element, as we have seen, was not always helpful.

Very early, Emperor Theodosius II said that the first concern of imperial authority was the protection of religion. And in a space of fifty seven years sixty-eight penal edicts against heretics were promulgated by the emperors with penalties which ranged from exile, confiscation of property and even death. When we journey to the core reason for the inquisitions, we run headlong into the brick wall of politics and wealth. Queen Isabella and King Ferdinand did not care one wit whether a Jewish-born Christian in their land was a practicing Catholic or not. They were concerned that the Jewish born Christian not undermine them, but support them in their wars with the Muslims. They were concerned that the *conversos* wealth fund their wars. They were concerned that the Jewish born Christian support them as king and queen. The Spanish Inquisition was concerned with property, with material possessions, with power in this life.

Torquemada was aware that he was playing with political fire, not the fire which comes from the Spirit of God. He was playing cards with a pope who was trying to make something Christian out of an Inquisition which was essentially non-Christian and a king and queen who had a political job to do. Perhaps he was both fascinated and intrigued by the game. He thought he could keep both pope, king and queen in the game -- to the pain and the suffering of 100,000 people who had to face his tribunal, and especially to the pain and suffering of those among them who faced torture and even death at his hands.

Chapter 14

DANTE, FLORENCE AND BONIFACE VIII

Many know of Dante Alighieri's work, now called *The Divine Comedy*. It is recognized as one of the greatest works of literature. It "enjoyed a fame that was immediate and enduring" (Ciardi, 1982, xiii). Dante's *Divine Comedy* stands tall in literary history, rivaling Shakespeare's works. However, few know the struggle of the man and his family due to charges generated by the city of Florence and the difficulties he and all of Europe faced from the reigning pope of the time, Boniface VIII. These difficulties undoubtedly refined the character of the man so he could write such a work. But history has few resources to relate the facts of his life. Reasons for the lack of history on the matter are simply these: few primary sources support the terrible events that happened, and Dante, who was a quiet, even bashful, man and a fugitive from the law did not spend time broadcasting his presence or his deeds. We will take the primary documents that do exist and connect the dots as best as possible in order to tell the frightening story of a great religious man and poet.

POPE BONIFACE VIII

Dante wrote of Boniface VIII:

> ...I shook with dread
> at the sight of an approaching lion.
>
> Raging with hunger, it was ready to attack me.
> Its enormous head
>
> held high, ready to strike a mighty blow
> at my vulnerable body (Dante, *Comedy*, 1:44-47 my translation).

The image of Boniface VIII in his *Comedy* is one of power moving against Dante. It shows Dante's intimidation and fear of the man.

In 1235, Boniface VIII was born in Anagni, 50 kilometers southeast of Rome. He was named Benedetto Gaetani. Benedetto was a bright young man who became an excellent canon lawyer (*Catholic Encyclopedia*). The knowledge he had of church law gave him a distorted vision of the church and the pope's position in it. He would have benefitted from a more scriptural balance.

No matter what church law might have said about the matter, Jesus was clear. The successor of Peter's position in the church was to be the servant of the people; the people were not supposed to be servants of the successor of Peter. Boniface VIII had this one issue turned upside down.

Benedetto Gaetani was elected Pope on January 23, 1294. He was 59 years old, ambitious and vain. He never did let his knowledge or common sense get in the way of either his ambition or his vanity. Boniface VIII knew that he was in the position of being the strongest and the richest force in all Europe (Rubin, 2004, 43-44). He was ready and willing to play that part.

Boniface VIII received his education at the University of Paris. Admittedly, he was a lover of the arts. During his reign as Pope, he did found the University of Rome, and he also vastly increased the number of volumes in the Vatican library.

Celestine V was Pope before him. Celestine V was a good and even saintly man, but he had been taken from a mountain cave in the wilds of Abruzzi to be pope, and he had few administrative skills. How he became pope is a mystery. Boniface VIII was one of the experts who convinced him to resign the papacy after only five months.

Celestine V thought that it would be good to get back to his cave in Abruzzi, but Boniface captured him and brought him back to Rome again and again. Finally, Celestine V took a boat to try to escape to a place where he would not be found, but, as luck would have it, he became shipwrecked. Boniface VIII then brought him back a final time and imprisoned him in a very narrow cell. The cell was so narrow that, when saying Mass, the saint's feet stood where his head lay when he reclined (*Catholic Encyclopedia*).[63] He died ten months later. We cannot but wonder today: why did Boniface think it necessary to so confine Celestine. Perhaps he was afraid that his supporters would rise up and reinstate the man. At the same time, Boniface VIII was not above trying to control all the people of the whole world.

Boniface VIII tried to stir up sentiments for a new crusade. When nobody was willing to go along with this idea. He then established himself as the Supreme Court for all the laws enacted in

---

63 The *Catholic Encyclopedia* quotes an authoritative article documenting this fact, "S Pierre Celestin et ses premieres Biographes," in *Analecta Bolland*, XVI, 365-487. The article states: "*Quod, ubi tenebat pedes ille sanctus, dum missam diceret, ibi tenebat caput, quando quiescebat.*"

Europe. He was the court of last resort, and because of the weak monarchies of the time, he had the power to do just that.

Furthermore, he then turned his sites on the city of Florence, which he wanted under the control of the Black Guelfs, the party that totally supported the church. This put him at odds with Dante and the White Guelfs.

DANTE ALIGHIERI

Dante was born in Florence in May, 1265. His family was of noble birth, but, after many years, it was no longer wealthy. When he was twelve years old, Dante's family committed him to marry Gemma of the then famous Donati family -- certainly a boon to the family's fading prestige.

When Dante was about twelve years old, approximately the same year that his family arranged his marriage to Gemma, he met Beatrice Portinari, who was nine years old. Beatrice was beautiful and stately standing before him. In his eyes, there was no one else in the room. She became the love of Dante's whole life, the feminine ideal image of his poetry. She was truly Dante's soul-mate, the angel of heaven. She influenced his poetry, especially the last two books of his *Comedy*, "Purgatorio" and "Paradiso" (Roberts-Moustaki, 2001, 2). But Dante, either because of shyness or because he was already committed to marry, never approached Beatrice: she was never aware of his devotion to her.

Dante studied at the University of Bologna, one of the most famous universities of the medieval world. Brunetto Latini taught there. He never actually taught Dante, but he understood Dante's poetry, and he advised and encouraged him. Dante had great respect for the man, even though he placed Brunetto in hell in his *Comedy*. Dante did not even give his friends a break in his *Comedy*: friends as well as enemies were in hell. Nonetheless, Dante continued to show

Brunetto professorial respect even when he met him in hell. He called him "Sir." According to Dante, Brunetto was in hell because of his sins of sodomy, which were completely frowned on by the whole medieval world (Dante, *The Divine Comedy*, inferno, xv, 30).

After Beatrice married a banker in 1277, Dante dutifully married Gemma Donati, and he had three children with her, two sons, Jacopo, the eldest of his children, Pietro, who became a successful lawyer in Verona, and one daughter, the youngest, whom Dante, not surprisingly, called Beatrice. But his wife was not his soul-mate. Beatrice had captured his imagination. At the end of his life, his daughter was the true Beatrice to Dante, because she took care of him in his last years.

Beatrice Portinari, the Beatrice of Dante's imagination, died at twenty-three years of age. Dante never stopped grieving for her. Memory is able to give the dead renewed life in our minds, and Dante made Beatrice as present as possible through her presence in the *Comedy*.

Italy was by no means united during Dante's day, no more than it was united during Francis of Assisi's youthful days. The city of Florence, like every other city in Italy, was a sovereign nation, not a city within a nation. In 1289, when he was 24 years old, we are told, Dante fought bravely for Florence at the battle of Campaldino, one of the city wars in Italy. Florence, then, had its own army. It had "its flag, its ambassadors, its foreign trade, its own coinage...."(Ciardi, 1982, xvi) Like every other city in Italy, it even had its own language.

THE GUELPHS AND THE GHIBELLINES OF FLORENCE

With a vengeance, the primacy of honor reigned in the city of Florence. It is exemplified by incidences that happened earlier in the history of the city: "In 1215 the jilting of an Amidei girl was avenged by the murder of the offending member of the Buondelmonti family, which, according to the chronicler Villani, originated the infamous Guelf-Ghibellini political factions" (Ciardi, 1982, xvi).

The Guelf-Ghibellini parties in Florence were different than the Democratic and Republican parties in the United States. In Florence, feelings between the two parties were deep, and blood flowed among the members of each party. Fighting between families broke out in the streets and people died. It was the retributions of the primacy of honor, part of the culture which ruled, and continues to rule even today, in the whole Mediterranean area.

During Dante's age, the papacy and the cities of the Holy Roman Empire were mortal enemies. Each claimed to be "king of the hill." Each claimed that God Himself gave him the right and the authority to be that "king." The Pope claimed that Jesus gave him the right to rule all spiritual and temporal matters when he gave infallibility to Peter and his successors. The Pope, then, thought that he had the God-given right to rule the whole world. The city officials of the Holy Roman Emperor claimed that God himself gave them the right to rule over the land and the people. It was called "the divine right of Kings," and it was supported by many theologians of the time.

By 1295, when Dante was 30 years old, he was, in his own way, engulfed in the politics of Florence. Dante belonged to the Guelph party -- members of the rising middle class: the scholars, the rich merchants, bankers, and landowners -- who traditionally supported the pope rather than the emperor. Traditionally, the Ghibelline -- members of the old aristocracy -- supported the emperor (Ciardi, 1982, 5-6).

Now it would have been less complicated if things remained as simple as we just stated it. Dante, whose family was Guelph, was an intellectual family, and in Dante's case, was often, but according to his nature, quietly, at odds with the reigning Pope Boniface VIII. He could and did support the spiritual leadership of the pope, but not his temporal leadership. He was called a White Guelph, a traitor within the Guelph party. Others remained true to the Guelph cause. They were the Black Guelphs, who continued to support the pope and everything that the pope said and did in the temporal and spiritual realm.

Dante, as a White Guelph, often sided with the intellectual Ghibellines, when they attacked the popes temporal leadership (Roberts-Moustaki, 2001, 2). Farinati, was the Ghibilline leader, at the time, in Florence. Dante admired him from a distance, but placed him in hell because he considered him a heretic. Dante could not agree with Farinati when he attacked the pope's spiritual leadership. In Dante's meeting with Farinati in hell, it is clear that Farinati never knew Dante. Dante had to explain that he was a member of the Alighieri clan -- the family Farinati knew well, but he did not know Dante (Dante, *The Divine Comedy*, inferno, x, 32-51).

Although *The Catholic Encyclopedia* denies it because of lack of evidence, Dante, apparently, with others from Florence, was sent on a peace mission to Rome in order to come to some agreement between the non-papal factions of Florence and the Pope. It is not surprising that lack of evidence should accompany anything Dante did. Dante always had deep feelings, but he tended to keep them to himself. We can understand why he would have been chosen for such a peace mission. He never had any problem with the spiritual authority of the pope, only the pope's claim to have secular powers over the nations of the world. The peace mission waited in Rome to make their papal appeal.

But the wily Pope Boniface VIII was setting a trap. He had no idea of making peace with Florence. During the respite, as he masqueraded as the prince of peace with the peace delegation in Rome, he was, in reality, buying time to move his own armies into Florence, turning the city over to the Black Guelfs, who completely supported him. The peace delegation was completely duped. Pope Boniface was a greedy man who wanted the treasures of Florence.

BATTLE FOR CONTROL OF FLORENCE

Boniface sent troops into Florence under the leadership of Charles Valois, the brother of Philip the Fair, starting unbelievable devastation. Riots began when a nobleman, Corso Donati, a White Guelf, came into the city with armed troops of his own, apparently winning the conflict. Then the Blacks commando units secretly set fire to the homes of their enemies, the Whites, and spread salt on the fields making them infertile. Boniface then threatened an inquisition on the city of Florence, and issued his decree *Unam Sanctam* in which he declared:

> The Roman pope has been selected by God as the judge of both the living and the dead, and has been granted all power, both in heaven and on earth. He rules above both kings and kingdoms ... above all mortals, he holds his power as a prince (Boniface VIII, *Unam Sanctam*).

The pope did not stop here. He went on to write:

> It is absolutely necessary for salvation that every human creature be subject to the Roman Pontiff (Boniface VIII, *Unam Sanctam*).

The pope obviously overstated his case. He claimed to be the judge of both the living and even the dead. He insisted that he had all power, both in heaven and on earth. However, the final word was that Boniface VIII's threats and his commando units turned Florence over to the Black Guelfs.

DANTE, THE EXILE

Dante learned of the change of power in Florence by the court order which he surprisingly received in Rome (Ciardi, 1982, 5-6). Dante had been black-listed by the Black Guelfs in Florence and by Pope Boniface VIII. While in Rome, with only the few clothes and personal items of a visitor, probably packed neatly by Gemma, official charges were made against Dante. On January 27, 1302, he and 359 others (Rubin, 2004, 3) were charged with graft, intrigue against the peace of the city of Florence, and hostility against the Pope. Dante was fined 5,000 florins, or 200,000 dollars in our money, which he was to pay in three days. He could not afford to pay that kind of fine. He also was ordered to report to the Council in Florence to defend himself.

In fact, he did not report. He knew that he would be facing a kangaroo court, and that court would have burned him at the stake. Because he did not appear and did not pay the fine, all his property was confiscated. He and his two sons, and many others, were banished from the city for life. If they were ever caught, they would have been burned at the stake (Roberts-Moustaki, 2001, 3). Surprisingly enough, little mention is made here of Dante's wife and daughter. Certainly, Gemma, his wife, and their daughter, Beatrice, were on the verge of being reduced to destitution. Undoubtedly, they went back to their Donati relatives.

Such banishment and confiscation of property was certainly the equivalent of capital punishment. Where would Dante now go? Where would he get clothes and food? Previously, Gemma probably got clothes out for him every day and cooked his dinner. He was a poor provider for his family because he thought more of writing than doing productive, salaried work. He was a man of books and ideas, and all those insights were kept carefully in vaults inside himself. He was now an exile, a fugitive from the law, a vagrant. He had to plot and connive. He had to consider carefully where he went and with whom he met. Everything had to be done in secret lest someone connected with the city of Florence capture him and turn him over to city officials for a fee. As Harriet Rubin says in *Dante in Love:*

> Exile is the death of identity…all that defines a man suddenly seems illusion….Some days on the road, he must feel as unsure as a ten year old; other days as an old man of a hundred….Wanderers are vulnerable to hailstorms, and a cloudless heaven can raise a plague of beetles from the cracked earth…. The exile straying from his native town in Italy in 1302 would lose his speech because there was no common language by which he could be understood. To move from one town to another less than thirty miles away called for sharp revision of attitude and knowledge. The roads Alighieri walked often gave way to overgrown paths, dense with briars, thick with trees hiding thieves. The paths led to swamps, where travelers would sicken and die in hours (Rubin, 2004, 11-12).

Physically, Dante was no hero of his age (Rubin, 2004, 10). He was no Hannibal, who took on the great Alps; he is no Gandhi, who saved a nation. He did not know how to act or what to do.

At first he entrusted himself to other political exiles, but he soon thought them stupid and foolish.

So for the next five to ten years, we lose track of him. We catch up with his movements by words mentioned in the *Comedy* and by eye-witness testimony given years later (Rubin, 2004, 13). Dante traveled through Italy and France. He might even have gotten as far as England. It is difficult to follow his exact movements because he was, after all, a fugitive from the law.

> Sometimes Dante is welcomed by friends, but more often he heads to the center of town, hangs his hat on a post and hopes some stranger will pick it up. The custom is that whoever takes a journeyer's hat promises him a night's free lodging, sometimes in a barn…(Rubin, 2004, 14).

Food was another problem. Dante lived on watered down squash soup and stale bread which kind persons offered him. Fresh bread was a luxury. Harriet Ruben goes on to write: "Dante will rue the salty bread of strangers. His wants seemed to be fed by petty thievery of his hosts -- not money, but a pen or a knife. (Rubin, 2004, 14)" One of his hosts was the nephew of Francesca, another friend whom Dante placed in hell for an illicit love affair (*The Divine Comedy*, inferno, v, 113).

The loss of all his resources led Dante to take stock of his own life and his own lack of discipline. This, of course, was not inevitable. He could have sulked, felt sorry for himself, and shriveled away into obscurity and nothingness after the manner of those he placed in hell for wasting their talents, not supporting any causes, and doing nothing with their lives (Dante, *The Divine Comedy*, *iii*).

But he did not sulk and pity himself. Although Dante

considered his exile a hell, he apparently knew that it was a hell that he had to go through in order to sharpen his creativity. God was a hidden God. Dante felt that he was called off the usual roads to find God in the briars, caves and mountain peaks of the world, in the very depths of hell. In deep thought as he walked, he was piecing together a masterpiece.

THE COMEDY

Dante begins his work straightway. He begins by talking about his own exile:

> Midway through my life's journey,
> I strayed through a dark woods
> wandering off the usual path into darkness.
>
> What a dire woods that was! I never saw anything so drear,
> It was such a difficult place for me to maneuver!
> The very thought of it renews my fear.
>
> So bitter was that place that death could not be worse!
> But through its trauma, good has come to me.
> From this dire place, much good has entered
> in. (Dante, *Comedy*, 1, 1-9)[64]

So Dante then wrote *The Divine Comedy*. Actually, Dante never called it that. The full title that he gave his work was *The Comedy of Dante Alighieri, Florentine by Citizenship, Not by Morals*. The very title of his work was an attack on his native Florence.

---

64 Many of the translations of the *Divine Comedy*, including *this section*, are my own.

The work was well-received and almost immediately attracted a large audience (Roberts-Moustaki, 2001, 3).

Furthermore, the work is intricate. Many persons are pictured in the narrative, and each one has a precise place. We can imagine that Dante worked on the *Comedy* during the totality of his exile, which was approximately twenty years. The work is composed of 14,233 verses, built into 100 cantos, each with a precise rhythm (Rubin, 2004, 90).

After a stint in Limbo, where he and Virgil meet the ancient poets and artists, Dante and Virgil tackle ugly hell. Hell is a gruesome place. The Marquis de Sade wrote nothing quite so ugly, although Dante did not labor over the details as did the Marquis.

Inferno

For Dante, counterstrike is one of the fundamental principles of hell:

> The law of retribution is the only law in hell. Reciprocal wounds bind victim to criminal. Dante comes upon Bertrand de Born, knight and troubadour, who lived in the year 1140-1215. Bertrand had instigated a quarrel between Henry II of England and his son, Prince Henry. That offense requires Bertrand to carry his head by its hair, separated from his body, swinging like a lantern to light his dark path. (Rubin, 2004, 74)

Then Dante goes on to state the basic principle of hell:

> an eye for an eye for all eternity:
> this is the law of hell observed by me (*Comedy*, Inferno, 28. 139-42; trans. my own).

THE CONSUMING FORCE

Dante begins at the very entrance of hell. We are in that place, and seemingly God speaks:

> LASCIATE OGNI SPERANZA, VOI CH' ENTRATE ...
> ABANDON ALL HOPE, YOU WHO ENTER HERE ... (*Comedy*, Inferno, Canto 3.9; trans. my own).

Notice that it is God who speaks. Dante is merely the scribe. If Dante's work did not become so popular, his flesh was meat for the flames of any inquisitor, any Bernard Gui, in Europe. For he is proposing his *Comedy* almost as a book of scripture.

The time was a devastating time in history. Dante was exiled. He was going from city to city not knowing how to communicate with the local people. The White Guelfs and the Ghibillines were fighting the Black Guelfs in Florence. The inquisition's flames were roaring. Bernard Gui, the Dominican, was a prime example. The Knights Templar were being hunted and burned in France. Hatred abounded. Leadership was waning throughout Europe. In summary, Europe was a living hell -- an easy time for Dante to write the Inferno.

Purgatorio

Dante writes about heaven, purgatory, hell, and limbo. Here we are dealing with the medieval mind. It was their way of dealing with an after-life. They thought in concrete terms, and in their minds, heaven, purgatory, hell, and limbo fit perfectly.

Souls arrive in Purgatory in "a boat so light, so quick /

that nowhere did the water swallow it" (2.40-41). All sins are purged there into a timeless desire. Beatrice is now leading Dante toward the goal of purgation.

Harriet Rubin infers in her book *Dante in Love* that before the period between 1160 and 1300, souls saw themselves going to either hell or heaven; there was no third possibility (Rubin, 2004, 144). Her inference is not true. What is true is that purgatory *as a place* came into existence with the rise of the merchants, money lenders and the communes in 1160 to 1180. Before this time, at death, some kind of purification was already recognized in pre-Christian Jewish literature (II Maccabees, 12:43-45), which stated that it was a good thing to pray for the dead. Also, in early Christian literature, starting with I Cor. 3: 15, when Paul states about a person, "He himself will be saved, but only as one fleeing from fire" (NAB). Readings from the Catacombs and *The Martyrdom of Perpetua and Felicity* in the second century refers to praying for the dead. Origen and Ambrose also use an analogy, saying, as did Paul before them, that it was like a purification by fire. Augustine of Hippo, in his *City of God* states: "Temporary punishments are suffered by some in this life only, by others, after death, by others both now and then; but all of them before the last and strictest judgment" (*City of God* 21:13).

Members of the communes of the twelfth century were more comfortable in solidifying this purification as a definite, concrete place, called purgatory. They knew that their moral life was not always on the up-and-up. They thought in concrete terms. They did not think they were so evil that they deserved such dire punishment as hell. They were comfortable with a place besides heaven and hell where they could go temporarily to be purged in the afterlife in preparation for heaven. They called this place purgatory. Purgatory, as a place, was the theological invention, not only of the theologians of the 1160's to 1180's. The theologians were pressed by the people of the era.

So Dante wrote about *the place* called purgatory. He also wrote about another theological fiction, a place called limbo, which was popular at the time. Limbo was a pleasant place, all things considered, where good non-baptized people went, but it was not heaven.

Why should Beatrice, the wife of a banker, be chosen by Dante to be his special guide through purgatory to heaven? She had died early in her life, and Dante throughout his life saw her as the ideal woman, the perfect woman in every way. There would be no stopping him now from seeing her as the one to lead him as he entered Purgatory and Heaven. Beatrice was the person in Dante's imagination who led him forward after Virgil had to be left behind. Harriet Rubin tells us: "When Beatrice meets Dante in upper Purgatory, she makes her 'bearded schoolboy' cry as if he were a child who betrayed her love with other women and unworthy pastimes" (Ruben, 2004, 146-7).

All the above does not limit Dante's genius one bit. Dante was not a theologian, but he was one of the greatest writers of history. He was a man of his time, and we cannot expect him to be anything else. The *Comedy* is a masterpiece.

Dante's first purgation was to wash off the dirt and darkness of hell. He had become filthy there, and it was simply improper for him to go to Purgatory in such a state.

In purgatory God is feminine. God is no longer the wrathful tyrant we found in hell. Suffering is endured not as an end in itself but as a purification. Individuals in purgatory are also pared down to their feminine selves. If God was feminine, so must these souls become. It is truly an exciting place. It is like going through the pains of preparing for a long and beautiful vacation. The women there are very beautiful. The suffering there is the suffering of transformation.

Paradiso

For Dante, *Paradiso* is the poem of desire fulfilled. On earth our desires are insatiable, and that insatiability is completely natural. But the satisfaction of these desires is heaven, paradise, Paradiso. In heaven we know and experience love in its totality, we experience God.

Dante soars through the fourth heaven, Mercury. Then he soars to the fifth, Mars. Then comes the sixth, Jupiter. Finally the seventh, Saturn. He sees heavenly spirits form words in the sky (18:70-72). By the time he reaches the eighth heaven, Beatrice's eyes transport Dante to the sphere of the stars (22.101). Dante's eyes clear as he ascends.

All he can know about God is that he can know nothing about him, the dark knowledge explained by John of the Cross. *Nada*, nothing is the essence of what he now sees of God.

Upon meeting St. Peter, Peter tells Dante that Pope Boniface will never receive mercy. History must end in justice, and justice brings the planets and stars into a kind of music and harmony.

In the ninth heaven, Dante sees God in a blinding light. God is more love than faith and hope. Dante can again see. Beatrice then "imparadises" his mind (28.3). Dante reaches the "Primum Mobile," the rim of the wheel on which heaven spins.

Then he tells Beatrice what he could not tell her all those years on earth or in their journey up to heaven:

> You have led me from my bondage and set me free
> by all those roads, by all those loving means
> that lay within your power and charity.
> through your power and your excellence alone
> have I recognized the goodness and the grace
> inherent in the things I have been shown (*Paradiso*
> 31.85-87, 31. 82-84; trans. Ciardi).

THE ESSENCE OF THE COMEDY

In order to understand the Divine Comedy today, it is necessary to set aside the medieval constructs of limbo, hell, purgatory and heaven. If these are set aside, Dante's life and ours can be set before our eyes. Dante was on the run, a fugitive from the city of Florence and from the pope. He was forced to be a vagrant, a bum. He lived a veritable hell. He had to be suspicious of everyone who treated him well, everyone who treated him poorly. His life was a life of despair, of utter horror. It is this type of life that every person has seen to some degree at some time in his or her life. He did not marry the person whom he truly loved, and the very thought of Beatrice lingered in his imagination.

When Dante dusted himself off in the Divine Comedy, it was a sign of him turning the corner. But dusting himself off was not inevitable. He could have sat in his hell and rotted. But he saw hope for the future; all was not lost. Then Dante flew through the universe, free as a bird in flight. He contacted every planet and then the stars. Love, joy, and God was now possible to him. And he enjoyed the vision of God who was all love and all energy. The same is true of every person. This is the reason the *Divine Comedy* is a classic of major proportions. It speaks to all about life and its possibilities. It is hope for all of us.

The nearer Dante gets to God, the more simple the poem becomes. Beatrice tells him to look at God, not her, and she slips away from him. His whole intent was to express the inexpressible. This is the reason that Dante is placed in volume two of *People's History*.

Dante died at Ravenna on September 13, 1321. He was buried there with due honors. Interestingly enough, Florence tried to get his body back. But not even the intercession of several popes was able to accomplish this. On a couple occasions, thieves tried to steal the body back to Florence, but they were caught each time. The body of Dante remains in Ravenna (Rubin, 2004, 21).

THE DEMISE OF BONIFACE VIII

Boniface VIII forbade Philip the Fair of France from taxing the clergy. The pope told Philip, "God has placed popes over kings and kingdoms." Philip had had enough. He sent his armies to Italy and they entered the papal bedroom at his retreat at Anagni on September 7, 1303. The pope had himself dressed in his papal robes, he sat on the papal throne for three days, the crucifix in one hand and the symbolic keys of St. Peter in the other (*Catholic Encyclopedia*). The pope was denied food and water for three days as he defiantly watched his palace plundered. When they demanded his resignation, he said in effect, "I would sooner die."

As a last ditch stand, Boniface VIII dusted off the document, *Unam Sanctam*, but one of the soldiers of Philip the Fair ripped it from the pope's hands and threw it into the fire. A copy of the document was smuggled out of the palace by one of Boniface VIII's attendants. Dante, who was willing to place many of his own friends in hell, was willing to side with Philip the Fair only to this extent: he placed him in Purgatory (Dante, *Comedy*, Purgatorio, XX, 50).

Public response among the people favored the pope. The people scattered the invaders, and they re-instated the pope. Legend states that hungry, barely standing, he stumbled to the marketplace and begged, "If there be any good woman who would give me alms of wine and bread, I would bestow upon her God's blessing and mine." He died three days later. Dante placed him in hell with the simoniacs (Dante, *Comedy*, Inferno, XIX, 52-53)

Boniface VIII may have been an excellent canon lawyer, but he failed miserably as a statesman and diplomat. He was openly cruel and unforgiving. His position on the power of the papacy is and was intolerable.

Epilogue: Synopsis of Events to Date

It is sad, but the common assumption among the members of any "in" group is that truth is owned by them, and heresy belongs to the "out" group. Alexander Pope (1688-1744) says it best in a poetic essay which he wrote when he was only twenty years old:

> Some valuing those of their own side or mind,
> Still make themselves the measure of mankind...
> (Pope, *Essay on Criticism*).

If we are "in," we think that truth stands before us and behind us, protecting us. Christianity is ours. Heresy is theirs. Heresy makes others much less than us; sometimes in history, it even made them worthless, fit to be destroyed. Even today, many tend to believe that the Christian church they attend has the truth, and the rest of the world lives in heresy. Certainly, the Muslims and other members of non-Christian sects are wrong, and we are right. It is an assumption that we might have been fed as youngsters. It is a psychological block which grounds us often in error. Maybe Christians ought to think it out again. Alexander Pope says it well when he describes human beings in the following ways:

> Created half to rise, and half to fall;
> Great lord of all things, yet a prey to all;
> Sole judge of truth, in endless error hurl'd
> The glory, jest, and riddle of the world (Pope,
> *Know Then Thyself*).

Persons who proposed to have truth are sometimes those who err the most. Anyone who stands up and makes a scene about truth or error in their midst might do best to note another quote from Alexander Pope:

> But you who seek to give and merit fame,
> And justly bear a critic's noble name,
> Be sure yourself and your own reach to know,
> How far your genius, taste, and learning go;
> Launch not beyond your depth, but be discreet,
> And mark that point where sense and dullness meet.
> Nature to all things fixed the limits fit,
> And wisely curbed proud man's pretending wit
> (Pope, *Essay on Criticism*).

Pope Urban II, who called the First Crusade, Eugenius III, who called the Second Crusade, Innocent III, who called the Fourth and Fifth Crusade and the Albigensian Crusade, and Gregory IX, who called the Albigensian Inquisition, claimed to have knowledge and truth. But all of them committed genocide. Pitifully, we are ashamed to say, they degenerated to the ranks of some of the vile dictators of our own day who kill the very people they were supposed to nurture.

Popes from Leo the Great onward claimed to have infallible truth. In recent years, popes have whittled down their proposed ability to have truth. They now claim to have infallibility only in faith and morals when giving special teachings, when speaking *ex cathedra* (literally, when speaking from the throne of St. Peter). Even so, such great knowledge does not exist in the human realm. Thomists claim that Thomas Aquinas was the Doctor of the Intellect, who gave primacy to truth. But all people, including Thomas and the popes, have struggled miserably with certain issues of truth.

Crusaders took an issue, their own Christianity, and they squeezed it until the truth they claimed to have in Christianity turned into a lie. I speak of the *tafurs* all the way up the line to even Saint Louis IX. Truth is not something that we can squeeze too hard or it turns on us. It must be touched lightly, with respect, in order to endure. The Crusaders killed many people in their attempts at righteousness. They destroyed too much that was human on earth.

The Albigensian Inquisition took place because Pope Innocent III claimed that he had the truth which he was anxious to impose on everyone in Languedoc in southern France. He imposed his will fiercely, with abandon. He squeezed people's bodies, stretched them, pierced them, burned them until some of them were dead. But Jesus demanded that we do not torture and kill human beings, but love, respect, and care for them.

Popes sat on their thrones and legislated it all. Quite frankly, they were often more interested in their own authority, pride, and dignity than truth or the dignity of others. Because of the popes' decrees, crusading, killing and burning chased "lies" from southern France to Jerusalem and then to Constantinople, and inquisitors burned the bodies of good people. Alexander Pope continues:

> Pride, where wit fails, steps in to our defense,

And fills up all the mighty void of sense.
If once right reason drives that cloud away,
Truth breaks upon us with resistless day.
Trust not yourself: but your defects to know,
Make use of every friend -- and every foe (Pope, *Essay on Criticism*).

When I was a boy, my brothers and I used to play with mercury in our hands. You see, in ages past, the popes were not the only ones who did unintelligent things. Whenever we would squeeze mercury, it would pop out of our grasp. We had to handle it very carefully. Truth is much like mercury. If we squeeze it too hard, it will pop out of our hands. We need a few guidelines for handling truth:

- If we find that our truth makes us better than another, it has slipped out of our hands. It has turned into a lie. Truth is borne only in humility.
- If truth drives us to hurt another physically, psychologically, mentally or spiritually, it has slipped out of our hands. It has turned into a lie. Truth is borne only in peace.
- If truth finds us taunting another, it has slipped out of our hands. Truth never says "I told you so"; it does not grow angry with someone who has yet to learn. Truth is always patient.
- If truth puts us higher on the hierarchy of human beings, certainly if it makes us infallible, it has slipped out of our hands. Truth is not authoritarian. It does not make us bigger or better than others. In humans, it is never infallible. It does not make anyone obedient to us. Truth is long-suffering and gentle.

It boils down to one simple fact which Alexander Pope says well:

> Good nature and good sense must ever join;
> To err is human, to forgive divine....
> 'Tis best sometimes your censure to restrain,
> And charitably let the dull be vain:
> Your silence there is better than your spite....
> For fools rush in where angels fear to tread (Pope, *Essay on Criticism*).

The example of Francis of Assisi comes to mind. He was an intelligent man. But he never presumed to know more than another. He listened as he walked from town to town in Italy, and he brought peace. He listened to his brothers, and his community grew to overwhelming numbers. He listened to the sultan, and his own spirituality grew to great heights. Oh, he certainly spoke, as well, but he never lost sight of his frail body and his frail mind, intelligent though he was. He knew he was still a weak human. He was a humble servant to those he met.

The journey now begun has become, for the most part, a horrendous, painful treck. Ambition and a thrust for power has taken over the Church of Jesus. It is time to evaluate and get Christianity back into Jesus' own hands. Pseudo-Christianity is no longer palatable. It is time to unwrap the essence of Christianity or it will die in the midst of the hubris and ignorance of humanity.

Many other events accompanied the happenings at this time. They are not so important as the events mentioned, but they do continue to paint a picture.

Elizabeth of Hungary died in 1231. She had been married at 14, widowed at 20, and died at 24. She was married to Louis IV of Thuringia, who died in the Crusades. Certainly she was a

THE CONSUMING FORCE

person of worth, who shared much with the poor. Elizabeth was quickly canonized by Gregory IX. While hers was a worthwhile canonization, it continued to perpetuate the fallacy of the age that only the nobility or people with connections could be recognized by the church as worthwhile human beings.

The Chronicler, Salimbene, wrote about a peace revival in 1233 called the Great Hallelujah movement. Gary Dickson tells us about it. Up to 10,000 processed across northern Italy, whipping themselves. These flagellants passed through Modena, Bologna, Reggio, and Parma with banners and crosses. They sang songs with great fervor, but their fervor was misplaced. The Franciscans and Dominicans tried with mixed success to organize the group into protesting the petty city wars in Italy. Salimbene, who was only twelve years old, joined the group, so he had first hand information about the event. People whipped themselves in imitation of the suffering of Jesus before he was crucified. Outside of their external fervor, little inner spirituality united the marchers, so the movement died quickly (Bornstein, 2006, 155).

A catastrophe beyond compare took place between 1237 and 1240 when the Mongol Empire invaded Russia, virtually destroying Moscow, Kiev, and the surrounding area.

In 1316, Edward Bruce was crowned King of Ireland. He was killed in the Battle of Farghart in 1318.

The scholastic tradition continued as the University College in Oxford was founded in 1249. The Paris school of the Sorbonne was founded by Robert de Sorbon in 1254.

The mystic Meister Eckhart was born in 1260. He died in 1327.

The future held little hope for recovery as inquisitions tore Europe like infernal lesions and the beginnings of the reformation further collapsed the church of Jesus. Both would have been inconceivable to the people who lived at the time of Christianity's origins.

In conclusion we recall words Karl Barth stated in his commentary on Paul's letter to the Romans:

> You are without excuse who judges another: for as you judge another, you condemn yourself. You who judge another is guilty of the same things. But we know that the judgment of God is judgment according to the standard of the truth (Romans 2:1-2).[65]

Barth continues:

> Those who do not know the unknown God (Romans 1:18-21) have neither occasion nor possibility of lifting themselves up. But so is it also with those who know him; for you too are a human being; you too belong to the world of time.... No actions or behavior, no disposition of mind or depth of feeling, no intuition or understanding is, by its own virtue, pleasing to God. Humans are humans, and we all belong to the world of human beings: *that which is born of the flesh is flesh.* Every concrete and tangible thing that we know belongs within the order of time.
>
> ... If you place yourself above the burden of the world by some pretended insight or vision, you do nothing but press the burden of the world more

---

[65] For readability's sake, we are taking the liberty of deleting the archaic "eths," etc. from Barth's text. Outside of these elements, Barth's translation is excellent.

heavily upon yourself than upon anyone else. By striding ahead of others, even though it be for their assistance, as though the secret of God were known to thee alone, you only show that you are completely ignorant of His secret; for by the act of removing yourself from your brothers and sisters, you render yourself incapable of assisting even the most helpless among them (Barth, 1953, 56).

I will go further. By birth, Jews are Jesus' brothers and sisters. Who can say more? Respect is the only thing that we can give them.

The Hindu relishes the state of *nada, nothing*. John of the Cross states that the state of *nada*, releasing ourselves from all desires and pleasures in this life and going deeply into ourselves, is the contemplative way, the way we meet our Jesus and our God. The Hindu way is not so strange to the modern Christian contemplative.

The Muslim faithfully prays five times a day, praising God for all he is and does. I am deeply a Christian, but I, like Francis of Assisi, sincerely admire the fact that the Muslim does that. Would it not be good to place ourselves in the state of *nada* at least five times a day, and find therein the God who made us and Jesus who holds us together as one?

I was born and raised Roman Catholic, so the presence of Jesus was always as close as the nearest Catholic Church. I believed from childhood in transubstantiation. The bread and wine was substantially changed into the body and blood of Christ. It is an exulted tradition, filled with mystery.

But, interestingly enough, "the Valley People" believed that Jesus was really and truly, but symbolically, present in the Eucharist. Now we think we know where some of the apostles went after Pentecost: Peter went to Rome and was crucified; John ended on the island of Patmos, and he was probably martyred there; James ended up, tradition tells us, in Spain; Bartholomew and Thaddeus went to Asia Minor, where they did magnificent work; Thomas went as far as India, according to tradition. Where did some of the disappearing apostles go? It is probable from various solid sources that one of them, or one of the disciples of one of the apostles, started the beautiful community in the Alps called "The Valley People." He or she probably taught the Valley People about the symbolic, but real presence of Jesus, which took place at Eucharist. Such a symbolic presence is also an exulted presence.

I have presented myself to celebrations of Jesus in churches that have no Eucharist, but only the word. They are also beautiful, and Jesus was obviously present there as well.

Then there are the agnostics and the aetheists. Who of us can say that at one time or other in our lives, we are not in their ranks? Persons facing the moment of death might say that they believe in God, and they probably basically do, but the fear manifested shows a lingering doubt. To some extent, most of us, maybe all of us, are to some degree agnostics. Teresa of Calcutta was undoubtedly a saint, but, at the end of her life, she wondered if she had wasted her life in the ghettos of the poor.

So who are we to judge? Within our human frame, we can only be people with humble hearts.

BIBLIOGRAPHY

Scripture Quotations are from *The New American Bible* (NAB). However, when quoting another who uses scripture quotations, the preferences of the quoted person are respected.

Richard Abanes, *End Time Visions: The Road to Armageddon*. New York, Four Walls; Eight Windows, 1998.

Allix Acland, *On the Churches of Piedmont,* 1827.

Hugh Dyke Acland, *A Compendious History of That People, Previous and Subsequent to That Event* as found in Henri Arnaud's *The Glorious Recovery of the Vaudois of Their Valleys*. London: John Murray, Albemarle-Street, 1827.

Bengt Ankarloo and Gustav Henningsen, ed. *Early Modern European Witchcraft: Centres and Peripheries,* Oxford, England, Clarendon Press, 1990

Henri Arnaud, *The Glorious Recovery of the Vaudois of Their Valleys, with a Compendious History of That People, Previous and Subsequent to That Event by Hugh Dyke Acland*. London: John Murray, Albemarle-Street, 1827.

John H. Arnold, *Inquisition and Power: Catharism and the*

Confessing Subject in Medieval History, University of Pennsylvania, 2001.

Thomas Asbridge, *The First Crusade: A New History.* Oxford University Press, 2004.

Aziz S. Atiya, *Crusade, Commerce and Culture.* Bloomington, Indiana, Indiana University Press, 1962.

Donald Attwater, *St. John Chrysostom: Voice of Gold.* Milwaukee, The Bruce Company, 1939.

Donald Attwater, *St. John Chrysostom: Pastor and Preacher.* London, Harville Press, 1959.

Augustine, *City of God*

Michael Baigent, Leigh, Richard; Henry Lincoln, *Holy Blood, Holy Grail,* New York: Dell, 1983.

Malcolm Barber, *The Cathars: Dualist Heretics in Languedoc in the High Middle Ages.* Edinburgh, Longman, an imprint of Pearson Education, 2000.

Julia Caro Baroja, "Witchcraft and Catholic Theology," chapter I of Ankarloo and Henningsen's *Early Modern European Witchcraft: Centres and Peripheries,* Oxford, England, Clarendon Press, 1990, pp. 19-43.

William Barry, *The Papal Monarchy from St. Gregory the Great to Boniface VIII,* T. Fisher Unwin, 1902.

Karl Barth, *The Epistle to the Romans,* 3rd Impression. Translated by Edwyn C. Hoskyns, Oxford University Press, 1953.

William Baum and Dietmar W. Winkler, *The Church of the East: A Concise History*. London: Routledge Curzon, 2003

Chrysostom Baur, *John Chrysostom and His Time*, vol. 1 Antioch. Tr., Sr. M. Gonzaga, The Newman Press, 1959.

S. Benko, *The Virgin Goddess: Studies in the Pagan and Christian Roots of Mariology*. Boston, Brill, 2004.

Bernard of Clairvaux, "Hortative Sermon to the Knights Templar," in Speed, Peter, *Those Who Prayed: An Anthology of Medieval Sources*, New York, Italica Press, 1997.

Marc Bloch, *Feudal Society*, translated by L. A. Manyon, University of Chicago Press, 1961.

Joseph Blotzer, "Inquisition," (transcribed by Matt Dean) *The Catholic Encyclopedia*, vol. VIII (K. Knight, 2003; original text from Robert Appleton Company, 1910)

Bonaventure, *Life of Francis of Assisi*.

Bongars, *Gesta Dei per Francos*, 1, tr. in Oliver J. Thatcher and Edgar Holmes McNeal, eds., *A Source Book for Medieval History*, New York: Scribners, 1905.

Pierre Bonnassie, *From Slavery to Feudalism in Southwestern Europe*, Cambridge, 1991.

Daniel E. Bornstein, ed., *Medieval Christianity*, Fortress Press, 2006.

Leonard E. Boyle, *The Setting of the Summa Theologica* of St.

Thomas. Toronto, Pontifical Institute of Mediaeval Studies, 1982.

Louis Brehier, "The Crusades," *The Catholic Encyclopedia.*

Robin Briggs, *Witches & Neighbors: The Social and Cultural Context of European Witchcraft.* New York, Viking Press, 1996

Peter Brown, *Power and Persuasion in Late Antiquity: Towards a Christian Empire.* , Madison, Wisconsin, University of Wisconsin Press, 1992 .

Raphael Brown, O.F.M., *Little Flowers of St. Francis [The Fioretti],* A modern English translation from the Latin and the Italian with Introduction and Notes, as found in Marion A.Habig, *St. Francis of Assisi: Writings and Early Biographies.* Franciscan Herald Press, 1972.

David Burr, *The Spiritual Franciscans,* University Park, Pennsylvania, 2001.

Daniel F.Callahan, "The Cult of the Saints of Aquitane," chapter t, pp. 165-183, Thomas Head and Richard Landes, eds., *The People of God: Social Violence and Religious Response in France around the Year 1000.* Ithaca, Cornell University Press, 1992.

Fabian Alejandro Campagne, "Witchcraft and the Sense-of-the-Impossible in Early Modern Spain: Some Reflections Based on the Literature of Superstition (ca 1500-1800) *Harvard Theological Review,* 96, 1 (2003)

Diana Fritz Cates. *Aquinas on the Emotions: A Religious-Ethical Inquiry.* Georgetown University Press, 2009.

Catholic Encyclopedia

I Celano, *Life of Francis of Assisi*

II Celano, *Life of Francis of Assisi*

Henry Chadwick, *The Church in Ancient Society: From Galilee to Gregory the Great.* Oxford: Oxford University Press, 2001.

Louis-Marie Chauvet, *Sacraments: the Word of God at the Mercy of the Body.* Collegeville, Minnesota, The Liturgical Press, 2001.

Robert Chazan, *In the Year 1096: The First Crusade and the Jews* Philadelphia, The Jewish Publication Society, 1996.

Noam Chomsky, *The Chomsky Reader* (ed. by James Peck; New York, Pantheon Press, 1987)

John Chrysostom, De compunctione.

John Chrysostom, De Genesis.

John Chrysostom, De Sacerdatione.

John Chrysostom, De Virginitate.

John Chrysostom, In Ephesianum.

John Chrysostom, In I Corinthianum.

John Chrysostom, In Matthaeum.

St. John Chrysostom, *Homilies on Genesis, 1-17. Fathers of the Church, a New Translation,* Catholic University of America Press, 1986.

St. John Chrysostom, *Old Testament Homilies, vol. One, Homilies on Hannah, David and Saul,* Holy Cross Orthodox Press, 2003.

St. John Chrysostom, *Old Testament Homilies, vol. two, Homilies on Isaiah and Jeremiah,* Holy Cross Orthodox Press, 2003.

St. John Chrysostom, *Old Testament Homilies, vol. three, Homilies on the Obscurity of the Old Testament; Homilies on the Psalms,* Holy Cross Orthodox Press, 2003.

John Ciardi, translator, *Dante Alighieri: The Inferno.* New American Library, 1954, 1982.

John Ciardi, translator, *The Divine Comedy, Dante Alighieri.* Norton, 1961, 1965, 1967, 1970, 1977.

Stuart Clark, "Protestant Demonology: Sin, Superstition, and Society (c. 1520-1630) Chapter 2 of Ankarloo and Henningsen, ed., *Early European Witchcraft, Centres and Peripheries,* Oxford, England, Clarendon Press, pp.44-81.

Norman Cohn, *Europe's Inner Demons: an Inquiry Inspired by the Great Witch-Hunt,* Sussex University Press, 1975.

Norman Cohn, *The Pursuit of the millennium: Revolutionary Millenarians and Mystical Anarchists of the Middle Ages.* New York: Oxford University Press, 1970.

Cyprian of Carthage

Cyril of Alexandria, Letters.

Rebecca Konyndyk Deyoung, Colleen McCluskey & Christina

Van Dyke. *Aquinas's Ethics: Metaphysical Foundations, Moral Theory, and Theological Context.* St. Louis University, 2009.

Fyodor Dostoyevsky, *Brothers Karamozov*

Georges Duby, *The Early Growth of the European Economy: Warriors and Peasants from the Seventh to the Twelfth Century,* (Translated by Howard B. Clarke, London, Weidenfeld & Nocolson, 1973.

Georges Duby, *The Three Orders: Feudal Society Imagined,* Translated by Arthur Goldhammer; Chicago, University of Chicago Press, 1980.

Jean Dunbabin, *Captivity and Imprisonment in Medieval Europe, 1000-1300* (New York, Palgrave Macmillan, 2002)

Jean Dunbabin, *France in the Making, 843-1180*, Oxford, 1985.

Durand of Huesca, *The Book against Heresy (Liber antiheresis),* 1180.

Will Durant, *The Age of Reason, A History of Medieval Civilization -- Christian, Islamic and Judaic -- from Constantine to Dante: A.D. 325-1300* New York: Simon and Schuster, 1950.

R. W. Dyson & Thomas Aquinas, *Political Writings (Cambridge Texts in the History of Political Thought*, Cambridge University Press, 2002. Susan B. Edgington, Susan B. and Sarah Lambert, ed. *Gendering The Crusades,* New York, Columbia University Press, 2002.

T. G. Elliott, *The Christianity of Constantine the Great.* Scranton, PA.: University of Scranton Press, 2003.

Omer Englebert, *Saint Francis of Assisi: A New Translation*, translated by Eve Marie Cooper, 2nd edition, revised and augmented by Ignatius Brady, O.F.M. and Raphael Brown, Chicago, Franciscan Herald Press, 1965.

Eusebius, *Life of Constantine*, Averil Cameron & Stuart G. Hall trans. & Commentary. Oxford: Clarendon Press,1999.

C. L'Estrange Ewen, *Witch Hunting and Witch Trials: The Indictments for Witchcraft from the Records of 1373, Assizes Held for the Home Circuit A. D. 1559-1736. (London: Kegan Paul, Trench, Trubner & Co., LTD, 1929.*

Benen Fahy, O.F.M., tr., *Major and Minor Life of St. Francis with Excerpts from Other Works by St. Bonaventure*, with Introduction by Damien Vorreux (tr. from the French by Paul Oligny, O.F.M.) edited by Marion A.Habig, *St. Francis of Assisi: Writings and Early Biographies.* Franciscan Herald Press, 1972.

Benen Fahy, O.F.M., tr. *The Writings of St. Francis.* Introduction and Notes by Placid Hermann, O.F.M. Chicago, Franciscan Herald Press & London, Burns & Oates, 1964; edited by Marion A. Habig.

Alberto Ferreiro, ed., *The Devil, Heresy and Witchcraft in the Middle Ages: Essays in Honor of Jeffrey B. Russell*, Boston, Brill, 1998.

Habig, *St. Francis of Assisi: Writings and Early Biographies. Chicago, Franciscan Herald Press, 1972.*

Donald Fairbairn, *Grace and Christology in the Early Church*, Oxford University Press, 2003.

Edward Feser, *Aquinas (A Beginners Guide)*. Oneworld Publications, 2009.

Heinrich Fichtenau, *Heretics and Scholars in the High Middle Ages, 1000-1200,* translated by Denise A. Kaiser, University Park, Pennsylvania, 1998.

George Park Fisher, *History of Christian Doctrine.* Charles Scribner Sons, 1896.

Peter Fox, ed , *Treasures of the Library: Trinity College Dublin.* Dublin, Trinity College.

Francis of Assisi, *Rule of 1221.*

Francis of Assisi, *Rule of 1223.*

Francis of Assisi, *Testament.*

Frederick II, "Letter from Frederick II to Henry III of England, 1229: The Imperial Achievement," as found in Peters, Edward, ed. Christian Society and the Crusades, 1198-1229, University of Pennsylvania Press, 1971.

W. H. C. Frend, *The Rise of Christianity,* Philadelphia, Fortress Press, 1985.

Reginald Garrigou-Lagrange, *The One God: A Commentary on the First Part of St. Thomas' Theological Summa.* Fifth printing. trans. by Bede Rose. Herder, 1943.

Paul Gavrilyuk, The Suffering of the Impassible God: The Dialectics of Patristic Thought. London: Oxford University Press, 2004.

Jenny Gibbons, "Recent Developments in the Study of the Great European Witch Hunt, http://www.cog.org/witch_hunt.html.

Jenny Gibbons, "Case Study: The European Witch Hunts, c.1450-1750.http:www.gendercide.org/case_witchhunts.html.

Jenny Gibbons, "Recent Developments in the Study of the Great European Witch Hunt," *The Virtual Pomegranate, 5.*

Mary E. Giles, ed., *Women in the Inquisition: Spain and the New World.* Johns Hopkins University, 1999.

Carlo Ginzburg, *Ecstasies: Deciphering the Witches' Sabbath.* Giulio Einaudi Editore, 1989 (Translated by Raymond Rosenthal, New York, Pantheon Books, 1991).

Rodolfus Glaber, *The Five Books of the Histories,* edited by Neithard Bulst and translated by John France and Paul Reynolds, Oxford, Clarendon Press, 1989.

Michael Goodich, Sophia Menache & Sylvia Schein, ed., *Cross Cultural Convergences in the Crusader Period: Essays Presented to Aryeh Grabois on His Sixty-Fifth Birthday.* New York, Peter Lang, 1995.

Gore, Charles, *Leo the Great.* London: Society for Promoting Christian Knowledge, 1887.

Elaine Graham-Leigh, *The Southern French Nobility and the Albigensian Crusade,* Rochester, New York, The Boydell Press, 2005.

Gregory VII, "Dictate of the Pope, 1075," Speed, Peter, ed., in

Those Who Prayed: An Anthology of Medieval Sources, New York, Italica Press, 1997

Wilfrid Griggs, *Early Egyptian Christianity: From Its Origins to 451 Ce*. Boston, Brill, 2000.

Marion A. Habig, *St. Francis of Assisi: Writings and Early Biographies*. Franciscan Herald Press, 1972.

Bernard Hamilton, *The Albigensian Crusade*, London, Cox and Wyman, Ltd., 1974.

Bernard Hamilton, *Monastic Reform, Catharism and the Crusades, 900-1300*, London, Variorum Reprints, 1979.

Paul W. Harkins, tr., *The Fathers of the Church: St. John Chrysostom on the incomprehensible Nature of God*, The Catholic University of America Press, 1984.

Jonathon Harris, *Byzantium and the Crusades*, London and New York, Hambledon and London, 2003.

Aideen M. Hartney, *John Chrysostom and the Transformation of the City*, Gerald Duckworth & Co. Ltd. Head, 2004.

Gustav Henningsen, *The Witches' Advocate: Basque Witchcraft and the Spanish Inquisition (1609-1614)*, Reno, Nevada, University of Nevada Press, 1980.

Placid Hermann, O.F.M., tr. and notes, *First and Second Life of St. Francis with selections from Treatise on the Miracles* of Blessed Francis I by Thomas of Celano, as found in Marion A. Habig, *St. Francis of Assisi: Writings and Early Biographies*. Franciscan Herald Press, 1972.

Placid Hermann, O.F.M., tr. *Sacrum Commercium; or Francis and His Lady Poverty*, tr. from the Latin, with Introduction and Notes, 1964, as found in Marion A.Habig, *St. Francis of Assisi: Writings and Early Biographies*. Franciscan Herald Press, 1972.

Johann Jakob Herzog. *The New Schaff Herzog Encyclopedia of Religious Knowledge: Embracing Biblical, Historical, Doctrinal and Practical Theology and Biblical, theological and Ecclesiastical Biography from the Earliest Times to the Present Day*, vol. 12. Funk & Wagnalls, 1908.

Hilary of Potiers, *Liber contra Auxentium*.

Robert Charles Hill, tr., *Commentary on the Psalms, vol. 1*, Brookline Massachusetts,1998.

Carole Hillenbrand , *The Crusades: Islamic Perspective*, University of Edinburgh, 2000.

Carole Hillenbrand, "Crusades Still Matter: Two Scholars Discuss a History Flashpoint and Its Relevance Today," Antonia Ryan, interviewer, *National Catholic Reporter*, 42, 17, February 24, 2006.

Ronald Hutton, *The Pagan Religions of the Ancient British Isles, Their Nature and Legacy*, Oxford, Blackwell, 1991.

Innocent VIII, *Summis Desiderantes, 1484, Bullarium Romanum* (Editio Taurinensis).

Trevor Jalland, *The Life and Times of St. Leo the Great*. London: Society for Promoting Christian Knowledge, 1941.

Henry Kamen, *The Spanish Inquisition*. New York, New American Library, 1965.

Henry Kamen, *The Spanish Inquisition: a Historical Revision*. Yale University Press, 1997.

J. N. D. Kelly, *Early Christian Doctrines*. Fourth Edition. London, Adam & Charles Black, 1978.

J. N. D. Kelly, *Golden Mouth: The Story of John Chrysostom—Ascetic, Preacher, Bishop* London, Gerald Duckworth, 1995.

Robert George Kennedy, *Thomas Aquinas and the Literal Sense of Sacred Scripture [Doctoral Dissertation]*. Notre Dame, Indiana, Medieval Institute, 1985.

Richard Kieckhefer, "Avenging the Blood of Children: Anxiety over Child Victims and the Origin of the European Witch Trials" as found in Ferreiro, Alberto, ed., *The Devil, Heresy, and Witchcraft in the Middle Ages*, 1998, p. 91-109.

David Koeller, *The Spanish Inquisition, 1478-1834* (David Koeller, 2001).

Henry Kramer, O. P. and Sprenger, James, O. P., *Malleus Mallificarum*.

R. A. Krupp, *Shepherding the Flock of God: The Pastoral Theology of John Chrysostom*. American University Studies, series VII, vol. 101, 1991.

Elisabeth Kubler-Ross, *Questions and Answers on Death and Dying*, Macmillan, 1974.

Elisabeth Kubler-Ross, *Death: The Final Stage of Growth*, Prentice-Hall, 1975.

Lactantius, *Divine Institutes*, v, 20.

Emmanuel LeRoy Ladurie, *Les Paysans de Languedoc (The Peasants of Languedoc)*. Doctoral Thesis, 1974.

Emmanuel Le Roy Ladurie, *Montaillou: The Promised Land of Error*. New York: George Braziller, Inc., 1975.

H. C. Lea, *The History of the Inquisition Spain*. New York, Harper, 1888-1906.

Matthew L. Lamb, O.C.S.O., tr. and intro., *Commentary on Saint Paul's Epistle to the Ephesians*. Albany, N.Y., Magi Books, 1966.

Landes, Richard, "Between Aristocracy and Heresy: Popular Participation in the Limousin Peace of God, 994-1033., pp 184-218 Thomas Head and Richard Landes, eds., *The People of God: Social Violence and Religious Response in France around the Year 1000*. Ithaca, Cornell University Press, 1992.

Landes, Richard, eds., *The People of God: Social Violence and Religious Response in France around the Year 1000*. Ithaca, Cornell University Press, 1992.

Landes, Richard, 1,*Relics, Apocalypse, and the Deceits of History: Ademar of Chabannes, 989-1034*. Cambridge, Harvard University Press, 1995.

Landes, Richard, 3 "While God Tarried: Disappointed Millenialism and the Making of the Modern West," *Deolog*, 4: 1, pp. 6-45., 1997

Lateran Ecumenical Council IV, Twelfth Ecumenical Council, Canons of Christian Lauranson-Rosaz, "Peace from the Mountains: The Auvergnat Origins of the Peace of God, chapter 5, pp. 104-134, Thomas Head and Richard Landes, eds., *The People of God: Social Violence and Religious Response in France around the Year 1000*. Ithaca, Cornell University Press, 1992.

The Legend of the Three Companions.

Acta Leonis XIII.

Robert E.Lerner, *The Heresy of the Free Spirit in the Later Middle Ages.* (Berkeley, University of California Press), 1972.

Richard Lim, *Public Disputation, Power, and Social Order in Late Antiquity.* University of California Press, 1995.

Vasiliki Limberis. *Divine Hieress: The Virgin Mary and the Creation of Christian Constantinople.* N.Y., Routledge, 1994.

Lester K. Little, *Religious Poverty and the Profit Economy in Medieval Europe* (Ithaca, New York, Cornell University Press.), 1978.

Simon Lloyd, "The Crusading Movement, 1096-1274," of Riley-Smith, Jonathan, ed., *The Oxford Illustrated History of the Crusades* Oxford University Press, 1995.

Gary Macy, "Nicolas Macy, Gary, "Nicolas Eymeric and the Condemnation of Orthodoxy," as found in Ferreiro, Alberto, *The Devil, Heresy, and Witchcraft in the Middle Ages: Essays in Honor of Jeffrey B. Russell*, Boston,, Brill, 1998.

Thomas Madden, *The New Concise History of the Crusades*, St. Louis University, 2005.

Wendy Mayer and Pauline Allen, *John Chrysostom.* London, Routledge, 2000.

Bernard McGinn, *Visions of the End.* New York, Columbia University Press, 1979.

Frederick G. McLeod, "Theodore of Mopsuestia Revisited," *Theological Studies,* vol. 61, 2000.

Robert T. Meyer, *Palladius: Dialogue on the Life of St. John Chrysostom* N.Y., Newman Press (Ancient Christian Writers, 45), 1985.

R. I. Moore, *The Birth of Popular Heresy.* London, Edward Arnold, 1975.

R. I. Moore, *The Formation of a Persecuting Society: Power and Deviance in Western Europe. 950- 1250, London, 1987.*

R. I. Moore, "Postscript: The Peace of God and the Social Revolution," Thomas Head and Richard Landes, eds., *The People of God: Social Violence and Religious Response in France around the Year 1000.* Ithaca, Cornell University Press, 1992, pp.308-326.

John Moorhead, *Am: Church and Society in the Late Roman World.* London and New York, Pearson Education, Ltd., 1999.

Colin Morris, *The Discovery of the Individual, 1050-1200* N.Y., Harper, 1972.

John Lawrence Mosheim, *An Ecclesiastical History*, London, William Tyler, Bolt Court, 1842.

Dana C. Munro, "Urban and the Crusaders," from *Translations and Reprints from the Original Sources of European History*, vol. 1-2 Philadelphia: University of Pennsylvania, 1895.

Verity Murphy, BBC Online, June 15, 2004.

Alexis Muston, *The Israel of the Alps: A History of the Waldenses*, Vol. 1, Blackie and Sons, 1875, AMS edition, 1978, 2001.

National Catholic Reporter

John J. O'Keefe, "Impassible Suffering? Divine Passion and Fifth Century Christology." Theological Studies, vol. 58, 1997.

Zoe Oldenbourg, *Massacre at Montsegur: A History of the Albigensian Crusade*. Translated by Peter Green. New York, Pantheon, 2001.

Origen, *Celsus*.

Kenan B. Osborne, *Christian Sacraments in a Postmodern World: a Theology for the Third Millenium*. Paulist Press, 1999.

Frans van de Paverd, *St. John Chrysostom, the Homilies on the Statues*, Rome, Pont. Institutum Studiorum Orientalium, 1991.

Frederick S. Paxton, "History, Historians, and the Peace of God," chapter 1, pp. 21-40, Thomas Head and Richard Landes, eds., *The People of God: Social Violence and Religious Response in France around the Year 1000*. Ithaca, Cornell University Press, 1992.

Richard J. Payne, *Apocalyptic Spirituality: Treatises and Letters of Lactantius, Adso of Montier-en-der, Joachim of Fiore, The Franciscan Spirituals, Savonarola.* New York, Paulist Press, 1979.

Edwin Pears, *The Fall of Constantinople, Being the Story of the Fourth Crusade* (New York, Harper & Brothers, 1886.

Mark Gregory Pegg, *A Most Holy War: The Albigensian Crusade and the Battle for Christendom.* Oxford University Press, 2008.

Edward Peters, ed. *Christian Society and the Crusades, 1198-1229* University of Pennsylvania Press, 1971.

Edward Peters, "Destruction of the Flesh – Salvation of the Spirit: The Paradoxes of Torture in Medieval Christian Society," as found in Ferreiro, Alberto's *The Devil, Heresy and Witchcraft in the Middle Ages: Essays in Honor of Jeffrey B. Russell,* Boston, Brill.

Edward Peters, *Inquisition.* Berkeley, California, University of California Press, 1988.

Philichdorfius, *In Haeresi Valdensium,* c.i. Bibliotheca Max.

Andrew Pinsent, *The Second Person Perspective in Aquinas's Ethics: Virtue and Gifts.*

Routledge Studies in Ethics and Moral Theory, Routledge, 1971.

Jean Plaidy, *Growth of the Inquisition.* New York, Citadel Press, 1965.

Jean Plaidy, *The Spanish Inquisition.* New York, Citadel Press, 1967.

Alexander Pope, *Essay on Criticism*.

Alexander Pope, *Know Then Thyself*.

James M. Powell, *Anatomy of a Crusade, 1213-1221*. University of Pennsylvania Press, 1986.

Diane Purkiss, *The Witch in History: Early Modern and Twentieth Century Representations*, London: Routledge, Taylor and Francis Group, 1996.

Robert D. D. Rainy, The Ancient Catholic Church: From the Accession of Trajan to the Fourth General Council, (A. D. 98-451) Charles Scribner Sons, 1902.

Jonathon Riley-Smith, "The Crusading Movement and Historians," in Riley-Smith, Jonathan, *The Oxford Illustrated History of the Crusades* Oxford University Press, 1995.

Nesta de Robeck, *Legend of the Three Companions*, with Introduction by Theophile Desbonnets, O.F.M. (tr. from the French by Paul Oligny, O.F. M.), 1964, as found in Marion A.Habig, *St. Francis of Assisi: Writings and Early Biographies*. Franciscan Herald Press, 1972.

Nesta de Robeck, *Legend of the Three Companions*, with Introduction by Theophile Desbonnets, O.F.M. (tr. from the French by Paul Oligny, O.F. M.), 1964, as found in Marion A.Habig, *St. Francis of Assisi: Writings and Early Biographies*. Franciscan Herald Press, 1972.

James Roberts and Nikki Moustaki, *Dante's Divine Comedy: Inferno*. N.Y., Hungry Minds, Inc., 2001.

Cecil Roth, *The Spanish Inquisition.* New York, Norton Press, 1964.

Harriet Rubin, *Dante in Love,* Simon and Schuster, 2004.

Norman Russell, Cyril of Alexandria, London: Routledge, 2000.

Antonia Ryan, interviewer, *The National Catholic Reporter,* February 24, 2006 (42, 17). Interviewees: Thomas Madden, professor and chair of history at St. Louis University, author of *The New Concise History of the Crusades* (2005) and Carole Hillenbrand, professor of Islamic culture at the University of Edinburgh, Scotland, author of *The Crusades: Islamic Perspectives,* 2000.

Paul Sabatier, *Life of St. Francis of Assisi,* translated by Louise Seymour Houghton, London, Hodder and Stoughton, 1919.

Sacrum Commercium; or Francis and His Lady Poverty.

G. E. M. de Ste. Croix, *Christian Persecution, Martyrdom and Orthodoxy.* Oxford, Great Britian: Oxford University Press, 2006.

Luigi Salvatorelli, *Life of Francis of Assisi,* New York, A. A. Knopf, 1928.

Isabella Sandwell, *Religious Identity in Late Antiquity.* Cambridge University Press, 2007.

Sellers, R. V., *The Council of Chalcedon: A Historical and Doctrinal Survey.* London: S.P.C.K., 1953.

Donald Senior, *Invitation to Matthew: A Commentary on the*

Gospel of Matthew with Complete Text from the Jerusalem Bible, Garden City, New York, Image Books, 1966.

Sylvia Shein, *Fideles Crucis: The Papacy, the West, and the Recovery of the Holy Land, 1274-1314,* Oxford, Clarendon Press, 1991.

Sylvia Shein, *Gateway to the Heavenly City: Crusader Jerusalem and the Catholic West (1099-1187),* Burlington, Vermont, Ashgate Publishing Company, 2005.

Lloyd Simon, "The Crusading Movement, 1096-1274," in Riley-Smith, Jonathan, *The Oxford Illustrated History of the Crusades* Oxford University Press, 1995.

Beryl Smalley, *The Study of the Bible in the Middle Ages.* Oxford, Basil Blackwell, 1952.

Ken Smits, O. F. M. Cap. "Has Ecumenism Gone into a Coma?" *Weekly Recap.* January 25, 2008.

Peter Speed, ed., *Those Who Prayed: An Anthology of Medieval Sources* New York, Italica Press, 1997.

Starhawk, *The Spiral Dance: A rebirth of the Ancient Religion of the Great Goddess.* New York: Harper and Row, 1979.

R. M. Stephens, *The Burning Bush,* United Kingdom, Rushden, Northhampton, Stanley Hunt Printers, Ltd., 1963.

W. R. W. Stephens, *Saint John Chrysostom: His Life and Times.* London, John Murray 1872.

Joseph R.Strayer, *The Albigensian Crusades* (New York, Dial), 1972 Reprint 1992.

Montague Summers, Translator's preface to Kramer, Henry, O. P., *Malleus Mallificarum*.

Jonathan Sumption, *The Albigensian Crusade* (New York, Faber and Faber, 1978.

Tedeschi, *A "Queer Story": The Inquisitorial Manuscripts*, including the censorship practices of post-Tridentine Rome, 19 volumes, with accompanying abjurations issued by the supreme Congregation of the Holy Office in Rome or by provincial Italian tribunals between 1564 to 1659, and four volumes spanning the years 1564-8 and 1564-59, which contains approximately 500 sentences, edited by Peter Fox, Treasures of the Library, Trinity College, Dublin, Ireland.

Tertullian, *Ad Scapulam.*

Jonathan Miriam Rita Tessera, "Philip Count of Flanders and Hildegard of Bingen: Crusading against the Saracens or Crusading against Deadly Sin?" *Gendering the Crusades,* ed. Susan B. Edgington and Sarah Lambert, N.Y., Columbia University Press, 2002.

Thomas Aquinas, *On the Power of God.* Newman Press, 1952.

Robert D., Tollison, Robert F. Hebert, Robert B. Ekelund, Jr., Gary M. Anderson, Audrey B. Davidson, , *Sacred Trust: The Medieval Church as an Economic Firm.* Oxford University Press, 1966.

Bernhard Topfer, "The Cult of Relics and Pilgrimage in Burgundy and Aquitaine at the Time of the Monastic Reform," chapter 2, pp. 41-57, Thomas Head and Richard Landes, eds., *The People of*

God: Social Violence and Religious Response in France around the Year 1000. Ithaca, Cornell University Press, 1992.

Leo Tolstoy, *Anna Karenina*, between 1873 and 1877, Quality Paperback Book Club, 1991.

Simon Tugwell, O.P., tr., ed., and intro., *Albert & Thomas: Selected Writings*. N.Y., Paulist Press, 1988.

The Twelfth Ecumenical Council: Lateran Council IV, Canons of, 1215.

Christian D. Von Dehsen. Philosophers and Religious Leaders. Phoenix: Oryx Press, 1999.

Andre Vauchez, *Francis of Assisi: the Life and Afterlife of a Medieval Saint*. tr. by Michael F. Cusato. Yale University Press, 2012.

Bruce Vawter, C.M., "The Gospel according to John," *Jerome Biblical Commentary*, vol. II, The New Testament and Topical Articles, 1968.

Geffroi Villehardouin, *Memoirs of the Crusades*, translated by Sir Frank T. Marzials, New York, E. P. Dutton, 2009.

Damien Vorreux, *Legend of Perugia*, tr. by Paul Oligny, O.F.M. from the annotated French version, with an Introduction by Theophile Desbonnets, 1968, as found in Marion A. Habig, *St. Francis of Assisi: Writings and Early Biographies*. Franciscan Herald Press, 1972.

Walter L. Wakefield, *Heresy, Crusade, and Inquisition in Southern France, 1100-1250*. California: University of California Press, 1974.

Brendan Walsh, *Fertile Ground: Journal of Peace House, the Kalamazoo Quaker/Catholic Worker,* 9, June, 2013.

Gerald G. S. J. Walsh; Bernard M. Peebles; Rudolph E. Morris; J. Reginald C. S. B. O'Donnell, trs. Fathers of the Church: Niceta of Rimesiana, vol. 7, Catholic University of America Press, 1949.

William Thomas Walsh, *Characters of the Inquisition.* New York: P. J. Kenedy & Sons, 1940.

Rene Weis, *The Yellow Cross: The Glory of the Last Crusade.* New York, Alfred A. Knopf, 2001.

James A. Weisheipl, O.P. *Friar Thomas D'Aquino.* Catholic University Press, 1974.

Robert Wilkin *John Chrysostom and the Jews in the Late Fourth Century* University of California Press, 1983.

D. H. Williams, "The Anti-Arian Campaigns of Hilary of Poitiers and 'The Liber Auxentium'" *Church History* 61:1 (1992), 7-24, 1992.

James Aithen Wylie, *The History of Protestantism,* vol. 1, Cassell, Petter & Galpin, 1878.

Howard Zinn, *A People's History of the United States.* Harper & Row, 1980.

Howard Zinn, *You Can't Be Neutral on a Moving Train.* Chicago Filmmakers, 1994.

ALSO BY TOM KESSLER

CHRISTIANITY: ENDANGERED OR EXTINCT

How the teachings of Jesus of Nazareth were transformed into an entirely different religion...

Written by two respectable religious scholars, this groundbreaking new book challenges some of our long-held beliefs about Christianity as we know it, detailing the origins of a great divide between Jesus of Nazareth's teachings and Christianity during its formative stages. With comprehensive historical research, authors Cragun and Kessler use the analysis of power and class struggle to reexamine Church history and the teachings of the theologians. They outline how the so-called "Fathers of the Church" took over the community of Jesus, destroyed its foundations, and built their own church edifice, which they then passed down to us. Though much of modern scholarship blames Constantine for the corruption of the Church, Christianity: Endangered or Extinct? shows how the corruption was a gradual process in which Platonic philosophy, power, and prestige gradually entombed the message Jesus actually gave us. This religion was carefully honed to be acceptable to emperors, rulers, and the elite, replacing Christ's original message of love, egalitarianism, communalism, pacifism, and servant leadership—concepts that are essential for the survival of humanity in the 21st century. This is a true People's History of Christianity in the tradition of Howard Zinn's People's History of the United States and one that will have you seeing Christianity in a brand-new light.

Learn more at: www.outskirtspress.com/ChristianityEndangeredorExtinct

www.ingramcontent.com/pod-product-compliance
Lightning Source LLC
Chambersburg PA
CBHW052048290426
44111CB00011B/1658